The New International Commentary on the New Testament

F. F. BRUCE, *General Editor*

THE EPISTLES OF
JOHN

by

I. HOWARD MARSHALL

WILLIAM B. EERDMANS PUBLISHING COMPANY

Library of Congress Cataloging in Publication Data

Marshall, I. Howard.
  The Epistles of John.

  (The New International Commentary on the New Testament)
  Includes indexes.
  1. Bible. N.T. Epistles of John—Commentaries. I. Title.
BS2805.3.M37   227'.94'07   77-28118
ISBN 0-8028-2189-2

CONTENTS

Editor's Preface   vii
Author's Preface   ix
Abbreviations   xiii
Commentaries and Other Works   xv

INVITATION   1

INTRODUCTION
1. THE SITUATION AND CHARACTER OF 2 AND 3 JOHN   9
2. THE SITUATION OF 1 JOHN   14
3. THE STRUCTURE OF 1 JOHN   22
4. THEORIES OF REARRANGEMENT AND REDACTION   27
5. RELATIONSHIPS BETWEEN THE JOHANNINE WRITINGS   31
6. THE AUTHORSHIP OF THE EPISTLES   42
7. THE EARLY HISTORY OF THE EPISTLES IN THE CHURCH   48
8. THE THOUGHT OF THE EPISTLES   49

THE SECOND EPISTLE OF JOHN
ADDRESS AND GREETING (1–3)   59
LIVING IN TRUTH AND LOVE (4–6)   65
BEWARE OF FALSE TEACHING (7–11)   68
FINAL WORDS AND GREETINGS (12–13)   75

THE THIRD EPISTLE OF JOHN
ADDRESS AND GREETING (1–4)   81
THE WRITER PRAISES GAIUS (5–8)   84
THE WRITER DENOUNCES DIOTREPHES (9–10)   88
THE WRITER PRAISES DEMETRIUS (11–12)   92
FINAL WORDS AND GREETINGS (13–15)   94

THE FIRST EPISTLE OF JOHN
PROLOGUE—THE WORD OF LIFE (1:1–4)   99

WALKING IN THE LIGHT (1:5–2:2)   108

KEEPING HIS COMMANDS (2:3–11)   120

THE NEW STATUS OF BELIEVERS AND THEIR
RELATION TO THE WORLD (2:12–17)   134

A WARNING AGAINST ANTICHRISTS (2:18–27)   147

THE HOPE OF GOD'S CHILDREN (2:28–3:3)   164

THE SINLESSNESS OF GOD'S CHILDREN (3:4–10)   175

BROTHERLY LOVE AS THE MARK OF THE CHRISTIAN
(3:11–18)   188

ASSURANCE AND OBEDIENCE (3:19–24)   196

THE SPIRIT OF TRUTH AND FALSEHOOD (4:1–6)   203

GOD'S LOVE AND OUR LOVE (4:7–12)   210

ASSURANCE AND CHRISTIAN LOVE (4:13–5:4)   218

THE TRUE FAITH CONFIRMED (5:5–12)   230

CHRISTIAN CERTAINTIES (5:13–21)   242

INDEXES

1. SUBJECTS   257

2. AUTHORS   260

3. BIBLICAL REFERENCES   264

4. EXTRA- AND NONBIBLICAL LITERATURE   272

EDITOR'S PREFACE

When it was decided to replace Dr. Alexander Ross's commentary on the Epistles of James and John by two separate volumes, it was necessary to secure two commentators. Happily, hard on Dr. James Adamson's acceptance of the invitation to write the commentary on the Epistle of James came Dr. I. Howard Marshall's consent to undertake the companion work on the Epistles of John.

Dr. Marshall is a graduate of the Universities of Aberdeen and Cambridge; he also spent a period of study under Professor Joachim Jeremias at Göttingen. For over twelve years he has been a member of the teaching staff of the Department of New Testament Exegesis at the University of Aberdeen, where he now holds the status of Reader.

He gave evidence of his interest in Johannine literature when, as a youthful scholar, he contributed the articles on the Gospel and Epistles of John to the *New Bible Dictionary* (1962). Since then he has proved his worth as a New Testament exegete and theologian in a succession of scholarly publications—some of a specialist nature and some more popular. In criticism and exegesis he has specialized thus far in Lukan studies, with his *Luke: Historian and Theologian* (1970) and *The Gospel of Luke: A Commentary on the Greek Text* (1978). He has written popular Scripture Union commentaries on *Mark* (1963) and *Kings and Chronicles* (1967). An important symposium on *New Testament Interpretation* appeared under his editorship in 1977. In New Testament theology his major work is a study of the doctrine of perseverance, *Kept by the Power of God* (1969). He is also author of *Christian Beliefs* (1963), *The Work of Christ* (1969), *The Origins of New Testament Christology* (1976), and *I Believe in the Historical Jesus* (1977). These works, together with a number of articles in learned periodicals, have placed him in the front rank of

British New Testament scholars, and the New International Commentary on the New Testament is to be congratulated on enlisting him among its contributors.

A fresh feature of this volume is the inclusion of an "Invitation" to the general reader as well as an "Introduction" for the specialist. Another fresh feature is a rearrangement of the traditional order of the three letters: 2 John and 3 John are studied before 1 John. This means that the two shorter letters are not relegated to the position of appendices but are treated as important documents of early Christianity in their own right.

Since writers of replacement volumes in the New International Commentary are left free to compose or select their own translations, Dr. Marshall has chosen to base his exposition on the *New International Version*.

With these prefatory words, the editor leaves Dr. Marshall to engage his readers' attention and appreciation by what he has to say in the following pages.

F. F. BRUCE

AUTHOR'S PREFACE

There are already so many commentaries on the various books of the New Testament that anybody who adds to their number should be obliged to give some defense of himself. The immediate occasion for the present work was a request by the editor of the New International Commentary on the New Testament that I should prepare a fresh volume on the Epistles of John. The original volume in the series by Dr. Alexander Ross also included the Epistle of James. The decision to publish a new, considerably fuller commentary on James in an individual volume meant that the treatment of the Johannine Epistles by Dr. Ross must also be replaced by a new volume at greater length.

It was my privilege to get to know Dr. Ross through his visits to the Aberdeen University Evangelical Union where he was a much-appreciated speaker. Both as a teacher in the Free Church of Scotland College and then during his active retirement as minister of the Free Church in Burghead, he exercised a gracious and scholarly ministry, and he was held in high esteem both inside and outside his own denomination. His commentary on these Epistles was one of the first books that I ever reviewed, and I am glad now to have this opportunity of paying respect to his memory.

Unfortunately Dr. Ross's commentary on the Johannine Epistles was limited in length and consequently in the amount of detailed exegesis of the text which it could provide. It was also written before the development of recent study of the Epistles. Writing in 1958, Dr. William Barclay could comment, with some exaggeration, that there were not many outstanding commentaries on these Epistles, although he then went on to list the works of B. F. Westcott, A. E. Brooke, and C. H. Dodd as the best, particularly the last mentioned. The situation has now changed. A year earlier than Ross's work there was published the first volume in a new German series. *Herders Theologischer Kommentar zum Neuen Testament* is a Roman Catholic production, intended to be on the scholarly level of the International Critical Commentary but with particular stress on theological exposition. This first volume was by R. Schnackenburg on the Epistles of John, and it remains unrivalled as a comprehensive and well-informed study of the Epistles; it is the fundamental work for the serious student. It was followed in 1957 by a full-length monograph by W. Nauck, *Die Tradition und der Charakter des ersten Johannesbriefes,* which opened up new viewpoints in the light of the Dead Sea Scrolls. The commentary by R. Bultmann which followed shortly after (1967) and would otherwise have been important in its own right had little that was fresh to offer in comparison with Schnackenburg's work; curiously it is Bultmann's work which has been translated into English rather than Schnackenburg's.

Among English works particular importance attaches to J. R. W. Stott's work in the Tyndale New Testament Commentaries, which is fuller than many of the other volumes in that series and remains the best general commentary on the Epistles, well based on sound scholarship but clear and practical. Nor can I fail to mention the work of my former teacher, J. N. S. Alexander, in the Torch Bible Commentaries, and the more recent work of J. L. Houlden in Black's New Testament Commentaries. But perhaps the most outstanding of the post-Schnackenburg era of commentaries is that by M. de Jonge; it is written in Dutch, which limits its availability, but its basic insights have been incorporated in the handbook on the Letters of John in the United Bible Societies' Helps for Translators series: this is an extremely valuable book, useful to all students and not merely to Bible translators.

Other works could be mentioned, but these I have found to be the most useful. The justification of the present commentary lies in its attempt to mediate to English readers the results of recent study, especially on the Continent, and to do so in such a way that the ordinary reader will not be distracted by the apparatus of scholarship. I have, therefore, attempted to separate off the technicalities from the exposition by rigidly confining the latter to the footnotes and also by writing a separate "Invitation" to the general reader and "Introduction" for the student. It is also arguable that too few commentaries attempt to expound the New Testament for the modern reader, and I have made some attempt to indicate how I think the

Epistles should be interpreted and applied in the contemporary situation. One further feature of the commentary is that it deliberately treats 2 and 3 John before 1 John, in the hope that readers will move from the easier books to the more difficult.

The English translation on which the commentary is based is that of the *New International Version,* and I am grateful to the New York Bible Society for the opportunity to use it here. It is an ideal translation for the present purpose, being sufficiently literal to form a good basis for exegesis and at the same time clear and modern in expression. Only in a few places have I wanted to question its renderings, and these did not seem sufficient in number to justify me in producing yet another translation of my own.

Martin Luther wrote of 1 John: "I have never read a book written in simpler words than this one, and yet the words are inexpressible" (WA 28, 183). I pray that something of the simplicity and the depth of these Epistles may emerge in this commentary. It is a not uncommon experience that the writing of a commentary opens up the mind and heart to new truth or fresh appreciation of the old; I trust that what I personally have experienced in writing this commentary may convey itself to the readers.

I. HOWARD MARSHALL

ABBREVIATIONS

AG	[Walter Bauer's] *Greek-English Lexicon of the New Testament and Other Early Christian Literature*, trans. and adapted by W. F. Arndt and F. W. Gingrich, Chicago/Cambridge, 1957
AH	*Against Heresies* (Irenaeus)
AV	*Authorized (King James) Version*
BD	Blass, F., and Debrunner, A., *A Greek Grammar of the New Testament* (trans. by R. W. Funk), Chicago/Cambridge, 1961
Bib	*Biblica*
BJRL	*Bulletin of the John Rylands Library*
BZ	*Biblische Zeitschrift*
CD	Book of the Covenant of Damascus (= Zadokite Work)
CH	*Corpus Hermeticum*
Diglot	*The General Letters: A Greek-English Diglot for the Use of Translators*, London, 1961 (incorporates the projected 3rd edition of the British and Foreign Bible Society text of the Greek New Testament prepared by G. D. Kilpatrick)
EQ	*The Evangelical Quarterly*
EvT	*Evangelische Theologie*
ExpT	*Expository Times*
HE	*Historia ecclesiastica* (Eusebius)
HTR	*Harvard Theological Review*
JBL	*Journal of Biblical Literature*
JTS	*Journal of Theological Studies*
Knox	Knox, R. A., *The New Testament*, Mission, KS/London, 1948
Metzger	Metzger, B. M., *A Textual Commentary on the Greek New Testament*, London, 1971
Moffatt	Moffatt, J., *The New Testament: A New Translation*, London, 1935
Moule	Moule, C. F. D., *An Idiom-Book of New Testament Greek*, New York/Cambridge, 1953
MH	Moulton, J. H., Howard, W. F., and Turner, N., *Grammar of New Testament Greek*, Naperville/Edinburgh, I, 1906; II,

	1929; III, 1963; IV, 1976
MM	Moulton, J. H., and Milligan, G., *The Vocabulary of the Greek New Testament*, Grand Rapids/London, 1914-29
NEB	*New English Bible*
NIDNTT	Brown, C. (ed.), *The New International Dictionary of New Testament Theology*, Grand Rapids/Exeter, 1975-77
NIV	*New International Version*
NovT	*Novum Testamentum*
NTA	*New Testament Abstracts*
NTS	*New Testament Studies*
RAC	Klausner, T. (ed.), *Reallexikon für die Antike und Christentum*, Stuttgart, 1941-
RB	*Revue Biblique*
RGG	*Religion in Geschichte und Gegenwart*
RHPR	*Revue d'histoire et de philosophie religieuses*
RSV	*Revised Standard Version*
RV	*Revised Version*
S	Codex Sinaiticus
SB	Strack, H. L., und Billerbeck, P., *Kommentar zum Neuen Testament aus Talmud und Midrasch*, München, 1956³
T.Dan, etc.	*Testament of Dan*, etc. (from *Testaments of the Twelve Patriarchs*)
TDNT	Kittel, G., and Friedrich, G. (ed.), *Theological Dictionary of the New Testament* (trans. by G. W. Bromiley), Grand Rapids, 1964-77
TEV	*Good News Bible: Today's English Version*
THAT	Jenni, E., und Westermann, C. (ed.), *Theologisches Handwörterbuch zum Alten Testament*, München, 1971-76
ThR	*Theologische Rundschau*
TLZ	*Theologische Literaturzeitung*
TNT	*Translator's New Testament*
TU	*Texte und Untersuchungen*
TZ	*Theologische Zeitschrift*
UBS	*The Greek New Testament* (3rd edition, United Bible Societies, London, 1975)
WA	Luthers Werke (Weimarer Ausgabe)
ZNW	*Zeitschrift für die Neutestamentliche Wissenschaft*
ZTK	*Zeitschrift für Theologie und Kirche*

COMMENTARIES AND OTHER WORKS

The books listed in this bibliography are referred to in the commentary simply by the author's name.

Alexander, J. N. S.   *The Epistles of John* (Torch Bible Commentaries), London, 1962.

Alford, H.   *The Greek Testament*, London, 1862², IV, 159-188, 421-528.

Balz, H.,   *Die "Katholischen" Briefe* (Das Neue Testament
und Schrage, W.   Deutsch), Göttingen, 1973¹¹, 150-216.

Barclay, W.   *The Letters of John*, Edinburgh, 1958.

Braun, H.   *Qumran und das Neue Testament*, Tübingen, 1966, I, 290-306.

Brooke, A. E.   *The Johannine Epistles* (International Critical Commentary), Naperville/Edinburgh, 1912.

Bruce, F. F.   *The Epistles of John*, Old Tappan/London, 1970.

Büchsel, F.   *Die Johannesbriefe* (Theologischer Handkommentar zum Neuen Testament), Leipzig, 1933.

Bultmann, R.   *The Johannine Epistles* (Hermeneia), Philadelphia, 1973.

Calvin, J.   *The Gospel according to St. John and the First Epistle of John*, Grand Rapids/Edinburgh, 1959-61, II, 227-315.

Chaine, J.   *Les Épîtres Catholiques* (Études Bibliques), Paris, 1939², 97-260.

Dodd, C. H.   *The Johannine Epistles* (Moffatt New Testament Commentary), London, 1946.

Findlay, G. G.   *Fellowship in the Life Eternal*, London, 1909.

Haas, C.,   *A Translator's Handbook on the Letters of John*
De Jonge, M., and   (Helps for Translators), London, 1972.
Swellengrebel, J. L.

Haenchen, E.   "Neuere Literatur zu den Johannesbriefen," in *Die Bibel und Wir*, Tübingen, 1968, 235-311; originally published in ThR nf 26, 1960, 1–43, 267-291.

Harvey, A. E.   *The New English Bible: Companion to the New Testament,* New York/Oxford/Cambridge, 1970, 758–779.

Hauck, F.   *Die Kirchenbriefe* (Das Neue Testament Deutsch), Göttingen, 1947[4].

Heise, J.   *Bleiben: Menein in der Johanneischen Schriften,* Tübingen, 1967.

Houlden, J. L.   *A Commentary on the Johannine Epistles* (Black's New Testament Commentaries), London, 1973.

Johnston, G.   "I, II, III John," in *Peake's Commentary,* London, 1962, 1035–1040.

de Jonge, M.   *De Brieven van Johannes* (De Prediking van het Nieuwe Testament), Nijkerk, 1973[2].

Koehler, M.   *Le Coeur et les Mains,* Neuchâtel, 1962.

Law, R.   *The Tests of Life: A Study of the First Epistle of St. John,* Edinburgh, 1914.

Morris, L.   "1 John, 2 John, 3 John," in *The New Bible Commentary: Revised,* Grand Rapids/London, 1970, 1259–1273.

Nauck, W.   *Die Tradition und der Charakter des ersten Johannesbriefes,* Tübingen, 1957.

O'Neill, J. C.   *The Puzzle of 1 John,* Naperville/London, 1966.

Plummer, A.   *The Epistles of S. John* (The Cambridge Bible for Schools and Colleges), Cambridge, 1883. See also *The Epistles of S. John* (Cambridge Greek Testament), Cambridge, 1894.

Ross, A.   *The Epistles of James and John* (The New International Commentary on the New Testament), Grand Rapids, 1954.

Schnackenburg, R.   *Die Johannesbriefe* (Herders Theologischer Kommentar zum Neuen Testament), Freiburg, 1953; 1975[5].

Smith, D.   "The Epistles of St. John," in W. R. Nicoll (ed.), *The Expositor's Greek Testament,* Grand Rapids/London, 1910, V, 149–208.

Stott, J. R. W.   *The Epistles of John* (Tyndale New Testament Commentaries), Grand Rapids/London, 1964.

Vawter, B.   "The Johannine Epistles," in *The Jerome Bible Commentary,* London, 1968, II, 404–413.

Wengst, K.   *Häresie und Orthodoxie im Spiegel des ersten Johannesbriefes,* Gütersloh, 1976.

Westcott, B. F.   *The Johannine Epistles* (Macmillan), London, 1883; reprinted, Abingdon, 1966.

Wilder, A. N.   "I, II, and III John," in *The Interpreter's Bible,*

Nashville, 1957, XII, 207–313 (with exposition by P. W. Hoon).

Williams, R. R. *The Letters of John and James* (The Cambridge Bible Commentary), New York/Cambridge, 1965.

Windisch, H. *Die Katholischen Briefe* (Handbuch zum Neuen Testament), Tübingen, 1951[3] (with additions by H. Preisker).

INVITATION

This is an invitation to you to read the Epistles of John. It is not an advertisement for the commentary which appears in this book. The task of the commentator is to serve the text and to help to make it comprehensible to the reader; no commentary was ever meant to be read for its own sake but only as a means to an end, the understanding of the text. John wrote his Epistles in Greek, a language not universally understood; the commentator must either use a translation in the language of his readers or produce a fresh one. The author and his readers lived in the past; the commentator must re-create the situation in which the Epistles were composed so that the modern reader can appreciate them in their original setting. The Epistles contain things which are hard to understand or ambiguous in meaning; the commentator must strive to establish the meaning and express it with all clarity. Finally, the Epistles form a part of Holy Scripture, the Word of God written; it is the commentator's supreme task to present their message to the modern reader, showing how they form part of God's Word to his people today. The commentator's duty is thus to be the servant of the text and its readers, so that the text may once again speak and be the vehicle of God's Word to a new generation.

Anybody, therefore, who wishes to hear the Word of God is invited to read the Epistles of John. They form an excellent starting place for the student who wants an introduction to the theology of the New Testament. In the *New English Bible* the First Epistle is given the heading "Recall to Fundamentals." It is an apt title, for this Epistle, and indeed all three, are concerned with the very fundamentals of Christian belief and life. The reader who grasps the message of these letters will have a sound basis in Christian doctrine, ready to be filled out by further study elsewhere in the New

1

Testament. In particular, he will have a good starting point for study of the Gospel of John; although the Gospel was probably written before the Epistles and forms the foundation for what they teach, it is probably easier in some ways for the reader to grasp John's message by beginning with the Epistles.

Again, these writings are among the shorter ones in the New Testament. In fact, 2 and 3 John are the shortest books in the New Testament. As a result, they have often been thought to be insignificant and unimportant alongside the other Johannine writings. Their position in the canon after 1 John has put them in its shadow, and readers who begin with 1 John may well conclude that there is nothing fresh to be found in them. But both 2 and 3 John do contain their own individual contributions to Christian thinking, and they can profitably be read as introductions to 1 John. I propose, therefore, to rescue them from their comparative obscurity by inviting the reader to look at them first, before turning to 1 John, and I believe that by reading the Epistles in this order students will come to a better appreciation of their intrinsic value. The New Testament order was probably arrived at simply on grounds of length; there is nothing sacrosanct about it. We shall do well to abandon that order in the interests of rehabilitating these valuable writings.

The student of the Greek New Testament is also well advised to begin his reading with these Epistles. Their Greek is the easiest to read in the whole of the New Testament. The total vocabulary of the New Testament is 5437 words; the number of different words used in 1-3 John is merely 303, and the majority of these are common words. To read a text with such a small vocabulary is a light undertaking. The general style and syntax of the Epistles is also simple and straightforward, and there are not many tricky passages to retard the beginner. Students who have not yet worked their way fully through an elementary Greek grammar can cut their teeth on these Epistles, and will have the rewarding experience of finding that they can actually read the New Testament itself without too much difficulty. It will pay any reader who has even a little knowledge of Greek to have his Greek Testament open in front of him as he proceeds through the commentary; while references to Greek words have been strenuously avoided in the text to make it as widely useful as possible, the footnotes will provide some help on problems met by the Greek student.

The Epistles of John are concerned with the fundamentals of Christian theology; they are brief in compass and simple to com-

2

prehend: what are they about? At the time of writing them their author, a man whom we know as John (although he does not in fact name himself), was apparently an old man. He had some kind of pastoral charge over a number of churches, probably somewhere in the neighborhood of Ephesus. Old people nowadays find rural travel difficult if they cannot drive. It must have been all the more difficult in the first century when there wasn't even a bus service to complain about. In order to keep in touch with his churches John had to rely on his pen and entrust his messages to younger men who could travel about more easily. Although, therefore, John could occasionally visit the churches under his care (2 Jn. 12; 3 Jn. 14), there were times when he felt that he must send them personal letters.

The writing of 2 John was occasioned by a couple of factors. John was worried by the fact that some of the traveling teachers who exercised an itinerant preaching ministry among the churches were putting forward doctrines which he felt to be out of harmony with genuine Christianity as he himself had accepted and taught it. Specifically they were denying that Jesus was the Christ and the Son of God. John feared that the members of one church in particular might be led astray by what was being presented as "advanced" Christian teaching. Fortunately just at this critical point some of the members of the church happened to visit John. Indeed, it may have been their reports which informed John about the danger affecting their church. So John seized the opportunity to send them back with a brief letter in which he warned his friends not to be taken in by this false teaching and not to assist its proponents by giving them hospitality for their mission. At the same time he was able to commend the church for the practical grasp of Christian truth and its expression in love which he found exemplified in the lives of its members. All this is said in a few lines of writing, but it presents us with a cameo of John's chief concerns: on the one hand, the importance of adherence to the truth, especially believing the truth about Jesus as the Son of God, and of living in Christian love, and, on the other hand, the dangerous threat posed by heresy. Truth and love constitute the two main positive features of John's Christianity.

The situation in 3 John is somewhat different. Here we have a letter addressed to a particular individual called Gaius. John expresses his good wishes for his health, and it may be that Gaius had been ill and was unable to attend the church some miles away. Gaius is commended for his faithfulness to the truth and for his love, shown in the way in which he opened his house to traveling preachers.

These preachers were colleagues of John, unlike the false teachers in 2 John. But there was a problem in the church. A man called Diotrephes was attempting to be leader in the church and rejected John's authority over it. He had suppressed a letter from John to the church, and he also refused to allow traveling teachers to minister in the church. John now wrote to Gaius, hoping that through him a message might get through to the church and his authority might be re-established, and he sent it by the hand of Demetrius, a traveling preacher whom he warmly commended to Gaius. The way in which John tells Gaius about the situation as though he was ignorant of it suggests that he lived some distance from the church and was not able to visit it very often, or that he belonged to a neighboring church. There is no suggestion in this letter that Diotrephes or the members of his church held any heretical views, but once again we find that John's characteristic stress on truth and love comes out in what he writes.

The same issues emerge, but much more broadly, in 1 John. This letter gives a full-scale expression of the kind of things that John wanted to say in 2 John. It is composed more like a sermon than a letter, but is obviously meant for a particular group (or groups) of Christians. From it we gain the impression that the heretical teaching which John opposed had become a more coherent system of thought, and that its adherents had set up their own rival church. Having themselves withdrawn from the church with which John had fellowship, they were now trying to persuade the rest of the church to follow them. This situation clearly produced considerable debate and uncertainty in the church. Here were the people who had left the church claiming that it was not necessary to accept Jesus as the Son of God in order to have knowledge of God. Indeed, they held that it was possible to live without sin on this basis, and that they had no need of the Christian doctrine of forgiveness through the death of Jesus. They based their view of Christianity on spiritual revelations for which they claimed divine authority. They may not specifically have denied the importance of love as a Christian virtue, but they certainly did not emphasize it in their teaching. They offered "Christianity without tears." It was bound to prove an attractive proposition to the congregation. No doubt some of them were tempted to accept it and join the seceders. The general effect, however, was to produce uncertainty in the minds of the congregation, even among those who remained loyal to John's teaching. If this "simplified" version of Christianity offered knowledge of God and sinlessness, what need was there for John's teaching? What did one have to believe and do in order to be a true Christian? What did it really mean to be a Christian?

These were the questions in the minds of John's readers, and in the light of them we can now understand the purpose of his letter: "I write these things to you who believe in the name of the Son of God so that you may know that you have eternal life" (1 Jn. 5:13). John addressed himself to his friends who were disturbed by the teaching of the seceders in order to reassure them that they really were true Christians since they accepted Jesus as the Son of God. John's purpose has sometimes been expressed as giving his readers "The Tests of Life." He lists the characteristics by which a person may know whether he has life and bids his readers test themselves accordingly. But in fact John's purpose is somewhat more positive. He is not so much encouraging his readers to test themselves and see whether they qualify for eternal life as assuring them that in fact they do qualify for eternal life.

But obviously we must fill this out in order to grasp the message of the letter as a whole. John has not written it according to any neat plan; attempts to get a tidy, three-point sermon out of 1 John are misguided. He conducts a tour through his subject, pausing at the points that interest him, returning to areas of interest, seeing familiar objects from different angles, and yet all the time progressing toward a conclusion. His starting place is firm and solid: it is the Word of life, the revelation of God in Jesus (1:1–4). His goal is clear: it is the possibility of fellowship between men and God through Jesus Christ, his Son. He begins from the nature of God as revealed by Jesus, a God who is light and who cannot therefore tolerate sin. No man is free from sin, and therefore the path to fellowship with God can only be opened up by cleansing from sin brought about through the death of Jesus. But freedom from sin is not merely negative. Positively there must be obedience to the commands of God, specifically to his command to love one another. All claims to knowledge of God by people who fail to love their brothers are false and deceitful. With these statements John is already implicitly attacking the false teachers. They did not believe that Jesus was the Son of God who died for the sins of the world, nor (in John's opinion) did they show love for their brothers. Such people were in fact still in the darkness, rather than in the light of God. They belonged to the sinful, rebellious world rather than to God. John in fact described them as "antichrists," people who were opposed to Christ

5

and who had therefore cut themselves off from God. The readers must not be led astray by them. Indeed, there was no need for them to be led astray because they had received the true teaching confirmed by the witness of the Spirit. Let them remain in that teaching and practice true holiness, and in due time they will see God.

Thus it emerges that one of the decisive differences between the true Christian and the false is that the former is free from sin, while the latter shows by his sin that he belongs to the devil. A further difference is that the true Christian loves his brothers—with real, sacrificial love, such as was shown by Jesus himself. Those who show these qualities really do have eternal life. But if the readers feel uncertain about this—and faced by such high ideals they could well feel uncertain—they are not to be worried. God is greater than their own feelings and accepts them. They can have confidence to come into his presence and pray with the assurance of being heard.

Those who have eternal life have received the Spirit of God. Yet it is necessary to remember that there are evil spirits as well as good. The seceders also claim spiritual inspiration. How can the two be distinguished? John's answer is that it depends on whether the person possessed by the spirit holds the true faith about Jesus.

Once again John returns to the theme of love and repeats his point that love is the mark of the Christian, since love is the characteristic of God himself. Not only so, but love is the sign that God lives in us, even though we cannot see him. This experience is confirmed by the gift of the Spirit, and it depends upon our acceptance of Jesus as the Son of God. It leads to confidence in prayer and takes away any slavish fear of God.

So Christian confidence depends upon our faith and love. It is through our faith that we can fulfil the commandment to love and all that this entails. But it must be emphasized that this is real Christian faith which is meant. It is faith that Jesus really was the Son of God, not merely (as the seceders taught) that a divine power came upon Jesus at his baptism and left him again before his crucifixion: the Son of God truly became incarnate in Jesus and died on the cross. This understanding of Jesus has been testified to by God through the Spirit, and to disbelieve it is to regard God as a liar.

Thus it is those who believe in Jesus who have eternal life. They can have confidence in praying to God. And therefore they should pray for any of their brothers whom they see committing sins which might deprive them of their confidence and assurance. There

6

are sins of another kind, which lead to death, and here John has nothing to say about the value of praying for those who commit them. He concludes by reiterating the certainties which have become apparent in the course of the letter: the sinlessness of God's children, the assurance that the readers are God's children, and the fact that Jesus Christ is the way to God.

From this quick summary of the letter we can see that John sums up the characteristics of the true Christian as right belief, righteousness, and love. These are the factors which he believes to be absent from the lives of the seceders. The true Christian has eternal life; he is in close fellowship with God and has received the gift of the Spirit. Real Christianity is based on the incarnation and sacrificial death of the Son of God. In such terms we can pinpoint the essential themes of Johannine Christianity.

All this is worth studying for its own sake, as a picture of an important area of first-century Christianity. But it also has relevance for our situation today. Although we must beware of the temptation to suggest that our circumstances today are just the same as in the first century, it is still true that we have some problems which are like those John faced. Today there is a variety of types of Christianity in existence, and we are bound to ask which of them is right, and what basis we have for discriminating among them. We are confronted by denial of the incarnation and atonement in various forms: has John anything to say that is relevant to these modern doctrines? Does it matter what one believes? Can one know God apart from his revelation in Jesus? Questions like these make John's message very relevant.

At the same time John's teaching has created problems for the Christian church. He says that Christians do not sin and holds out the prospect of sinlessness. He speaks about the possibility of God's love being made complete or perfect in us. Are these things really possible? Can a Christian live a life that is free from sin and full of love? Or again: John says that everyone who loves has been born of God: does this mean that all you need to be a Christian is love? Or again: John talks about a kind of sin which leads to death; does he mean that it is possible for a Christian to sin beyond hope of forgiveness? These are some of the problems which are raised by this Epistle. The answers to them will, we hope, appear in the course of the commentary, and we do not propose to short-circuit the process of reading through the Epistles with the assistance of the commentary by offering quick answers at this point. What we hope is

7

that the reader's attention will have been sufficiently stimulated to encourage him to proceed now to read the Epistles.

At this point, therefore, the ordinary reader may go straight on to the commentary. The Introduction, which follows at this point, is more technical and is intended to provide the kind of fuller information needed by students and scholars.

INTRODUCTION

1. THE SITUATION AND CHARACTER OF 2 AND 3 JOHN

Unlike 1 John, 2 and 3 John fall into the category of personal letters. Each of them is the length of an ordinary private letter of the time which could be written on a standard-sized piece of papyrus (about 25 cm. by 20 cm.), and each of them has the typical "form" of a letter with a more or less stereotyped introduction and conclusion.[1] The form of 3 John in particular can be closely paralleled from that of the following letter, dating from the second or third century AD and discovered in Egypt:

> Irenaeus to Apollinarius his dearest brother many greetings. I pray continually for your health, and I myself am well. I wish you to know that I reached land on the sixth of the month Epeiph and we unloaded our cargo on the eighteenth of the same month. . . . Many salutations to your wife and to Serenus and to all who love you, each by name. Goodbye. Mesore 9.
> (Addressed) to Apollinarius from his brother Irenaeus.[2]

There is no doubt that 3 John is a real letter from the elder to his friend Gaius, fitting in with the pattern of ancient letter-writing, but transformed by Christian usage. 2 John follows the same general pattern; it has been suggested that it is more formal and artificial in style, and hence that it is not really a letter but a literary fiction,

[1]See R. W. Funk, "The Form and Structure of II and III John," JBL 86, 1967, 424–430; W. G. Doty, *Letters in Primitive Christianity*, Philadelphia, 1973; P. Vielhauer, *Geschichte der urchristlichen Literatur*, Berlin, 1975, 58–66. For 3 John see also C. W. Keyes, "The Greek Letter of Introduction," *American Journal of Philology* 56, 1935, 28–44.
[2]*Berliner griechische Urkunden* 27; cited by C. K. Barrett, *The New Testament Background: Selected Documents*, New York/London, 1956, No. 22.

based on the pattern of 3 John.[3] This is a most improbable suggestion, since the letter can be well understood as what it claims to be,
namely a real letter written to a concrete situation.

The situation in which 2 John was written can best be explained in a fuller discussion of the problems confronting the author
of 1 John. All that needs to be said here is that 2 John appears to
have been written to the same Christian community as 1 John but at
an earlier date (since the false teachers evidently still had access to
the church in 2 John, but had seceded from it in 1 Jn. 2:19), or else it
was written to a different church.

Although 2 John is apparently written to an individual, the
"chosen lady" (2 Jn. 1), it is probable that this is in fact a way of
personifying a community. By contrast 3 John is written to a specific
person, Gaius, and it deals with ecclesiastical rather than theological
problems. Its background appears to lie in the growth of a new type
of church organization.[4] At first the various churches were to
a considerable extent under the guidance and leadership of apostles
and evangelists (like Paul, Timothy, and Titus) who traveled from
place to place and maintained a general supervision over the
churches placed under their care. In this type of situation the role
and authority of the local leaders whom they appointed was corre-

---

[3]For the view that 2 John is a literary fiction by a different author from that of
3 John see Bultmann, 1; Heise, 164–170. Heise argues that 2 John offers a correction
of Johannine teaching intended to make it acceptable to orthodox Christians. He
makes the following points: (1) The vague address of the letter is intended to give it
a "catholic" circulation. The use of ἐκλεκτός is not Johannine. (2) The form of
address is copied from 3 John, lacks concrete features, and is not spontaneous.
(3) 2 John 4 refers vaguely to *all* Christians. (4) 2 John 5f. summarizes 1 John 2:7;
3:11; 5:3. (5) 2 John 7 is based on 1 John 2:18, 19, 26; 4:1–3; and the change in the
tense of the confession indicates a difference in authorship. (6) 2 John 8 teaches
the unjohannine idea of reward. (7) 2 John 9 places "teaching" alongside the Son;
contrast 1 John 2:23b. (8) The treatment suggested in 2 John 10f. goes beyond
that advocated in *Didache* 11f. and is different from the method of dealing with
heresy in 1 and 3 John. These points are part of a case that 2 John is not by the
author of 1 John or 3 John. Only the first three points are relevant to the question
of the epistolary character of 2 John. They are not impressive. The opening of the
letter can equally well be addressed to a specific community, so well known to the
writer that further identification was unnecessary. In so brief a corpus of writings
no weight can be placed on ἐκλεκτός as a word not found elsewhere. The correspondence with the form of address in 3 John is only natural in two letters written
by the same person. The suggestion that the letter is written to Christians generally
comes to grief on the clear indications that a concrete situation is envisaged. On
the question of authorship see below, section 5, especially n. 70.
[4]B. H. Streeter, *The Primitive Church*, London, 1928, 83–97; G. Bornkamm,
TDNT VI, 670–672; E. Schweizer, *Church Order in the New Testament*, London,
1961, 12c, 14a.

spondingly restricted. But as time passed and churches increased in number, a new situation began to arise. The apostles and their colleagues were growing old, or had actually died. There was no defined universal system of succession, and it was natural that local churches should begin to develop a more powerful leadership of their own. At the same time there was a tendency toward the concentration of leadership. In the early days church leaders constituted a group of elders or of bishops and deacons. Now this "team ministry" was giving way to the idea of one man as the bishop who occupied a position of leadership over the other church officials. It looks as though Diotrephes was trying to encourage this process in his own church—naturally with himself as the appointed leader. He was seeking autonomy for his own church by trying to get rid of the influence of John and John's emissaries, and he was claiming authority for himself within the church. It does not necessarily follow that Diotrephes had already become the authorized leader in his own church, but simply that he was desirous of this position.[5] We have not yet reached the state of development reflected in the Epistles of Ignatius, where each local church has its own bishop, elders, and deacons.[6]

Since 1 and 2 John were written to churches which faced problems caused by heresy, some commentators have been tempted to find the same problem in 3 John also. This view was adopted by W. Bauer:

> To be sure, 3 John does not contain an explicit warning against false teachers. Nevertheless, its close connection with 2 John is a sufficient indication of its thrust. And the assurance repeated no less than five times in this brief writing that the brethren who support the elder possess the "truth"—that entity which in 2 John and also in 1 John distinguishes the orthodox believer from the heretic—renders it very unlikely, to my way of thinking, that we are here dealing merely with personal frictions between the elder and Diotrephes. . . . Since 2 John shows the elder to be a determined opponent of a docetic interpretation of Christ, we need not spend time in searching for the real reasons that time and again prompt him to

---

[5]Dodd, 161–165; Schnackenburg, 329. Cf. H. von Campenhausen, *Ecclesiastical Authority and Spiritual Power in the Church of the First Three Centuries*, Stanford/London, 1969, 122 n. 326, who cites the opinion of T. Craig, "It is clear that this Diotrephes not only *loved* the pre-eminence but he *had* it." Diotrephes was certainly claiming the leadership of the church, but it seems doubtful whether he held a lawfully constituted and recognized position.

[6]For Ignatius see H. von Campenhausen, *op. cit.*, 97–106.

renew his efforts to maintain contact with the beloved Gaius through letters like 3 John, and with the church of Diotrephes through emissaries.[7]

Bauer's argument is clearly largely based on silence. We may well wonder why an author who expresses himself so strongly against heresy in 1 and 2 John does not also say something on precisely this point in a letter which refers to one of his opponents by name. It is not surprising, therefore, that this thesis has not found acceptance among scholars.[8]

Indeed, so weak is the evidence that Diotrephes was a heretic that E. Käsemann felt himself able to propound precisely the opposite hypothesis.[9] He argued that it was in fact the elder who had Gnostic sympathies and wrote a Gospel which could, at the very least, be misunderstood in a Gnostic direction. Diotrephes thus emerges as the champion of orthodoxy who went so far as to excommunicate the elder on account of his heretical views; the letter then represents the elder as trying to regain support from the church. R. Bultmann expressed some sympathy for this hypothesis, although he claimed that Käsemann had pushed it too far: there is no evidence whatever that the elder was, as Käsemann held, an elder in Diotrephes' church who had been excommunicated by the latter and yet clung to the title of elder; nevertheless, Käsemann is right in regarding Diotrephes as the representative of orthodoxy over against the elder.[10] Other scholars have been less impressed than

---

[7]W. Bauer, *Orthodoxy and Heresy in Earliest Christianity*, Philadelphia/London, 1972, 93. Bauer's general position regarding the first- and second-century church has come under increasing fire; see I. H. Marshall, "Orthodoxy and heresy in earlier Christianity," *Themelios* 2:1, September 1976, 5–14.

[8]See Haenchen, 290–294.

[9]E. Käsemann, "Ketzer und Zeuge," ZTK 48, 1951, 292-311, reprinted in *Exegetische Versuche und Besinnungen,* Göttingen, I, 1960, 168–187; note the modification in *ibid.*, II, 1964, 133f. See the summary by Haenchen, 295–297. Käsemann drew attention to the fact that the elder never reproaches Diotrephes for holding false doctrine, although the bitter situation between them could have arisen only on the basis of doctrinal differences. Evidently, therefore, the elder did not feel certain of his own ground, and this could only be because it was he himself who was accused of false teaching. He had in fact been excommunicated by Diotrephes and was now trying to reverse the position. As the author of the Gospel of John he had written much that could be misunderstood as Gnostic in character. The elder in fact was campaigning on two fronts, against Gnostic Docetism and against those who doubted his own orthodoxy. His title of "elder" indicated not that he was a universally respected church leader, but rather that he was simply an elder in Diotrephes' church; and this explains how he could be the victim of excommunication.

[10]Bultmann, 101 and n. 8; similarly P. Vielhauer, *op. cit.*, 478–480. Both of these scholars deny that the elder wrote the Gospel, and that he was an elder in Diotrephes'

Bultmann. Acceptance of Käsemann's viewpoint demands that we find evidence of Gnostic sympathies in the elder. Such evidence is lacking.[11] It also surely requires some evidence that doctrinal points were at issue between the elder and Diotrephes, and of this there is no sign. The Johannine writings are in fact a powerful weapon against Gnosticism.[12]

We return, therefore, to the ecclesiastical understanding of the situation. This view was largely developed by A. von Harnack, who visualized a large-scale mission with John at the center and many traveling missionaries sent out by him.[13] This picture is undoubtedly exaggerated.[14] Over against it E. Haenchen suggests that the evidence merely supports the view that the elder was the leader of a neighboring church to that of Gaius and Diotrephes who was disturbed by Diotrephes' attitude to the traveling preachers who ministered to the churches.[15] This is probably too strong a reaction. It does not do justice to the authority with which the elder writes, nor to the way in which he can refer to himself as "*the* elder." More probably we should think of the elder as holding a position analogous to that of Timothy or Titus, as portrayed in the Pastoral Epistles, men charged to maintain oversight over a group of churches. Against this view Haenchen claims that in 2 John the elder appears as the leader of a neighboring church who has to write with extreme delicacy when intervening in the affairs of a church over which he has no pastoral authority.[16] But this is probably to move too far in the opposite direction from Harnack's suggestion of a central organization. A mediating position is occupied by H. von Campenhausen, who argues that the elder was a man with a wide influence by means of his letters and the traveling preachers. He was not

---

church who was excommunicated by him. See the discussion of the first of these points below; the second would command general assent.

[11]See the criticisms made by Haenchen, 297–299; Schnackenburg, 299f.; G. Bornkamm, TDNT VI, 671 n. 121. These scholars rightly argue that there is no evidence whatever of doctrinal differences between the elder and Diotrephes, that the elder's views in the Epistles cannot be understood as heretical (quite the contrary!), that there is no evidence whatever that the elder had been excommunicated, and that his use of the title of "*the* elder" hardly fits one who was merely one of a collegiate group of elders in a local church.

[12]See further below, section 2.

[13]A. von Harnack, *Über den dritten Johannesbrief* (TU 15:3), Leipzig, 1897.

[14]Haenchen, 286–290.

[15]Haenchen, 301–304.

[16]Haenchen, 304–307. Schnackenburg, 300f., notes that Haenchen's exegesis of the letters is close to his own, but argues that the elder adopts a position of greater authority than Haenchen allows to him.

a "superintendent" with an official position, but "figures rather as a prophet or teacher of the earlier type, one of those 'elders' and fathers to whose testimony Papias and Irenaeus later appealed." The elder trusted to the power of the truth when conflict arose with a church where his authority met with resistance. "He is deeply angered, but he does not put forward his own rights in opposition to those of the other man, nor does he waste time discussing his opponent's claims. He falls back on the living authority with which he is endowed by the 'truth'; and thus armed he proposes to confront Diotrephes face to face, to convict him and overcome him—in just the same way as Paul did with his opponents in Corinth."[17] This suggestion has the most to commend it; it does full justice to the various factors in the situation.[18]

2. THE SITUATION OF 1 JOHN

In contrast to 2 and 3 John, 1 John lacks the typical stylistic features of a letter. Nevertheless, it is not to be regarded as a literary or fictitious "epistle," or even as a "catholic" epistle, written to all Christians everywhere. It bears all the marks of being addressed to a specific situation in some church or group of churches known to the author. It is probably best to regard it as a tract written to deal with a specific problem; it is a written sermon or pastoral address. It deals with the same problem as had arisen in the church addressed in 2 John, but does so at considerably greater length and in much more detail.

A crisis had arisen in the church due to the rise of teachers who were advocating an understanding of Christianity different from that upheld by John and his colleagues. The point had been reached where they had actually left the church, presumably to set up their own rival institution (1 Jn. 2:19), but, although they had left the church, they were still in contact with its members and were causing considerable uncertainty among them regarding the true character of Christian belief and whether the members of the church could truly regard themselves as Christians. John considered it necessary to write a careful statement of the apostolic understanding of Christianity for the benefit of his friends so that they might see where it

---

[17]H. von Campenhausen, *op. cit.*, 121–123.
[18]We thus in effect return to a milder form of Harnack's basic point.

was distorted by the seceders and confirm their own understanding of it and their place in the company of God's people.

These false teachers were forerunners of the heretics who were responsible for the developed Gnostic sects of the second century. The seeds of Gnosticism were already to be found in the New Testament period, although it is misleading to use the actual term "Gnosticism" to describe the incipient Gnosticism or "pre-gnosticism" of this period.[19] It is still not proved that Gnosticism properly so called existed in the first century.[20]

It is hard to tell exactly what the false teachers opposed by John positively believed and taught; it is easier to say what features of the orthodox faith they denied, since John directs his attention mainly to these. Further, we should beware of supposing that every attitude which John condemns must necessarily be attributed to the false teachers, or that their teaching formed a coherent, complete system of thought. (False TEacheRS)

It seems likely that the claims which John denies at the beginning of the Epistle represent those of the false teachers. They were people who claimed to have fellowship with God and to be sinless (1:6, 8, 10). They said that they knew God (2:4). Very possibly they believed that God was light and said that they lived in the light (2:9). What lies beyond any doubt is that they held unorthodox views about Jesus. They did not believe that Jesus was the Christ or the Son of God (2:22; 5:1, 5); they denied that Jesus Christ had come in the flesh (4:2; cf. 2 Jn. 7). When John affirms that Jesus came not only by water, but by water and blood (5:6), it would seem that this statement was one denied by the false teachers. If they denied that Jesus was the Christ, they probably also denied that his death had any significance; if they claimed that they had no sin, it would follow that they felt no need of atonement and cleansing by the blood of Jesus. At the same time it also seems that they did not accept the validity of any commands given by Jesus (2:4). It is not clear whether they disbelieved in the resurrection of Jesus; one of the curious facts about this Epistle is that the resurrection is not mentioned, although John clearly presupposes it. Although the false teachers did not accept the commands of Jesus, there is no evidence that they lived in a conspicuously immoral manner; it may be that in

[19]See R. M. Wilson, *The Gnostic Problem*, London, 1958; *Gnosis and the New Testament*, Oxford, 1968.
[20]E. M. Yamauchi, *Pre-Christian Gnosticism: A Survey of the Proposed Evidences*, Grand Rapids/London, 1973.

15

2:15–17 we have a side glance at their way of life, but this is as far as John goes. He certainly condemns them for lack of brotherly love, but there is no evidence of open vice on their part. Very probably the false teachers claimed a deeper knowledge of God than ordinary Christians (2:20, 27); theirs was an "advanced" understanding of religion (2 Jn. 9). It was apparently based on prophetic revelations which they claimed to be inspired by the Spirit (4:1).

What conclusions are we to draw from this summary?

(1) It is sufficiently obvious that we are dealing with a genuine case of false teaching, a developed system of doctrine which stood over against orthodox Christianity. Recently it has been possible for M. D. Hooker to raise the question, "Were there false teachers in Colossae?", and to set some questions marks against the usual assumption that Paul was opposing a coherent, organized heresy in that church.[21] However plausible or otherwise her case may be, such a case can certainly not be made out for the church addressed by John. It is true that an attempt was made to argue this by F. Büchsel, who argued that the trouble was nothing more than an outbreak of Christian prophecy run riot.[22] This view has found no acceptance. It does not do justice to the facts that a group had seceded from the church and that something more coherent than the babblings of ecstatic prophets is reflected in the Epistle.[23]

(2) A second view which no longer finds favor is that two or three different heresies were being confronted by John.[24] While it is true that John reckons with a number of adversaries to the church, there is no suggestion that they held a variety of different beliefs.

(3) Since the Gospel of John is intended, in part at least, to deal with Jewish denials that Jesus was the Messiah and the Son of God, it is plausible to assume that the Epistle also deals with this same danger. This thesis was defended by A. Wurm, who noted that the opponents of John claimed to know the Father although they denied that Jesus was the Messiah.[25] This description would fit Jewish opponents of the Christian faith. But although this view has a certain attractiveness, it faces the objection that the false teachers

---

[21]M. D. Hooker, "Were there false teachers in Colossae?", in B. Lindars and S. S. Smalley (ed.), *Christ and Spirit in the New Testament*, New York/Cambridge, 1973, 315–331.
[22]Büchsel, 4–5.
[23]See Schnackenburg, 17.
[24]Brooke, xxxix–xli.
[25]A. Wurm, *Die Irrlehrer im ersten Johannesbrief*, Freiburg, 1903 (as noted by Schnackenburg, 16f.).

had once been members of the church (2:19), something which cannot have been true of non-Christian Jews.[26] More important is the fact that claims to guidance by the Spirit and to sinlessness do not fit a merely Jewish outlook. Above all, the elaborate way in which John attempts to deal with the christological heresy of his opponents suggests that something more than a Jewish view of Jesus is involved.

(4) Perhaps the most widely accepted view of the heresy is that it was related to Gnosticism, and in particular that it was akin to the views of Cerinthus. Gnostic thinking was based on a sharp dualism between spirit and matter. The spiritual was regarded as divine and good, while the material was created and evil. It followed that the material world could not have been directly created by the supreme God, and different Gnostic systems of thought devised various ways of explaining how the world had come into existence. One method was to postulate a series of beings or "aeons" emanating from God and forming a long and complicated series, rather like a genealogical tree turned upside down, so that God is at the top and successive groups of aeons occupy different, lower levels, until at last one of the aeons farthest away from God creates the world. By this means the supreme God could be relieved of responsibility for creating the world. But if God could not create the world, neither could he, nor his immediate relations, be united with the evil, material world in any real or lasting sort of way. Consequently, a real incarnation of the Son of God was impossible. One way of getting around this difficulty and yet holding an apparently Christian belief in Jesus as the Son of God was to hold that the Son of God merely "seemed" to be incarnate in Jesus; upholders of this view came to be known as "Docetists" (from *dokeō,* "to seem"). Views of this kind were held by Cerinthus, a first-century heretic, and by Basilides in the second century.[27] Cerinthus argued that the "Christ" descended upon Jesus at his baptism, but that he departed from Jesus before his crucifixion; thus there was no lasting union of the Christ with Jesus, and the Christ did not suffer, something that would have been impossible for a spiritual being. The fact that John

[26]Schnackenburg, 17.
[27]"A certain Cerinthus in Asia taught that the world was not made by the first God, but by a power which was widely separated and remote from that supreme power which is above the all, and did not know the God who is over all things. Jesus, he suggested, was not born of a virgin, for that seemed to him impossible, but was the son of Joseph and Mary, just like all the rest of men but far beyond them in justice and prudence and wisdom. After his baptism Christ descended upon him in the form of a dove, from the power that is over all things, and then he proclaimed

17

emphasizes that Jesus came by water and blood is very plausibly interpreted as a polemic against this type of outlook. We also have information from Irenaeus that John was an opponent of Cerinthus, and would not even bathe in the same bathhouse at Ephesus with that "enemy of the truth."[28] All this suggests that the teaching opposed by John was closely related to that of Cerinthus.[29]

But this identification can be questioned from two sides. On the one hand, it has been noted that certain features of Cerinthus's teaching are not reflected in the Epistle. There is, for example, no reference in the Epistle to Cerinthus's distinction between the supreme God and the inferior being who created the universe. Nor do we hear any echo of Cerinthus's view that Jesus was the son of the inferior creator-god.[30] Above all, there is no trace of a developed Gnostic cosmological myth with a series of aeons. On the other hand, there are features of the teaching of the heretics reflected in 1 John which are not found in our other accounts of Cerinthus's teaching. We do not, for example, know that claims to sinlessness were made by Cerinthus and his followers, or that they claimed to rest their teaching on spiritual revelations. For reasons such as these the identification of the heresy as Cerinthianism has become much less popular.

(5) R. Schnackenburg in particular has argued against detecting Cerinthianism in the Epistle and holds that more attention should be paid to the Docetist heretics who are attacked by Ignatius and who flourished in Asia Minor in the early second century. In his

---

the unknown Father and accomplished miracles. But at the end Christ separated again from Jesus, and Jesus suffered and was raised again, but Christ remained impassible, since he was pneumatic" (Irenaeus, AH 1:26:1; cited from W. Foerster, *Gnosis*, Oxford, 1972, I, 35f.). See further G. Bardy, "Cérinthe," RB 30, 1921, 344–373; Wengst, 24–34. The teaching of Basilides is summarized thus by Irenaeus: "The unoriginate and ineffable Father, seeing their disastrous plight, sent his first-born Nous—he is the one who is called the Christ—to liberate those who believe in him from the power of those who made the world. To their [the angels'] nations he appeared on earth as a man and performed miracles. For the same reason also he did not suffer, but a certain Simon of Cyrene was compelled to carry his cross for him; and this [Simon] was so transformed by him [Jesus] so that he was thought to be Jesus himself, and was crucified through ignorance and error. Jesus, however, took on the form of Simon, and stood by laughing at them" (AH 1:24:4; W. Foerster, *op. cit.*, 60). There is a different account of Basilides' thought in Hippolytus, but here too it seems that only the bodily part of Jesus underwent suffering (*Refutatio omnium haeresium* 7:27:10; W. Foerster, *op. cit.*, 73f.).
[28]Irenaeus, AH 3:3:4.
[29]Westcott, 183; Law, 36–38; Windisch, 127 (with caution); Ross, 114–117; Bultmann, 38 n. 17 (as one possibility); Stott, 47–50. See further n. 38.
[30]Schnackenburg, 19f.

Letter to the Smyrnaeans Ignatius was grateful that his readers were "fully persuaded as touching our Lord that He is truly of the race of David according to the flesh, but Son of God by the Divine will and power, truly born of a virgin and baptized by John that all righteousness might be fulfilled by Him, truly nailed up in the flesh for our sakes under Pontius Pilate and Herod the tetrarch. . . . For He suffered all these things for our sakes [that we might be saved]; and He suffered truly, as also He raised Himself truly; not as certain unbelievers say, that He suffered in semblance. . . . For I know and believe that He was in the flesh even after the resurrection."[31] Ignatius here commends his readers for not sharing the views of certain Docetic heretics who claimed that Jesus merely seemed to suffer. He also comments that these people "have no care for love, none for the widow, none for the orphan, none for the afflicted, none for the prisoner, none for the hungry or thirsty. They abstain from eucharist [thanksgiving] and prayer, because they allow not that the eucharist is the flesh of our Saviour Jesus Christ, which flesh suffered for our sins, and which the Father of His goodness raised up."[32] The christological heresy and the ethical failure of Ignatius's opponents give a close parallel to the teaching and way of life attacked in John's Epistle. Nevertheless, as Schnackenburg notes, there are also significant differences: the heretics attacked by Ignatius had strong links with Jewish beliefs and practices, of which there is no trace in 1 John.[33] Schnackenburg also claims that John's opponents do not seem to have been real Docetists of the kind attacked by Ignatius. He concludes that the opponents of John cannot be identified with any other group of heretics presently known to us.[34]

---

[31]Ignatius, *Letter to the Smyrnaeans* 1–3; cf. 5:2; *Letter to the Magnesians* 11; *Letter to the Trallians* 9f. According to U. B. Müller, *Die Geschichte der Christologie in der johanneischen Gemeinde*, Stuttgart, 1975, 53–68, John's opponents were Docetists who did not separate Jesus from the Christ (as in Cerinthianism), but rather argued that, although Jesus was the Christ and the Son of God, he did not suffer and die to save men; they regarded Jesus as a glorious figure but not as a savior. Jesus' sufferings were thus merely "apparent" and not real. It is, however, hard to believe that John's criticisms were directed merely against the denial that Jesus was a savior and not rather against the denial that he was truly the Son of God (e.g. 1 Jn. 2:22f.).

[32]Ignatius, *Letter to the Smyrnaeans* 6:2.

[33]Schnackenburg, 22; cf. Ignatius, *Letter to the Magnesians* 9f.

[34]For the same point of view see de Jonge, 122–124; Balz, 151f. Bruce, 17 and n. 11, notes that we cannot be sure that the views of Cerinthus are exclusively in John's mind, and refers to R. M. Grant's view that possibly Menander of Antioch is in mind (*A Historical Introduction to the New Testament*, New York/London,

(6) A fresh attempt to deal with the problem has been made by K. Weiss. In the first of two articles he defended the view that John was working in a situation where the boundaries between orthodoxy and heresy were still unsettled.[35] In a second, fuller treatment of the theme he examined the views of the heretics more carefully, taking as his starting point the fact that they are characterized as "antichrists." Their error was not so much Docetism as a total denial of the character of Jesus as Christ and Son of God; they had no interest in the person of Jesus, the quality of his life as an ethical example, or his death as a means of atonement. For them Jesus was simply a man. They did not deny the existence of God, but claimed to know him as Father; possibly they thought of him as combining good and evil. They regarded the orthodox Christians as belonging to "the world," or possibly they identified themselves with the world. They had no doctrine of salvation by the work of Christ, but probably claimed to possess eternal life thanks to their direct knowledge of God; they even claimed to have seen God. They did not need forgiveness and cleansing because they claimed to be sinless, and yet they ignored both the ethical teaching of the Old Testament and the commandments of Jesus. Although they were not libertinists, they lacked love.

This type of outlook is related to Gnosticism. There is nothing specifically Christian about it. But there are no developed Gnostic features either. If they had a place for "Christ" in their system, it was as one of the heavenly aeons. According to Weiss there is no indication that they regarded the world as belonging to the realm of evil. On the contrary, it is John who stands closer to Gnostic dualism. The heretics themselves are closer to the opponents of Paul in Corinth, and in both cases Weiss finds contacts with popular Greek philosophy rather than with Gnosticism.[36]

On this view it is a mystery how John's opponents could have regarded themselves as Christians or ever formed part of a Christian

---

1963, 233). The account of Menander's teaching in Irenaeus, AH 1:23:5, however, shows no clear contacts with the heresy opposed by John. Wengst, 37, argues that John's opponents were not Docetists, since they did not deny that Jesus was a real man; rather they attached no theological importance to Jesus and laid all the weight on the heavenly being, Christ. This produced the same theological effect as Docetism, but the manner of expression was different.
[35]K. Weiss, "Orthodoxie und Heterodoxie im I. Johannesbrief," ZNW 58, 1967, 247–255.
[36]K. Weiss, "Die 'Gnosis' im Hintergrund und im Spiegel der Johannesbriefe," in K.-W. Tröger (ed.), Gnosis und Neues Testament, Gütersloh, 1973, 341–356.

church. The impression that we get from John is that it was possible for the orthodox to misunderstand the teaching of the heretics as real Christianity; it would surely have been impossible for this to happen if there was so little of specifically Christian content in their teaching. We are also left wondering why John stresses that Jesus Christ came not merely by water but by water and blood; here Weiss's explanation is not convincing.[37] At other points also Weiss's picture is unconvincing. The suggestion that "Christ" was a Gnostic aeon at this early stage is highly unlikely.

It emerges that there is considerable difference of opinion regarding the identity of John's opponents.[38] Links can be found with Paul's opponents at Corinth, with Cerinthus, and with Ignatius's opponents. It seems most likely that the opponents were Christians who felt that they had moved beyond the elementary stages of orthodox theology to a new position which called orthodox affirmations into question. They were like men kicking away the ladder on which they have climbed to the heights and leaving themselves without any visible means of support. Relying on their belief that they were inspired by the Spirit and claiming a direct knowledge of God, they thought that they no longer needed Jesus or his teaching. Under the influence of Docetism they argued against a real incarnation of the Son of God in Jesus, and probably adopted a view like that of Cerinthus or Basilides, that the Christ or Son of God inhabited Jesus only for a temporary period. Probably Weiss goes

---

[37]K. Weiss, ibid., 348, suggests that the emphasis on the blood arose from John's insistence on the importance of the blood and death of Jesus as a means of atonement; since his polemic was directed primarily against the denial of this by his opponents, this is why he emphasized the place of the blood.

[38]In the most recent discussion of the problem K. Wengst has strongly defended the view that the heresy represents a stage on the way to Cerinthianism. He states that the heretics were not true Docetists, since they did not deny the real humanity of Jesus. What they did deny was the real, permanent incarnation of the Son of God in Jesus. Their heresy could have arisen from a misunderstanding of John 1:32/34; 19:30, or rather it was possible for them to reinterpret these verses in accordance with their own theological views and thus claim support for them. The heresy showed Gnostic traits, and Wengst draws useful parallels with later Gnostic writings. One of the most interesting features of his discussion is when he turns to John's reply to the heretics. John's case is that Christian love has its basis in the love of God shown concretely in the incarnation and death of his Son. Thus apart from the true christological confession of Jesus as the Son of God Christians have no reason to believe in the love of God and no basis in ultimate reality for the love-command. So far from John being a representative of an early catholicism which defends orthodoxy simply for its own sake, he has demonstrated the inner connection between right belief and ethical exhortation and shown how the latter depends on the former.

21

too far in saying that they attached no significance at all to Jesus; it is more likely that he had a nominal importance for them. On the whole, then, a combination of reliance on spiritual experiences and a Gnostic type of world-view led the opponents to a form of Christianity in which Jesus Christ no longer occupied a central position.

One further possibility should be mentioned at this point, namely the suggestion that the heresy arose from overstressing the "Gnostic" aspects of the teaching of the Gospel of John.[39] The Epistle would then be in the nature of a rearguard attack by a proponent of a more orthodox understanding of Johannine thought. We shall defer discussion of this point to a later stage when we consider the background of John's thought.

3. THE STRUCTURE OF 1 JOHN

The structure of 1 John is determined by its author's purpose, which was to provide an antidote to the false teaching which confronted his readers. It is, however, extremely difficult to find a pattern in the author's thinking, and many different suggestions have been offered.

(1) A classical view is that the thought of the Epistle proceeds in the form of a spiral, the same ideas being repeated several times at ever higher levels of discussion. This view is particularly associated with R. Law, who offered the following analysis:

> Prologue. 1:1–4.
> 1. First Cycle. 1:5–2:28. The Christian Life as fellowship with God (walking in the Light), tested by righteousness (1:8–2:6), love (2:7–17), and belief (2:18–28).
> 2. Second Cycle. 2:29–4:6. Divine sonship tested by righteousness (2:29–3:10a), love (3:10b–24a), and belief (3:24b–4:6).
> 3. Third Cycle. 4:7–5:21. Closer correlation of righteousness, love, and belief.[40]

The weakness of this scheme is that it breaks down in the third "cycle" where the three themes common to the first and second cycles do not occur in the same manner.

(2) A more elaborate scheme was adopted by A. E. Brooke:

---

[39]Houlden, 11–20.
[40]Law, 1–24. For earlier views see the discussion between B. F. Westcott and F. J. A. Hort, "The Divisions of the First Epistle of John," *The Expositor* 7:3, 1907, 481–493. Cf. Westcott, xlvi–xlvii.

Introduction. 1:1–4.

A. 1. Ethical Thesis—Walking in the light as the true sign of fellowship with God. 1:5–2:17.

2. Christological Thesis—Faith in Jesus as the Christ as the test of fellowship with God. 2:18–27.

B. 1. Ethical Thesis—Doing of righteousness as the sign that we are born of God. 2:28–3:24.

2. Christological Thesis—The Spirit which is of God confesses Jesus Christ come in the flesh. 4:1–6.

C. Combination of the two Theses:

1. Love as the basis of faith. 4:7–21.

2. Faith as the basis of love. 5:1–12.

Conclusion. 5:13–21.[41]

Although this scheme has found a certain amount of support among commentators,[42] it seems a highly artificial way of presenting one's material, and I find it difficult to believe that anybody would plan his material in this kind of way.

(3) A quite independent view is that of C. H. Dodd:

Exordium. 1:1–4.
What is Christianity? 1:5–2:28.
Life in the Family of God. 2:29–4:12.
The Certainty of the Faith. 4:13–5:13.
Postscript. 5:14–21.[43]

This has an attractive simplicity about it, and Dodd rightly remarks that it is a fairly broad and arbitrary way of dividing up the Epistle.

(4) A return to Law's type of analysis is to be found in the detailed dissection of the Epistle offered by E. Malatesta:

Prologue. 1:1–4.

1. First exposition of criteria of new covenant communion with God. 1:5–2:28.

A. Walking in the light and freedom from sin. 1:5–2:2.

B. Knowledge of communion with God and observance of the new commandment of love. 2:3–11.

C. Believers contrasted with the world and with antichrists. 2:12–28.

2. Second exposition of criteria of new covenant communion with God. 2:29–4:6.

---

[41]Brooke, xxxii-xxxviii, following T. Häring.
[42]Bruce, 29; W. G. Kümmel, *Introduction to the New Testament*, Nashville/London, 1966, 306f.
[43]Dodd, xxii.

   A. Doing right and avoiding sin. 2:29–3:10.
   B. Love: its nature, exigencies, and signs. 3:11–24.
   C. Discernment of spirits. 4:1–6.
  3. Third exposition of criteria of new covenant communion with
God. 4:7–5:13.
   A. (missing).
   B. Love comes from God and is rooted in faith. 4:7–21.
   C. Faith in the Son of God is the root of love. 5:1–13.
  Epilogue.[44]

On this view the first section is considered in terms of light, the second in terms of God's righteousness and our sonship, and the third in terms of love. However, the neatness of the scheme manifestly comes to grief in the third section where division A. is missing. Nevertheless, Malatesta's analysis is instructive in its detailed attempt (not reproduced here) to show how John links up the smaller units of material.

    (5) Yet another attempt to structure the Epistle along similar lines is offered by P. R. Jones:

Prologue. 1:1–4.
I. God is light. 1:5–2:27.
   A. Communion with God and confession of sin. 1:5–2:2.
   B. Communion with God and obedience. 2:3–11.
   C. Attitude toward the world. 2:12–17.
   D. Warning against the antichrists. 2:18–27.
II. God is righteousness. 2:28–4:6.
   A. The righteous children of God. 2:28–3:10.
   B. The righteous love of the children of God. 3:11–18.
   C. Confidence before God. 3:19–24.
   D. Warning against the spirit of antichrist. 4:1–6.
III. God is love. 4:7–5:12.
   A. The nature of true *agapē*. 4:7–21.
   B. Cruciality of faith in Jesus. 5:1–12.
Epilogue. 5:13–21.[45]

It will be observed that in its main lines this analysis is close to that of Malatesta.

    (6) A somewhat different analysis is given by R. Schnackenburg:

---

[44]E. Malatesta, *The Epistles of St. John: Greek Text and English Translation Schematically Arranged*, Rome, 1973.
  [45]P. R. Jones, "A Structural Analysis of I John," *Review and Expositor* 67, 1970, 433–444.

Preface. 1:1–4.

1. Fellowship with God as walking in the light and its realization in the world. 1:5–2:17.

    A. Fellowship with God and sin. 1:6–2:2.

    B. Knowledge of God and keeping the commandments. 2:3–11.

    C. Application to the readers. 2:12–17.

2. The present situation of the Christian church. 2:18–3:24.

    A. The false teachers and the struggle against them. 2:18–27.

    B. The Christians' expectation of salvation. 2:28–3:3.

    C. The religio-ethical task now. 3:4–24.

3. The separation of those who belong to God from the 'world' by true faith in Christ and love. 4:1–5:12.

    A. Dividing the spirits. 4:1–6.

    B. Love as the sign of birth from God. 4:7–5:4.

    C. True faith as power to overcome the world. 5:5–12.

Conclusion. 5:13–21.[46]

The significance of this analysis is the fact that the most important modern commentary on the Epistle offers a quite different understanding of the structure from the other suggestions that we have considered. Schnackenburg explicitly warns against attempts to trace too neat a scheme in the Epistle. He finds, however, clear breaks at 2:18 and 4:1, on the basis of which he offers the main divisions suggested above. And he insists that the analysis must be plausible as representing the mind of the author of the Epistle.

(7) Yet another scheme has been proposed by A. Feuillet, who divides the Epistle into two major sections, within each of which a parallel structure can be discerned:

Prologue. 1:1–4.

I. The demands of communion with God who is light. 1:5–2:28 (29).

    A. Avoid sin. 1:8–2:2.

    B. Keep the commandments. 2:3–11.

    A'. Avoid the world's outlook. 2:12–17.

    B'. Avoid the errors of false teachers and remain faithful to the truth. 2:18–28.

II. The demands of communion with God who is love—or the conduct of genuine children of God. (2:29) 3:1–5:12.

    A. How to distinguish the children of God and of the devil. 3:3–10.

    B. Brotherly love. 3:11–18.

[46]Schnackenburg, vii-viii, 10f.; cf. Haas, 13–15.

C. Assurance as the prerogative of God's children. 3:19–24.
A'. Discernment of false prophets. 4:1–6.
B'. Brotherly love. 4:7–21.
C'. Victory as the prerogative of God's children. 5:1–12.
Epilogue. 5:13–21.
Conclusion. 5:13.
Postscript. 5:14–21.

This analysis is more natural than some of the others.[47]

Nevertheless, even this scheme is not free from difficulty, and it seems preferable to regard the Epistle as being composed of a series of connected paragraphs whose relation to one another is governed by association of ideas rather than by a logical plan.[48] This does not mean that John is illogical, but rather that his Epistle is not meant to be divided into large sections on a logical basis. We therefore propose the following outline:

Prologue—the Word of life. 1:1–4.
Walking in the light. 1:5–2:2.
Keeping his commands. 2:3–11.
The new status of believers and their relation to the world. 2:12–17.
A warning against antichrists. 2:18–27.
The hope of God's children. 2:28–3:3.
The sinlessness of God's children. 3:4–10.
Brotherly love as the mark of the Christian. 3:11–18.
Assurance and obedience. 3:19–24.
The spirits of truth and falsehood. 4:1–6.
God's love and our love. 4:7–12.
Assurance and Christian love. 4:13–5:4.
The true faith confirmed. 5:5–12.
Christian certainties. 5:13–21.

It will be seen that this analysis adopts essentially the same major paragraph divisions as Schnackenburg. Where it differs from his analysis is in its refusal to divide up the Epistle into three large main sections. If, however, major sections are to be seen in the Epistle, then Schnackenburg's scheme commends itself as best. The decisive objection to all such schemes, however, is that it is hard to gather all the material in any one main section under one single theme, and at

---

[47]A. Feuillet, "Étude structurale de la première Épître de Saint Jean," in H. Baltensweiler und B. Reicke (ed.), *Neues Testament und Geschichte* (Festschrift O. Cullmann), Zürich, 1972, 307–327. Feuillet finds a parallel with the structure of the Gospel of John.
[48]Cf. de Jonge, 9–11.

the same time material characteristic of any one section can also be found in the others.[49]

4. THEORIES OF REARRANGEMENT AND REDACTION

In view of the difficulty experienced in reducing the contents of the Epistle to an orderly plan, it is not surprising that many attempts have been made to explain the present form of the Epistle in terms of rearrangement of the original order, the use of sources, and editorial revision.

(1) The simplest rearrangement is that proposed by K. To-moi, who suggested placing 4:1–6 between 4:21 and 5:1; the effect would be to bring together the teaching on love in 3:11–24 and 4:7–21 and the teaching on true confession of Jesus in 4:1–6 and

[49]Malatesta's scheme works in terms of the three perspectives that God is light (1:5), just (2:29), and love (4:8, 16). It is strange, however, that in 2:29 the rubric "he is righteous" is introduced so casually in comparison with the solemn affirmations "God is light" and "God is love." Further "he is righteous" probably refers to Jesus (Schnackenburg, 166; Haas, 75). We may also observe that the thought of light and darkness is found only in 1:5–2:11 and not in the remainder of the first main section, that the concept of righteousness is likewise confined to the first half of the second section (2:28–3:10), and that the theme of love, including God's love, is strongly present in the second section (3:1, 10–18, 23), long before we reach the third section. In general, the various themes associated by Malatesta with his three main sections of the Epistle are spread more evenly throughout the Epistle. For the earlier analysis by Law, see the criticisms by P. R. Jones, *art. cit.*, 434f.

P. R. Jones himself has useful insights in the course of his study, particularly when he notes that "abiding in Christ" is the key metaphor in the Epistle, and notes how this metaphor is related to orthodoxy and orthopraxy. However, his adherence to Law's scheme imposes a rigidity upon John's thinking which is scarcely justified by the text itself. None of the writers who adopt Law's type of analysis is able to account adequately for the presence of paragraphs with themes which simply do not fit into the overall patterns postulated for the main sections; the Achilles' heel of all such schemes is 4:1–6, and a similar role is played by 2:12–14, 15–17. Nor can these schemes explain adequately the transition from love to faith in 4:13–5:12.

The above schemes all find a major caesura at 2:27/28 (or 2:28/29). By contrast R. Schnackenburg finds the caesura at 2:17/18. This latter view is preferable. 2:12–17 is a "bridge section" which is hard to fit into any analysis, and this suggests that a new theme begins at 2:18 rather than a continuation of the theme in 1:5–2:11. But the way in which sections like 2:12–17 and 4:1–6 are hard to fit into an overriding pattern strongly suggests that it is misguided to look for such a pattern.

A totally different kind of analysis of the Epistle, based on the number of syllables in each section, has been offered by J. S. Sibinga, "A Study in 1 John," in *Studies in John presented to Professor Dr. J. N. Sevenster*, Leiden, 1970, 194–208; on this view the Epistle presents a carefully balanced chiastic structure, with 1450 syllables in 1:1–2:26, 1370 syllables in 2:27–4:6, and 1450 syllables in 4:7–5:21. See the brief but effective criticism in De Jonge, 304f.

5:1–12.[50] There is, however, no objective evidence for this transposition, and in fact it disturbs the catch-word connection at 3:24/4:1 ("Spirit"–"spirits") and the close association of ideas in 4:21 and 5:1.

(2) More weight must be given to theories regarding the incorporation of sources in the Epistle. The lead in this direction was provided by E. von Dobschütz, who drew a distinction between a series of carefully structured antithetical statements which he found in 2:29; 3:4, 6–10 and attributed to a source, and the homiletical expansions of these which he attributed to an editor. He argued that the four sets of antitheses which he discovered were linked in content and had an "ethical" quality compared with the more "physical" character of the surrounding homily.[51]

(3) Von Dobschütz's work was followed up by R. Bultmann, first in an article published in 1927. He argued that two different styles of writing could be traced throughout the Epistle, and attributed one to a source and the other to the author. The source was to be associated with the "revelatory source" which figured in Bultmann's understanding of the origins of the Gospel of John. The source contained the following verses (or parts thereof): 1:5–10; 2:4f., 9–11, 29; 3:4, 6–10, 14f., (24); 4:7 (8), 12, 16; 5:1, 4; 4:5, 6 (?); 2:23; 5:10, 12; (2 Jn. 9). Later, in 1951, Bultmann took his analysis further by claiming that the completed Epistle was subjected to an "ecclesiastical" revision which added 5:14–21 and various interpolations dealing with eschatology (phrases in 2:28; 3:2; 4:17) and atonement (a phrase in 1:7; the whole of 2:2 and 4:10b).[52] In his commentary Bultmann made some slight alterations in his hypothesis, and in particular urged that 1:5–2:27 represented the original draft of the Epistle, which is then followed by a loosely organized set of paragraphs on the same themes.[53]

(4) As in the case of the Gospel of John, Bultmann's analysis of the possible sources of the Epistle has become the basis for most of the subsequent discussion. It soon became the target for critical

[50]K. Tomoi, "The Plan of the First Epistle of John," ExpT 52, 1940–41, 117–119.
[51]E. von Dobschütz, "Johanneische Studien I," ZNW 8, 1907, 1–8.
[52]R. Bultmann, "Analyse des ersten Johannesbriefes," in *Festgabe für A. Jülicher*, Tübingen, 1927, 138–158 (reprinted in R. Bultmann, *Exegetica*, Tübingen, 1967, 105–123); *idem*, "Die kirchliche Redaktion des ersten Johannesbriefes," in W. Schmauch (ed.), *In Memoriam Ernst Lohmeyer*, Stuttgart, 1951, 189–201; reprinted in R. Bultmann, *Exegetica*, 381–391.
[53]In his commentary Bultmann no longer assigned 1:9; 4:12, 16; 5:6, 10 and possibly 1:5b to the source, but now assigned 2:23 to the source (see P. Vielhauer, *op. cit.*, 463 n. 8).

debate, being accepted by H. Windisch and rejected by F. Büchsel.[54]
H. Preisker (writing independently of Bultmann's second article)
claimed that the author of the Epistle had used a second source
alongside the one postulated by Bultmann, and to this he ascribed
the eschatological teaching in the Epistle.[55] This source was isolated
on grounds of content rather than style. At the same time H. Braun
carried out another examination of Bultmann's theory and offered a
revised version of it.[56] Subsequent critics have been singularly
unimpressed by these theories, and it is interesting that both the
fairly conservative Catholic R. Schnackenburg and the radical Prot-
estant E. Haenchen have united in claiming that the criteria used to
distinguish source material and redaction are ineffective.[57]
Schnackenburg in particular argues that the different types of style
in the Epistle are related to the varying purposes of the author,
polemical teaching directed against his opponents and homiletical
encouragement to his friends; the attempt to separate tradition and
redaction often breaks down for lack of clear evidence; the alleged
theological differences between source and redaction can be explained on the assumption of the theological unity of the Epistle;
and, finally, the alleged form of the source document as a collection
of antitheses would be unparalleled.[58]

(5) Another attempt to distinguish source from redaction is
that of W. Nauck, who has effectively criticized the views of
Bultmann and his followers and offered his own, simpler theory.

---

[54]Windisch, 136; F. Büchsel, "Zu den Johannesbriefen," ZNW 28, 1929, 235–241.
[55]Windisch, 168–171.
[56]H. Braun, "Literar-Analyse und theologische Schichtung im ersten Johannesbrief,"
ZTK 48, 1951, 262–292; reprinted in H. Braun, Gesammelte Studien, Tübingen,
1962, 210–242. Whereas Bultmann regarded the source as being Gnostic in character,
Braun held that it was Christian.
[57]Schnackenburg, 10–15; Haenchen, 242–246, 250–255.
[58]The essence of Bultmann's solution is accepted by P. Vielhauer, op. cit., 463–466.
He argues that John used a written source, and that 5:14–21 is a later addition to
the Epistle. His main arguments are that a source composed of antithetical statements is perfectly conceivable, that there is a difference in style between different
parts of the Epistle, and that opponents of source-theories have offered no convincing explanation of these stylistic differences. The question thus reduces to
one of whether there are irreconcilable stylistic differences between different parts
of the Epistle; despite Vielhauer's claims to the contrary, I find it impossible to
believe that a single author could not be responsible for the varieties in style in
the Epistle.
Other scholars who resist the idea of use of sources include E. Käsemann,
ZTK 48, 1951, 307, who holds that John was influenced by two kinds of tradition;
O. A. Piper, "I John and the Didache of the Primitive Church," JBL 66, 1947,
437–451; de Jonge, 11–14; Houlden, 26–29.

Going back to von Dobschütz's original suggestion he offers a revised set of antitheses which he believes to have been incorporated in the present Epistle. These are to be found in 2:29–3:10; 1:6–10; 2:4–11, and according to Nauck they reflect the "genre" of divine law found in the Old Testament and in the Qumran documents, which was then taken up and used in Christian baptismal instruction. Where Nauck differs decisively from Bultmann is in his view that the source material was composed by the author of the Epistle himself, who used his earlier composition as the basis for his later work.[59] Nauck's work has been reviewed sympathetically by F. F. Bruce,[60] but he suggests that it is more probable that John was using material from his oral teaching rather than citing a document of any kind. Schnackenburg and Haenchen are more critical, and both point out the difficulty of supposing that the author had to destroy the character of his earlier composition in order to fit it into his later work.[61]

(6) J. C. O'Neill has argued that the author of the Epistle took up twelve poetic admonitions of a Jewish character and put them into a Christian framework in order to produce a document showing the fulfilment of Judaism in Christ. On this view John's opponents were Jews who had refused to become Christians—a view that we have already seen reason to dispute. The establishment of this view depends upon the acceptance of a number of guesses regarding the original wording of the text and the postulation of a glossator who inserted a number of phrases that O'Neill cannot otherwise account for.[62] It is completely speculative, and has won no adherents.

The result of half a century of analysis has been to show that the Epistle cannot be explained in terms of written sources; we have to reckon rather with the utilization of tradition by its author.[63]

[59]Nauck, 1–127.
[60]F. F. Bruce, review of Nauck's book in EQ 30, 1958, 115f.; cf. Bruce, 29f.
[61]Schnackenburg, 13f.; Haenchen, 243–246, 254f.
[62]O'Neill accepts, for example, doubtfully attested textual readings in 2:8 and 27 in order to bolster his theory. He attributes the references to the Spirit in 3:24 and 4:13 and also the whole of 5:4b and 6 to a glossator; 5:7f. is then attributed to a "sacramentalist." Other glosses are also found in 1:7; 2:8, 17; 3:20. A theory which has to rewrite the text to this extent is clearly suspect. Further objections have been lodged by de Jonge, 11 n., who observes that 4:2 (cf. 2 Jn. 7) is hardly directed against Jewish opponents, that some of the concepts in the postulated source have no Jewish parallels, and that other alleged Jewish parallels are unconvincing. The merit of the theory is that O'Neill does bring out the affinities of the Epistle to Jewish teaching.
[63]Haenchen, 255.

5. RELATIONSHIPS BETWEEN
THE JOHANNINE WRITINGS

Most scholars have regarded the three Johannine Epistles as stemming from the one author. There was, however, some uncertainty on the matter in the early church. Eusebius mentioned the possibility that 2 and 3 John were not written by the author of the Gospel and 1 John,[64] and similar doubts were expressed by Jerome and Ambrose.[65] In his encyclopaedic Introduction to the New Testament J. Moffatt cited a number of earlier scholars who held this view, and he himself supported it, arguing that "The two notes have a distinctiveness of form and even of language which justifies the hypothesis that their origin is not that of 1 John and the Fourth Gospel."[66] This view was firmly rejected by subsequent commentators on the Epistles,[67] but recently it has again achieved some popularity. We have already noted that some writers consider that 2 John is a literary fiction, following the pattern of 3 John. The evidence for this view is not compelling.[68] It has also been claimed that 2 and 3 John cannot be by the author of 1 John since the concept of "truth" in the two sets of writings is not the same: in 1 John it is used in a dualistic framework and stands in contrast to "error," while in 2 and 3 John it simply means the content of the Christian faith.[69] This argument, however, is also without force, and the common authorship of all three Epistles remains the overwhelmingly probable hypothesis.[70]

[64]Eusebius, HE 3:25:3, refers to "the so-called second and third Epistles of John which may be the work of the evangelist or of some other with the same name." Eusebius, of course, assumed that the evangelist (i.e. the author of the Gospel) also composed 1 John.

[65]Jerome, De Viris Illustribus 9, 18; Ambrose, Epistle 11:4; cf. also the Decretum Gelasianum.

[66]J. Moffatt, An Introduction to the Literature of the New Testament, Naperville/ Edinburgh, 1918³, 479–481.

[67]Brooke, lxxiii-lxxix; Dodd, lx-lxvi; Schnackenburg, 297f.; R. H. Charles, The Revelation of St. John, Naperville/Edinburgh, 1920, I, xxxiv-xxxvii.

Moffatt's specific arguments were: "idiosyncrasies like εἴ τις for the Johannine ἐάν τις, ἐρχόμενος ἐν σαρκί for ἐληλυθὼς ἐν σαρκί, κοινωνεῖν for κοινωνίαν ἔχειν, εἰς οἰκίαν for εἰς τὰ ἴδια, etc. The collocation of χάρις, ἔλεος, εἰρήνη is not Johannine, and there are other resemblances to Pauline language, apart from the apparent acquaintance with 1 Peter which 2 John betrays" These differences in wording, concerned as they are with single phrases, are either of no significance, or are demanded by their contexts. Resemblances with other parts of the New Testament are no argument against unity of authorship with 1 John.

[68]See n. 3 above for the views of Heise and Bultmann.

[69]R. Bergmeier, "Zum Verfasserproblem des II und III Johannesbriefes," ZNW 57, 1966, 93–100; P. Vielhauer, op. cit., 481.

[70]R. Schnackenburg, "Zum Begriff der Wahrheit in den beiden kleinen Johannes-

There is much less unanimity over the relationship of the Epistles (more specifically 1 John, since 2 and 3 John are too brief to permit adequate comparisons) and the Gospel of John. J. Moffatt was able to give a lengthy list of supporters for his view that the works were by different authors,[71] and this theory has commanded increasing support, especially in view of its advocacy by C. H. Dodd.[72] Even R. Schnackenburg, who in earlier editions of his commentary supported unity of authorship, has now declared a shift of opinion.[73] The discussion has been rendered all the more complicated by the current tendency to regard the composition of the Gospel as taking place in several stages at the hands of different authors or editors; the problem then becomes which, if any, of these part-authors of the Gospel can be identified with the author of the Epistles. It is probably true that few scholars at present defend unity of authorship for the Gospel and Epistles, although weighty names can be cited in favor of this view.[74]

We shall consider in turn the various kinds of argument which have been thought relevant to the problem.

(1) Older scholars attached considerable importance to the linguistic differences between the Gospel and 1 John. It is not difficult to draw up a list of stylistic differences, including such facts as the scantier vocabulary of prepositions, adverbial particles, conjunctive particles, and compound verbs in 1 John, together with differences in idiomatic expression. These differences have been carefully examined by W. F. Howard and W. G. Wilson, who have

---

briefen," BZ nf 11, 1967, 253–258 (as summarized in NTA 12, 1968–69, §659), has shown that the idea of "walking in truth" is common to both sets of writings. See also Houlden, 162f. Some of the points made by Heise (n. 3 above) are relevant to the question of common authorship. He claims that 2 John simply summarizes certain verses in 1 John, but does not examine the possibility that both sets of teaching may come from one mind. He argues that the tense of the verb "coming" in 2 John 7 as compared with 1 John 4:2 is a sign of difference of authorship. He also claims that 2 John 9 puts the "teaching" in the place of Christ (contrast 1 Jn. 2:23b). In neither case does he allow the author some degree of variation in expression. Finally, he holds that the treatment of heretics in 2 John 10f. is different from that in 1 John and 3 John—but does not ask whether different situations may be reflected. The case is accordingly completely unconvincing.

[71]J. Moffatt, *op. cit.*, 589–593.

[72]Dodd, xlvii–lvi; C. H. Dodd, "The First Epistle of John and the Fourth Gospel," BJRL 21, 1937, 129–156.

[73]Contrast Schnackenburg, 34–38, and 335 (the addendum to the fifth edition of the commentary).

[74]Brooke, i–xix; Law, 339–363; W. G. Kümmel, *op. cit.*, 310–312; MH IV, 132–138. See also n. 75.

been able to question their force.[75] In general, however, the application of statistical methods and stylistic comparisons is a method of limited applicability. R. Morgenthaler has rightly observed that even if statistical investigations of this kind can produce fruitful results, they must always be carried out with very great caution; taken by themselves statistics can be deceptive.[76] Again, the fact that similar differences can be established between books whose common authorship is scarcely in doubt should make us diffident about attaching too much significance to these findings for the Johannine literature.[77] In every case it is necessary to inquire concerning the possible causes of stylistic differences, such as the use of sources or different amanuenses and differences in literary genre. Finally, in the present case it can be noted that the Epistles of John stand closer to the Gospel in style and content than do any other writings to one another in the New Testament; the close stylistic similarities are quite sufficient to outweigh the differences that have been discovered. For such reasons as these critics are generally agreed that the linguistic differences between the Gospel and Epistles are certainly not adequate to bear the weight of proof of different authorship.[78] Accordingly, this argument has dropped from the forefront of contemporary discussion.

(2) A second type of argument is concerned with the absence of various words and word-groups which are characteristic of the Gospel from the Epistle. These include such themes as: salvation and destruction; Scripture; glory; send and seek; above and below; and judgment. These motifs have been carefully discussed by W. F.

---

[75]W. F. Howard, "The Common Authorship of the Johannine Gospel and Epistles," JTS 48, 1947, 12–25; reprinted in *The Fourth Gospel in Recent Criticism and Interpretation*, London, 1955[4], 281–296; W. G. Wilson, "An Examination of the Linguistic Evidence adduced against the Unity of the First Epistle of John and the Fourth Gospel," JTS 49, 1948, 147–156; cf. A. P. Salom, "Some Aspects of the Grammatical Style of 1 John," JBL 74, 1955, 96–102.

[76]R. Morgenthaler, *Statistik des neutestamentlichen Wortschatzes*, Zürich, 1958, 65.

[77]The linguistic differences between Luke and Acts detected by A. C. Clark, *The Acts of the Apostles*, New York/Oxford, 1933, 393ff., and more recently by A. W. Argyle, "The Greek of Luke and Acts," NTS 20, 1973–74, 441–445, have rightly failed to persuade scholars of difference in authorship; see W. L. Knox, *The Acts of the Apostles*, Cambridge, 1948, 1–15; B. E. Beck, "The Common Authorship of Luke and Acts," NTS 23, 1976–77, 346–352.

[78]P. Vielhauer, *op. cit.*, 467. See further G. Klein, "'Das wahre Licht scheint schon' Beobachtungen zur Zeit- und Geschichtserfahrung einer urchristlichen Schule," ZTK 68, 1971, 261–326, especially 265 n. 25. To be sure, both writers claim that while the linguistic arguments in themselves cannot settle the matter, they can form part of a cumulative case against identity of authorship.

Howard, who is able to offer reasonable explanations for their absence. The general point is that there are differences of emphasis between the Gospel and Epistles which arise from their being written in different situations, against different opponents, and for different purposes; it would be foolish to expect different books to have identical contents. Some remarkable omissions and differences can be found when the Epistles of Paul are compared with one another; even within one Epistle surprising omissions can be observed, such as the total absence of the word "church" in Romans 1–15 and the absence of "faith" in the whole of the section Romans 5:3–9:30 (except for 6:8).[79]

(3) More importance attaches to the establishment of theological differences between the Gospel and Epistles. This point must be considered in two stages. In the first place a number of differences in theological emphasis have been detected between the two groups of writings. These may be listed as follows:

(a) In 1 John there is a transference to God of functions which in John are reserved for Christ. Christians are said to be "in God," whereas in John this relationship is mediated through Christ (Jn. 10:7, 9; 14:6; 15:5; 1 Jn. 2:5; 3:21; 4:4; 5:14).

(b) In 1 John eternal life depends on correct belief about the person of Christ rather than on faith in him.

(c) Christ is identified with Life rather than with Logos (1 Jn. 1:1–4; Jn. 1:1–18).

(d) There is a stronger emphasis on sin and the need for propitiation in 1 John.

(e) There is no mention in 1 John of the signs which authenticate the Messiahship of Jesus.

(f) There is a greater emphasis on the parousia and the day of judgment.

(g) The Holy Spirit is less personal than in the Gospel, and has become simply a witness to orthodox belief rather than an indwelling presence in believers.

(h) The thought in 1 John is nearer to Gnosticism than is that of John.[80] The force of these points is varied. Moffatt himself saw no great significance in (f); there is in fact clear teaching about the

---

[79]See W. F. Howard, *op. cit.,* 287–292.

[80]For the above points see J. Moffatt, *op. cit.,* 591–593. See also E. Schweizer, "Der Kirchenbegriff im Evangelium und den Briefen des Johannes," in *Neotestamentica,* Zürich, 1963, 254–271, who notes differences in ecclesiology between the Gospel and Epistles, but leaves the question of authorship open.

parousia and the judgment in John (5:21–29; 12:47f.). As for point (e), the messianic signs are ignored in the Epistle because it is directed against a different type of unbeliever from that addressed in the Gospel. The doctrine of the atonement (d) is adequately presented in the Gospel (Jn. 1:29), even if the terminology of propitiation is missing. The Spirit is represented as an indwelling presence in the Epistle (g) (1 Jn. 3:24; 4:13; cf. 2:20, 27; 3:9). Christ is identified as Life in John 1:4; so that point (c) is robbed of its force. The stress on correct belief (b) is due to the exigencies of polemic, and the alleged nearness of the Epistle to Gnosticism is probably due to the same reason: it is inevitable that polemic against heresy reflects the language of the heretics. Finally, it is doubtful whether there is a significant difference in function between Jesus and God in the two works (a): the Epistle makes it quite clear that nobody can have a relationship with the Father unless he believes in the Son. On the whole, there is nothing here that requires us to postulate difference in authorship.

(4) There is, however, a second level at which the argument can be conducted. This is to consider the use of common ideas with the aim of showing that different use is made of them in the Gospel and 1 John and that 1 John represents a later accommodation of Johannine thought (as expressed in the authoritative text of the Gospel) to common Christian thinking.

Thus M. Dibelius argued that union with God is the final goal of union with Christ in John but is the common possession of all Christians in 1 John. In John 1:18 "no man has ever seen God" establishes the uniqueness of the revelation given in Jesus, but it has lost this sense in 1 John 4:20 and is used to back up the exhortation to love our brothers whom we can see. Similarly, the claim that the believer has already passed from death to life (Jn. 5:24) is also linked with brotherly love in 1 John 3:14, so that the presence of life is something self-evident and can be verified by the presence of brotherly love, a thought which would be impossible in the Gospel.[81]

This type of approach was taken further by H. Conzelmann, who drew attention to the way in which "the beginning" refers to the beginning of the world in John 1:1 (cf. 1 Jn. 1:1; 2:13f.; 3:8) but in 1 John 2:7, 24; 3:11 and 2 John 5f. to the beginning of the church. This latter use is a development from John 6:64; 15:27; 16:4 where the phrase refers to the beginning of discipleship. "From the begin-

---

[81]M. Dibelius, "Johannesbriefe," RGG² III, 346–349, especially 347.

ning" now refers to the origin of Christian tradition, the message and the commands (1 Jn. 1:5; 2:7; 3:11, 2 Jn. 5f.), which are "old." He concludes: "The church relates itself to its origin, and understands this as an absolute date beside which no other (in salvation history or world history) is of any interest at all. The eschatological self-consciousness has been transmuted as a result of contemplation of the historical existence of the Christian society." Conzelmann hinted that other changes in Johannine concepts could be traced in the Epistle, and argued that in 1 John we have a later reinterpretation of the ideas expressed authoritatively in John.[82]

These seed thoughts were brought to full maturity in a lengthy and difficult article by G. Klein.[83] The author begins by attempting to show a difference between the use of the term "light" in John and 1 John. According to John light and darkness are chronologically undifferentiated powers at work in the past, present, and future of the world; nevertheless this is merely the self-evident presupposition beneath the author's theological reflection, which is concerned with the difference between light and darkness on the level of existential time. From this point of view it can be said with regard to the past that men had no time for the light, with regard to the present that they are offered a new opportunity for the light, and with regard to the future that unless they decide at once there will be no more time for the light. In 1 John, however, and especially in 2:8, it is taught that until Christ came darkness was in exclusive control of the world, not merely in the sense that men preferred it but as a matter of principle. But the coming of Christ brought a new epoch in which the darkness is coming to an end and the first phase of a new era of light is beginning. This means that a difference in the understanding of "light" has emerged. The light/darkness antithesis is no longer existential so much as historical. At the same time there is another important shift in that whereas in John light is a description of the Revealer, in 1 John it is now a description of God himself; it is the reality behind revelation rather than revelation itself. How is this shift to be explained? Klein suggests that as a result of the chronological limitation of the period of light to the ministry of Jesus it was necessary to find a way of making the concept relevant to the

[82]H. Conzelmann, "Was von Anfang war," in *Neutestamentliche Studien für R. Bultmann,* Berlin, 1954, 194–201; reprinted in H. Conzelmann, *Theologie als Schriftauslegung,* München, 1974, 207–214.
[83]G. Klein, *art. cit.* See also the summary of this approach in P. Vielhauer, *op. cit.,* 467–470.

whole life of the believer. Finally, the continued shining of the light is dependent on the proclamation of the church about Christ.

Second, Klein takes up the concept of the "hour," which refers to the eschatological event of revelation which binds together past, present, and future in John. This is to be contrasted with the idea of the "last hour" in 1 John, where the use of "last" suggests a series of "hours," whereas the "hour" in John is *sui generis*. But the term "hour" has no comparable use in eschatological expressions elsewhere, and must be derived from the usage in John. The "hour" has become the last in a temporal series, and can be empirically seen to have arrived in the presence of the antichrists. It is a distinct expression from the "last day" in John (due to a redactor); and it is unlikely that the author of 1 John and the redactor of John should be identified.

Third, Klein considers the use of "new" and "old" in 1 John 2:7f. Here too there is the sense of a continuing period of Christian history which works in chronological terms; hence the eschatological sense of "new" in John 13:34 is weakened in 1 John.

Thus 1 John is seen to operate with the idea of the present time as part of a continuing epoch. Having looked at the relation of present to past, Klein finally turns to the place of the future in Johannine thought. He finds little concern about the future in the Gospel, provided that references to the future are carefully ascribed to a redactor or otherwise deprived of their force. But the future is important for 1 John, as is seen in his use of "now" and "not yet" (1 Jn. 3:2) and of the term "hope" in 1 John 3:3. The thought of 1 John has been influenced by the traditional ecclesiastical eschatology, and this can be further seen in the use of apocalyptic terminology with reference to the parousia and day of judgment.

In Klein's view this shift in theological understanding between the Gospel and 1 John demands a change of authorship. Two questions must be addressed to this line of argument. The first is whether the alleged differences between the two works rest on correct exegesis; the second is whether such differences in thought as may be substantiated are of such a character as to suggest difference of authorship. In general it may be said, first, that Klein's case in particular rests upon an existential interpretation of the Gospel derived from R. Bultmann, and this is certainly open to question. Second, Klein assumes without argument that the Gospel of John is primarily a source for the theology of the Evangelist, who was expressing his own theological viewpoint; he thereby fails to take into account the degree to which the Evangelist was controlled by the teaching of Jesus and the tradition of that teaching which it was his task to pass on to others; in other words, the authoritativeness of the Gospel as tradition for the author of 1 John was the authority of the tradition rather than the authority of the Evangelist, and hence it would have been possible for one person to compose the Gospel and also to express his own theological reflection on the tradition in the Epistle. To be sure, it is generally agreed that the Gospel represents to some extent the theological thinking of its author, but he may well have felt more bound to the tradition in the Gospel than was the case in the Epistle. Third, it is not impossible that there was a time-gap between the composition of the Gospel and the composition of 1 John, sufficient to allow for some modification in the author's manner of expression.

In the light of these general considerations, it is not surprising that the author of 1 John should be conscious of a new era introduced by the coming of Jesus and should draw contrasts between the present time, the beginning of the new era, and the future consummation. The "new" commandment was indeed "old" by the time of the Epistle, but it was "new" when Jesus gave it. There was indeed a "beginning" to the new era, and it was important to look back to that beginning. Again, the coming of Jesus could certainly be understood as the coming of light in a new way into the world, and the stress on light as the character of God may be explained in terms of the author's need to counter the claims of his opponents to have fellowship with God while living sinful lives. Along lines such as these it can be argued that the differences in theological expression between the Gospel and Epistle are not such as to demand difference in authorship.[84] Nevertheless, the possibility cannot be absolutely excluded, especially if there are other grounds for supposing that there was a "Johannine" group or "school" who shared a common theological outlook and manner of literary expression.

(5) The problem of determining the relation between the Gospel and Epistles of John is rendered all the more difficult to solve by the current state of opinion regarding the composition of the Gospel. Most contemporary scholars reckon with a number of stages in the writing of the Gospel, whether by the author himself or by several writers. If the latter is the case, there were clearly two or

---

[84]Klein's position demands fuller consideration than I have been able to give here, and I hope that I may examine the issues involved more fully on another occasion. See also Wengst, 76 n. 184, who finds that the different accents in 1 John are due not so much to a new understanding of time as to a different polemical situation.

more writers each capable of writing in a common Johannine style and idiom, and sharing a fairly similar theological outlook. This makes literary analysis of the Gospel extremely difficult and explains why there is such a confusing set of varying opinions among scholars.[85] It also indicates why it is difficult to identify the author of the Epistles with any one of the postulated writers of the Gospel rather than with any other. Until there is some degree of consensus regarding the composition of the Gospel, there is little progress that can be made with regard to the relation between the Gospel and the Epistles.

The tendency of recent scholars is to argue that the Epistles represent a more "ecclesiastical" theology than that of the Gospel, and to associate them with the kind of more orthodox theology found in the final redaction of the Gospel, as postulated by R. Bultmann and his followers.[86] More particularly, it has been suggested that the type of heresy combatted in 1 John represents a one-sided development of ideas found in the Gospel, and that the Epistle is an attempt to restate Johannine theology over against this perversion of it.[87] The exponents of this view differ as to whether the Gospel itself was heretical or was merely open to a heretical interpretation.[88]

[85]See the very useful survey by M. de Jonge, "Ontwikkelingen binnen de Johanneïsche Theologie," *Vox Theologica* 43, 1973, 205–226. Broadly speaking, there is considerable difference of opinion regarding: (1) the existence of a "signs-source," possibly with a rather naive "divine man" christology (see R. T. Fortna, *The Gospel of Signs*, Cambridge, 1970; W. Nicol, *The Semeia in the Fourth Gospel*, Leiden, 1972); (2) the question whether the main core of the Gospel is Docetic or anti-docetic (see J. Becker, "Wunder und Christologie," NTS 16, 1969–70, 130–148); (3) whether the Gospel underwent a "second edition" by the author (B. Lindars, *Behind the Fourth Gospel*, Naperville/London, 1971; *The Gospel of John*, Greenwood, S.C./London, 1972; R. E. Brown, *The Gospel According to John*, New York/London, 1971) or a reviser (J. Becker, "Aufbau, Schichtung und theologiegeschichtliche Stellung des Gebetes in Johannes 17," ZNW 60, 1969, 56–83; "Die Abschiedsreden Jesu im Johannesevangelium," ZNW 61, 1970, 215–246; "Beobachtungen zum Dualismus im Johannesevangelium," ZNW 65, 1974, 71–87; H. Thyen, "Johannes 13 und die 'Kirchliche Redaktion' des vierten Evangeliums," in G. Jeremias *et al.* [ed.], *Tradition und Glaube* [Festschrift K. G. Kuhn], Göttingen, 1971, 343–356); (4) whether the Gospel underwent a further "ecclesiastical" redaction (R. Bultmann, *Das Evangelium des Johannes*, Göttingen, 1959). For fuller details see H. M. Teeple, *The Literary Origin of the Gospel of John*, Evanston, 1974, and on the Gospel generally see S. S. Smalley, *John: Interpreter and Evangelist*, Exeter, 1978.

[86]J. Becker, ZNW 61, 1970, 233–236, argues that there is a closeness in thought between 1 John and John 15–17, which he regards as an ecclesiastical addition to the Gospel.

[87]Houlden, 1–20.

[88]M. de Jonge, *art. cit.*, 217f., apparently adopts the latter view, holding that the opponents solved the eschatological tension in the Gospel by overstressing the

It is not possible here to discuss adequately the questions about the Gospel which are raised by this type of theory. The possibility of various stages in the composition of the Gospel is not to be rejected out of hand.[89] Nor is it impossible that, since John's opponents had departed from the church, the church was the place where they developed their heretical views. But we must ask whether this was at all likely. According to the reconstruction of their views which we attempted earlier, the heretics denied the incarnation and the atoning significance of the death of Jesus, they claimed to know God and to be in the light, they laid claim to guidance by the Spirit, and they were indifferent to the command to love one another. We may well ask whether such views could have arisen out of a reading of the Gospel of John. Certainly in its present form the Gospel could not have been interpreted in this fashion. Suppose, however, that we assume an earlier form of it, one in which it lacked the prologue (Jn. 1:1-18), references to the last day and the final judgment, such passages as John 6:51b-58; 19:31-37; and 20:24-29, the "variant" form of the farewell discourse in John 15-16 (and 17), and the epilogue (Jn. 21); could a heretical interpretation be placed on what is left?[90] Even in this form it is hard to see how the Gospel could have given rise to the heresy. The identity of Jesus with the Son of God remains firmly established.[91] It is true that the Gospel has been described as Docetic, but the error of the heretics appears to have been rather to deny that Jesus had any significance in bringing men to a knowledge of God.[92] The Gospel is not concerned with human knowledge of God apart from men's knowledge of Jesus, and hence it is hard to see how the heretics could have come to believe that Jesus was dispen-

---

"present eschatology" and that John's christology in the Gospel could be the basis for a Docetic view of Christ. Similarly, Wengst, 24, 43, 45, 53, 61, argues that the opponents could have claimed support for some of their views in a Gnostic understanding of texts from John (e.g. Jn. 1:29-34 and 19:30 could be made to support their christology, Jn. 1:13; 3:6 their claim to divine birth, and 14:7 their claim to knowledge of God).

[89]De Jonge follows the view of Lindars and Brown that one author may have composed and revised the Gospel. R. Schnackenburg, however, finally concludes for additions made by others than the Evangelist himself (*Das Johannesevangelium*, III Teil, Freiburg, 1975, 463f.).

[90]I make this assumption purely for the sake of the argument, to see whether the kind of truncated Gospel postulated by contemporary scholars could have given rise to the heresy opposed in 1 John.

[91]John 1:34, 49; 3:16-18; 5:23; 11:27; 20:31.

[92]For the view that the Gospel is Docetic see especially E. Käsemann, *The Testament of Jesus*, London, 1968. For the contrary view see G. Bornkamm, "Zur Interpretation des Johannes-Evangeliums," EvT 28, 1968, 8-25.

sable on this basis.[93] Similarly, the atoning significance of the death of Jesus is firmly embedded in the Gospel.[94] Finally, the need to obey Jesus' commandments, including the commandment to love one another, is clearly stated in the Gospel. All this suggests that it is impossible to explain the theology of John's opponents as arising from a misreading of the Gospel. The point can of course be put more subtly, by arguing that they shared the dualistic outlook found in the Gospel and developed it in their own manner. But this hypothesis too is extremely unlikely: the Johannine dualism is firmly tied to the coming of Jesus with the light of revelation to the sinful world, whereas the heretics appear to have dispensed with Jesus more or less completely as the revealer of God.

The effect of these remarks is to suggest that attempts to derive the views of the heretics from their interpretation of Johannine theology have so far not been successful. It would follow that there is the less reason to regard 1 John as a deliberate correction of the Gospel in order to avoid unorthodox deductions being drawn from it. On the contrary, the author of 1 John clearly respects the teaching in the Gospel as authoritative.

These considerations show that there is little reason to attribute the outlook found in 1 John to an author of different outlook from that of the main body of the Gospel. It is, therefore, possible that both works come from the same author. In any case, however, the Gospel and Epistles stand so close together in terms of theological outlook that they must at least have been written by authors who stood very close to each other.

A brief comment must be made on the relation of the Epistles of John to the Revelation. There is no doubt that there is a close relation between Revelation and the rest of the Johannine literature; the wealth of common theological concepts mark off the five Johannine books as forming a distinct group. Although one can cite significant opinions in favor of the common authorship of all five books,[95] the majority of scholars would endorse the opinion of

[93]Human knowledge of God is found in John 14:7; 17:3 but only in association with knowledge of Jesus; cf. 8:55; 16:3 for denial that men know God, and also (using οἶδα) John 7:28; 8:19; 15:21.

[94]John 1:29, 36; 10:11, 15, 17f.; 11:50–52. The attempt to demonstrate the contrary view by J. T. Forestell, *The Word of the Cross*, Rome, 1974, is hardly successful.

[95]E. Lohmeyer, *Die Offenbarung des Johannes*, Tübingen, 1953², 198f., 202f.; P. Feine und J. Behm, *Einleitung in das Neue Testament*, Heidelberg, 1954¹⁰; W. Michaelis, *Einleitung in das Neue Testament*, Bern, 1954²; D. Guthrie, *New Testament Introduction*, Downers Grove/London, 1970.

Dionysius of Alexandria that this is impossible on linguistic grounds.[96] The only way around this difficulty is to suppose that the author wrote Revelation himself, but entrusted the Gospel and Epistles to an amanuensis who improved his Greek for him.[97] This hypothesis is not very likely. J. Moffatt argued that 2 and 3 John and Revelation had a common author, but his evidence is very thin.[98] On the whole, it is improbable that the author of the Epistles also composed Revelation.

6. THE AUTHORSHIP OF THE EPISTLES

The Johannine Epistles do not name their author, but in 2 and 3 John he refers to himself as "the elder." Our problem regarding the authorship of the Epistles would be solved if we could identify the bearer of this title.

The word originally meant an old man, but it also came to be used quite naturally for a person exercising oversight and leadership. As such it was used for leaders in Jewish communities, and it came to be used for groups of leaders in early Christian churches. A further important use was to refer to distinguished Jewish teachers of an earlier generation.[99]

One possibility of interpretation is thus that the writer of 2 and 3 John was simply an old person held in high respect. A second possibility is that he was merely referring to himself as an elder in a local church,[100] but this is unlikely, since he claims an authoritative position which goes beyond that of a local church elder.

Light has often been sought from a passage in the introduction to a treatise entitled *Interpretation of the Oracles of the Lord* by Papias:

> If ever anyone came who had followed the presbyters, I inquired into the words of the presbyters, what Andrew or Peter or Philip or Thomas or James or John or Matthew, or any other of the Lord's

---

[96]Dionysius's comments are preserved in Eusebius, HE 7:25; cf. W. G. Kümmel, *The New Testament: The History of the Investigation of its Problems,* Nashville/London, 1973, 15–18, for a translation.

[97]D. Guthrie, *op. cit.,* 940–962.

[98]J. Moffatt, *op. cit.,* 480f.

[99]G. Bornkamm, TDNT VI, 651–680; cf. L. Coenen, NIDNTT I, 192–201.

[100]E. Käsemann, ZTK 48, 1951, 301; Haenchen, 307–311; see, however, the criticisms by G. Bornkamm, TDNT VI, 671 n. 121; de Jonge, 239f.

disciples had said, and what Aristion and the presbyter John, the Lord's disciples, were saying.[101]

Here Papias refers to a number of disciples of the Lord, all of them bearing names which appear in the list of the Twelve, and describes them as elders. The use of the past tense to describe what they "had said" suggests that they were dead at the time when Papias sought information from their followers. He then goes on to mention two living disciples, Aristion and the presbyter John, and what they "say." Two Johns thus appear in the list, and Eusebius, to whom we owe the preservation of the passage, adds his own comment that Papias was referring to two different men called John, and that for his own part he regards the former John as the Evangelist and the latter as the probable author of Revelation.[102]

A number of scholars have argued that Papias was in fact referring to only one person called John; on this view Papias mentions the name twice because only John was still alive out of the first group, and therefore he had to be listed both in the first group, consisting of members of the Twelve, and also in the second, smaller group, consisting of persons still alive. Such early church writers as Irenaeus and Polycrates appear to have known of only one John.[103] If so, "the elder John" would be a title for John the apostle, a usage which is perhaps paralleled in Peter's description of himself as "your fellow-elder" in 1 Peter 5:1. Since, further, the most plausible interpretation of 1 John 1:1–4 is that the author claimed to be an eyewitness of the earthly life of Jesus, and since we know that the Gospel of John was attributed to one of Jesus' earthly disciples (Jn. 21:24), it is an attractive solution to our problem to say that John, the son of Zebedee, known as "the elder," was the author of the Gospel and the Epistles.[104] On this view, the term "elder" would denote one of the venerated older generation of Christian leaders who had had personal contact with Jesus.

This hypothesis faces a number of objections of varying strength. First, it has been argued that it is incredible that Diotrephes would have attacked the elder in the way he did if the

---

[101]Eusebius, HE 3:39:4. See especially J. Munck, "Presbyters and Disciples of the Lord in Papias," HTR 52, 1959, 223–243.
[102]Eusebius, HE 3:39:5–7.
[103]Plummer, 213–216.
[104]So especially T. Zahn, *Introduction to the New Testament*, London, 1909, II, 452; similarly Plummer, 213–216; Smith, 159–162; Ross, 125–129; Stott, 35–39; D. Guthrie, *op. cit.*, 866–869, 884–890.

elder had held the authoritative position of an apostle, and that the elder should not have appealed to his apostolic authority in replying to him.[105] This is not a strong argument. The apostolic authority of Paul was certainly attacked by his opponents, especially in Corinth, and his claim to be an apostle was denied. It is true that Paul stressed his authority when dealing with his opponents, whereas the elder did not do so, but this difference may be explained by the difference in temperament between the two men, and also by the fact that the controversy in Paul's case centered on the fact of his apostleship as such.

Second, it is debated whether the Gospel can be the work of an eyewitness of the life of Jesus: its contents are often held to be incompatible with apostolic authorship, and the slowness of the church to accept it as canonical might suggest the existence of doubts about its authorship. These are points which belong to a discussion of the Gospel, and it must suffice to say that in our opinion they do not constitute decisive objections to the hypothesis of John's authorship.[106]

Third, we have already suggested that it is unlikely that one and the same person wrote the Epistles and the Revelation. To accept apostolic authorship for the Gospel and Epistles would thus entail denying it for Revelation. Yet it can be argued that the external evidence for the apostolic authorship of Revelation is as strong as, if not stronger than, in the case of the Gospel.[107] On the other hand, it can be argued that it would be very natural for second-century writers to assume that a prophet who called himself "John" *simpliciter* (Rev. 1:1, 4, 9) was the apostle.

Fourth, the interpretation of the passage from Papias on which this hypothesis rests is extremely doubtful. It is generally agreed that if Papias meant to refer to only one person called John, then he did so in a very clumsy manner. The majority of scholars, however, think that he was referring to two separate persons called John. However, even if Papias was referring to two Johns, this is not necessarily a fatal objection to the hypothesis of apostolic

---

[105]E. Käsemann, *art. cit.,* 295.

[106]The simple truth is that nobody knows what the intellectual capabilities of John, the son of Zebedee, were; arguments based on Acts 4:13 carry little conviction. The reticence of the church to accept the Gospel as Johannine was probably due to the use made of it by the Gnostics, who claimed to find support in it for their own views.

[107]Justin Martyr, *Dialogue* 81; *Apocryphon of John* 22 (W. Foerster, *Gnosis,* I, 106).

authorship of the Epistles, since it is clear that Papias refers to the apostles as elders,[108] and therefore that John the apostle could have been known as the elder. It must be admitted, however, that it would be strange if there were two Johns, each called "the elder."

Scholars who feel the weight of these objections have accordingly suggested that the Epistles (and possibly the Gospel) should be attributed to the second John mentioned by Papias. M. de Jonge notes how elsewhere Papias could refer to John the elder simply as "the elder," and suggests that this is how he was known.[109] Whether this John was a disciple of the earthly Jesus is uncertain; according to Papias he was a "disciple of the Lord," and according to I John 1:1-4 the author was an eyewitness of the ministry of Jesus, but many scholars doubt Papias's reliability on details and argue that a broader interpretation of the preface to 1 John is possible.[110]

Adoption of this solution raises the question of a possible relationship between John the apostle and John the elder. It has been suggested that the elder was a disciple of the apostle.[111] Such a view would do justice both to the evidence that John the apostle is the authority behind the Gospel and also to the difficulties caused by assigning the Gospel and Epistles directly to his pen. But it must be emphasized that we have no evidence whatever that John the elder was a disciple or associate of John the apostle; this part of the theory is pure speculation, although it may be regarded as an attractive and by no means impossible speculation.

Both of the theories based on Papias's evidence associate the Epistles with an "elder" named John. Various scholars who recognize their hypothetical nature, and are skeptical of the value of Papias's evidence are content with framing a less precise hypothesis. Recognizing the kinship between the various Johannine writings, they postulate the existence of a "school" or group of Christian thinkers gathered around the figure of John, various members of which produced the different Johannine writings. On

---

[108]Against the assertion of G. Bornkamm, TDNT VI, 677, to the contrary, see J. Munck, art. cit., 236f.

[109]De Jonge, 239. J. Munck's view, art. cit., 238, that the same person could not be known as "the elder" and as "John the elder," ignores the fact that Papias speaks of the same person in both ways (Eusebius, HE 3:39:15).

[110]Schnackenburg, 56f.; de Jonge, 271. But both authors would admit that the narrower interpretation is perfectly possible.

[111]B. H. Streeter, The Four Gospels, London, 1930⁴, 430-461. Similarly, A. M. Hunter, The Gospel according to John, New York/Cambridge, 1965, 12-14.

this view, the inspiration of the different writings can be traced ultimately to the apostle, although he himself was not personally the author of any of them. The authorship of the individual writings then remains uncertain, and the Gospel may indeed be the work of several hands.[112]

In attempting to come to a conclusion we have to ask what "the elder" signifies in 2 and 3 John, and to whom the title refers. For Papias the elders are "members of the older generation who are regarded as mediators of the authentic tradition and reliable teachers."[113] What is not clear is whether one of this group would refer to himself by this title; it appears to be more of a title conferred upon a respected figure than a title that one would claim for oneself. It is, however, possible that a person might refer to himself by the title by which he was known to his followers (compare perhaps Jn. 13:13). It is also possible that by reason of his age and charismatic authority the author of the Epistles might have come to be known as "the elder," especially if the local church organization did not involve a plurality of elders. This usage might then have been transferred to refer to such early church leaders in respect of their position as mediators of the apostolic tradition. In this way we may perhaps make a link between the usage in the Epistles and the usage of Papias.

There remain substantial difficulties in the way of the early church's identification of the John who wrote the Revelation, the elder who wrote the Epistles, and the "disciple whom Jesus loved" with John the apostle. So far no convincing alternative has been suggested. The most that can be suggested here is that the Revelation was written by a prophet called John, and that the Gospel and Epistles are either by John the apostle, who was known as "the elder," or by a follower of the apostle who was known as "the elder."[114]

---

[112]C. K. Barrett, *The Gospel according to St. John,* New York/London, 1955, 113f.
[113]G. Bornkamm, TDNT VI, 676.
[114]The author of Revelation claims no higher status that that of a prophet, and the way in which he refers to the apostles in Revelation 21:14 perhaps suggests that he did not belong to their number. He does not use the title "the elder" of himself. It is unlikely, therefore, that he was the apostle or the elder. It would, however, be natural for the early church to identify this "John" with the son of Zebedee. The author was in any case linked in some way with the author(s) of the Johannine works, as is evidenced by the close links in thought. It still seems most probable to me that the "beloved disciple" in John is to be identified with John, the son of Zebedee, although there are important arguments to the contrary (R. Schnackenburg, *Das Johannesevangelium,* III, 449–464). It is possible that he was known as "the elder"

The long-established view that the Epistles were addressed to communities in Asia Minor is still the most probable. If the teaching opposed in 1 John is connected in any way with Cerinthus, this would strengthen a case which is firmly based on the traditions connecting John (whether the apostle or the elder) with Asia Minor.[115] A case has been made out for linking the Epistles with Syria,[116] but the evidence for this is very weak.[117]

The date of composition cannot be determined with any certainty. It has long been customary to date the Epistles fairly late in the first century, largely on the basis of a similar dating for the Gospel of John. If the heresy attacked in the Epistles is associated with Cerinthus, this probably points in the same direction, although it should be noted that there is no firm evidence regarding the precise date of Cerinthus's activity. But it must be remembered that while the heresy opposed is like that of Cerinthus, it was not necessarily identical with it. Recently J. A. T. Robinson has attempted to re-open the whole question of the dating of the books of the New Testament, and has argued that none of them needs to be dated after AD 70.[118] Whatever be the merits of his case as regards the rest of the New Testament, he has certainly demonstrated the weakness of many of the arguments for a late dating of the Gospel, and indeed shown that there is very little concrete evidence one way or the other. We must allow adequate time for the growth of the false teaching reflected in 1 John and the development of the ecclesiastical situation, both of which show links with the situation behind the Epistles of Ignatius early in the second century; there is also the general consciousness in 1 John that the

---

by reason of his age and authority in the church, and that he wrote or was responsible for the Gospel and the Epistles. But the possibility cannot be excluded that "the elder" was a disciple of the apostle who wrote on his authority, although this view is hard to harmonize with the eyewitness claim made in 1 John 1:1–4. It remains very dubious whether "the elder John" of Eusebius was the author of the Johannine literature, especially since Papias himself says nothing on this matter; Papias merely conveys what "the elder" said about Matthew and Mark.

[115]The tradition goes back to Irenaeus, who was himself dependent on "all the presbyters who had been associated in Asia with John" (Irenaeus, AH 2:22:5; 3:3:4; cited in Eusebius, HE 3:23:3f.). The same tradition is attested by Polycrates, bishop of Ephesus (Eusebius, HE 3:31:2f.; 5:24:3f.).

[116]Nauck, 165.

[117]Nauck's view depends on his interpretation of 1 John 5:6f., which has not found general acceptance. The title "ad Parthos" found in some Latin authorities is of no historical value; see Brooke, xxx–xxxii; Schnackenburg, 40.

[118]J. A. T. Robinson, *Redating the New Testament*, Philadelphia/London, 1976; see pp. 284–292 on the Johannine Epistles.

commandment of Jesus is now "old." These factors suggest that we should not date the Epistles too early, but all in all a date between the sixties and nineties of the first century seems appropriate; it would be rash to attempt greater precision in the lack of more concrete evidence.[119]

7. THE EARLY HISTORY OF THE EPISTLES IN THE CHURCH

A careful distinction must be made between knowledge of a New Testament writing by a subsequent author, citation of it as authoritative, and attribution of it to a particular author. The earliest citations of 1 John come from Polycarp, *Philippians* 7, and Justin, *Dialogue* 123:9; the former of these writings is dated *c.* AD 110–140 and the latter *c.* 150–160. There are possible allusions in Ignatius, *Ephesians* 7:2; *Diognetus* 10:3; *Gospel of Truth* 27:24; 31:4f.[120] According to Eusebius, HE 3:39:17, whose testimony there is no reason to doubt, it was used by Papias. When we come to Irenaeus, toward the end of the second century, we find that he accepted the Epistle as the work of John the disciple of the Lord,[121] and this view was shared by such authorities as Tertullian, Clement of Alexandria, Origen, and the Muratorian Canon.[122] Indeed Eusebius states that its authenticity was never questioned (HE 3:24:17; 25:2).

The position with the two shorter Epistles is not so clear. There is a lack of early evidence concerning them, which is not surprising in view of their brevity and comparative unimportance. The Muratorian Canon certainly includes the Epistles of John, but it is not clear whether it intends to refer to all three Epistles or

---

[119]For a date around AD 100–110 see de Jonge, 276f., who stresses the links with Ignatius and also Polycarp.

[120]See Bruce, 18–20; Brooke, lii–lxii; Chaine, 97–103, 225–231; Stott, 13–16; de Jonge, 272–276.

The use of 1 John 4:2 or 2 John 7 in Polycarp, *Philippians* 7, is quite certain. Justin, *Dialogue* 123:9, equally certainly alludes to 1 John 3:1 and 2:3. When Ignatius, *Ephesians* 7:2, speaks of "God having become in flesh" this could be based on 1 John 4:2f. *Diognetus* 10:3, "how greatly will you love Him who so loved you first?" looks like a reminiscence of 1 John 4:19. The alleged allusions in *Gospel of Truth* 27:24; 31:4f. are very doubtful.

[121]Irenaeus, AH 3:16:5, 8, quotes from 1 John as the epistle of John the disciple of the Lord.

[122]Clement, *Stromateis* 2:15:66 (see further Brooke, lvi); Tertullian, *Adversus Marcionem* 5:16:4 (see further de Jonge, 275); Origen, *In Joannem* 5:3 (see Eusebius, HE 6:25); Muratorian Canon, 26–34.

merely to the first two.[123] The second Epistle was quoted twice by Irenaeus, although he attributes one of the verses cited to 1 John, no doubt by oversight,[124] and also by Aurelius a Chullabi.[125] Eusebius tells us that Clement of Alexandria commented on all the canonical Scriptures (HE 6:14:1), but the fragments of his *Adumbrationes* which have survived do not include comment on 3 John.[126] Origen was aware of doubts concerning their status,[127] and Eusebius had to list them among those books which were disputed by some but nevertheless generally recognized in the church (HE 3:24:17; 25:2f.)—thus placing them in company with other books which all became part of the canon of the New Testament. Jerome too testifies to doubts concerning them,[128] and Theodore of Mopsuestia and Chrysostom made no use of 2 and 3 John.[129]

On the basis of this and other evidence T. W. Manson argued that 1 and 2 John became known in the Latin-speaking church in the West before 3 John, which was translated separately into Latin.[130]

In the eastern church in Syria the Catholic Epistles were late in being accepted into the canon. 1 John was included in the *Syriac Peshitta* translation of the New Testament along with James and 1 Peter, but 2 and 3 John were accepted only much later in the Philoxenian version (AD 508).

8. THE THOUGHT OF THE EPISTLES

Although modern scholarship has rightly recognized that the study of the Old Testament in the early church forms the "sub-structure" of New Testament theology,[131] this judgment might not seem to apply to 1–3 John. Direct allusions to the Old Testament are few,

---

[123]For the view that all three Epistles are mentioned see J. Moffatt, *op. cit.*, 478f.; P. Katz, "The Johannine Epistles in the Muratorian Canon," JTS ns 8, 1957, 273f. For the view that only two are mentioned see T. W. Manson, "Entry into Membership of the Early Church. Additional Note: The Johannine Epistles and the Canon of the New Testament," JTS 48, 1947, 32f.; Bruce, 18f.
[124]Irenaeus, AH 1:16:3 (2 Jn. 11); 3:16:8 (2 Jn. 7f.).
[125]Brooke, lix.
[126]Brooke, lx.
[127]Origen, *In Joannem* 5:3 (see Eusebius, HE 6:25); Brooke, lvii.
[128]Jerome, *De Viris Illustribus* 9.
[129]Vawter, 404f.
[130]T. W. Manson, *art. cit.*
[131]C. H. Dodd, *According to the Scriptures: The Sub-structure of New Testament Theology*, London, 1952.

being confined to references to the devil and to Cain (1 Jn. 3:8, 12); there are no citations from the Old Testament. Nevertheless, a number of conceptions in the Epistles have been drawn from the Old Testament, such as the idea of sin, the possibility of sin that leads to death, and forgiveness through the atoning death and blood of Jesus (1 Jn. 5:16f.; 1:7; 2:1). Behind the statements in 1 John 2:12–14 there may lie the thought of the new covenant, as prophesied by Jeremiah.[132] More generally the theological and ethical atmosphere of the Epistles is thoroughly Jewish, and reflects the Jewish background which is common to the New Testament writings.

Attempts have been made to define more precisely the forms of Judaism which may be reflected in the Epistles. Here a prominent place must be assigned to the Dead Sea Scrolls. The enthusiasm which surrounded their discovery led to attempts to find parallels and influences in them to every part of the New Testament, and the Johannine writings offered an obvious candidate for such comparisons.[133] A more sober note was sounded by H. Braun, who probably reacted too far in the opposite direction by pointing out the differences between the Qumran documents and the Johannine writings.[134] Now that there has been time for reflection it is possible to reach a more balanced verdict. There are undoubted parallels in thought between the Scrolls and the Johannine Epistles. These are to be seen particularly in the dualism of light and darkness, truth and error, which governs the thought of 1 John. It may also be seen in the resultant division of men into two groups and the association of one group with the Spirit of God and the other with the spirit of error. The stress on love within the community is also a feature of both groups. It must be insisted, however,

[132]See commentary *ad loc.* A. T. Hanson, *Studies in the Pastoral Epistles,* Naperville/London, 1968, 91–96, has argued that 1 John 1:7–2:9 is the work of an author who was familiar with the use of Psalm 130 (LXX 129) in the context of baptism and allowed it to color his words when writing what may perhaps be a baptismal homily. The Psalm is concerned with confession of sins, the provision of ἱλασμός and redemption from lawless acts, themes which recur in 1 John.

[133]Nauck; R. E. Brown, "The Qumran Scrolls and the Johannine Gospel and Epistles," in *New Testament Essays,* Milwaukee, 1965, 102–131; M.-É. Boismard, "The First Epistle of John and the Writings of Qumran," in J. H. Charlesworth (ed.), *John and Qumran,* London, 1972, 156–165.

[134]Braun, I, 290–306. This work has the form of a commentary on the New Testament, discussing in turn each section where Qumran influence has been detected by scholars; a second volume is devoted to general essays on the theme. See also Haenchen, 255–260.

that the two groups of writings do not use identical terminology, and that there are considerable differences between the two groups in their practical understanding of what is involved in belonging to the realm of light. Salvation for the Qumran sect lay in strict observance of the law of Moses, but for the Johannine community it was associated with obedience to the law of love given by Jesus. The attempt to trace connections between the ritual practiced at Qumran and the initiatory rites practiced in the Johannine community has not been successful.[135] The evidence shows that the Dead Sea Scrolls and the Johannine Epistles exhibit some striking resemblances and to some extent have a similar conceptual background, but direct evidence of influence from Qumran upon the Epistles is much less easy to find.

Although the attempt of J. C. O'Neill to find a Jewish document at the base of 1 John has failed to attract any supporters,[136] he has nevertheless performed the useful service of emphasizing once again the essentially Jewish background of thought of the Epistle, and in particular its affinities with the type of piety and ethical teaching found in the *Testaments of the Twelve Patriarchs*. The stress on keeping God's commandments and on brotherly love is especially characteristic of these documents.[137]

The Jewish affinities of the Epistles may also be seen in the character of the author's Greek style, which is unmistakably Semitic and may reflect a number of Hebrew constructions.[138]

Undoubtedly, however, the major influence on the Epistles is to be sought in early Christianity, specifically in its Johannine version.[139] Whatever be the relationship between the Gospel of

---

[135]See commentary on 1 John 5:8, especially 239 n. 29.

[136]See above, section 4 (6).

[137]O'Neill, 15, 39. See *Testament of Dan* 5:1; *Testament of Reuben* 6:9; *Testament of Gad* 4.

[138]J. Héring, "Y a-t-il des Aramaïsmes dans la Première Épître Johannique?", RHPR 36, 1956, 113–121, answers his own question affirmatively. He suggests that in a number of cases the Aramaic relative conjunction d^e has been mistranslated: in 1:1, 3 the neuter ὅ is a mistranslation for the masculine form ὅς (cf. Jn. 17:24); in 2:8 ὅ is a mistranslation for ἥ; in 2:12–14 the repeated ὅτι is a mistranslation for the relative form οἵ (cf. Jn. 8:53; 9:17); and in 3:2 ὅτι is a mistranslation for ὅτε. He further suggests that in 5:4 (cf. Jn. 17:2) *kōl* ("every") has been mistranslated as neuter instead of masculine, and that in 2:10 ἐν αὐτῷ refers back to ἐν τῷ φωτί (cf. NIV mg.). These examples are not particularly convincing. See further Schnackenburg, 7; and especially MH IV, 135–137. The most convincing Hebraisms are to be found in 1 John 1:6 ("to do the truth") and 2 John 2 (participle coordinate with a main verb), and also the use of *casus pendens* (1 Jn. 2:5, 24).

[139]Haenchen, 266f.

John and the Epistles, it is undeniable that they all belong to the same area of Christian thought and practice, and it may be argued that the thought of the Epistles is simply derived from that which is reflected in the Gospel. We have already discussed this relationship and seen that the Epistles reflect a later stage than the Gospel. The problem of the origins and nature of Johannine Christianity lies beyond the horizon of the present introduction.

A particular problem is whether the thought of the Epistles owes anything to the syncretistic and Gnostic influences which appear to have affected the opponents of the writer.[140] The topic of the new birth or divine generation in particular has no terminological background in Judaism, and it is arguable that the vocabulary has been influenced by Hellenistic considerations. The Johannine dualism has also been traced to Gnosticism, and it is arguable that the concepts of divine "anointing" and "seed" stem from the same source. We need not fight shy of admitting that John has used terminology from such sources in the interests of making his message comprehensible to his readers. It is a different question when it is implied that the content of the Gospel has been fundamentally altered by such borrowings, or that what can be traced to Hellenistic sources cannot be a means of divine revelation.

It remains, however, very doubtful whether Gnosticism in the full sense of the term existed in the first century,[141] and it is important to notice that what John condemns is a Docetic or similar christology and a lowering of Christian ethical standards rather than the full-blown Gnostic system of teaching. Nor is there any evidence that he himself had adopted a Gnostic standpoint. The most that can be said is that some of the terminology which he adopted may have been drawn from Hellenistic sources.

The theological emphases of the Epistles are obviously due in some measure to the nature of the situation in which John was writing. Nevertheless, it is clear from the less polemical tone of 3 John that truth and love were two of the fundamental terms in his theology, and it would not be difficult to write a summary of his thought centered on these two terms.

---

[140]See Haenchen, 260–265, who apparently holds that 1 John uses some Gnostic concepts but is by no means Gnostic in outlook; Schnackenburg, 29–32.

[141]See nn. 19 and 20. A discussion of L. Schottroff's attempt to prove that the Gospel of John is "the first detailed Gnostic system known to us which has adapted Christian traditions" (*Der Glaubende und die feindliche Welt*, Neukirchen, 1970, Kap. 6) cannot be undertaken here.

His doctrine of God emphasizes his character as light and as love. He is the Father, known as such only through his Son, Jesus Christ, and he can be known as Father by believers. His love is the origin of human salvation, and, although he is presented as the righteous judge, it is he who sent his Son to deliver men from their sins.

Jesus is presented as the Christ, the Son of God, and the reality of the incarnation of the preexistent Word of God is stressed. His life is the ethical model for believers, his teaching contains the divine commands by which they must live, and his death is the atoning sacrifice for their sins. They look forward to his parousia, and through him they enjoy eternal life. John does not refer in so many words to the resurrection of Jesus, but he clearly presupposes it.

The Spirit is regarded as the source of the truth, by which the Word is implanted in believers. The experience of his presence is a source of assurance that believers truly belong to God.

The nature of God stands in the sharpest contrast to the devil and the world which are characterized by lies, hatred, and evil. This contrast, present throughout the New Testament, is depicted in absolute terms without any intermediate shades of grey between the light of God and the darkness of sin. In this situation mankind is divided into two groups, those who belong to God through divine birth and faith in Jesus Christ and those who belong to the world. The life of the former is characterized by righteousness and love, and that of the latter by sin and hatred.

It is precisely at this point that John's manner of expression leads to problems. It is open to the danger of suggesting that mankind is arbitrarily divided into these two groups without there being any way for an individual to move from the one to the other. It is also open to the difficulty, clearly felt by John himself, that the fact of sin in God's people stands in tension with the sinlessness which should characterize them. A further possible consequence of John's outlook is that believers may lack concern and love for the sinful world around them.

These items will be taken up at the appropriate points in the commentary. Meanwhile it may be observed, first, that the dualism characteristic of John is present throughout the New Testament, even if it is disguised in different terminology and not expressed in such a rigorous fashion. Second, although John appears to see mankind as being divided into two camps, nothing suggests that those who belong to the light were placed there by some act of God without their cooperation; on the contrary it is clear that God sent his Son to be an atoning sacrifice for the sins of the world, and that anybody who believes in him can have eternal life. Third, John is too much of a realist to deny the fact of sin in the lives of believers, although he claims that those born of God cannot sin. He recognizes that believers must be urged to live in righteousness and love, and to seek cleansing and forgiveness for their sins. He may not be able to explain the tension between sin and righteousness in the Christian life, but he does not turn a blind eye to it. Finally, John's tendency to concentrate attention on relationships within the church must be balanced by his clear statements that Jesus died for the whole world and by the open-ended character of the term "brother" when used to indicate the object of our love.

If John's theology raises such problems as these, it also has its strengths, and it has a valuable contribution to make to Christian thought. We can best sum up this contribution in terms of John's understanding of faith.

He insists, first, on the character of faith as orthodoxy. He reminds us in no uncertain terms that faith must have a proper understanding of the person of Jesus as the Son of God. Faith must be based on truth; otherwise it is a sham and has no saving power. Faith is the complement to divine revelation; it is not human subjective opinion, but is based on Christian tradition, more precisely on the apostolic tradition which is now enshrined in Scripture.

Second, John insists that faith cannot be separated from love. Mere orthodoxy is not Christian faith. Christian faith must issue in brotherly love, and the absence of love is proof of the absence of faith. It is, of course, also true that love without faith is not real Christian love.

Third, John claims that faith expresses itself in righteousness and sinlessness. The believer keeps the commandments of God and does not fall into sin. There is no place for antinomianism in John's view of things. Lack of moral concern is an indication of lack of true faith. John's insistence on sinlessness and perfect love places before us the divine ideal for the Christian life and reminds us that this is meant to be an attainable ideal for those who have been born of God.

Finally, John links together faith and assurance. The believer can know that he has eternal life; he can have communion with God, and so he is able to come confidently before him in prayer.

John's ultimate aim in his first Epistle is to give his readers solid grounds for assurance that they have eternal life through belief in Jesus Christ.

Such teaching is clearly vital for the church and the world today. Despite all the differences between the first century and ours it may be urged that the fundamental similarities make it possible to apply Johannine teaching to our situation without much difficulty. The church today needs to learn the lessons that faith must rest on God's revelation of himself in his Son, Jesus Christ, that faith and love cannot be separated from one another, that Christians are called to a life of perfect love, and that they can enjoy assurance and certainty in their knowledge of God.

The Second Epistle
of
JOHN

TEXT, EXPOSITION, AND NOTES

ADDRESS AND GREETING (1–3)

1. *The elder,*
To the chosen lady and her children, whom I love in the truth —
and not I only, but also all who know the truth — 2. *because of the*
truth, which lives in us and will be with us forever:
3. *Grace, mercy and peace from God the Father and from Jesus*
Christ, the Father's Son, will be with us in truth and love.

1 Unlike a modern letter-writer who leaves his reader guessing his identity until he reaches his signature at the end of the letter, ancient writers of letters began by naming themselves and their readers in a formal salutation.[1] To understand the letter we need to put ourselves in the situation of the original readers and see whether the writer's message to them still has something to say to us in our different situation.

The writer of this letter does not give his personal name. He writes like a modern clergyman who might sign a pastoral letter to members of his congregation with "Your vicar" or "Your pastor" without adding his name (which would of course be familiar to them). What matters is his position rather than his personal name. This is indicated by the phrase "the elder." The word simply means an old man, and hence a (usually old) person exercising oversight and leadership. Elsewhere in the New Testament it refers to groups

---

[1]The usual form of greeting in a Greek letter was "A (says) to B, Greeting" (Acts 15:23; 23:26; Jas. 1:1). Christian letters follow an oriental model in which the greeting proper has become an independent address to the recipient (Dan. 4:1). See E. Lohse, *Colossians and Philemon,* Philadelphia, 1971, 5f., where fuller references are given.

of leaders in local churches.[2] This meaning is unlikely here since the writer refers to himself in the singular as "*the* elder," and since he is probably writing to a church of which he was not a member. It is possible that he was simply a venerable figure in the church known with affectionate reverence as "the old man." More precisely he may have been one of a group of persons with links with the earlier days of the church who were known as elders.[3] But since ecclesiastical terms were used loosely in the early days of the church, it is also possible that the writer was what we would now call a "superintendent" or "bishop" with responsibility for a group of churches.[4] In any case, he has a position of authority over against his readers.

He addresses his readers as "the chosen lady and her children." This is a metaphorical way of saying "the church and its members."[5] If the letter was sent to a particular church,[6] there was no need to specify more particularly which church was meant—and this may have been indicated on the package containing the letter.[7] The personification of a community was not uncommon in ancient writings. Jerusalem was regarded by the Jews as the mother of the nation,[8] and it was natural for Christians to think similarly of the church. When Peter writes about her "who is in Babylon, chosen together with you" (1 Pet. 5:13), he is using the same idea.[9] The word translated "lady" is a respectful term meaning "mistress." It is the feminine form of the word "lord"; possibly there is a hint of the church being the bride of the Lord, so that her children are the

---

[2]Acts 11:30; 14:23; 1 Timothy 5:17; James 5:14; 1 Peter 5:1, *et al*. The Jews also used the word for venerated scribes (Mk. 7:3, 5) and for religious and community leaders (Mk. 8:31, *et al*.). See G. Bornkamm, TDNT VI, 651–683; L. Coenen, NIDNTT I, 192–201.

[3]For details, see the Introduction, section 6.

[4]Admittedly we have no other evidence for such a usage, which must have been local in extent and of limited duration. But there is no reason in principle why one person should not have come to be "the elder" in a specific church situation.

[5]Older scholars (e.g. Plummer, 57f.; Smith, 162f.; Ross, 129f.; Morris, 1271) took the phrase literally as a reference to a particular lady and her children. But the interchange of singular and plural in the letter and the reference to the lady's sister all support the view that the writer is personifying the church. For detailed argument in support of this position see Brooke, 167–170.

[6]Bultmann, 107f., thinks that the letter is a "catholic" epistle to be taken to a number of churches. But to justify this view he has to argue that the details in the letter which suggest one particular destination are fictitious.

[7]Dodd, 145, notes the possibility that the name of the addressees was omitted for prudential reasons during a time when the church was being persecuted.

[8]See Isaiah 54:1–8; Baruch 4:30–37; 5:5; Galatians 4:25; Revelation 12:17.

[9]Both here and in 1 Peter 5:13 it is the local church which is meant. The one church is visible in its local manifestations.

spiritual offspring of the Lord and his church.[10] She is "chosen," an adjective often applied to Christians to denote that it was God who called them to be his people; the word always signifies those who have responded to this call and thus actually become the people of God.[11]

Although the writer is following the standard pattern of an ancient letter, he is not bound by it, and before moving on to the greeting which should follow at this point he assures his readers of the love which he has for them. He uses the Greek word which often functions in the Greek Old Testament and in the New Testament to express the particular kind of love shown by God to men and which must be shown by men to God and to one another. The use of this word, rare in secular writing, shows how a new word was needed to bring out the special elements in Christian love.[12] It contains such thoughts as caring for other people, showing loyalty to them and seeking their good, in contrast with other words which are more expressive of seeking one's own enjoyment in the object of love or of mutual attractiveness and affection.[13] Christian love is first and foremost *giving* love, although it does not lack other elements such as affection.

But even Christian love can be counterfeited by people who present the appearance without the reality. So the elder adds that he loves "in truth." By itself this phrase could simply mean "truly, really," indicating that the elder's love is genuine and springs from his heart. It is not a merely outward attitude, perhaps taken up to hide some ulterior motive, nor is it anything less than wholehearted.[14] But in view of the significant role which "truth" plays in these letters, a deeper sense may already be present here.

---

[10]For κυρία see W. Foerster, TDNT III, 1045. For the thought of the church as the spiritual mother of believers see Cyprian, *De Unitate* 6; J. Calvin, *Institutes* IV:1:1: "To those to whom (God) is a Father, the Church must also be a mother."

[11]Cf. 1 Peter 5:13. See G. Schrenk, TDNT IV, 181–192; L. Coenen, NIDNTT I, 536–543.

[12]G. Quell and E. Stauffer, TDNT I, 21–25; W. Günther, H.-G. Link, and C. Brown, NIDNTT II, 538–551. However, the word ἀγαπάω can also be used of other kinds of love (e.g. 2 Sam. 13:15 LXX; 2 Tim. 4:10).

[13]Thus ἔρως, which does not occur in the New Testament, on the whole expresses passionate longing. φιλέω is a more neutral word, used of the love which exists between friends. It does not occur in 1–3 John, but is used frequently in John, where its meaning is scarcely distinguishable from that of ἀγαπάω. See especially C. S. Lewis, *The Four Loves*, New York/London, 1960. See also notes on 1 John 2:5; 3:16; 4:8.

[14]Cf. Schnackenburg, 307. On this view ἐν ἀληθείᾳ is equivalent to ἀληθῶς (Jn. 1:47) or ἐπ' ἀληθείας (Mk. 12:32). Note that this attitude is precisely the opposite of the hypocritical spirit which Jesus so often condemned (Mt. 23:13ff.; Lk. 12:1–3).

The elder loves in a way that is consistent with the Christian revelation that has been received by both him and his readers. In other words, the "reality" with which the elder loves the church is the true, divine love revealed in the Christian message.[15]

The fact that the elder is writing to a church rather than an individual family is confirmed by his further assertion that his love is shared by all who know the truth.[16] To know the truth means to know and accept the Christian message.[17] Such knowing goes beyond merely knowing facts or doctrines to a positive acceptance of the truth and commitment to it. All who have come to know the truth in this way are brought into the same bond of mutual love which exists between the elder and this congregation. Acceptance of the truth involves active love; where love is absent, it is a sign that the truth has not been accepted.

2 The fact that knowing the truth issues in love is emphasized by the phrase "because of the truth," which perhaps sounds repetitious after the previous two uses of "truth." But the elder has a tendency to round off his paragraphs by a repetition of the opening thought,[18] and in this case the effect is to accentuate the point and deepen it. The point here might simply be that Christians love because the revelation of the truth contains the command, "Love one another," but the elder's point is deeper. The truth is something which has come to stay in the members of the church, and it exercises an inner dynamic on them to love. What is said in the Gospel about the Spirit of truth (Jn. 14:15–17) is here affirmed of the truth, so that the truth has become a personal influence within Christians.[19] Somewhat loosely the writer adds that the truth will be with

[15]Brooke, 170; Dodd, 145; Stott, 202; see also Haas, 13f. The difficulty with this view is that there is no article with the phrase (cf. 2 Jn. 3, 4; 1 Jn. 3:18; 3 Jn. 1, 3b). But the writer appears to use the phrase with or without the article without any obvious difference in meaning (cf. 2 Jn. 4 and 3 Jn. 3 with 3 Jn. 4; and 3 Jn. 3a with 3b), and in 1 John 3:18 it is difficult not to give ἀλήθεια its full force alongside ἔργον.

On ἀλήθεια see G. Quell and R. Bultmann, TDNT I, 232–251; C. H. Dodd, *The Interpretation of the Fourth Gospel*, New York/Cambridge, 1954, 170–178; R. Schnackenburg, *Das Johannesevangelium*, Freiburg, 1971, II, 265–281.

[16]The perfect tense is used to signify those who have come into a lasting knowledge of the divine reality revealed in the Christian message.

[17]For the elder "truth" signifies what is ultimately real, namely God himself. Hence it can refer to the expression of God in his incarnate Son and in the Christian message. In 2 John 2 it becomes evident that the truth is tantamount to the Spirit of truth who can enter into the believer. The truth stands in contrast to the ultimately unreal and deceptive lies which stem from the devil.

[18]See Malatesta's schematic presentation of the Epistles of John (Introduction, section 3).

[19]ἐν ἡμῖν refers to the writer and his readers.

his readers forever; his thoughts are carried beyond the immediate issue to the horizon of Christian experience.[20]

3   After naming the writer and recipients, the customary opening of a Greek letter included some form of greeting. Just as the former element was often developed to indicate the Christian status of the persons involved, so too the greeting took on a Christian form. We can trace this new type of greeting especially in the letters of Paul, and it may be that he was largely responsible for developing it.[21] The elder makes his own characteristic use of the Christian formula "Grace and peace to you from God our Father and the Lord Jesus Christ."[22] His greeting is a positive affirmation rather than a wish, since he is sure that it will be fulfilled, and he includes himself in the circle of blessing.[23] "Grace and peace" figure in the typical Pauline greeting, but the elder includes "mercy." "Grace" signifies the love and favor shown freely to men by God, and "mercy" has very much the same meaning; "peace" represents the sum total of the spiritual blessings given to men by God in his grace and mercy.[24] None of these words is characteristic of the letters of John.[25] They are part of the conventional language of the church, just as we may use in prayer words which are not part of our normal Christian vocabulary (e.g. we rarely refer to "trespasses" except when we are saying the Lord's Prayer). But the fact that they are not words that sprang automatically to the elder's lips does not weaken their force. If he himself preferred to speak of love, this is not very different from "grace" and "mercy," and similarly he would have preferred to speak of "eternal life" rather than its equivalent, "peace."

The greeting goes on to specify the source of these blessings

---

[20]The use of καὶ . . . ἔσται . . . after a participle produces anacolouthon and reflects Hebrew style (cf. Jn. 5:44; BD 442[6]; 468[3]). For εἰς τὸν αἰῶνα see the same phrase used of the Paraclete in John 14:16.

[21]See 59 n. 1.

[22]Galatians 1:3. A simpler form is found in 1 Thessalonians 1:1.

[23]The textual variant ὑμῶν is poorly attested (K 69 pm lat sy[h]; TR) and is clearly a simplification of the text to what the scribe expected to read.

[24]For the combination "grace, mercy, peace," see 1 Timothy 1:2; 2 Timothy 1:2; Jude 2. The Jewish form "mercy and peace" (2 Bar. 78:2; cf. Gal. 6:16) appears to have influenced the usual Christian "grace and peace," which was itself probably formed from the Jewish greeting by the substitution of "grace" for "mercy." On "grace" see W. Zimmerli and H. Conzelmann, TDNT IX, 372–402; H.-H. Esser, NIDNTT II, 115–124; on "mercy" see R. Bultmann, TDNT II, 477–485; H.-H. Esser, NIDNTT II, 593–601; and on "peace" see G. von Rad and W. Foerster, TDNT II, 400–417; H. Beck and C. Brown, NIDNTT II, 776–783.

[25]Only εἰρήνη recurs in 3 John 15, again as part of a greeting. For χάρις see John 1:14, 16f.; for εἰρήνη see John 14:27; 16:33; 20:19, 21, 26. It would seem that the use of the three terms here reflects accepted usage adopted by the writer.

as God the Father and Jesus Christ, the Son of the Father. God is given the title which had taken on a new significance for Christians in the light of the revelation of Jesus as his Son; "father" was a word already used in the Old Testament and in Judaism to describe God, but only in Christianity was the thought of God's personal, loving relationship to the individual developed.[26] As the elder insists elsewhere, it is through the revelation of his Son that God is known as the Father, not merely of the Son but also of all believers; it follows that rejection of the Son means rejection of the way in which God has revealed himself to be the Father. To say "no" to God's way of revealing himself is to say "no" to God himself, for he will not let himself be known by men except on his own terms.[27] The elder, therefore, gladly used this fixed form of words which expressed so clearly his own thinking; it is one of the typical "binitarian" formulae which have come down from the early church and place the Father and the Son on the same level of reality.[28] But the elder draws out the meaning in his own characteristic way. His description of Jesus as "the Father's Son" makes explicit the significance of naming God as Father. He also writes that the blessings of the Father and Son will be with his readers "in truth and love." These words prepare the readers for the central theme of the letter in verses 4–11. Their immediate purpose is to indicate that the "conventional" blessings of "grace, mercy and peace" are accompanied by truth and love. The revelation of God in Jesus takes place in truth and love (cf. Jn. 1:14, 17) and its effect is to lead believers into truth and love; it is as Christians grow in truth and love that they go on to experience the fulness of God's blessing.[29] By these alterations in the conventional greeting, the elder has succeeded in repristinating its language for his readers so that its familiar words make a fresh and meaningful impact upon them. Today we perhaps need some way of giving fresh life to "truth" and "love," especially the latter of these two words.

---

[26]See G. Quell and G. Schrenk, TDNT V, 945–1014; O. Hofius, NIDNTT I, 615–621; J. Jeremias, *The Prayers of Jesus,* Naperville/London, 1967.

[27]1 John 2:23; 4:15; 5:10.

[28]O. Cullmann, *The Earliest Christian Confessions,* London, 1949; V. H. Neufeld, *The Earliest Christian Confessions,* Grand Rapids/Leiden, 1963.

[29]The precise linking of the phrase to the rest of the sentence is not clear. For the three possibilities suggested see Dodd, 147; Schnackenburg, 309; Stott, 204.

LIVING IN TRUTH AND LOVE (4–6)

4. *It has given me great joy to find some of your children living by the truth, just as the Father commanded us.* 5. *And now, dear lady, I am not writing you a new command but one we have had from the beginning. I ask that we love one another.* 6. *And this is love: that we live in obedience to his commands. As you have heard from the beginning, his command is that you live a life of love.*

4 Ancient letters, like their modern counterparts, often began with an expression of joy on the part of the writer for good news concerning his readers. Paul's letters sometimes begin with an expression of thanks to God for the spiritual progress of his readers (e.g. 1 Thess. 1:2f.). If the elder adopts a more "secular" form of expression here, this does not lessen the Christian content of what he says.[1] He describes the great joy which he felt when he learned that some of the members of the church[2] were living by the truth. The phrase "some" may carry the implication that other members of the church were not living as they should; in this case the following injunctions would be addressed particularly to these members of the church.[3] But while it is quite possible that some members of the church were not living as they should, it is more likely that the elder is thinking of the personal contact which he has had with some members of the church. Presumably they had visited him, and were now returning home with this letter of greeting. It was the fact of being able to see for himself that they were living by the truth that gladdened the elder's heart. He felt that what was true of them was true of the church generally, so that he could use the opportunity provided by the visit of his friends to write an appeal to the church based on its existing hold on the truth.[4]

[1]Cf. 3 John 3; Polycarp, *Philippians* 1:1; also 1 Corinthians 16:17; Philippians 4:10. The aorist ἐχάρην is not epistolary, but refers back to the time when the elder met the members of the church; Schnackenburg, 310 n., suggests that it is ingressive, but this suggestion seems unnecessary.

[2]The perfect tense εὕρηκα suggests that the writer believes that what he discovered in the past is still true. It is not clear whether εὕρηκα here means that the elder "found" certain people who were living by the truth (so Schnackenburg, first edition, 276 n. 2) or that he had found that certain people were living by the truth (on the basis of some evidence) (Schnackenburg, 310 n. 2). The former view is preferable.

ἐκ τῶν τέκνων σου is a partitive phrase (supply τινάς); cf. Luke 21:16; John 16:17; BD 164².

[3]Brooke, 172; Schnackenburg, 310 n. 2; Bultmann, 110f. Houlden, 143, goes so far as to suggest that those who lived by the truth were a minority in the church.

[4]So Schnackenburg, first edition, 310 n. 2. εὕρηκα strongly suggests personal

After his initial stress on truth, it is not surprising that the elder commends his friends for living by it. "Living" translates a verb which literally means "walking" and was used to describe the whole of a person's existence and behavior.[5] To live "by the truth" means to live in accordance with God's revelation in the gospel and by the standards contained in it.[6] It is the same as living "in the light" (1 Jn. 1:7). Those who live in this way are fulfilling the commandment of the Father. Probably the elder is thinking specifically of the teaching in 1 John 3:23: "This is his command: to believe in the name of his Son, Jesus Christ, and to love one another as he commanded us." The difficulty with this view is that the elder then goes on to speak about mutual love as if this was a further command. But it is probable that he felt it necessary to repeat this particular aspect of what it means to live by the truth for the benefit of the church as a whole. The fact that the commandment is ascribed to the Father (rather than to Jesus) indicates that he is thought of as the ultimate source of the message declared by Jesus (Jn. 7:16f.) and by his followers (1 Jn. 1:5).

5 The elder now issues the first of two exhortations to the church as a whole; the address, "dear lady,"[7] shows that he is addressing all the members and exhorting them to live in the same way as the members with whom he has had personal contact. He makes his request on his own authority as a pastor, but the request is simply one which he passes on from Jesus himself and whose authority is that of God himself. It is as a pastor or teacher who communicates the Word of God that he has authority to command his congregation, but this authority is complemented by the note of personal urgency which comes from his own love for those over whom he has been set.

---

experience, and the parallel in 3 John 3 suggests that the elder has been visited by members of the church. Had the elder faced a church whose membership was partly or largely heretical, it is probable that his injunction would have been to truth rather than to love (v. 5).

[5] 1 John 1:6f.; 2:6, 11; 3 John 3f.; Mark 7:5; John 8:12; 12:35; Romans 6:4; and frequently; the usage is derived from the Old Testament (Gen. 17:1; 2 Kings 20:3; G. Bertram and H. Seesemann, TDNT V, 940–945).

[6] See above, 62 n. 15. Bultmann, 110, translates "really, in an authentic way," which is not satisfactory. Schnackenburg, 310, traces a background in 1 Kings 2:4; 2 Kings 20:3; 1QS 5:25; 7:18; 8:5.

[7] "Dear" is an addition in translation, since the simple address as "lady" or "madam" (κυρία) is unacceptable in contemporary style. The use of the vocative here underlines the personal appeal which is being made by the writer. On the structure of the petition see T. Y. Mullins, "Petition as a Literary Form," NovT 5, 1962, 46–54.

In the light of all this, it is not surprising that the elder has no new teaching or command to give to the church. It is true that Jesus once spoke of his command as a new one (Jn. 13:34) and that the elder himself could also describe it as still new because it expressed the way of life of the new era initiated by the coming of Jesus (1 Jn. 2:8), but the years had gone past, and the readers would already have been familiar with a command that was well known in the church.[8] Although, then, it went back to the beginning, i.e. the commencement of the new era (or possibly the beginning of creation; cf. 1 Jn. 3:11f.), the commandment could bear repetition. Christians must love one another. This is the basis of Christian living to which all believers constantly need to be recalled. For the elder it meant practical, costly caring for the needy, even readiness to sacrifice oneself for the sake of others (1 Jn. 3:16–18); but at the same time it included real affection for one's fellow-believers. It has often been objected that we cannot be commanded to show an emotion such as love. The objection is met by observing that Christian love is a matter of active caring for others rather than an emotional feeling, but it is difficult not to care for other people and to be conscious for their needs without feelings of sympathy, compassion, and affection developing spontaneously.

6   Since the word "love" can have a variety of senses and loving has a number of aspects, the elder draws attention to one particular feature which he felt needed emphasis. Love means living[9] according to the Father's commands. We can readily understand that love *for the Father* would involve keeping his commands: the person who loves somebody else will be anxious to please him by doing what he wants. But the elder says that love *for one another* involves keeping the Father's commands. A further difficulty is that the elder oscillates between "the command" and "the commands."[10] These two difficulties are solved when we grasp that "*the* command" is that we should love one another, while "the commands" are the detailed requirements which unfold the structure of this central command. In Romans 13:8–10 Paul asserts that the various social commands in the second part of the Ten Commandments are

---

[8]This would be especially the case for churches which used John as their Gospel.

[9]The verb used is again περιπατέω, "to walk."

[10]The singular is used in 1 John 2:7f.; 3:23; 4:21; 2 John 4, 5, 6; and the plural in 1 John 2:3f.; 3:22, 24; 2 John 6. Cf. John 13:34; 15:12 and 14:15, 21; 15:10 respectively. See G. Schrenk, TDNT II, 544–556, especially 554f.; H.-H. Esser, NIDNTT I, 331–339.

summed up in the one rule of loving one's neighbor, so that love is the fulfillment of the law. If Paul's point is to show that all the commands issue out of love and can be regarded as expressions of love, the elder's point is to show that love must issue in various detailed types of action in accordance with God's commandments. It may be that the elder was thinking of people who did not realize the incompatibility of saying that they loved their fellow Christians and yet stealing from them or coveting their property. The elder insists that loving one another will be seen in obedience to the commands which unfold the nature of love. Such commands include the social aspects of the Ten Commandments, but also Jesus' positive command that we should do good to one another in the same kind of way as we would like to be treated ourselves (Mt. 7:12).

The final sentence in this section has the effect of rounding it off into a coherent and self-contained whole. The elder underlines that what he is telling his readers is something that they have heard all along, right from the beginning of Christianity; it is the command that they should live in love.[11] Perhaps the stress is particularly on the word "live": the readers must see to it that they put into practice what they have so frequently heard.[12] For this is the supreme command contained in the Christian revelation.

The relevance of the elder's point is obvious in the modern situation where we are sometimes told: "All you need is love." Such advice is meaningless if the nature of love is not defined and unfolded. Love expresses itself in following the divine guidelines. At the same time, merely to keep the commands out of a sense of duty or constraint or fear of punishment is not true love. Love means obedience from the heart and true concern for the good of others.

BEWARE OF FALSE TEACHING (7–11)

7. *Many deceivers, who do not acknowledge that Jesus Christ has come in the flesh, have gone out into the world. Any such person is the deceiver and the antichrist.* 8. *Watch out that you do not lose what you have worked for, but that you may be rewarded fully.* 9. *Anyone who runs ahead and does not continue in the teach-*

---

[11]ἐν αὐτῇ probably means ἐν ἀγάπῃ (Westcott, 228), not ἐν τῇ ἐντολῇ (vg; Brooke, 174), which creates a tautology.

[12]Schnackenburg, 312. Note that the stress on the "oldness" of the commandment may be a polemical point against the "novel" teaching of the heretics who are opposed in these Epistles.

ing of Christ does not have God; whoever continues in the teaching has both the Father and the Son.   10. If anyone comes to you and does not bring this teaching, do not take him into your house or welcome him.   11. Anyone who welcomes him shares in his wicked work.

7 A new section begins here, marked in the NIV by the commencement of a new paragraph and the absence of any connective word at the beginning. In the Greek text, however, the verse begins with a "because," which indicates that it gives the reason for what has preceded. In fact the connection is rather loose,[1] and the new section is not simply an explanation of what has preceded but culminates in the second of the elder's main exhortations. It is probably best to regard the "because" as a link with the whole of verses 4–6: the elder was glad to know that the church was living by the *truth,* and he exhorted it to show *love* because there was a danger of it being corrupted by *falsehood,* which would in turn lead to lack of mutual love.[2] The elder feared that those who accepted false teaching on doctrine would no longer practice Christian love, and that thus there would be a split in the church.[3]

Jesus had prophesied the appearance of false prophets who would attempt to deceive God's people (Mk. 13:5f., 22), and now his prophecy had come true. They had gone out into the world, i.e. as missionaries for their particular brand of Christianity (cf. 3 Jn. 7 of orthodox missionaries going out),[4] but their influence was not confined to the outside world. Whether they were "members of the church" is hard to say. It may be anachronistic to pose the question in this form. There were no doubt various small groups of people calling themselves Christians at this time, and there was no denomi-

---

[1]For the use of ὅτι here cf. 1 John 3:11; 5:7.

[2]Brooke, 174, makes a different connection: "The command to mutual love grounded on true faith must be obeyed so as to find expression in action and conduct. Otherwise the forces which make against obedience will be too strong." Cf. Schnackenburg, 304: "Inner unity and brotherly union are clearly the strongest guarantee for the immovability of the church in the face of the dangerous influences to which it was exposed through the false teachers."

[3]The entry of false teaching would prevent the community being united in love, since not all its members would then know the truth (2 Jn. 1). At the same time, the false teachers did not even show love among themselves (1 Jn. 2:9f.; 4:20).

[4]It is less likely that the elder means that they had gone out from the church to form their own group (as in 1 Jn. 2:19). Bultmann, 112, suggests that if they have come from anywhere, it is from the antichrist. "World" (κόσμος) here means the world as the sphere in which Christians live, not the world as the ungodly world which stands over against the church; see 1 John 2:15 n.

national organization gathering them all together. It would be quite possible for "Christians" who held different views of the faith from their colleagues to set up their own groups. Consequently, when traveling preachers came around, it may have been difficult for a small church group to know whether they shared the same understanding of the faith, although orthodox and unorthodox leaders alike probably did their best to indicate which groups were acceptable from their own point of view. Here the elder proposes a clear test by which the church to which he is writing may test the orthodoxy of any suspect preachers, and at the same time warns the church that such people may well visit them.

He describes the acceptance of Christian truth as "confession,"[5] a word which was characteristically used of declaring one's allegiance to Jesus in situations of persecution. Here, however, the word has become associated with allegiance to a particular expression of the Christian faith, so that the content of a Christian confession can be tested for its doctrinal orthodoxy. In this case the elder cites an orthodox confession, failure to accept which is the sign of unorthodoxy. Literally it ran: "[I believe that] Jesus Christ [is] coming in flesh." The present continuous tense used is surprising when compared with 1 John 4:2: "Jesus Christ has come in the flesh." We might have expected a simple past tense, "Jesus Christ came in the flesh" (cf. 1 Jn. 5:6), as a confession of the historical reality of the incarnation in a point of past time. It seems unlikely, therefore, that the false teachers simply denied the reality of the incarnation.[6] The use of the present and perfect tenses becomes significant if the point is that Jesus Christ had come *and still existed* "in flesh." We know that some Gnostic thinkers taught that a heavenly power (the Christ) came upon Jesus at his baptism in the form of the Spirit, but that it departed from him again before the crucifixion, so that there was no lasting union of the divine Christ with the human Jesus, and hence no real, lasting incarnation.[7] The elder's formulation of the orthodox faith in Jesus Christ seems to be designed to exclude such inter-

[5]Cf. 1 John 2:23; 4:2, 3, 15; O. Michel, TDNT V, 199–220, especially 210; D. Fürst, NIDNTT I, 344–348.

[6]Schnackenburg, 313, thinks that the participle simply expresses the supra-temporal significance of the incarnation. The use of the present participle in a future sense to refer to the parousia is ruled out by the clear evidence elsewhere in 1 John that it was the incarnation which was being denied.

[7]The teaching opposed by the elder appears to have been similar to that ascribed to Cerinthus and Basilides by Irenaeus. According to Irenaeus, Cerinthus taught that "after his baptism Christ descended upon (Jesus) in the form of a dove, from the

pretations of the person of Jesus. For him it was axiomatic that there had been a true incarnation, that the Word had become flesh and remained flesh.[8] It is a point which receives much stress in 1 John (2:18–27; 4:1–6; 5:5–8).

Certainly the elder is so convinced of the danger of taking up this position that he brands any person who adopts it as (the) deceiver and (the) antichrist. He means that such a person is the deceiver *par excellence,* since his denial cuts at the very root of Christian belief. Indeed, he has made himself the opponent of Jesus. The word "antichrist" is found only here and in 1 John 2:18, 22; 4:3. Whatever it means elsewhere,[9] here it is used to characterize people who are radically opposed to the true doctrine about Christ and are thus supremely his opponents, even if they protest that they hold the truth about him and are Christians. The elder says that anybody who denies the truth is a very antichrist, just as we might speak of a supremely evil person as "the very devil."

There could be no stronger condemnation of error and deceit in the realm of Christian doctrine. But it should be noted that the elder's attack is on those who strike at the heart of Christian belief, not at those who may have happened to differ from him on theological points of lesser importance. When, however, the central citadel

---

power that is over all things, and then he proclaimed the unknown Father and accomplished miracles. But at the end Christ separated again from Jesus, and Jesus suffered and was raised again, but Christ remained impassible, since he was pneumatic" AH 1:26:1). Similarly, Basilides is said to have taught that "The . . . Father . . . sent his first-born Nous—he is the one who is called the Christ—to liberate those who believe in him from the power of those who made the world. . . . He appeared on earth as a man and performed miracles. . . . He did not suffer, but a certain Simon of Cyrene was compelled to carry his cross for him; and this [Simon] was transformed by him [Jesus] so that he was thought to be Jesus himself, and was crucified through ignorance and error. Jesus, however, took the form of Simon, and stood by laughing at them" (AH 1:24:4; citations from W. Foerster, *Gnosis,* Oxford, 1972, I, 36, 60). See Introduction, section 2, and 1 John 2:22; 5:6 nn.

[8]If this interpretation is correct, the elder's terminology would appear to have been different from that of Paul, who insisted that "flesh and blood cannot inherit the kingdom of God" (1 Cor. 15:50). For Johannine thought, however, it is the Word made flesh in whom can be seen the divine glory which in Paul's thought is associated with the exalted and returning Lord (Jn. 1:14; 2 Cor. 4:4–6; Phil. 3:21).

[9]Apocalyptic thought prophesied the coming of a supremely evil antagonist of God in the last days—the lawless one (2 Thess. 2:1–12) or the beast (Rev. 13). This figure is certainly opposed to Christ and attempts to emulate his powers. He could well have been designated as *the* Antichrist, but in fact the word is never attested with this meaning. When 1 John 2:18 prophecies that "the antichrist is coming," the allusion is no doubt to this expectation. The elder's point is that the spirit of opposition to Christ is already present in those who oppose the truth about Christ (cf. W. Grundmann, TDNT IX, 571f.; E. Kauder, NIDNTT I, 124-126).

of the faith is under attack, there is need for clear speaking.[10]

8 Having stated the danger, the elder now warns against the dangers of succumbing to it. If despite this warning regarding the falsity of the teaching his readers are taken in by it, they stand to lose what they have worked for and will fail to receive the full reward which they would otherwise obtain. Although the NIV has "what *you* have worked for," the correct text may be "what *we* have worked for."[11] If so, the elder is expressing his fear that his missionary and pastoral work will have been a failure since his readers have turned aside from the truth which he and his colleagues committed to them. The Christian life leads in the end to a reward, and failure to persevere in the truth (and in right conduct) can lead to loss of what God has promised to his people. The elder's language suggests that only a partial loss of reward is contemplated, but in the next verse he indicates that persons who do not hold fast to the truth sever their relationship with God. It may be that the elder reckoned that persons who succumbed to the false teaching would thereby show that "they did not really belong to us" (1 Jn. 2:19), but it is hard to be sure that he excludes the possibility of genuine believers embracing heresy; certainly he warns them in the clearest terms about the dangers attendant on dabbling with heresy.[12]

9 The reason why failure to abide in the true doctrine leads to loss of reward is now indicated. The "teaching of Christ" is the tradition about Christ taught by the elder himself and handed down by authoritative tradition in the church.[13] "Teaching" thus means "orthodox teaching," a phrase which the elder uses rather than "the

---

[10]It is not immediately apparent why the elder regarded this error as being of such fundamental significance. From verse 9 it is, however, clear that he believed that a false view of the person of Jesus destroyed the possibility of a religious relationship with God. From 1 John it is apparent that for the elder "Christ" and "Son of God" were virtually synonymous; hence denial that Jesus was the Christ was a denial that God's Son had truly become incarnate and revealed the love of God by dying as an atoning sacrifice for sin. The historical basis of Christian faith was thus removed. The elder rightly saw that such views led straight to Gnosticism.

[11]The reading εἰργάσασθε is supported by S A 1739 latt sy$^{p, h}$ Ir^{lat} (Schnackenburg, 314; Bruce, 141; Haenchen, 306); ἠργασάμεθα is read by B* al sy^{hms} (cf. εἰργασάμεθα, K L P al; TR; UBS). Metzger, 721, considers it more likely that the delicate nuance present in "that you do not lose what we (your teachers) have worked for" is due to the author than to copyists. Other scholars think that copyists wished to stress the author's role as a missionary. The Byzantine text has the first person throughout (ἀπολέσωμεν . . . ἀπολάβωμεν, K L P 69 al; TR), but this reading cannot stand against the superior external evidence for the second person.

[12]See I. H. Marshall, *Kept by the Power of God*, Minneapolis, 1975, 186–190.

[13]Most commentators regard "of Christ" as a subjective genitive, i.e. "the teaching given by Christ" (cf. Jn. 7:26; 18:19; Brooke, 177; Schnackenburg, 314f.). But the

truth."[14] Anybody who does not "continue" in this teaching—be he a false teacher from outside or a member of the church who abandons his former belief—can be said to "run ahead."[15] Perhaps this is a sarcastic reference to the way in which the false teachers themselves proudly claimed to be offering "advanced" teaching; the elder claims that they have "advanced" beyond the boundaries of true Christian belief. The warning is still a valid one: any teaching which goes beyond the plain message of Scripture should at once put us on the alert lest it actually contradicts the truth revealed in Scripture. When the teaching of the Bible needs to be supplemented by some "key" to the Bible or by some new revelation, it is a sure sign that "advanced" doctrine is being put forward.

People who reject the truth about Christ no longer "have God." No doubt they claimed that they did have God, but the elder's point is that anybody who fails to have a proper understanding of Jesus Christ cannot have a true relationship with God.[16] Those who deny the coming of Jesus Christ, the Son of God, in the flesh have a false understanding of God and of the way to God, since the Son is the only way to the Father (Jn. 14:6; 1 Jn. 2:22f.). It is impossible to separate the Father from the Son in Christian experience: you cannot have fellowship with the one without having it with the other. But, if so, it also follows positively that those who accept the teaching[17] have spiritual fellowship with both the Father and the Son. It goes without saying that the elder is not suggesting that mere orthodoxy in doctrine leads to spiritual life: his emphasis on the conduct which issues from acceptance of the truth shows that he is thinking of real commitment to the truth contained in the teaching; that truth is ultimately God himself. The warning thus culminates in a promise of spiritual blessing for those who heed it.

10 Those who accept "the teaching" should not give any

---

context suggests that the author is thinking rather of teaching *about* Christ (objective genitive; Bultmann, 113). Moreover, the elder does not use "Christ" by itself as a name for the earthly Jesus.

[14]For the elder "the truth" is the divine reality to which testimony is borne in the apostolic teaching ("*this* teaching," as opposed to that of the false teachers, 2 Jn. 10); on the concept see K. H. Rengstorf, TDNT II, 135–165, especially 143f., 163–165.

[15]Instead of προάγων, the TR has παραβαίνων, "transgressing," an interesting slip in which the wish was perhaps father to the thought.

[16]To "have God" means to have a spiritual relationship with God (cf. 1 Jn. 2:23); the background of the phrase is to be found in Jewish Greek writings (3 Macc. 7:16; T.Dan 5; T.Iss. 7; H. Hanse, TDNT II, 822–824).

[17]τῇ διδαχῇ is read by S A B Ψ 33 81 1739 vg sa; other authorities clarify by adding τοῦ Χριστοῦ or αὐτοῦ.

kind of practical encouragement to the false teachers. The situation was one in which the evangelistic and pastoral ministry of the church depended largely on Christians who were prepared to travel around the countryside, preaching the gospel as they went and ministering in the various church groups. For their hospitality and keep they depended on the generosity of the members of the church. Such hospitality is not to be offered to preachers with a false message; it can be taken for granted that they were not to be allowed to minister in the church. Nor are the members of the church to "welcome," literally "greet," them.[18] Such a greeting would have been regarded as no mere formality but as a positive expression of encouragement.

11 The adoption of these measures would obviously curb the influence of the false teachers. It is clear, however, that the elder is more concerned with the danger of members of the church aligning themselves with them. To welcome them was to express solidarity with them; even if one professed to reject their views, hospitality was a way of sharing in their work, and those who helped them in this way were in danger of coming under the same condemnation as the false teachers themselves. The church must be kept from contamination by error.

The elder's point needs reiterating in an age when the church had become much more tolerant of deviation and heresy. It can be objected that he is recommending an unloving attitude toward those who are guilty of error, and that the church is unlikely to win back to the truth those to whom it refuses to offer love and fellowship.[19] More basically, it can be urged that at a time when the content of Christian truth is uncertain and formulations of doctrine are increasingly diffuse we have no right to regard those who differ from us as upholders of "false doctrine"; rather we all hold inadequate concepts of Christian truth and must help one another to a better understanding of the faith. Today's heresy may well become tomorrow's orthodoxy.

It should be noted, however, that the elder's injunctions are addressed to the church rather than merely to the individuals who compose it; he is no doubt thinking of action that would be sanctioned by the church rather than unilateral action by individu-

---

[18]χαίρειν was the common Greek greeting, used orally and in letters (Acts 15:23; 23:26; Jas. 1:1). The Jewish equivalent was εἰρήνη (Lk. 10:5f.); in Christian usage it acquired a deep significance as an expression of salvation, but here the thought is rather of fellowship and encouragement. For the thought see Ignatius, *Letter to the Smyrnaeans* 4:1; cf. 7:2; *Ephesians* 9:1.

[19]Dodd, 151f.

als. Further, he is not suggesting that the church should refrain from showing love and concern for those who hold erroneous views, but rather that the church should not encourage and help them in their propaganda. There is a difference between giving a person love and even hospitality and providing him with a base for his work. The elder was writing in a situation where the provision of hospitality to traveling preachers was a means of helping their work; in the modern church situation things are different in some respects, and the provision of hospitality to persons who are in error need not necessarily be understood as an expression of solidarity with their views. Jesus was prepared to take meals with persons of whose way of life he disapproved—and to take the risk of misunderstanding which this involved (Mt. 9:11; 11:19). Finally, the elder would have rejected any suggestion that the content of the teaching was uncertain and open to discussion and dialogue. He firmly believed that what had been handed down as apostolic tradition was true and inspired by the Spirit, and that Christians possessed of the Spirit would recognize it as such. Moreover, his concern was, as we have seen, about the central affirmation of the faith and not about matters on which Christians may legitimately have differences of opinion.[20] It can be claimed that the church today is too ready to profess doubt even as regards the centralities of the gospel and too ready to tolerate dissent from the faith once and for all handed down to the people of God.[21]

FINAL WORDS AND GREETINGS (12–13)

12. *I have much to write to you, but I do not want to use paper and ink. Instead, I hope to visit you and talk with you face to face, so that our joy may be complete.*

13. *The children of your chosen sister send their greetings.*

[20]Ross, 231f.

[21]It is one thing to doubt the central doctrines of the Christian faith. It is another thing to rethink them in order to understand them more fully and to express them in language and thought-forms which will communicate them effectively in the modern world. The point is well put in the *Interim Report (April 1972)* on *Multilateral Church Conversation in Scotland:* "The primary or privileged witness to Jesus Christ in Scripture is definitive. In a sense it is final; nothing can take its place or occupy the same place. But in another sense it is not final: for what is there said must be again said. *There is nothing other to be said: but the same has to be otherwise said.* The idea of translation is helpful here. To translate is not to transmute—the two are contradictory. Translation implies (*a*) absolute fidelity to what is the inviolable original, and (*b*) immense sensitivity to the present circumstances which must determine the mode of expression" (Edinburgh, 1972, 8; my italics).

12 Despite the sternness of the warning which he had felt impelled to give the church, the elder was basically confident of its loyalty to the truth and was attached to it by warm Christian love. Although, therefore, he could say more to them in his letter, he prefers to look forward to the possibility of a personal meeting which will provide the opportunity for personal conversation with the members of the church—no doubt on subjects more congenial than false teaching; such a meeting will give him and his readers greater joy than is possible by means of correspondence.

The language used to express this wish is somewhat formal; it is repeated almost word for word in 3 John 13f.,[1] but in both cases it expresses genuine feeling. We can only speculate what else the elder would have written if he had not contented himself with this brief note; the developed discussion in 1 John shows the kind of things that were especially on his mind. Nor can we do any more than speculate as to why the elder felt it necessary to send this letter if he hoped to visit the church soon. But it would surely be entirely natural for him to wish to nip incipient danger to the church in the bud; it would be equally natural for him to take advantage of the presence of visitors from the church to have them take a message home with them. No doubt the elder could have contented himself with a verbal message, but it is clear from Paul's example that special importance was attached to the actual writing of an authoritative letter by a church leader, and that this served in some measure as a substitute for his own presence.[2] When such a visit is possible, however, the joy that the elder has in the church, and the church in him,[3] will be full and complete.

13 Finally, the elder conveys greetings to the church from its sister-church, i.e. the church with which he himself was associated.[4] Such a greeting would add the church's authority to his own, as well as being a genuine expression of Christian love. The

---

[1]ἐβουλήθην is an epistolary aorist; the writer puts himself in the temporal position of his readers, for whom his act of writing took place in the past. (On the usage see Schnackenburg, 126 n. 1, correcting BD 334.) ὁ χάρτης is papyrus, and τὸ μέλαν is ink (2 Cor. 3:3; 3 Jn. 13). These were the normal writing materials for letters.

[2]See R. W. Funk, "The Apostolic *Parousia:* Form and Significance," in W. R. Farmer (*et al.*), *Christian History and Interpretation: Studies Presented to John Knox,* New York/Cambridge, 1967, 249–268.

[3]ἡμῶν should be read (S K L P Ψ 614 syph. h; TR) rather than ὑμῶν (A B; Brooke, 180), which is probably due to the influence of the surrounding pronouns; cf. Metzger, 722.

[4]The language is based on 2 John 1, so that the metaphor of the two sisters provides the frame for the letter as a whole.

formal language of greeting thus becomes the vehicle of Christian love and affection, just as the simple words "I do" uttered formally in a marriage ceremony can be charged with fulness of emotion and conviction.

The Third Epistle
of
JOHN

TEXT, EXPOSITION, AND NOTES

ADDRESS AND GREETING (1–4)

1. *The elder,*
To my dear friend Gaius, whom I love in the truth.
2. *Dear friend, I pray that you may enjoy good health and that all may go well with you, even as your soul is getting along well.*
3. *It gave me great joy to have some brothers come and tell about your faithfulness to the truth and how you continue to live according to the truth.* 4. *I have no greater joy than to hear that my children are living according to the truth.*

1 This is one of the few letters in the New Testament addressed to an individual Christian.[1] His name was Gaius, which was as common then as John or James today. We must assume that a more precise identification of the recipient was written on the package containing the letter or that fuller instructions regarding delivery were given to the messenger (probably Demetrius, v. 12) who carried it; in the letter itself it was sufficient to address the recipient by his personal name. We know nothing about him beyond what can be gleaned from the letter. He was a member of one of the churches over which the writer of the letter exercised some oversight, but there is no indication whether or not he held any particular office in it. There are no positive reasons for identifying him with any of the other bearers of the same name in the New Testament, although this

---

[1]The letters to Timothy and Titus were probably meant to instruct a wider group of people than their addressees, since they contain teaching which must already have been well known to the persons named; they would be intended to be read in the churches where the addressees ministered. Although the letter to Philemon includes his family among the persons addressed, it is basically a personal letter, and thus affords the closest analogy to 3 John.

81

has not stopped earlier commentators from offering guesses.

The writer refers to himself simply as "the elder."[2] He thus writes in token of the position of authority and respect which he holds in the church, so that this is not a private letter but rather has the force of an official communication. Presumably the writer was not known to his friend by his personal name, perhaps because of his greater age and the respect which went with it. But although there is this sense of distance between the two men, there is certainly no lack of warmth in the tone of his greeting. He speaks of Gaius with affection as his friend, literally his "beloved,"[3] and strengthens what could have degenerated into a conventional expression by commenting that he loves him in truth. While this phrase could simply mean "truly, really,"[4] the usage elsewhere in these letters suggests that the elder is thinking of the kind of love which is consistent with the Christian revelation; it is not only genuine and heartfelt, but is the kind of love shown by God himself.[5]

It is surprising that the letter does not contain a specific word of greeting at this point, as is universally the case in other letters in the New Testament (see especially 2 Jn. 3).[6] It is possible that "whom I love in the truth" or the following expression of good wishes is regarded as an equivalent; but since it was normal to include both a greeting *and* a prayer, this explanation is not altogether satisfactory. Nor does the presence of a closing greeting (v. 15) compensate for the omission here.[7]

2 Whatever be the reason for the omission of the greeting, the elder follows conventional practice in expressing good wishes to his friend. In Christian letters this element often took the form of a prayer of thanksgiving to God, sometimes at considerable length.[8] "I pray" may mean little more than "I wish,"[9] although the following verses suggest that the thought is somewhat stronger. The wish is a perfectly natural and proper one for Gaius's physical well-being,

---

[2]See on 2 John 1.
[3]Cf. 3 John 2, 5, 11; 1 John 2:7; 3:2, 21; 4:1, 7, 11.
[4]Bultmann, 96. Dodd, 157, cites two Greek letters where this is the meaning of the phrase, but opts for a deeper meaning in its Johannine context. See on 2 John 1.
[5]The TNT renders the phrase "within the fellowship of the truth," which brings out one aspect of the meaning: the elder loves those who share with him in knowledge of the truth.
[6]On salutations in New Testament letters see on 2 John 1–3. Omission of the greeting appears to be at least highly unusual; cf. Schnackenburg, 320 n. 2.
[7]A closing greeting would be normal practice in any case.
[8]See on 2 John 4.
[9]Bultmann, 97; Haas, 149.

for this is as much the concern of a Christian friend as is spiritual well-being. The particular wish here for good health allows, although it does not necessarily demand, that the elder had some reason for making it. The phrase would be perfectly possible in a letter to somebody with robust health, that he may continue to enjoy it, but there is some probability that Gaius was not in the best of health (see on v. 9).[10] At the same time the elder wants him to prosper in every way.[11] This verb literally means "to have a good journey" (Rom. 1:10), but here (and in 1 Cor. 16:2) it is metaphorical.[12] The elder knows that Gaius's soul is prospering and bases his assurance that all will go well with him on this fact. The phrase may simply mean "as you are indeed already prospering,"[13] but more probably it expresses the hope that Gaius will prosper physically in the same way as he is making progress spiritually.[14] Even though a person is ill or in poor material circumstances, he may still be spiritually prosperous, and conversely material success is not necessarily a guide to spiritual progress. In the case of Gaius the elder had no doubt that to wish him physical well-being commensurate with his spiritual well-being was to wish the very best for him.

3 The elder now gives the reason for his confidence in Gaius's spiritual progress.[15] He has had news of him from some visitors who were able to testify to the quality of his life. These "brothers" may simply have been ordinary Christians whose business had brought them to the town where the elder lived, or they may have been missionaries who traveled from church to church; they had enjoyed Gaius's hospitality and were now visiting the elder.[16] The verb used[17] indicates that several visits had been paid to

[10]Vawter, 413. For ὑγιαίνω cf. Luke 5:31; 7:10; 15:27; U. Luck, TDNT IX, 308–313; D. Müller, NIDNTT II, 169–171. For conventional use of the language see MM 647; Schnackenburg, 321 n. 3.

[11]περὶ πάντων means "in all respects," and is not equivalent to πρὸ πάντων, "above all" (as is suggested in BD 229²); cf. AG 650. Note that the NIV inverts the order of the verbs for ease in translation (cf. Haas, 150).

[12]On εὐοδόομαι see W. Michaelis, TDNT V, 109–114.

[13]Bultmann, 97.

[14]E. Schweizer, TDNT IX, 651f. Cf. Schnackenburg, 321f., who emphasizes that the contrast is not so much between body and soul as between physical and spiritual well-being, both of which are important; there is no devaluation of the body.

[15]Scribes who failed to see how verse 3 is linked to what precedes omitted the connective γάρ, but it is well attested. The NIV leaves it untranslated.

[16]It is possible that ἀδελφός was used especially to refer to Christian workers, although usually it refers to Christians in general; see E. E. Ellis, "Paul and his Co-Workers," NTS 17, 1970–71, 437–453, especially 448.

[17]The present participles indicate repetition.

the elder, possibly by different groups of Christians. They bore testimony to Gaius's truth, i.e. to the concrete evidence of his adherence to the truth. Soundness in doctrine is no doubt included in the thought, but the basic point is that Gaius's life of loving hospitality for other Christians (vv. 5–6) indicated his adherence to the truth. The last clause, "and how you continue to live according to the truth," can be understood as an expression of what the brothers told the elder,[18] or it may express the elder's conviction, based perhaps on his own knowledge of Gaius, that their testimony was in accord with the facts.[19]

4 It was the news of this which had given great joy to the elder (v. 3),[20] and he now emphasizes that this was no merely conventional remark by affirming that he cannot have any greater cause of joy[21] than the knowledge that his spiritual "children" are living according to the truth. "Children" is a word used especially by Paul to refer to his own converts (1 Cor. 4:14; Gal. 4:19; Phil. 2:22); in the same way the implication here may be that the elder had led Gaius to faith in Jesus Christ, but he may simply be using this phrase to refer to people under his pastoral care, to whom he adopted a fatherly attitude.[22] In any case, the elder makes it clear that his supreme concern as a pastor is to help other people to know the truth and to live by it.

THE WRITER PRAISES GAIUS (5–8)

5. *Dear friend, you are faithful in what you are doing for the brothers, even though they are strangers to you.* 6. *They have told the church about your love. You will do well to send them on their way in a manner worthy of God.* 7. *It was for the sake of the Name that they went out, receiving no help from the pagans.* 8. *We ought therefore to show hospitality to such men so that we may work together for the truth.*

[18]On this view καθώς is used to introduce indirect speech and is equivalent to πῶς or ὡς (AG 392; Schnackenburg, 322); cf. Acts 15:14.
[19]Schnackenburg, first edition, 287; Bultmann, 98 n. 6. Haas, 150, offers both possibilities.
[20]Cf. 2 John 4.
[21]χαρά is here concrete, "cause of joy." The variant reading χάριν (B vg bo; Westcott, 237; Chaine, 253) is probably a scribal error, perhaps due to substitution of the more common New Testament word, which is, however, rare in the Johannine literature. Contrast 2 Corinthians 1:15.
[22]Schnackenburg, 323; cf. 1 John 2:1, *et al.*; for the view that converts are meant see Bultmann, 98.

5 Having spoken in general terms of Gaius's commendable way of life, the elder now refers to one particular aspect of it which is important in view of the main theme of the letter. We have seen in 2 John how much of the evangelistic and teaching ministry of the church was dependent on the work of traveling missionaries who served the various churches and who were dependent on the hospitality and the gifts which they received from the members of the churches which they visited. Gaius had been conspicuous for his hospitality to such travelers on their various visits to his area,[1] and this was no doubt part of the news which had been brought back to the elder by "the brothers" (v. 3). The elder describes his action as "faithful." It is unlikely that this means that the act was an expression of his faith. Rather it demonstrated his faithfulness to the truth and was commensurate with his adherence to it. There may be the more precise thought that Gaius was showing his faithfulness to the elder and his friends over against the attitude of Diotrephes (vv. 9f.) who disapproved of the travelers and those who welcomed them.[2] In the ancient world it was difficult for travelers to find decent accommodation except with their friends. It was a signal feature[3] of Gaius's hospitality that he was prepared to extend it to people who were otherwise unknown to him and had no claims on him except that they formed part of the company of those who like him had come to know the truth (cf. 2 Jn. 1).

6 So impressed had the brothers been by Gaius's kindness that they had made special mention of it when they had told their story at a meeting of the church[4] attended by the elder. Such action clearly sprang from true Christian love, the virtue which the elder especially valued alongside adherence to the truth. In view of this the elder felt that he could confidently ask Gaius to continue to help traveling brothers on their visits. "You will do well" is an idiom that means "please" and expresses a polite request.[5] Sending the mis-

---

[1]The use of ὃ ἐάν with the subjunctive is indefinite and implies an unspecified number of ways or occasions of helping the brothers. For the use of ἐργάζομαι cf. Galatians 6:10; Colossians 3:23.

[2]Cf. Westcott, 238, although his explanation of the actual phrase is improbable; Schnackenburg, 323 n. 4.

[3]καὶ τοῦτο (1 Cor. 6:6; Phil. 1:28; Eph. 2:8). On the importance of φιλοξενία in the early church see 1 Timothy 3:2; 5:10; Titus 1:8; Romans 12:13; Hebrews 13:2; 1 Peter 4:9; Hermas, *Similitude* 9:27; Justin, *Apology* 1:67; Barclay, 171f.

[4]After the preposition ἐνώπιον the article is not required with ἐκκλησίας (1 Cor. 14:19, 35; BD 255).

[5]For this idiomatic use of καλῶς ποιέω with a participle see Acts 10:33.

sionaries on their way involved providing for their journey—supplying them with food and money to pay for their expenses, washing their clothes, and generally helping them to travel as comfortably as possible.[6] But there are various levels at which such help can be given, and the elder wanted it to be offered in a way that would please God and be worthy of the one who gives generously and richly to his servants.[7] While Christian missionaries needed to beware of the temptation to make a good thing out of their work, and churches had to beware of being taken in by charlatans,[8] it was perhaps more important to remind the churches not to treat the missionaries like beggars and so bring discredit on the name of the God to whom they were looking for their support.

The point is still relevant. Christian ministers and missionaries live in the faith that God will encourage his people to provide for their needs; it is better that such provision err on the side of generosity than stinginess.

7 The elder's appeal to Gaius rests on this fact that missionaries are wholly dependent on God's people for their support. This is because they set out on their missionary work[9] for the sake of the Name and get no support from the people whom they evangelize. The "Name" is of course that of Jesus,[10] and the missionaries labored on behalf of its Bearer and therefore made it the content of their work.[11] They were thus entitled to expect support from the One whom they served as ambassadors (2 Cor. 6:1). In not claiming support from the people whom they evangelized they were motivated by Jesus' principle: "Freely you have received, freely give"

---

[6]προπέμπω can mean "to accompany" (Acts 20:38; 21:5; Rom. 15:24) or "to send someone on his way" (Acts 15:3; 1 Cor. 16:6, 11; 2 Cor. 1:16; Tit. 3:13). In the latter case it must mean more than simply saying good-bye.

[7]For ἀξίως τοῦ Θεοῦ cf. Colossians 1:10; 1 Thessalonians 2:12.

[8]On the problems caused by support for traveling preachers see *Didache* 11: "Let every apostle, when he cometh to you, be received as the Lord; but he shall not abide more than a single day, or if there be need, a second likewise; but if he abide three days, he is a false prophet. And when he departeth let the apostle receive nothing save bread, until he findeth shelter; but if he ask money, he is a false prophet. . . . And whosoever shall say in the Spirit, Give me silver or anything else, ye shall not listen to him; but if he tell you to give on behalf of others that are in want, let no man judge him."

[9]ἐξέρχομαι is to go out from the church (or from God) into the world, regarded as a field for evangelism.

[10]Acts 5:41; Romans 1:5. This is the nearest that the elder comes to actually naming Jesus in this letter.

[11]ὑπέρ can mean "on behalf of" and also "concerning."

(Mt. 10:8).[12] To take payment for the gospel would be to nullify the offer of free grace. At the same time it would have reduced the missionaries to the level of the various popular philosophers and religious preachers who sought payment for their services.[13] In addition, Paul's example shows that refusal to accept payment for preaching the gospel and even subsistence from the churches (1 Cor. 9:11f.) was not incompatible with doing manual or other work for one's keep: a "tent-making ministry" is not excluded by the elder's principle (Acts 18:1–4; 1 Thess. 2:9). And, perhaps paradoxically, the right of men to receive the gospel for nothing does not absolve those who have accepted the gospel and become members of the church from supporting the Christian mission and sharing their material goods with those who give them spiritual instruction (1 Cor. 9:11; Gal. 6:6), so that the workers may receive what is due to them (1 Cor. 9:14). There is thus a difference between demanding payment for the gospel and encouraging those whose hearts have been transformed by grace to show their thanks for God's generosity to them in tangible form.

8 As is his custom, the elder rounds off his appeal by repeating the main thought. In view of the missionaries' resolve to act as ambassadors for the Name and to refrain from seeking support from pagans, all Christians (the "we" is emphatic) stand under an obligation to help them. As sharers in the truth themselves, they must prove to be fellow-workers in practice.[14] The NIV assumes that the elder and his readers are to work together with the missionaries for the benefit of the truth,[15] but it is also possible to translate so that all Christians are thought of as fellow-workers with the truth itself.[16]

---

[12]Houlden, 152, is therefore wrong in ascribing the attitude of the missionaries to "the intensely inward-looking quality of the Johannine consciousness"; it was common Christian practice, and it was motivated not by an inward-looking attitude but by the desire to present the gospel freely.
[13]An inscription describes a slave of a Syrian goddess who went out begging and never brought back less than seventy bags of money for her (Dodd, 160; A. Deissmann, *Light from Ancient East*, London, 1927, 108ff.).
[14]For this use of γίνομαι see John 15:8; AG 159.
[15]So apparently Bultmann, 99.
[16]So AG 795; Brooke, 187. In favor of this view is the use of the verb συνεργέω with the dative of helping somebody. See D. R. Hall, "Fellow-Workers with the Gospel," ExpT 85, 1973–74, 119f. On the whole, the former rendering fits better in the context here, where the elder is urging Gaius to continue to help the missionaries in the cause of the truth.

THE WRITER DENOUNCES DIOTREPHES (9–10)

> 9. *I wrote to the church, but Diotrephes, who loves to be first, will have nothing to do with us.* 10. *So if I come, I will call attention to what he is doing, gossiping maliciously about us. Not satisfied with that, he refuses to welcome the brothers. He also stops those who want to do so and puts them out of the church.*

9 The letter now reaches its climax, for which all that has preceded has been in some sense a preparation. The elder informs Gaius that he had written a letter[1] to the church but that someone called Diotrephes was refusing to accept "us."[2] This must mean that Diotrephes was refusing to accept whatever was said in the letter, and possibly also that when the letter came into his hands he did his best to suppress it. This letter must have contained some commendation of the traveling preachers. It cannot, therefore, have been 1 John. There is a better case that it was 2 John, but this too is improbable. If we accepted the identification, it would follow that Diotrephes objected to the elder's denunciation of the false teachers (2 Jn. 7–11) and retaliated by refusing to accept preachers associated with the elder. But there is nothing in the letter to suggest that Diotrephes was sympathetic to false teaching, and therefore it is best to assume that the letter in question has been lost—which would not be surprising if Diotrephes was its recipient.[3]

A further puzzle concerns the identity of the church to which the elder had written. The simple phrase "the church" surely implies that it was the local congregation to which Gaius himself belonged.[4] Against this it has been objected that Gaius would not have needed to be told the story of Diotrephes by the elder if he was already familiar with it. Hence many commentators think that another church must be in mind, and that this fits in with the way in which Diotrephes is said to lord it over *them*.[5] Nor does the elder

---

[1]Literally, "I wrote something" (τι), implying that it was a letter of modest size. The variant ἔγραψα ἄν found in later MSS was motivated by the desire to avoid the suggestions that the elder's letter had been lost or that its authority had not been accepted.

[2]ἐπιδέχομαι can mean "to accept the authority of" or (v. 10) "to welcome." The plural "us" will refer to the elder and his associates.

[3]Older scholars identified the letter mentioned here with 2 John (e.g. V. Bartlet, "The Historical Setting of the Second and Third Epistles of St. John," JTS 6, 1905, 204–216), but the decisive arguments against the identification are of equal age (Brooke, 187f.).

[4]So most commentators.

[5]ὁ φιλοπρωτεύων αὐτῶν.

suggest that Gaius should intervene in order to deal with Diotrephes; he merely exhorts him not to follow his example. This view is a possible one,[6] but it does not do justice to the use of "*the* church." If we accept it, it is possible that Gaius belonged to a different church, and that the elder feared that Diotrephes' influence might spread to it.

But perhaps there is something to be said in favor of the first view. Two possibilities, which are not mutually exclusive, arise. It is possible that the elder, having had his letter to the church suppressed by Diotrephes, made a second attempt to communicate with the church by writing to his friend Gaius, hoping that Gaius would share the letter with the church; he therefore wrote at this point in a somewhat formal manner so that the church would know that he was cognizant of the situation and proposed to act with reference to it. The other possibility is that Gaius may have lived at some distance from the church, possibly in a village where his was the only Christian household. This would explain the significance of his house as a stopping place for missionaries on their travels if the various churches were more than one day's travel from one another. At the same time we may wonder whether his health was such that, although he could entertain guests at home, he was not able to make the journey to the church and confront Diotrephes. This would explain his ignorance of the situation and the fact that he is not apparently asked to do anything about it. In the nature of the situation some speculation is inevitable, and this is only one of several possible reconstructions of the situation, but it may be claimed that some such suggestion does justice to the meager evidence at our disposal.[7]

As for Diotrephes, he appears only here in the New Testament and has gone down in history as the man who wanted to lead the church.[8] He appears to have resented the elder and his influence over the church. He represented the cause of independency at a time when the system of oversight by apostles and evangelists was beginning to be replaced by the development of independent churches, and the informal organization of earlier days was being replaced by something more complex and formal. Such, at least, is a common reading of the situation, and it represents an

[6]So Windisch, 140; Dodd, 161.
[7]On this view αὐτῶν (v. 9) simply refers back to τῇ ἐκκλησίᾳ and is masculine plural *ad sensum;* it may refer particularly to those members of the church who accepted Diotrephes' authority.
[8]φιλοπρωτεύω appears here for the first time in Greek literature, but the noun φιλόπρωτος is well attested; see AG 868.

attempt to see things from Diotrephes' point of view.[9] But, whether
or not this was the background, it would not be unnatural in any
local church for a person who possessed gifts of leadership or was
fired by ambition to seek a position of control and establish himself
as *the* leader. By the early second century we can trace the growth
of the so-called "monepiscopate," in which a "bishop" came to
occupy a position superior to the "elders" in a local church.[10]
Whatever official terminology was in use—if any at all—Diotrephes
coveted such a position. He appears to have felt thwarted by the
influence of the elder. Perhaps he thought that he had justifiable
grounds for impatience. The old man may have been standing in the
way of younger men; he may have held on to his position instead of
in effect resigning in favor of younger men; he may have seemed
conservative and even reactionary in his ways when the times were
demanding new and vigorous measures. We simply do not know. All
that we have is the elder's own view of the situation and his verdict
that Diotrephes was basically moved by ambition and displayed it in
an unchristian way. It was a danger that had arisen in Jesus' own
lifetime, and the Gospels contain warnings against love of position
which were especially relevant for such a situation as this (Mt.
23:5–12; cf. 24:20–28). Diotrephes is a standing warning against the
danger of confusing personal ambition with zeal for the cause of the
gospel. It should be noted that there is no suggestion that Diotrephes
disagreed with the elder on any vital point of doctrine.[11] He did not,
however, express his adherence to the truth in love (cf. 2 Jn. 4–6).

10 Action was called for. The elder hoped to visit the area
before long, and if he did so,[12] he would not hesitate to take
Diotrephes to task for what he was doing. The translation "I will call
attention to what he is doing" is too mild; the elder intends to "take

---

[9]See Introduction, section 1.

[10]This type of episcopacy is to be distinguished from the "diocesan" variety found
today in which a bishop has jurisdiction over a number of churches rather than just
one.

[11]For this view see W. Bauer, *Orthodoxy and Heresy in Earliest Christianity,*
Philadelphia/London, 1972, 93; it is criticized by Haenchen, 290–294. The suggestion
is reversed by E. Käsemann, "Ketzer und Zeuge," ZTK 48, 1951, 292–311, who
thinks that it was the elder who was regarded as heretical by the orthodox Diotrephes
and that consequently the elder replied in a mild fashion and did not dare raise the
question of doctrine (similarly, Bultmann, 101). See Introduction, section 1.

[12]The conditional form does not necessarily place the likelihood of the visit in doubt
(cf. 1 Jn. 2:28; Westcott, 240).

up the matter" with him and to seek satisfaction about it.[13] Presumably he intended to do this on a personal level in the first instance rather than openly in church, although since the matter concerned Diotrephes as a leader in the church rather than as a private individual the latter is possible. In any case, the elder was prepared to exercise his authority in the matter. It is not Christian to refrain from exercising legitimate authority when there is need to do so; the modern church is perhaps too chary in exercising brotherly admonition and even discipline when it is required.

Certainly the elder felt that Diotrephes merited censure—and there is no reason to doubt his verdict on the matter. Diotrephes had been "gossiping maliciously" about him, i.e. making unjustified accusations against him.[14] He had moved from words to deeds by refusing to accept into his house any traveling missionaries who were associated with the elder[15] and by refusing to allow other members of the church to receive them; if anybody did receive them, he put them out of the church.[16] If Gaius lived at a distance from the church, this would explain why he himself had not been ejected as well. Diotrephes' action was clearly very serious, and it is noteworthy that the elder's censure appears comparatively mild: he was determined not to fight a battle of words and descend to his opponent's level.[17]

---

[13]ὑπομιμνῄσκω is literally "to remind." The sense here is similar to that in Wisdom of Solomon 12:2: "For this reason thou dost correct offenders little by little, admonishing them and *reminding* them of their sins, in order that they may leave their evil ways." See also 2 Timothy 2:14 where the verb is used of instruction by a church leader.

[14]φλυαρέω can be used of babbling and talking nonsense (cf. the adjective in 1 Tim. 5:13) and hence of making empty, groundless accusations.

[15]This is more likely than that Diotrephes refused to welcome them into the church.

[16]It is probably anachronistic to think of official excommunication; in any case we have no evidence that Diotrephes had the authority to practice it. It must be presumed that Diotrephes had some backing in the church. Some commentators wish to regard κωλύει and ἐκβάλλει as merely conative in force (Westcott, 241; cf. Jn. 10:32; 13:6), but the close coordination of these verbs with οὔτε . . . ἐπιδέχεται, which is factual, makes this suggestion less attractive (Schnackenburg, 328).

[17]Some commentators have suggested that the elder's mild response was because he was not sure of his ground, perhaps because he and his friends were in a minority position. But in fact the elder characterizes Diotrephes in fairly strong terms in the letter, and the explanation offered above is therefore preferable: the elder is not acting out of weakness, but with loving restraint in the face of provocation.

THE WRITER PRAISES DEMETRIUS (11-12)

> 11. *Dear friend, do not imitate what is evil but what is good. Anyone who does what is good is from God. Anyone who does what is evil has not seen God. 12. Demetrius is well spoken of by everyone—and even by the truth itself. We also speak well of him, and you know that our testimony is true.*

11 Having spoken about the conduct of Diotrephes, the elder now urges Gaius to imitate what is good rather than what is evil. The use of the word "imitate"[1] shows that Gaius is being urged to copy the example of good people and to refrain from copying evil. The position of the sentence and the order of words[2] strongly suggest that Diotrephes is the evil example and that the good example is typified by Demetrius who will figure in the next verse. The verse is thus basically an appeal to Gaius not to be misled by Diotrephes and to follow his example, even if he may be placed under considerable personal pressure to conform to Diotrephes' instructions. Although the elder was surely confident regarding Gaius's attitude, he judged it wise to reinforce it. He assumes that Gaius will recognize what is good and what is evil, especially in view of his known adherence to the truth and his hospitality to the elder's colleagues. Now he strengthens his appeal to him by remarking tersely that a person who does good is from God, i.e. is on the side of God and draws his will and strength to do good from God.[3] By contrast, a person who does evil—such as Diotrephes—has not seen God. He has no real Christian experience, and his conversion must be judged to have been an illusion.[4] It is clear that the lack of Christian character is to be regarded as a mark of the absence of true Christian experience. Evil, unloving conduct calls in question a person's profession to be a Christian: "For anyone who does not love his brother, whom he has seen, cannot love God, whom he has not seen" (1 Jn. 3:20).

---

[1] For the thought of imitating godly men see 1 Corinthians 4:16; 11:1; 1 Thessalonians 1:6; 2:14; 2 Thessalonians 3:7; Hebrews 6:12; 13:7; such an example is binding only as the objects to be imitated themselves imitate the Lord (1 Cor. 11:1; 1 Thess. 1:6; cf. Eph. 5:1). See W. Michaelis, TDNT IV, 659-674; W. Bauder, NIDNTT I, 490-492.

[2] The verse forms a chiasmus: "evil . . . good . . . good . . . evil," which suggests that the primary force is one of warning.

[3] Cf. John 8:47; 1 John 2:21; 3:10; 4:2-7. The person who is "from God" has been born from God and possesses his spiritual power.

[4] Cf. 1 John 3:6. The elder presumably regarded Diotrephes as possibly being one who did not truly belong to the church (1 Jn. 2:19). But the statements are quite general, and are not directly applied to members of the two parties in the church.

12   Without any warning the elder introduces the figure of Demetrius. He is doubtless meant as an example of the good which Gaius is to imitate, but the real reason for mentioning him here at the end of the main part of the letter is to write a note of commendation for him to Gaius.[5] It can be taken as virtually certain that he was the bearer of the letter (cf. Rom. 16:1f.) and as highly probable that he was a traveling missionary, possibly one of the group which had been made unwelcome by Diotrephes. He was, however, a stranger to Gaius, and in the present situation the elder judged that he needed to commend him to Gaius, even though Gaius was known to welcome strangers. In the situation of tension created by Diotrephes' action a letter of commendation was necessary, and refusal to heed it would indicate a flouting of the elder's authority.

The elder could speak in the warmest terms of Demetrius and produces a threefold testimony to his character. He had a good testimony from "everyone," i.e. from every Christian who knew him but perhaps especially from those in the elder's immediate circle. He could also receive a testimonial from "the truth itself." This can be taken to mean that if the truth could speak, it too would testify that Demetrius's life was in accord with its own standards. It is possible for a person to miss obtaining human favor and yet to enjoy God's favor. Even if Diotrephes and his group might disapprove of Demetrius, yet he would be upheld at God's bar (cf. 1 Cor. 4:3f.). On this view "truth" is virtually personified.[6] But it is also possible that the elder simply means that the behavior of Demetrius, which was in accord with the truth, bore testimony to his uprightness of character.[7] Finally, the elder adds his own testimony,[8] and reminds Gaius that he knows him to be a truthful witness.[9] The elder's word can be trusted over against any possible insinuations from Diotrephes. Thus the full complement of three witnesses (Deut. 19:15; 1 Jn. 5:8) is provided to uphold Demetrius.

---

[5]See C. W. Keyes, "The Greek Letter of Introduction," *American Journal of Philology* 56, 1935, 28–44.

[6]Plummer, 193; Windisch, 142f.; Bultmann, 102. The "truth" here is not Jesus or the Spirit (Jn. 14:6; 1 Jn. 5:6) but rather the Christian revelation personified (cf. Papias, in Eusebius, HE 3:39:3). Schnackenburg, 330f., thinks that a common figure of speech is being used and warns against over-interpretation.

[7]Westcott, 241f.; Brooke, 193; Dodd, 167; Stott, 229.

[8]The first person plural is used here, presumably to indicate the elder's close colleagues, as distinct from the broader group mentioned earlier in the verse.

[9]Cf. John 19:35; 21:24 for the wording.

FINAL WORDS AND GREETINGS (13–15)

> 13. *I have much to write to you, but I do not want to do so with pen and ink.* 14. *I hope to see you soon, and we will talk face to face.* 15. *Peace to you. The friends here send their greetings. Greet the friends there by name.*

13 The elder had already announced his intention of visiting the church (v. 10). In view of this anticipated visit he feels that he is released from the obligation[1] which would otherwise have rested upon him to say considerably more in his letter.[2]

14 He hopes that instead of writing he will be able to see his friend without delay and to have a leisurely personal talk with him. The language used is very similar to that in 2 John 12, and if the note of joy at the thought of the impending meeting is not explicit here, as it is in 2 John 12, we may well assume that it is nevertheless implicit.[3]

15 The letter closes with greetings. First, the elder conveys his own greeting to Gaius, "Peace to you."[4] Its presence here may perhaps compensate for the absence of an opening greeting, but it was normal to close a letter with some such wish. Here the elder takes over the well-known Jewish greeting which had already been filled with deeper significance for Christians by its use by Jesus (Jn. 20:19, 21, 26) and figures in several New Testament letters (Eph. 6:23; 1 Pet. 5:14).[5]

Second, the "friends," i.e. the members of the elder's church,[6] add their greetings to the writer's, and thus associate themselves with the elder's sentiments and back up his requests with their authority.

Finally, the elder asks that his greetings be conveyed to "the friends" individually.[7] These may be the members of Gaius's

---

[1]εἶχον is an example of the imperfect being used to express obligation or duty (BD 358).

[2]The aorist γράψαι expresses the writing of a single letter containing what the writer felt obliged to say; the present γράφειν indicates the continuation of the present letter. The wording is similar to that in 2 John 12. κάλαμος is here used of a reed pen.

[3]The sense of urgency, absent from 2 John 12, is conveyed by εὐθέως.

[4]The secular greeting was ἔρρωσο, literally, "be strong" (Acts 15:29). With the phrase εἴη (optative, expressing a wish) should be supplied.

[5]Paul especially liked to conclude a letter with an expression referring to peace (Rom. 15:33; 16:20; 2 Cor. 13:11; Gal. 6:16; Phil. 4:9; 1 Thess. 5:23; 2 Thess. 3:16; cf. Heb. 13:20).

[6]Cf. Luke 12:4; John 15:14f.; Acts 27:3; and see G. Stählin, TDNT IX, 162f., 166.

[7]κατ᾽ ὄνομα is found in this sense in Greek letters (Schnackenburg, 332).

household or the members of the church who sided with him rather than with Diotrephes. Perhaps the elder hoped that, although Diotrephes had suppressed his letter to the church, Gaius would share this letter with the church when opportunity permitted, and therefore it includes greetings to all who lived according to the truth and thus were in the fullest sense "friends" of the writer.

The First Epistle
of
JOHN

TEXT, EXPOSITION, AND NOTES

PROLOGUE—THE WORD OF LIFE (1:1–4)

1. *That which was from the beginning, which we have heard, which we have seen with our eyes, which we have looked at and our hands have touched—this we proclaim concerning the Word of life.* 2. *The life appeared; we have seen it and testify to it, and we proclaim to you the eternal life, which was with the Father and has appeared to us.* 3. *We proclaim to you what we have seen and heard, so that you also may have fellowship with us. And our fellowship is with the Father and with his Son, Jesus Christ.* 4. *We write this to make our[a] joy complete.*

[a]Some early MSS read *your.*

1 This writing begins without any of the formal features characteristic of a letter, such as we found in 2 John and 3 John. Since the conclusion also lacks any typical features of a letter,[1] we must conclude that the writing is not so much a letter as a written sermon or address. The close relationship which is evident between the writer and his readers, however, and the occasional reference to a specific situation (2:19) show that the author was writing for the benefit of a particular group or groups of readers, so that the writing is in effect a letter. The writer does not name himself or his readers. His identity would of course be known to them, and we may assume that he was the same person who wrote 2 and 3 John.

His message begins in a lofty but difficult manner. In the original Greek the first three and a half verses form one long sen-

[1]See, however, F. O. Francis, "The Form and Function of the Opening and Closing Paragraphs of James and 1 John," ZNW 61, 1970, 110–126, who notes that ancient letters could end without a formal conclusion.

tence; this has been broken up into shorter sentences for ease of understanding in modern English versions. Again, in a normal sentence we have the basic word order "subject–verb–object." Here the writer has placed the object first for emphasis and keeps us waiting for the subject and verb (which formed one word in Greek). To make matters still worse, the object consists of a string of parallel relative clauses—and it is expanded by a parenthesis (v. 2)[2] which describes one of the elements in the object more fully. As a result of this set of complications the writer repeats the substance of verse 1 in verse 3 before he finally reaches the main verb "we proclaim." In order to simplify this complicated construction the NIV has inserted the verb "we proclaim" in verse 1 as well as in verse 3 so that the reader is not kept too long in suspense; other modern translations follow various devices to get around the same difficulty.[3]

The result—which is important—is that the opening emphasis falls on the nature of the object which is proclaimed rather than on the activity of proclaiming it. The writer's purpose is to remind his readers of the character of the Christian message rather than to draw attention to the actual act of preaching it. What, then, is this object? It is "that which was from the beginning." If the readers were familiar with the Gospel of John and with the book of Genesis,[4] it is highly likely that they would recognize the echo of John 1:1, which in its turn echoes Genesis 1:1. If so, they would equate "that which was from the beginning" with the "Word" which was with God in the beginning.[5] The writer, however, does not use the term "Word" at this precise moment (although he will do so by the end of

[2]Francis's claim that the parenthesis is not really a parenthesis but one part of a two-pronged statement of the theme of the Epistle is not convincing.

[3]The NEB is particularly successful here: "It was there from the beginning; we have heard it; we have seen it with our own eyes; we looked upon it, and felt it with our own hands; and it is of this we tell. Our theme is the word of life. This life was made visible; we have seen it and bear our testimony; we here declare to you the eternal life which dwelt with the Father and was made visible to us. What we have seen and heard we declare to you, so that you and we together may share in a common life, that life which we share with the Father and his Son Jesus Christ." By contrast the RSV offers a strictly literal translation which expresses well the underlying Greek sentence structure.

[4]Both of these assumptions are highly likely. Despite the lack of direct allusion to the Old Testament the Epistle works with Jewish categories of thought, and it is probable that the writer shared these with his readers. The prologue to the Gospel is probably an earlier composition than the present writing.

[5]The phrase ἀπ' ἀρχῆς has been taken by some scholars to mean "from the beginning of the Christian dispensation" (cf. 2:7, 24; 3:11; H. H. Wendt, "Der 'Anfang' am Beginn des I Johannesbriefes," ZNW 21, 1922, 38–42). H. Conzelmann, "Was von Anfang war," in *Theologie als Schriftauslegung*, München, 1974, 207–214 (originally

the verse), and he thus leaves open the question of what it was that "was from the beginning."[6] He goes on quickly to describe it as something that he and others had "heard."[7] This confirms that it is the "Word" which he has in mind, and it indicates that what had been with God from the beginning had now come into the area of human experience. God's message has come to men so that they can hear it.

So far the object could be simply a word or message. But now the writer goes on to add "we have seen with our eyes." It is a strange message which is visible, and the qualification "with our eyes" leaves no doubt that literal seeing is meant. The point is hammered home by the further statement that the writer had gazed upon it[8] and had touched it with his hands.[9] These descriptions of something perceived by the senses mean that the writer cannot be thinking merely of a message that is heard. He must be thinking of the appearance of the "Word" described in John 1:1–18 who was made flesh as Jesus Christ.

But why does the writer say this in such an ambiguous manner? He is thinking of two things, which are nevertheless one. On

in W. Eltester [ed.], *Neutestamentliche Studien für R. Bultmann*, Berlin, 1954, 194–201), rightly argues that it refers to the absolute beginning. Since there is no mention of the creation (contrast Jn. 1:3) and the wording differs from that in John 1:1 (ἐν ἀρχῇ), the reference is to eternity past rather than to the beginning of creation (Schnackenburg, 59; cf. 2:13f.; G. Delling, TDNT I, 481f.).

[6]The writer uses the neuter form here, although the Greek word λόγος is masculine. Elsewhere too he uses the neuter when a masculine form would have been expected (5:4f.; cf. Jn. 3:6; 4:22; 6:37, 39; 17:2, 10; BD 138[1]). Here the use of the neuter suggests that the writer has in mind the Christian message which was incarnated in Jesus; he has therefore deliberately used this more general form of expression.

[7]The writer uses the perfect form which expresses an act in the past with lasting consequences; cf. the frequent New Testament use of γέγραπται with Old Testament citations to give the sense "it stands written (and is still valid)." The object of the "hearing" is still deliberately vague; the writer is thinking of hearing Jesus, which includes hearing what he said.

[8]It is not clear whether there is a different nuance in the use of θεάομαι alongside ὁράω. Westcott, 6, thinks that the verb denotes "calm, intent, continuous contemplation," while Brooke, 4, says that it is "to 'behold' intelligently, so as to grasp the meaning and significance of that which comes within our vision." The latter view is over-subtle, and ignores the fact that another verb of simple sense perception follows. Schnackenburg, 60, argues that the verb is used for reasons of rhythm and literary variation in the construction of the two sets of rhythmically parallel clauses. The shift in tense to the aorist in the second set of verbs is not significant.

[9]A reference to touching Jesus is to be found in John 20:24–29, and the same verb ψηλαφίζω occurs in Luke 24:39, again in the context of demonstrating the reality of the resurrection. The reference here, however, is broader, and there is possibly a polemical point against the Docetists, who denied the real physical incarnation of the Son of God (cf. Ignatius, *Smyrn.* 2f.).

the one hand, he is thinking of the Christian message which is the object of Christian proclamation and is heard by men; he himself is proclaiming it to his readers so that they may enjoy the blessings which come to those who receive it (v. 3). This message was preached by Jesus himself. On the other hand, Jesus himself can be described as the Word. The message takes concrete form in him. I may send a girl a message saying that I love her; I can also send her a costly ring which will be immediately recognizable to her as a tangible message of love. Jesus is both the preacher of God's message and the message itself. Paul could say, "We preach Christ" (1 Cor. 1:23; cf. 2 Cor. 4:5), showing that the message and the person are ultimately identical. Similarly, the writer to the Hebrews can tell how "God spoke to our forefathers through the prophets at many times and in various ways, but in these last days he has spoken to us by his Son" (Heb. 1:1f.). Our writer here wants to emphasize that the Christian message is identical with Jesus; it took personal form in a person who could be heard, seen, and even touched.[10]

At this point we could expect to find the verb which governs the object which has just been stated, and it is in fact inserted here by the NIV. But before the writer himself comes to it he inserts a qualifying phrase which he then develops in the parenthetical statement in verse 2. What he is describing is "concerning the Word of life."[11] The term "life" is the most general term for the spiritual experience which is the object of religious longing and is given to

[10]There has been much debate whether John is thinking primarily of the gospel message or the personal Word of God in this passage (see, for example, the discussion between J. E. Weir and K. Grayston in ExpT 86, 1974–75, 118–120 and 279). For the former view see especially Dodd, 1–6; Bruce, 35; and for the latter see Schnackenburg, 61; Haas, 29. The discussion is bedeviled by the fact that commentators have not distinguished clearly between (a) the antecedent of the relative clauses, and (b) the phrase ὁ λόγος τῆς ζωῆς. It is not clear that these are to be identified. While the relative clauses in our opinion indisputably refer to the concrete manifestation of the Word in a person who could be seen, heard, and touched, it is possible that "the word of life" could mean "the message about life." The matter is further complicated by the syntactical uncertainty at this point; see the next note.

[11]The phrase περὶ τοῦ λόγου τῆς ζωῆς is syntactically uncertain. (a) It may be taken closely with the preceding relative clauses. What the writer has heard, seen, and touched with regard to the word of life—that is what he proclaims. So Dodd, 3, who suggests that the phrase indicates the theme of the announcement, while the relative clauses state the contents (similarly, Bultmann, 8 n. 5). (b) Most commentators regard the phrase as summing up the relative clauses and providing a second object to the verb "we proclaim" (for ἀπαγγέλλω περί see Lk. 7:18; 13:1; Jn. 16:25). If so "this phrase defines the area with which what we have heard, seen and felt is concerned" (Houlden, 50; cf. Schnackenburg, 60f.; Haas, 21, 29). As Houlden comments, the difference between the two constructions is not very great. The former construction seems much more natural.

men by God. The writer believes that ordinary men may possess physical life but lack spiritual life; from a spiritual point of view they are dead (3:14; Jn. 5:24). Jesus, however, is the source of spiritual life; those who believe in him go through a spiritual experience comparable to physical birth and thus obtain the gift of life (Jn. 3:16, 36, cf. 3–8). Often this life is qualified as "eternal" (v. 2), but this adjective simply brings out a characteristic that is inherent in the concept itself; it stands to reason that the spiritual life into which God admits believers will be of the same eternal quality and duration as his own (cf. Lk. 20:36).

The "Word of life" can mean the message which conveys this life to men or which tells them about it (Acts 5:20; Phil. 2:16). The phrase would then be a description of the Christian message preached by the writer and his colleagues. But if we glance back at John 1:4 we find that "in him [sc. the Word] was life," and in John 11:25; 14:6 Jesus says that he is life. Here, therefore, Jesus himself may be meant as the Word who is the source and substance of eternal life.[12] Probably the phraseology is again deliberately ambiguous, although the writer is perhaps thinking more of the Christian message.[13]

2 Although the Christian message is the means of bringing eternal life, it was of supreme importance to the writer to make it clear beyond all possibility of mistake that the life to which it bears witness was revealed by God in the historical person of Jesus. This is why he now includes this slightly awkward parenthesis which interrupts his line of thought. Its very awkwardness calls attention to its importance: the life that God gives to men was revealed historically in Jesus. Indeed it is identical with Jesus, so that the writer can say that he has actually seen it. Because of this he is qualified to testify to it, i.e. to bear his personal witness to what he himself has actually seen and experienced.[14] His proclamation thus consists of an act of testimony. But still his emphasis is not on the act of proclamation but on the historical reality of that to which he bears witness. It is the eternal life, he says, which was with the Father and then appeared to us. The language used here is precisely that which was used of the personal Word which was with God in the beginning (Jn.

---

[12]The NIV indicates its acceptance of this interpretation by its use of the capital letter with "Word." Similarly, Schnackenburg, 61; Bultmann, 8 n. 5; Haas, 23f.
[13]So Westcott, 6f.; Brooke, 5; Stott, 66-68; Bruce, 36f.; Houlden, 50–52. De Jonge, 37–39, stresses the difficulty of coming to a decision.
[14]See H. Strathmann, TDNT IV, 497–499.

1:2). It was the personal manifestation of eternal life in the historical person of Jesus which was of crucial importance for the writer—and his readers.

3 The parenthesis is concluded, and the writer resumes his sentence with a recapitulation of verse 1: "what we have seen and heard." Now at last he comes to the principal verb of the sentence[15] and tells his readers that he is sharing his message with them too, so that they too may have fellowship with him. But, he goes on, he and his colleagues enjoy fellowship with the Father and his Son, Jesus Christ. The implication is surely that his readers also will share in this fellowship with the Father and the Son as a result of their fellowship with him.

"Fellowship" renders a Greek word which literally means "having in common." Two or more persons can be said to have fellowship with one another when they have something in common. James and John were sharers with Simon in their common pursuit of fishing (Lk. 5:10). Paul and Titus shared in a common faith (Tit. 1:4; cf. Jude 3). Believers share in the grace of God (Phil. 1:7), in Jesus Christ (1 Cor. 1:9), and in spiritual gifts generally (Rom. 15:27). As a result fellowship has two aspects. There is the element of participation in some spiritual gift or in Christian service, and there is the element of union with other believers as a result of common enjoyment of some spiritual privilege or common sharing in some Christian activity.[16] Here in this verse the writer clearly wants to make known his message to his readers so that by their acceptance of it they may become and remain his partners and thus be joined together in that Christian love which unites those who have a common faith in Jesus Christ. But[17] the fellowship which the writer enjoys includes the Father and the Son. Here the thought of union with God is uppermost, and the thought of participation in some common object has dwindled to the point of vanishing.[18]

4 Verse 3 has expressed the purpose of the writer's presentation of the Christian message. Now he adds a subsidiary reason. He

---

[15]The verb ἀπαγγέλλω has in fact already been used in verse 2, so that verse 3 is somewhat of an anticlimax.

[16]See H. Seesemann, *Der Begriff* KOINΩNIA *im Neuen Testament*, Giessen, 1933; F. Hauck, TDNT III, 797–809.

[17]The use of καὶ . . . δέ serves to develop and intensify the thought. Moule, 165, renders "Yes, and. . . ." Cf. 3 John 12.

[18]It is possible that the thought is of the participation of believers in the Father and Son, but the close parallelism with the preceding clause makes this improbable. For the thought of union between believers and God in John see especially Bruce, 38f.

is writing this—i.e. the letter—in order that his joy[19] may be complete.[20] He has the heart of a pastor which cannot be completely happy so long as some of those for whom he feels responsible are not experiencing the full blessings of the gospel.

Our exposition of the prologue to the Epistle has left a number of questions unanswered. Above all, we have not seen why the writer expressed himself in this particular way to his readers. At first sight he appears to be addressing them as if they were not Christians; he wants them to hear his message so that they may share in Christian fellowship with him. Yet later on in the writing it is quite certain that he is writing to Christian believers: "I write these things to you who believe in the name of the Son of God so that you may know that you have eternal life" (5:13). His concern is rather that they should not be led astray from their Christian faith and that they should have assurance that they really are Christians. It is probable, therefore, that the writer felt anxious about their spiritual state. Some of the members of the church had left it and had thereby shown that they had never truly belonged to it. The writer feared perhaps that there were others in the church who did not truly believe or that some members of the church might be misled by his opponents into the acceptance of a false message which would cut them off from genuine fellowship with God. We could interpret verse 3 to mean that he is expressing his understanding of the Christian message so that his readers might know where he stood and hence whether they could have fellowship with him on the basis of a common acceptance of the same message; he was quite certain that his message was the true one, and that only by acceptance of it could one have true fellowship in the church, a fellowship which brought God and man together in spiritual union. On this view, verse 3 is not necessarily prescribing the condition for entry to fellowship, but for continuance in fellowship.[21]

---

[19]There are textual variants here. Instead of ἡμεῖς (S A* B P Ψ 33 z cop^sa ms) most authorities have ὑμῖν, which critics generally regard as a correction. The authorities are divided between "our joy" (ἡμῶν, S B L Ψ 049 z cop^sa al) and "your joy" (ὑμῶν). Since the two words were pronounced almost identically, confusion was easy. Most critics judge that the thought is of the writer's own pastoral joy, and that scribes failed to recognize this point and/or were influenced by John 16:24. The reading "your" is defended by J. H. Dobson, "Emphatic Personal Pronouns in the NT," *Bible Translator* 22, 1971, 58–60, but his reasoning is not compelling.

[20]πληρόω has the note of fulness, whereas τελειόω has more the idea of attainment of an end. Cf. 2 John 12; John 15:11; 16:24.

[21]The use of the continuous ἔχητε rather than the punctiliar σχῆτε ("to obtain") may be significant.

The nature of the writer's understanding of the Christian message is already apparent in the prologue, but receives fuller clarification later. He states that he and his colleagues have fellowship with the Father and with his Son, Jesus Christ. In some way or other, the opponents of the writer claimed that it was possible to have life and fellowship with God without Jesus playing any significant part. It was some form of Christless religion. The writer makes two points by way of reply. He emphasizes that Christian fellowship is with the Father and the Son, and later on in the Epistle he will make it abundantly clear that nobody can enjoy a relationship with God without a relationship with Jesus (2:23). At the same time, he emphasizes that eternal life is found only in Jesus. He incorporates the life of God, which was with God at the beginning, and it is in him that God has revealed his life; the content of the Christian message is Jesus, the Word of life.

What the writer states most emphatically of all, however, is that certain people can testify to these facts because they had personal experience of Jesus. They heard and saw him, they even touched him, and they saw in him the incarnation of divine life. The writer associates himself with others who had shared in this personal experience. He uses the "we" form of expression to include himself and others who had known Jesus personally and who were thus qualified to witness to others and draw them into the circle of Christian fellowship. There cannot be any real doubt that the writer claims to have been an eyewitness of the earthly ministry of Jesus.

Nevertheless, this interpretation has been questioned. In 4:14 the writer can say "we have seen and testify that the Father has sent his Son to be the Savior of the world"; here it seems probable that the "we" refers to Christians generally, just as in the preceding verse 13. May not the same be true here in 1:1–3? More important is the consideration that for many scholars it is unlikely that 1 John was written by an eyewitness of the ministry of Jesus. If so, some other explanation must be found. One possibility is that the writer is referring to the whole event of the coming of Jesus and the realization of his significance in the church: it is the church's experience of salvation in Jesus which is the object of testimony. Another possibility is that the writer is associating himself and other, later Christians with the experience of the eyewitnesses, claiming their experience as something in which the whole church could be said to share. The often-cited parallel is that of a spectator returning home after watching a football game and saying "We won," although what he really means is "the team which I support won." The Jews shared this outlook; every Jew was to regard himself at the passover feast as if he had personally taken part in the Exodus from Egypt.[22]

Neither of these explanations carries conviction.[23] The structure of the passage is different from that in 4:13f., and the group denoted by "we" here stands over against the Christian readers of the letter. This excludes the second explanation. The first is also unlikely, since the reference to "touching" can only indicate personal acquaintance with the historical Jesus and cannot be watered down to mean knowledge of the Christian message. The writer here expresses himself as a member of the group of eyewitnesses of the ministry of Jesus, and his claim must be a genuine one; had it been false, his readers would have known not to believe him, and his message would have carried no force.

John's prologue highlights two dangers which still confront the church. The one is the assumption that Christian fellowship is possible other than on the basis of common belief in Christ. Some people would almost go so far as to say that Christian unity means Christians of different beliefs coming together in fellowship; it is easy enough, they say, to have Christian unity with those of like mind, but the real test of Christian unity is whether we are willing to have it with those with whom we disagree. There is a sense in which this is true; where matters not of the substance of the faith are concerned, it is all too easy for us to avoid Christian unity with people whose way of doing things or whose general culture is different from ours, and we need to pull down such barriers. But it is not true that there can be fellowship between persons who disagree on the central affirmations of the faith. There cannot be unity between denominations which differ in their understanding of the way of salvation, and there cannot be unity between those who accept and those who do not accept Jesus Christ—crucified for our sins and raised for our justification—as Savior. There is no common ground in such cases.

The other danger is the assumption that it is possible to have a

[22]See the citations from *Mishnah Pesahim* 10:5b; Amos 2:10f.; Joshua 24:7; Tacitus, *Agricola,* 45, in Bultmann, 10.
[23]There is a detailed discussion in Schnackenburg, 52–58. For the possibilities rejected here see Bultmann, 10f., who thinks that the reference is to the "eschatological" contemporaries of Jesus, and Dodd, 9–16, who uses the idea of the solidarity of the church with the eyewitnesses. Wengst, 65 and n. 149, holds that the "we" is a pseudonymous device to suggest the author's identity with the author of John, who also refers to himself as "we" in his prologue.

true relationship with God while rejecting Jesus Christ as the way, the truth, and the life. As this Epistle will go on to make clear, the Father can be known only through the Son. There is "none other name."

WALKING IN THE LIGHT (1:5–2:2)

5. *This is the message we have heard from him and declare to you: God is light; in him there is no darkness at all.* 6. *If we claim to have fellowship with him yet walk in the darkness, we lie and do not put the truth into practice.* 7. *But if we walk in the light, as he is in the light, we have fellowship with one another, and the blood of Jesus, his Son, purifies us from every sin.*

8. *If we claim to be without sin, we deceive ourselves and the truth is not in us.* 9. *If we confess our sins, he is faithful and just and will forgive us our sins and purify us from all unrighteousness.* 10. *If we claim we have not sinned, we make him out to be a liar, and his word has no place in our lives.*

2:1. *My dear children, I write this to you so that you will not sin. But if anybody does sin, we have one who speaks to the Father in our defense — Jesus Christ, the Righteous One.* 2. *He is the atoning sacrifice for our sins, and not only for ours but also for the sins of the whole world.*

Although the prologue to the Epistle has given strong hints that the problem facing the writer was the existence of doubts about the historical revelation of God the Father in his Son, Jesus Christ, he begins his main discussion at a different point. His aim was that his readers might stand in a position of real fellowship with himself and so with God and Jesus. But there are conditions attached to such fellowship, and in addition to the doctrinal condition already hinted at (which will be developed later) there is also a moral condition which arises out of the character of God.

5 John, therefore, begins his argument with a statement about the nature of God which, he declares, he has heard from Jesus.[1]

---

[1]John writes of the message which has been heard from him (ἀπ' αὐτοῦ). His use of pronouns in this Epistle is sometimes vague, but here the reference to hearing and the fact that the content of the message is about God both suggest that Jesus is the author of the message (cf. Jn. 1:18; 3:32). John bases his teaching, over against that of his opponents, on the authority of what he has heard in the historical revelation of God in Jesus. ἀκούω is normally constructed with παρά, but here John uses ἀπό (cf. Acts 9:13).

God is light. This description of God is admittedly not found in the teaching of Jesus in the Gospels in so many words. The coming of Jesus, however, was regarded as a revelation of light (Mt. 4:16; Lk. 2:32; Jn. 1:4–9; 3:19–21). According to John Jesus identified himself as the light of the world (Jn. 8:12; 9:5; cf. 12:35f., 46), and Matthew tells us how he commanded his disciples to take up the same role (Mt. 5:14–16). All this implies that the character of God himself is light, and that Jesus was the incarnation of divine light for men. To speak of God in this way was to employ a well-known symbol which was capable of several facets of meaning and which was used in many religions. Fundamentally John's thought was derived from the Old Testament. Light was an obvious symbol for God, especially since on occasion God revealed himself in fire and light. God could be said to be clothed in light and glory (Ps. 104:2) and hence too bright for man to behold (1 Tim. 6:16). Specifically two notions became associated with God as light. One was that of revelation and salvation (Ps. 27:1; 36:9; Isa. 49:6). Light provides illumination in dark places and is an appropriate symbol for the way in which God reveals himself to men to show them how to live. The other is that of holiness; light symbolizes the flawless perfection of God. The comparison of good and evil with light and darkness is a familiar one, and it was current in the ancient world. It was typical of Iranian religion (Zoroastrianism) and was taken up in Gnosticism, but it was also at home in Jewish thought: in the Rule of the Qumran sect the members were exhorted to love all the sons of light and hate all the sons of darkness (1QS 1:9f.).[2]

The author takes up this symbolism when he announces his basic thought: God is light. He is fond of emphasizing his propositions by a restatement of them in negative form, and so he at once adds "in him there is no darkness at all." The contrast between God and darkness is expressed as strongly as possible. The point is not so much that God did not create darkness[3] but rather that living in the darkness is incompatible with fellowship with God. This makes it clear that the writer is thinking of light and darkness predominantly in ethical terms; it is his way of saying: "God is good, and evil can have no place beside him."

6 This basic thesis is now followed by a series of criticisms

---

[2]On "light" see H. Conzelmann, TDNT IX, 310–358; there is a brief note in Stott, 70–72.

[3]John does not raise the question of the origin of the darkness. Bultmann, 17, goes too far in claiming that John is merely presenting a "dualism of decision."

of positions which are incompatible with acceptance of it. John takes up three claims which people make, but which must be assessed in the light of their real character and in relation to this thesis. It is probable that these claims were real statements made by people in the church to which John was writing, and that they reflect the outlook of the people who were causing trouble in the church. The claims were:

(1) We have fellowship with him.
(2) We are without sin.
(3) We have not sinned.

In each case, the writer's reply is to compare the statement with the actual way of life of the persons who made it and hence to show that the claims were false. Then he goes on to indicate in each case how people who wished to have fellowship with God could really have it.

The first claim was made by people who alleged that they had fellowship with God; they probably claimed to have a true relationship with God without accepting the particular teaching of the writer. The writer combatted their claim by alleging that they were still living in darkness.[4] Now there is a sense, of course, in which all Christians live in the darkness. They live in this world which is opposed to God (see 2:15–17) and characterized by darkness. But the situation of the Christian is like that of a person walking on a dark stage in the circle of light cast by a spotlight which is focused on him; he moves slowly forward so that he can walk in its light without fear of stumbling and losing his way. To live in the glare of the spotlight involves living a life that is compatible with being in the light, a life that is free from sin. To live in the darkness means to live without the benefit of divine illumination and guidance and so to live in sin. What John is saying is that it is not possible to have fellowship with God and yet to live in sin because to have fellowship with God means walking in the light while to live in sin means to walk in the darkness. It is improbable that the people actually said, "We can have fellowship with God and yet walk in darkness"; that was a contradiction that they would not have accepted any more than John would. Rather, John was drawing attention to certain features of their way of life and branding these as sinful, and hence as signs of living in the darkness.

Such persons were deceiving themselves. They claimed to

---

[4]The NIV preserves the literal rendering "walk" for περιπατέω; see 2 John 4.

have fellowship with God, but because of the incompatibility between the character of God as light and their own character as men living in the dark they were self-deceived. They were deceived in thinking that they could have fellowship with God while they practiced sin, and they were deceived in thinking that the experience which they thought was fellowship with God was really fellowship with him. This last point is implied in the writer's comment that they do not put the truth into practice.[5] We have seen already in 2 John that the truth is the ultimate reality of God revealed in Jesus and in the Christian message, and that this reality is moral in quality. To practice the truth means to live according to the way revealed by God and so as those who belong to the divine sphere. John says that those who practice sin demonstrate that they do not belong to God; in other words, they do not have fellowship with God.

7 Now comes the writer's contrast. The opposite of living in the darkness is living in the light, i.e. being responsive to the divine revelation of the truth which shows us how we ought to live. To live in the light is to come into the sphere where God himself is to be found, or rather to live in the same way as God himself. The metaphors used are quite plastic, so that there is nothing strange in the writer saying both that God is light and that he is in the light. It follows logically that those who live in the light have fellowship with God, since these two expressions refer to different aspects of the same reality. To live according to God's light brings a man into the relationship of fellowship with God. But this is not in fact what the writer says. Earlier he had written that his purpose was that his readers might have fellowship with himself and his colleagues; now, using the preacher's "we," which includes speaker and congregation or writer and readers, he says that walking in the light brings us into fellowship with one another, i.e. with the whole company of God's people. This is an interesting surprise. Haas puts the point neatly: "The false teachers whose opinions he is quoting and refuting in these verses boasted of their fellowship and communion with God, but they neglected the fellowship with men. John wants to remind them that they cannot have fellowship with God unless they have fellowship with other Christians."[6] Persons who cut themselves off from fellowship with other Christians cannot have fellow-

---

[5]"To put the truth into practice" translates a phrase which appears to have a Semitic background; cf. 1QS 1:5; John 3:21.
[6]Haas, 35.

ship with God. But if they are prepared to live by God's light, they will come into fellowship with them and with God himself.

As soon as a person does this, however, he will become conscious of his sin; the very thing which separates him from God is shown up in the light. What is he to do? He may simply dodge back out of the circle of light into the darkness because he knows that his deeds are evil, and he does not want them to be shown up, nor does he want to be separated from them (Jn. 3:20). Alternatively, he comes, sin and all, into the light, and to his amazement discovers that the dark blemishes disappear. The blood of Jesus, God's Son, cleanses from sin. This thought is essential to what the writer is saying, and scholars who regard it as a secondary addition to the text by a pedantic redactor[7] have misunderstood the situation. "Blood" is a symbolical way of speaking of the death of Jesus. In the Old Testament the "blood" was the result of the death of the sacrificial victim, and its application to the person offering the sacrifice indicated that the effects of the sacrifice applied to him. The effect of the death of Jesus was to purify us from sin. To say that the blood of Jesus purifies us is to say that our sin is removed and forgiven;[8] its defiling effects no longer condemn us in the sight of God. Although as Christians who walk in the light we may be conscious of sin, yet this does not prevent our fellowship with God, for God himself removes our sin.[9]

8 We have seen that in verse 6 the writer accused his opponents of claiming fellowship with God although they walked in the darkness, i.e. committed sin. It would appear that their response to this accusation was to deny it. "We are without sin," they replied—whether this was their actual answer to John or the answer which he could imagine them making to his accusation is unimportant.[10] They argued that they did not need cleansing from sin be-

---

[7]Bultmann, 20; similarly, O'Neill, 10, excises the words "the blood of Jesus his Son."

[8]It was in connection with this verse that Westcott, 34–37, developed his extraordinary thesis that "The Blood always includes the thought of the life preserved and active beyond death." Despite the support which has been given to this view, it undoubtedly misrepresents biblical teaching; see J. Behm, TDNT I, 172–176; A. M. Stibbs, *The Meaning of the Word "Blood" in Scripture,* London, 1954²; L. Morris, *The Apostolic Preaching of the Cross,* ch. 3. For καθαρίζω see below, 114 n. 14.

[9]O'Neill, 10, argues that the subject of the clause was originally God. He also argues that instead of ἀλλήλων in the first part of the main clause we should read αὐτοῦ, which has weak textual attestation. Both conjectures are highly improbable.

[10]It is not clear how far John is citing actual slogans of his opponents in the Epistle. It is

cause they had no sin from which to be cleansed. Actions which John evidently regarded as sinful—we shall see later what they were—did not appear sinful to them.

To John it was self-evident that these men were sinners. His reply to them is simply that they are *deceiving themselves and the truth is not in them*. This doesn't mean simply that they are telling a lie, but that they have no share in the divine reality despite their claims to the contrary. There is a certain paradox in this statement. The converse is that if we do say that we are sinners, the truth is in us; the resolution of the paradox is that to admit our sin is to face up to reality instead of pretending, and it is as we confess our sin that it is cleansed and no longer stands against us. If, however, we do not admit our sin, it remains unconfessed and unforgiven, and hence the truth is not in us. The temptation to deny one's sin is common to both the non-Christian and the Christian. John's opponents included persons whom he did not regard as Christians (2:19), who had cut themselves off from forgiveness by their denial of their sin and of Christ's ability to save; he feared that others in the church might follow their example and claim a sinlessness which could interrupt their fellowship with God. Later on, he will argue that the Christian does not, and cannot sin (3:6, 9; 5:18); the resolution of the further paradox occasioned by that statement in relation to the present one must be attempted in due course.

9 Again, as in verse 7, the writer presents the contrary position to that which he has just outlined. Instead of claiming that we are without sin, we ought to *confess our sins*. Although the statement lies in a conditional clause, it has the force of a command or obligation: we ought to confess our sins, and, if we do, *he is faithful and just.* . . . To confess sins is not merely to admit that we are sinners, but to lay them before God and to seek forgiveness.[11] If we do so, we can be sure of forgiveness and purification on the grounds

---

probable, however, that he accurately depicts the kind of things that they said, although "to have sin" is a Johannine expression (Jn. 9:41; 15:22, 24; 19:11; Brooke, 17f.).

[11]ὁμολογέω is used elsewhere of confession of faith (2:23; 4:2, 3, 15; 2 Jn. 7); ἐξομολογέω is more commonly used of confessing sin (Prov. 28:13; Mt. 3:6; Acts 19:18; Jas. 5:16). The practice of confessing sins is found in the Old Testament (Lev. 16:21; Ps. 32:5; Prov. 28:13; Dan. 9:20) and Judaism (1QS 1:24–2:1; CD 20:28f.). Schnackenburg, 85f., holds that public confession before God by the individual is meant, but denies that the church acts in any way as God's intermediary in forgiving the sins confessed.

of God's character. He is faithful and just[12] to[13] forgive confessed sin. The faithfulness lies in his adherence to his promises that he will forgive his people: "Who is a God like thee, pardoning iniquity and passing over transgression for the remnant of his inheritance? He does not retain his anger forever because he delights in steadfast love. . . . Thou wilt show faithfulness to Jacob and steadfast love to Abraham, as thou hast sworn to our fathers from the days of old" (Mic. 7:18–20). The justice lies in the inherent rightness of the act; if the conditions are fulfilled, God would be wrong to withhold forgiveness. His forgiveness is not, therefore, an act of mercy which stands in opposition to his justice, for his mercy and justice are ultimately one. The description of God's act is an expansion of that in verse 7. The thought of purification from sin is expanded in terms of forgiveness of sin and purification from unrighteousness. Sin is regarded as making us guilty in the sight of God, and therefore in need of forgiveness, and also as making us unclean in God's sight, and therefore in need of purification. Most commentators regard the two terms as synonymous, but it is possible that purification signifies the removal not only of the guilt of sin but also of the power of sin in the human heart.[14]

10 For the third time John takes up the kind of things said by his opponents and members of the church who might be misled by them. He cites their statement, "we have not sinned." It is puzzling to see why he quotes this saying after verse 8, "we are without sin," and commentators have attempted to find some difference in emphasis between the two statements. Westcott thought that verse 8 referred to the presence of the sinful principle in a man; a person may recognize "the natural permanence of sin as a power within" and "may yet deny that he personally has sinned."[15] This view is followed by many commentators. Since, however, John has interpreted the claim in verse 8 in terms of the need for forgiveness of sins (plural) in verse 9, it is unlikely that he saw the claim in verse 8

---

[12]The phraseology is reminiscent of Deuteronomy 32:4. Cf. Romans 3:25; Hebrews 10:23.

[13]The ἵνα clause expresses the way in which God expresses his faithfulness and justice; it is equivalent to an infinitive of result (BD 391⁵).

[14]To purify is to remove the defiling effects of sin, either by the avoidance of sinful acts (2 Cor. 7:1; Jas. 4:8) or by the pardon of sins already committed (Eph. 5:26; Heb. 1:3; 10:2). Here the thought is primarily of pardon through Christ's atoning blood, but the fact that John speaks of *both* forgiveness *and* cleansing may suggest that he is also thinking of the destruction of sinful desires which defile us in God's sight. See Calvin, 241; Westcott, 25. "Unrighteousness" is a synonym for "sin" (cf. 5:17).

[15]Westcott, 25.

merely as a denial of the presence of a sinful power within. It is possible that there were people who both denied present sinfulness (v. 8) and past acts of sin (v. 10): even if you claim not to sin now, you certainly sinned in the past, may be the thought in John's mind. Perhaps, however, we should regard the two claims as virtually identical; if so, John is making the point that those who make such claims do not merely deceive themselves (v. 8); they actually make God a liar (v. 10) by denying his verdict on men that they are sinners.[16] Paul's statement that "all have sinned" (Rom. 3:23) is no isolated remark; it sums up the teaching of Scripture on the universality of sin.[17] Not only so; the scriptural revelation of God emphasizes his character as a God who forgives sin, and this description would be pointless if men had no sins to be forgiven. Those who deny their sin thus fall into the serious sin of making God out to be a liar. By no stretch of the imagination can they be said to have his word in them. The message of God, mediated through Christian tradition, has not affected their belief or their conduct.[18]

2:1 At this point there is a brief pause in the thought, indicated by the writer's address to his readers as "my dear children."[19] In the preceding verses he has had his opponents very much in mind, and has been citing the kind of things which they said, by which other members of the church might be led astray. Now he turns his attention more directly to the members of the church and issues an appeal to them. His choice of the term "children" indicates the affectionate concern which he feels for them. When he describes them as God's children, he uses a different Greek word (3:1).[20] It is interesting that although the disciples were commanded not to call one another "father" (Mt. 23:9), the relation of the pastor to his congregation is often likened to that of a father to his children, and the pastors had no compunctions about addressing their congregations as "children" (e.g. 1 Cor. 4:14, 17; Gal. 4:19; 1 Tim. 1:2; Phm. 10; 3 Jn. 4).

---

[16]Schnackenburg, 88 and n. 2.

[17]1 Kings 8:46; Psalm 14:3; Job 4:17; 15:14–16; Proverbs 20:9; Ecclesiastes 7:20; Isaiah 53:6; 64:6.

[18]The word of God is here tantamount to the truth (v. 8). Cf. John 17:17. The reference is not to the personal Word of God, which is not said to dwell in men. Rather John is speaking of hearing and accepting the Christian message.

[19]The Greek τεχνίον, literally "small child," a diminutive form expressing affection, is rendered "dear child" by the NIV.

[20]For τεχνίον see 2:12, 28; 3:7, 18; 4:4; 5:21. John also uses παιδίον (2:14, 18) in the same sense.

It was possible that the readers might interpret what John had just written[21] with its emphasis on the fact that Christians were not free from sin as a license to sin. If sin was a characteristic of Christians, and forgiveness was freely available, the readers might well have reacted like the people who asked, "Shall we go on sinning, so that grace may increase?" (Rom. 6:1). John, therefore, had to make it quite clear that his purpose was that Christians should not sin. Unconfessed sin was incompatible with fellowship with God. John's aim, therefore, was that his readers would both recognize their sin and confess it—and also seek to live without sin. It is easy to live without sin if one denies that one's acts are really sinful. John wished that his readers would recognize the all-pervasive character of sin—and yet live without sinning.

Having inserted this almost parenthetical note, he returns for the third time to the question of forgiveness. There is a remedy for those who sin and confess it, and it lies in the fact that "we have one who speaks to the Father in our defense." This is the NIV's paraphrase of a Greek word which is generally rendered as "advocate." The English word is based on the Latin *advocatus*, which in turn corresponds to the Greek word *parakletos*, and literally means "one called alongside (to help)." In the present context the word undoubtedly signifies an "advocate" or "counsel for the defense" in a legal context. It means a person who intercedes on behalf of somebody else. That this was one of the meanings of the Greek word is well attested, and the idea of intercession before God was at home in the Old Testament and Jewish background of the New Testament. Paul too speaks of Jesus as the one who is at God's right hand and makes intercession for us (Rom. 8:34), and he also refers to the work of the Spirit as the one who assists us in our feeble prayers by his intercession for us (Rom. 8:26). This is the idea that is present here. We have nothing that we can plead before God to gain us forgiveness for our sins, but Jesus Christ acts as our advocate and enters his plea for us.[22] He is described as being righteous. John is fond of this adjective with reference to Jesus, especially when he is thinking of Jesus as an example for Christians to follow (2:29; 3:7). Peter also de-

---

[21] ταῦτα refers back to what has just been written, but the author may be thinking of the Epistle as a whole; cf. 5:13.

[22] The meaning of παράκλητος in John 14–16 may be different from what it is in the present passage; it does not need to be discussed here. See J. Behm, TDNT V, 800–814; R. E. Brown, *The Gospel according to John*, New York, 1967, and London, 1971, II, 1135–1144; O. Betz, *Der Paraklet*, Leiden, 1963.

scribed Jesus in this way when he contrasted the innocence of Jesus with the wickedness of those who put him to death (Acts 3:14; cf. 7:52), but above all he spoke of him as the righteous One who died on behalf of the unrighteous so that he might bring them to God (1 Pet. 3:18).[23] It is this thought which is present here. Jesus Christ not only has no sins of his own for which he must suffer; but as one who is not contaminated by sin he is qualified to intercede for others. He can, as it were, plead his own righteousness before God and ask that sinners be forgiven on the basis of his righteous act.[24]

2   But what precisely is the ground on which the Advocate rests his case? John goes on to elucidate the thought by describing Jesus as "the atoning sacrifice" (hilasmos) for our sins. This word, which is found elsewhere in the New Testament only in 4:10,[25] has aroused considerable debate, not to say controversy. When the word appears outside the Bible, it conveys the thought of an offering made by a man in order to placate the wrath of a god whom he has offended. It was a means of turning the god from wrath to a favorable attitude, and it operated by giving the god something that made up for the offense that he had suffered. In the Greek version of the Old Testament, however, the meaning is debated. Westcott and Dodd both argued that, while in secular Greek the corresponding verb takes as its object the god who has been offended, in the Old Testament the object is the offense itself, and from this they concluded that "the scriptural conception . . . is not that of appeasing one who is angry, with a personal feeling, against the offender; but of altering the character of that which from without occasions a necessary alienation, and interposes an inevitable obstacle to fellowship."[26] This view was strengthened by noting that God himself may be the provider of the sacrifice. The conclusion was that in secular sources the word means "propitiation," i.e. a means of placating an offended person, but in the Bible it means "expiation," i.e. a means of neutralizing and cancelling sin. Since neither of these words is in common usage today, most modern translations offer a

[23]J. Jeremias, TDNT V, 707, holds that we have here a traditional, messianic title ultimately based on Isaiah 53:11; cf. 1 Enoch 38:2; 53:6.
[24]Possibly there is the thought that his defense is not based on any false pleading.
[25]Other words from the same root are used: ἱλάσκομαι in Luke 18:13 and Hebrews 2:17; ἱλαστήριον in Romans 3:25 and Hebrews 9:5; and ἵλεως in Matthew 16:22 and Hebrews 8:12.
[26]Westcott, 85–87; C. H. Dodd, "ἱλάσκομαι, its cognates, derivatives and synonyms in the Septuagint," JTS 32, 1931, 352–360; reprinted in The Bible and the Greeks, London, 1935, 82–95.

paraphrase. The NIV, with its rendering "atoning sacrifice," combines the two ideas, since "atonement" is something made for sin, and "sacrifice" is an offering to God. The TEV rendering, "the means by which our sins are forgiven," is neutral, while the NEB has "the remedy for the defilement of our sins," which stands closer to "expiation."

Westcott and Dodd's interpretation of the evidence has been strongly challenged by L. Morris and D. Hill.[27] These two scholars have shown that in the Old Testament the idea of placating the wrath of God or some other injured party is often present when the word-group in question is used. They conclude that the same is true in the New Testament. The meaning of the present passage would then be that Jesus propitiates God with respect to our sins.[28] There can be no real doubt that this is the meaning. In the previous verse the thought was of Jesus acting as our advocate before God; the picture which continues into this verse is of Jesus pleading the cause of guilty sinners before a judge who is being petitioned to pardon their acknowledged guilt. He is not being asked to declare them innocent, i.e. to say that there is no evidence that they have sinned, but rather to grant them pardon for their acknowledged sins. In order that forgiveness may be granted, there is an action in respect of the sins which has the effect of rendering God favorable to the sinner. We may, if we wish, say that the sins are cancelled out by the action in question. This means that the one action has the double effect of expiating the sin and thereby propitiating God. These two aspects of the action belong together, and a good translation will attempt to convey them both.[29]

The atoning sacrifice is, of course, the death of Jesus. This is clear from the fact that in the parallel statement in 1:7 it is the blood

---

[27]L. Morris, *The Apostolic Preaching of the Cross,* London, 1965³, chs. 5 and 6; D. Hill, *Greek Words and Hebrew Meanings,* Cambridge, 1967, ch. 2. See further R. R. Nicole, "C. H. Dodd and the Doctrine of Propitiation," *Westminster Theological Journal* 17, 1954–55, 117–157; *idem,* " 'Hilaskesthai' Revisited," EQ 49, 1977, 173–177; N. H. Young, "C. H. Dodd, 'Hilaskesthai' and his critics," EQ 48, 1976, 67–78.

[28]Greek περί; cf. 4:10; 1 Peter 3:18. See also Hebrews 5:3; 10:6, 8, 18, 26; 13:11; H. Riesenfeld, TDNT VI, 53–56.

[29]The problem is whether the action envisaged is primarily concerned with expiating the sin or with propitiating God. The common argument, that propitiation cannot be in mind because it is God who provides the means, cannot apply in the present passage because God is the object of the Son's advocacy. (For this reason, H. Clavier is wrong when he interprets the passage more of God offering the propitiation to men to win them over from their opposition to him: "Notes sur un mot-clef du johannisme et de la sotériologie biblique: *hilasmos,*" NovT 10, 1968, 287–304.) The fact would seem to be that the word-group can have different nuances in different contexts, and in some cases it bears more the sense of expiation (cf. 2 Kings 5:18; Ps. 25:11; Sir.

of Jesus which cleanses us from sin; blood is a metaphor for a sacrificial death.

Two important points must be noted. The first is that Jesus is both the advocate and the atoning sacrifice. What he pleads on behalf of sinners is what he himself has done on their behalf. It is this that constitutes him a righteous advocate for them. The second thing is that the language of advocacy and sacrifice appears to place Jesus over against God as if God had to be persuaded by a third party to forgive us. It is an inherent weakness in the picture which is employed here that it is in danger of presenting God as an unwilling judge from whom forgiveness has to be wrested by the advocate for sinners. But this would be a false conclusion to draw. Already in 1:9 John has emphasized that it is God himself who is faithful and just and forgives our sins, and in 4:9f. he adds his powerful voice to the New Testament chorus which declares that it was God the Father who gave Jesus his Son to be the atoning sacrifice for our sins. It is God himself who provides the means of our forgiveness and pays the cost of it. The language of advocacy is thus ultimately inadequate to express the paradox of the offended God who himself pardons our offenses by giving his own Son to be our Savior.

Nor is that the full extent of the wonder.[30] With one of his typical afterthoughts John adds that the efficacy of this sacrifice is not confined to the sins of his particular group of readers. It reaches out to all mankind.[31] The universal provision implies that all men have need of it. There is no way to fellowship with God except as our sins are forgiven by virtue of the sacrifice of Jesus. At the same time John rules out the thought that the death of Jesus is of limited efficacy; the possibility of forgiveness is cosmic and universal. As usual, Charles Wesley has caught the thought admirably:

> *The world He suffered to redeem;*
> *For all He hath the atonement made;*
> *For those that will not come to Him*
> *The ransom of His life was paid.*[32]

---

[30]5:5f.), while in others it bears more the sense of propitiation. See further J. D. G. Dunn, "Paul's Understanding of the Death of Jesus," in R. J. Banks (ed.), *Reconciliation and Hope*, Grand Rapids/Exeter, 1974, 125–141, especially 137–139.

[30]Note the odd use of δέ very late in this clause (BD 475²).

[31]The NIV has "but also for *the sins of* the whole world," supplying the words italicized from the context; cf. John 1:29. Westcott's view (44f.) that we should translate "but for the whole world" seems over-subtle.

[32]"Father, whose everlasting love" (*The Methodist Hymnbook*, London, 1933, No. 75).

John's teaching in this section stands fast against errors in the church of today that reflect those of the first century. The message that "God is light" has received new emphasis in Great Britain at the beginning of the last quarter of this century in a campaign to expose what is ugly and sordid for what it really is and to demonstrate that in the light of truth, righteousness, and love there is the possibility of rich and satisfying life. But two errors still die hard. One is that acts of sin do not cut us off from access to God. Modern men treat sin lightly, and insofar as they do believe in God, they believe that he makes considerable allowances for our weaknesses and failures. The message that God is light is not taken with sufficient seriousness. Probably few people would deny that acts of deliberate, clear-cut evil are incompatible with true religion. What they do deny is that any of their own acts fall into that category. There is a refusal to measure actions by the standards of God. The other error is the claim to be sinless. Whatever may be said later in this Epistle, John here stands firm against all claims to perfection that Christians may make. None of us is free from sin; none of us can claim that we do not need the cleansing offered by Jesus for sinners.

KEEPING HIS COMMANDS (2:3–11)

3. *We can be sure we know him if we obey his commands.* 4. *The man who says, "I know him," but does not do what he commands is a liar, and the truth is not in him.* 5. *But if anyone obeys his word, God's love is truly made complete in him. This is how we know we are in him:* 6. *Whoever claims to live in him must walk as Jesus did.*

7. *Dear friends, I am not writing you a new command but an old one, which you have had since the beginning. This old command is the message you have heard.* 8. *Yet I am writing you a new command; its truth is seen in him and you, because the darkness is passing and the true light is already shining.*

9. *Anyone who claims to be in the light but hates his brother is still in the darkness.* 10. *Whoever loves his brother lives in the light, and there is nothing in him[a] to make him stumble.* 11. *But whoever hates his brother is in the darkness and walks around in the darkness; he does not know where he is going, because the darkness has blinded him.*

[a]Or *it*

The theme of the previous section is continued in this one. This can be seen from the way in which the writer is still taking up the kind of claims that might be made by his opponents (2:4; cf. 2:9) and showing that they are incompatible with certain ways of life. It can also be seen by the way in which the thought of light, which introduced the earlier section (1:5), reappears for the last time in the Epistle to round off the present section. But the teaching is now directed more to John's readers in the form of exhortation, than against his opponents. The Christian's relationship to God, which was expressed earlier in terms of fellowship with him, is now spoken of as knowledge of God living (literally, "abiding") in him. If the accent earlier was on recognition of one's sinfulness and taking steps to deal with this barrier to fellowship with God, now John speaks more positively of the commands which Christians ought to fulfil.

3 The thought of knowledge of God appears here for the first time, although we have already come across the idea of knowing the truth in 2 John 1. The abruptness of the new idea is mitigated by the fact that the writer's earlier references to fellowship with God (1:3, 6, 7) are alternative ways of expressing the same reality. Nevertheless, the connection of thought with the immediately preceding verses is not obvious. Probably the key lies in verse 4 where we have another slogan of John's opponents which stands in the same series as the slogans in chapter 1; if so, John was simply moving on from the opponent's claims to live in the light (1:6) to their claims to know God, and, as in 1:5 he inserts his own basic point before proceeding to evaluate his opponents' claims in terms of it, so he does the same here by stating his own belief first.

Knowledge of God was a favorite theme of ancient religion. It was particularly common in a group of religions which have come to be known as "Gnostic" (from Gk. *gnōsis,* "knowledge"). Although they flourished in the second century, some of their basic motifs were already current earlier and their roots stretched a long way back. For some religions of this kind "knowledge" of God meant some kind of mystical experience or direct vision of the divine. For others it meant knowledge of esoteric myths, sometimes given in visions, which conveyed salvation to those who were initiated in them. In both cases knowledge was a purely religious attainment and had little, if any, connection with moral behavior. The evidence which we have already gathered from this Epistle suggests that John's opponents were not too concerned about sin and evil, and did not think that sin was a barrier to fellowship with God.

121

In the Old Testament it is comparatively rare to find the thought that men know God, although this was something for which the prophets hoped (Jer. 31:34; cf. Heb. 8:11). On the contrary, it is more often the case that the prophets complain that the people do not know God (Job 36:12; Jer. 9:6; Isa. 1:3; 5:13; 1 Sam. 2:12) and need to be told to know him (1 Chron. 28:9; Jer. 9:24). The sign of knowledge of God is obedience to his commands and recognition of the way of life that he expects from his people. When Hosea, for example, complains that there is no knowledge of God in the land, he immediately follows this up by saying "there is swearing, lying, killing, stealing, and committing adultery" (Hos. 4:1f.). To know God thus involves knowledge of his character and requirements and obedience to these requirements.[1]

When John speaks of knowing God he uses the perfect tense.[2] This manner of expression indicates that he is thinking of a past experience which has continuing results: "we have come to know him."[3] By "him" he probably means God the Father; it is true that the nearest person to whom the pronoun might refer is Jesus (v. 2), but John is not too careful about such matters. In practice God the Father and God the Son cannot be sharply distinguished as the objects of Christian experience, and the pronouns used reflect this ambiguity.[4]

But how does a person know that he knows God? This is the question which is in John's mind and which he answers by saying "we can be sure [literally, we know] that we know him." It is the question of religious assurance. For many people today it arises in

[1]On "knowledge" see R. Bultmann, TDNT I, 689–714; C. H. Dodd, *The Interpretation of the Fourth Gospel,* New York/Cambridge, 1954, 151–169; W. Schottroff, THAT I, 682–701; M.-É. Boismard, "La connaissance de Dieu dans l'Alliance Nouvelle d'après la première lettre de S. Jean," RB 56, 1949, 365–391; Schnackenburg, 95–101.

[2]This is obscured in the NIV, which translates by the present tense.

[3]Cf. 2:4, 13, 14; 3:6, 16; 4:16; 2 John 1; BD 340.

[4]A reference to God is found by Chaine, 154; Schnackenburg, 82; Bultmann, 24; Haas, 44. Heise, 121f., argues that Jesus is meant on the grounds that only so can John produce an argument against the opponents who claimed to know God apart from Jesus, and that in verses 7f. "his commandments" have become identified as the commandment of Jesus. These arguments are unconvincing. αὐτός in verse 3 can hardly have a different meaning from that in verse 4 where it must refer to God (in a claim by John's opponents), and while it is true that John has in mind Jesus' commandment to love in verses 7f. he does not characterize it as coming from him, but as being true in him. It may be truer to say with Westcott, 46f., that John "assumes a general antecedent 'Him to whom we turn as God' without special distinction of Persons" (cf. Dodd, 31), but it remains probable that if John were pressed to give an answer, he would say that he was thinking primarily of God (Haas, 44).

the form, "How can I know that I am a Christian? I don't feel any different. I haven't had any religious experience." Others may have had some kind of experience, and their question is, "How can I know whether my experience was a religious experience? Was it perhaps something that can be explained in natural terms?" John is writing in the present verse with a positive purpose, to reassure his readers that their experience of God was genuine. We can know by this, he says:[5] The test is whether we keep his commandments. This test is deliberately put as a condition, since it may or may not be true of each of the readers; each one must ask himself whether he fulfils the conditions. Bultmann makes the valuable point that the writer is not suggesting that certain conditions have to be fulfilled before a person can come to know God; obeying God's commands "is not the condition, but rather the characteristic of the knowledge of God. There is no knowledge of God which as such would not also be 'keeping the commandments.' "[6]

In 2 John 4–6 we saw that love for God is expressed in keeping his commandments. This fact removes any suggestion that keeping the commandments is a condition of salvation or a means of securing the favor of God by our own efforts. It is rather the result of love for God, the tangible evidence of the presence of that love. John does not detail their contents at present, although it is clear from verses 10f. that he has in mind principally the obligation for Christians to love one another.

Here, then, is the test by which the readers can be sure that they know God. It may be hard to know whether one's spiritual experience is a genuine knowledge of the invisible God; it is easier to look at one's own conduct and see whether it is in conformity with God's commands. Nevertheless, there is a difficulty here which should not be overlooked. Keeping the commandments is the sign of knowing God, while sinning is the sign of ignorance of God. How absolute are these conditions? It would surely be as unreasonable to say that perfect obedience was the necessary sign of true spiritual knowledge as it would be to say that a person must be totally sunk in sin before we can say that he is ignorant of God. Plainly, therefore, John cannot be saying that perfect obedience to God's commandments is necessary before we can say that we know him; otherwise,

---

[5]The Greek is literally translated: "And by this we know that we have come to know him, (namely) if we keep his commandments." John uses ἐν τούτῳ to point forward to the following clause; see on 2:5.
[6]Bultmann, 25.

he would be contradicting his own teaching that none of us can say that we are without sin. The question is whether I am trying (and to some extent succeeding) to keep God's commandments.[7]

4 The writer now turns to the negative side of the matter and issues a warning to any who claim to have come to know God and yet do not keep God's commandments. As has already been suggested, the slogan "I know him" must have emanated from the same people as those who claimed fellowship with God in 1:6. John, therefore, is repeating the same point in different words. These people were indifferent to the commandments of God. John has no hesitation in stating that their claims to know God must be false[8] and that God's truth is not in them (1:8).[9] He has thus attacked their claims to knowledge of God by pointing to their sins of commission (1:6) and omission (the present verse).

5 The writer's thought in verses 3–5 has an "A B A" pattern; having stated a contrast to his original point, he now restates the latter once more. His aim was to reassure his readers who kept God's commands that they really did know God and to exhort those who were under the influence of his opponents' teaching to follow his own instruction. So now he takes up the condition expressed in verse 3 and speaks of the reward which is in store for those who fulfil it. Instead of speaking, however, of keeping God's commandments, he speaks more broadly of keeping God's word, that word which is *not* kept by those who deny that they have sinned (1:10). This expression moves beyond the thought of obeying God's commands and includes the thought of receiving and believing his promises. If a person does this, he does not merely have the truth of God in him (the expected converse of the statement in v. 4), but "God's love is truly made complete in him."[10]

Commentators dispute whether "the love of God" means (a) "God's love for man" (the undoubted meaning in 4:9), or (b) "man's love for God" (the probable meaning in 2:15 and 5:3), or (c) "God's kind of love." The fact is that all three interpretations are possible here; de Jonge rightly asks whether John was conscious of the kind

---

[7]Calvin, 245f.; Stott, 90.
[8]The point here is that they are telling lies and deceiving other people by their false claims; in 1:6 the point is rather that they are deceiving themselves.
[9]This does not mean merely that their statement is false (which would be a simple repetition of the preceding phrase); rather the truth of God has not taken control of their thinking. Cf. Brooke, 31.
[10]Morris, 1263.

of distinctions made by modern grammarians. It is, of course, true
that our love for God is a reflection of God's love for us and a
response to it, so that our keeping of God's word could be a sign that
God's love had done its full work in us. On the other hand, the
parallel expressions in 2:15 and 5:3 strongly support the view that
John is thinking primarily of our love for God rather than of the
divine love which produces this response in us. One might also
suggest that "love of God" stands parallel with "knowledge of God"
in verses 3f.[11]

Such love is "truly made complete." "Truly" suggests that
the writer is thinking of the realities of the situation as compared
with the possibly empty claims of the man who says "I love God"
(4:20). "Made complete" means that the Christian's love is entire
and mature.[12] It was this and other references in this Epistle (4:12,
17f.) which led John Wesley to his doctrine of "perfect love" as the
characteristic of the mature Christian.[13] This phrase is scriptural,
whereas the closely related phrase "Christian perfection" is not and
is open to misunderstanding. Wesley's concept expresses what John
evidently regarded as the normal characteristic of the Christian. To
receive and obey God's word is to be made perfect in love; the
thought of pleasing and serving God is supreme in the Christian's
motives and molds his conduct. Nevertheless, it is staggering to
think that "perfection" can be attributed to the love shown by the
ordinary Christian.[14] We must bear in mind two things: first, that
perfection is not incompatible with further progress and development, and, second, that John's statement here must be placed
(paradoxically) alongside his earlier assertion that it is wrong for us
to say "we are without sin." What he puts before us here is a divine

[11](a) God's love for man (subjective genitive): Westcott, 49; Bultmann, 25; Houlden,
68; Haas, 46f. (with hesitation); Wengst, 73 n. 172;

  (b) man's love for God (objective genitive): Brooke, 32; Dodd, 31; Stott, 91; Bruce,
51.

  (c) God's kind of love (genitive of quality): Schnackenburg, 103; de Jonge, 77f.

  Schnackenburg and Haas hold that there is a parallel between "truth" (v. 4) and the
love of God, which speaks against view (b), but this does not seem compelling. On the
basis of 4:20 and 5:2f. Bultmann claims that our love cannot be directly oriented to
God, but the texts do not support this remarkable statement.

  On the whole, the primary sense here appears to be (b). See further on 2:15; 3:17;
4:9, 12; 5:3.

[12]See G. Delling, TDNT VIII, 81f. (who thinks that the reference is to God's love for
us).

[13]J. Wesley, A Plain Account of Christian Perfection, London, 1952 edition.

[14]The point still holds if we take the phrase to mean the love of God for men; in this
case the thought is that it achieves its perfect work in men.

promise rather than a statement that we might proudly make on our own behalf.

Indeed much of the criticism of teaching about perfect love has arisen from the danger of its proponents claiming perfect love for themselves and so falling into the sin of pride. But anyone who proudly claims to have perfect love shows by his very claim that he has misunderstood the nature of Christian love. It will become apparent later in the Epistle that by "love" John means the kind of love which God showed in giving his Son to be the Savior of the world. It is the sort of love which does not look for personal reward but for the benefit of the person loved. Much (but not all) human love is of the "getting" variety, where the lover is really seeking his own pleasure; "I love ice cream" is a fairly harmless example of this attitude, although such love for anything may stand in the way of fulfilling our obligations. God's love is of the "giving" variety, where the lover is seeking the benefit of the beloved, and his own pleasure is found in giving pleasure to others. Human pride is incompatible with this sort of love, since it means that the lover is really seeking his own selfish pleasure by his action.[15]

The verse concludes with the words "This is how we know we are in him." Unfortunately it is not clear whether the "this" is a signpost pointing backward or forward. If it points forward (as in the NIV), the test by which we may know whether we are in him is to be found in verse 6 and consists in determining whether we "walk as Jesus did." If, however, the signpost points backward, then the test lies in determining whether we keep his word or whether we experience fulness of love.[16] In substance there is not much difference between the two views. If the sentence does refer backward, verse 6 is in effect a recapitulation of verse 5a expressed in the form of an exhortation. If it refers forward, verse 5a contains the principle out of which the test in verses 5b–6 is developed. In any case, there is no real difference between keeping God's word and walking as Jesus did. The latter is the concrete, practical expression of the former. If we must make a decision, however, probably we should follow the NIV.[17]

---

[15]On love see 213 n. 4.

[16]Reference backward: Westcott, 50; Schnackenburg, 104; Bultmann, 26; Haas, 47; reference forward: Dodd, 32; Stott, 91; Bruce, 52; Houlden, 55; Heise, 122f.

[17]The expression usually points forward (2:3; 3:16, 24; 4:2, 9, 10, 13); it may refer backward in 3:10, 19; 4:17; 5:2 (see notes on these verses), but at least in 3:10 it appears to look both ways. Statistical probability thus supports the NIV here; the

John here employs yet another expression for the state of the true Christian. He is "in him," i.e. in God.[18] The phrase is synonymous with "Live [literally, abide] in him" in verse 6. Elsewhere John speaks of Christians abiding in Jesus (Jn. 15:4–10; cf. 1 Jn. 2:27, 28; 3:6) or of Jesus abiding in them: men are in the Son and the Son is in men (Jn. 14:20, 23; 17:21, 23, 26; 1 Jn. 5:20). He also speaks of the Father being in men (Jn. 14:23; 1 Jn. 4:4) and of men being in the Father (Jn. 17:21; 1 Jn. 5:20). By such expressions John denotes the close communion between believers and the Son or the Father. He uses similar language to indicate the relationship between the Son and the Father (Jn. 14:10, 11, 20; 17:21, 23).[19]

6 The test is now expressed in terms of living (literally, abiding) in him.[20] Being in him and living in him are to be regarded as synonyms, the latter word perhaps emphasizing the permanence of the relationship and the need for perseverance on the part of men. John is thinking of persons who claim to enjoy this relationship. It is not certain whether this was a specific claim of his opponents; the way in which it is expressed is typically Johannine; hence either the opponents had picked up John's manner of expression, or he is putting the kind of claim they made into his own words. But there need not be any polemical tone; John may simply be saying, "If you want to be able to claim that you live in him, you must do this." The test is whether we walk (1:6)[21] as Jesus did.[22] John uses a strong demonstrative pronoun, "that one," for Jesus here and elsewhere.[23]

---

reference is probably forward, but the test given is derived from the principle in verse 5a.

[18]So most commentators, as in 2:3. Heise, 123 n. 125, however, thinks that Jesus is meant, as in verse 3.

[19]See C. H. Dodd, *The Interpretation of the Fourth Gospel,* 187–200.

[20]See Heise for a detailed study of all the occurrences of μένω in the Johannine writings; his conclusions are often open to criticism. The treatment in TDNT IV, 574–576 (F. Hauck), is thin; it is better in Schnackenburg, 105–110.

[21]Heise, 123–126, claims that the background to the use of περιπατέω in 1 John is to be found in Gnosticism, which sees the whole of life as a journey leading to God and salvation; the "walk" of Jesus leads from the Father into this world and back again and is characterized by obedience to the Father and love for his disciples. This usage is to be differentiated from the Pauline usage which is more concerned with the moral aspects of life; cf. H. Seesemann, TDNT V, 945; R. Bultmann, *Das Evangelium des Johannes,* Göttingen, 1959, 261 n. 1. There is, however, as Heise has to admit, so little of the Gnostic outlook present, that it seems unnecessary to postulate its presence here. (For the Jewish background see Schnackenburg, *Johannesevangelium,* II, 242.) The difference from the Pauline usage is more imaginary than real, since here too a moral condition is present.

[22]οὕτως is bracketed in UBS; it is omitted by A B d vg sa.

[23]3:3, 5, 7, 16; 4:17.

Christians were so used to talking about Jesus that "that One" was a self-evident term. The interesting thing is that here the earthly life of Jesus is being presented as an example to Christians (cf. Jn. 13:15; 1 Pet. 2:21). John can assume that his readers were familiar with the picture of one who "went around doing good" (Acts 10:38), although he gives no concrete description of the life of Jesus in his Epistle.[24] The test of our religious experience is whether it produces a reflection of the life of Jesus in our daily life; if it fails this elementary test, it is false.

7 It is tempting to regard a new section of the Epistle as beginning here; having concluded his discussion of his opponents' slogans, John now turns to a positive statement of the Christian way of life (2:7-17). But we have already noted that verses 9-11 are linked closely with 1:5f., and there is something of a break at 2:11/12. It is preferable, therefore, to see here the beginning of a new sub-section closely linked to what precedes. Some support for the thought of a new beginning might be seen in the writer's new address to his readers as "dear friends," literally "beloved" (cf. 3 Jn. 1).[25] This is a frequent form of address, which indicates that he is writing to those who already stand in the circle of Christian love; here the choice of words is an appropriate bridge to a discussion of the need for them to show love.

Just as in John 13 the example of Jesus' love and humility is associated with a statement of how his disciples ought to live, and followed by the giving of the new commandment of love, so here the reference to Jesus' way of life and the statement that disciples should live in the same way are followed by an exposition of the commandment. It is not unknown for new sects to impose new patterns of behavior on their adherents; one has only to think, for example, of the early Mormons. It does not seem likely that any such new rules were being put forward by John's opponents, so that he would have had to put up some alternative of his own. Rather, it looks as though they thought that he was putting up some novel rules which they could ignore. This suspicion might have been confirmed in their minds by his talk of a "new" commandment (cf. 2 Jn. 5). So he begins his elucidation of the commandments (vv. 3f.) by em-

[24]In general, the Epistles make no direct reference to the ministry and teaching of Jesus; it appears to have been considered inappropriate to do so. Cf. I. H. Marshall, *Luke: Historian and Theologian*, Grand Rapids/Exeter, 1970, 48.
[25]Some MSS have ἀδελφοί (K L *al;* TR), but the attestation for ἀγαπητοί is better (S A B C P *al* vg syᵖ ʰ sa bo arm); the latter suits the context better and fits in with John's style (he uses "brothers" only in 3:13); see Brooke, 34; Metzger, 709.

phasizing that the commandment which Christians should obey is not new, but old. The switch from the plural "commandments" (2:3f.) to the singular is because John regards all the commandments as being summed up in one. If the readers were familiar with the Gospel, they would know that Jesus had spoken of a "new" commandment (Jn. 13:34), that of mutual love (Jn. 15:12; 1 Jn. 3:23; 2 Jn. 5). Clearly this is the commandment which is meant. But although it was "new" when Jesus gave it,[26] it had now been in circulation among Christians for some years, and it had often been heard before by the readers. In that sense it was no longer "new" but "old." The readers had had it "since the beginning," i.e. from the start of their Christian experience, in the Christian proclamation which they had heard.[27]

8 Yet[28] there was a sense in which the writer could refer to the commandment as "new." It remains new in that it remains true and is continually being realized and actualized in the life of Jesus and his followers in the new age. The NIV is not altogether adequate here, and the force of the Greek is better expressed in the TNT: "Yet it is a new commandment that I am writing to you. The truth of that is seen both in Christ and in you; for the darkness is passing away and the true light is already shining." This translation makes it clear that the "truth" refers to the whole of the previous clause; it is not so much that the commandment is "true" as the fact that it is "new."[29] Moreover, "truth" conveys more the idea of the realization of the commandment in the lives of Jesus and the disciples.[30] It

---

[26]The newness of the commandment lies in the fact that it rests on the example of God's supreme love seen in Jesus himself and that it offers the possibility of a new kind of life. It does not mean that Jesus was the first to tell men to love one another (cf. Lev. 19:18). He was, however, the first to reveal fully the self-giving love of God which constitutes the pattern for his disciples to follow.

[27]"From the beginning" refers primarily to the readers' own Christian experience, more broadly to the beginning of the church's experience, i.e. the beginning of the Christian era (Westcott, 51). The possible view that the writer's thought goes even further back to the beginning of creation (cf. 3:11f.; Brooke, 33f.) is probably to be rejected. The repetition of the phrase ἀπ' ἀρχῆς at the end of the verse (K L *pm;* TR; *Diglot*) is secondary; Metzger, 710.

[28]πάλιν usually means "again," but can have the force "on the other hand"; cf. Luke 6:43; AG, *s.v.*

[29]The relative clause is introduced by the neuter ὅ, whereas ἐντολή is feminine; it refers to the preceding clause as a whole. Law's view (376), that we should render it, "I write to you, as a new commandment, what is true in him . . .," is cited by Moule, 130f., but was already rightly rejected by Westcott, 53, on grounds of symmetry with verse 7.

[30]Fulfilment of the commandment has become a reality, rather than that the commandment has been shown to be true. (Strictly speaking, a commandment cannot be

was Jesus who showed the reality of this new kind of love in a concrete manner (Jn. 10:14–18; 15:12f.), and the same thing was to be seen in the disciples who followed his example. We might almost translate: "Its fulfilment is seen in him and in you." The newness of the commandment lies in the fact that it is being fulfilled in a way that had not happened previously. To put it differently, the darkness of the old age, in which men did not love in this sort of way, is disappearing, and the light of the new age, in which Christian love is shown, is already shining.[31] The picture is that of a world in the darkness of night, but the first rays of the dawning sun have already begun to shine; more and more areas are becoming light instead of dark, and the light is getting brighter. There are still dark places, completely sunk in shadow, but there are places where there is bright light, and it is here that the disciples are to be found, walking in the light and themselves shedding light. This is how John expresses the thought of the two overlapping eras of the old and new creations. The light, of course, is not that shed by the approaching parousia of Jesus, heralded as it is by a period of twilight (Rom. 13:12; 1 Cor. 7:31; 2 Pet. 1:19).[32] The light of the world has already dawned in the coming of Jesus (Jn. 8:12; cf. 1:19; 3:19; 9:5; 12:35f., 46), but it shines like a beacon in the continuing darkness, and will blaze out gloriously at the parousia. Hence men have the choice of remaining in the darkness or coming to the light. The light is described as "true."[33] It is the real thing. Possibly there is a polemical thrust here. John is rejecting the idea that there can be any other source of light than that provided by Jesus and the Christian message.[34]

---

true or false, but it could be said to reflect the truth.) Cf. Dodd, 34f. (citing Moffatt's rendering, "realized in Him and also in yourselves"); R. Bultmann, TDNT I, 248. Schnackenburg, 112 n. 1, cites Acts 12:9 as a good parallel and refers to the use of ἀληθῶς, meaning "really."

[31]The connection between the ὅτι clause and what precedes is discussed by Haas, 50, who concludes that it explains in what situation the new commandment is *being realized* by referring to the fact that the true light is already shining. The NEB takes it as an explanation of the *newness* of the commandment, while the TEV combines both possibilities.

[32]This was Brooke's view, 36f.

[33]John used a different adjective here, ἀληθινός (cf. 5:20). G. D. Kilpatrick, "Two Johannine Idioms in the Johannine Epistles," JTS ns 12, 1961, 272f., suggests that John uses ἀληθής predicatively and ἀληθινός attributively. This rule, however, does not apply to the Gospel.

[34]The term φῶς means the light brought by Jesus, rather than simply Jesus himself as the light of the world (Schnackenburg, 112f.).

9 The close association which John has made between the new commandment and the light has an inevitable consequence. If a person claims to be in the light (as John's opponents claimed to be, 1:6) and yet hates his brother, he is still in the darkness—even though the light has already begun to shine![35] John is here assuming that his readers know that the new commandment is about loving one's brothers, and that if a person does not love his brother, he hates him. This is not how we would put it. We would say that there are persons whom we do not love, but this is not the same thing as hating them. Our attitude is a neutral one. We might in fact point out that there are lots of people in the world, including people we meet in daily life, with whom we cannot have a relationship of love, since our contacts with them are so slight; I can hardly be said to "love" the garbage collector, with whom I have at the most a nodding acquaintance. But John will have none of this. His concept of love is caring for the needs of others, even to the point of self-sacrifice. If I am unwilling to do that for somebody in need, I love myself more than him; I am not being merely neutral, but am actually hating him. Moreover, he is writing about our fellow-Christians, and is thinking no doubt about relationships in a comparatively small community where everybody could know everybody else; in this situation failure to care for others was all the more heinous. John's comment is a shocking one, for here and elsewhere he is deliberately awakening us to the need for radical love if we claim to follow Jesus. Even the garbage collector must be the object of my love; if I do not treat him with courtesy and give him the help he needs, but say "he is just the garbage collector" and treat him accordingly, then I hate him.

Critics have pointed out, however, that John says nothing about loving the garbage collector—or anybody else outside the Christian community. He has been criticized for restricting Jesus' command to love our enemies not merely to love for our friends but to love for our Christian friends. The criticism, however, loses its force when we bear in mind that John was writing to a specific situation in which members of the church (or former members) were not loving their Christian brothers. He is dealing with this particular problem and concentrates all his attention on it.[36]

---

[35]"Still" renders ἕως ἄρτι, literally "until now," i.e. "even now."
[36]See Wengst, 68–70, who claims that refusal to love one's brother is the same as love for the world (2:15; 3:17). Love for the world thus does not mean helping a group of

10 As is his manner, John goes on to state the converse of the proposition which he has just offered and to make a fresh point (which he will then develop again in a negative contrast in the next verse). It is significant that he does not write: "Whoever *says* that he loves his brother lives in the light." He is concerned with action, not with words which may not correspond to reality. In any case, the man who loves his brothers does not go around telling everybody that he does. Such people live in the light; they are in no danger of wandering off into the darkness.[37]

So far verse 10 has simply stated the antithesis to verse 9, but now a fresh thought is added. There is nothing in him[38] to make him stumble. The Greek wording leaves it uncertain whether the thought is that the man himself does not stumble (NIV) or does not cause other people to stumble. Since verse 11 is concerned with the personal fate of the man who hates his brother and does get lost in the darkness, it is probable that we should follow the first interpretation here.[39] To stumble is to fall into sin or apostasy. The person who loves his brother is not going to succumb to temptation because he has his principles right and will not be deflected from them by the attractions of a self-centered existence; he recognizes temptation for what it is and says "No" to it.[40]

11 Finally, John returns to the case of the man who hates his brother. He has already commented that such a person is still in the darkness. Now he repeats the point but with greater emphasis, using ideas arising out of verse 10. First, he goes on to say that such a person walks in the darkness. This is a stronger expression: while a person may feel comparatively safe in one place in the darkness, once he tries to move around and find his way to a better place he

---

"false" people, but refusing to give help wherever it is needed, whether inside or outside the church.

[37]Bultmann, 26 n. 9, rightly notes that "abide" answers the question "until when? how long?"; the verb expresses persistence and faithfulness. Heise, 126–130, ignores the point.

[38]The pronoun could refer to "it," i.e. the light (NIV mg.; RSV; Schnackenburg, 115); but the analogy of 1:8, 10; 2:4f., 8 supports the personal interpretation (Haas, 52).

[39]For the thought of causing others to stumble see John 6:61; 16:1; Matthew 16:23; Romans 14:13; Revelation 2:14. For the thought of causing oneself to stumble (using προσκόπτω) cf. John 11:9f. For the first view see Westcott, 56 (apparently); for the second, see Brooke, 39f.; Haas, 52. Bultmann, 28, follows AG, *s.v.*, in translating σκάνδαλον by "stain, blemish." See further G. Stählin, TDNT VII, 356f., and Nauck, 39f., who cite Judith 5:20; 1QS 2:12, 17; *Jubilees* 1:21.

[40]A σκάνδαλον is a trap, hence something which causes a person to stumble, a temptation or cause of ruin; G. Stählin, TDNT VII, 339–358.

will quickly land in trouble. It is good advice to mountaineers lost in a mist without a compass to stay where they are until the mist clears or help comes, rather than to wander around without any sense of direction. "Walk" is thus being used in a fairly literal sense. This is confirmed by the second statement: the man does not know where he is going (cf. Jn. 12:35), i.e. he does not know what to do, or how to find his way to salvation. He cannot find lasting satisfaction in life because he is blind. Having chosen to live in the darkness, he now finds that his eyes can no longer see the light; in other words, having yielded to sin, he finds that his heart has become so hardened that he cannot respond to the call of God and he falls into further sin.[41] This is the divinely permitted result of sin (Jn. 12:40).

Already in this section another of John's major lessons is forcefully expressed. At the beginning of the Epistle he emphasized that the reality of a person's claims to spiritual life is to be tested by his sin. It is sin which cuts a person off from fellowship with God, and John warns against the attitude which is blind to one's own sin and treats it with indifference. Now in this section he sets forth the converse, that the reality of spiritual life is to be seen in acceptance of God's commandments and obedience to them. It is not just the absence of sin which characterizes the true Christian; it is also the positive presence of love. Too often we think of Christian maturity in terms of freedom from sin. Provided that we think of sins of omission rather than commission, that is fair enough. But John wants us to see that spiritual life is characterized by positive acts of love, and that such love will be seen in the fellowship of the church as well as in our attitude to other people generally. The writer remembers the reaction of some of the members of a prominent evangelical church to their new minister: "He is always preaching on ethics," they said, and the implication was that he was not preaching the gospel, perhaps indeed that it was doubtful if he was a thoroughgoing evangelical. Maybe his sermons were touching them in sensitive areas. In any case, it is unlikely that they would have fared any differently with John as their minister. For the gospel is about "faith expressing itself through love" (Gal. 5:6), and anything else is counterfeit.

[41]H. Conzelmann, TDNT VII, 444, claims that "darkness" is not a sphere or power opposed to God, but is rather an expression for the state of living in sin and apart from God. The statement that the darkness blinds a person's eyes is metaphorical; Westcott, 57, thinks that a physical effect of the darkness on the eyes is meant, but Brooke, 40, holds that John simply means that a man's eyes are useless in the dark. The point is that sinning leads to moral and spiritual blindness; cf. W. Schrage, TDNT VIII, 292.

THE NEW STATUS OF BELIEVERS AND THEIR RELATION TO THE WORLD (2:12–17)

12. *I write to you, dear children,*
      because your sins have been forgiven on account of his
      name.
13. *I write to you, fathers,*
      because you have known him who is from the beginning.
    I write to you, young men,
      because you have overcome the evil one.
14. *I write to you, dear children,*
      because you have known the Father.
    I write to you, fathers,
      because you have known him who is from the beginning.
    I write to you, young men,
      because you are strong,
      and the word of God lives in you,
      and you have overcome the evil one.
15. *Do not love the world or anything in the world. If anyone loves the world, the love of the Father is not in him.* 16. *For everything in the world—the cravings of sinful man, the lust of his eyes and his pride in possessions—comes not from the Father but from the world.* 17. *The world and its desires pass away, but the man who does the will of God lives forever.*

12–14 Verse 11 concluded a section in which the contrast between light and darkness was expressed in terms of keeping the new commandment that believers must love one another. We now come to a brief section, which stands out from its surroundings by its careful expression in parallel clauses, and which it is hard to relate to what precedes or to what follows. In content it is a series of statements about the spiritual state of the readers which might be regarded as summing up some of the preceding teaching and stressing that it is true of the readers.[1] At the same time, there are new ideas present which find fuller expression later in the Epistle, such as the thought of overcoming (4:4; 5:4f.). There is, however, no very clear connection in terms of vocabulary with the immediately following section (vv. 15–17) which contains a warning not to love the world. What appears to be a quite new section begins at verse 18. It seems probable, therefore, that verses 12–14 are intended to assure the readers of their Christian status; they are based partly on teaching

[1]For verse 12 see 1:9; for verses 13a, 14a and b see 2:3; for verse 14c see 1:8, 10.

134

already given earlier in the Epistle, and they provide the basis for the command in verses 15–17. Haas argues that verses 12–14 are not a mere introduction to the command but are of equal weight with it: the two sections give the positive and negative application of the preceding part of the Epistle.[2] They indicate the true position of believers over against the false claims of the opponents of John, and they warn such believers against falling into the worldliness which inspired the false teachers (4:5).

The understanding of the passage in detail is difficult. There are four general problems of interpretation: (1) The writer gives us two sets of three parallel statements, the second of which largely repeats the first. What is the explanation of this repetition? (2) The first set of statements is introduced by "I write" (present tense) while the second set is introduced by "I wrote" (aorist tense).[3] Is there any significance in the change of tense? (3) The Greek word rendered "because" could equally well be translated "that" in each case. Is John explaining *why* he is writing to his readers, or stating *what* he has to say to them? (4) Each set of statements is directed in turn to children, fathers, and young men. Are we to take this literally, or metaphorically, or in some other way?

The repetition of the statements in slightly different language is perhaps the most difficult thing to account for. Bruce thinks that we may have two drafts of the same basic material, both of which have been incorporated in the present Epistle.[4] This leaves the problem as to why the author included them both. It is also possible that he was making use of some existing forms of saying used in oral teaching in the church and included two versions of what was essentially the same material.[5] Yet another view builds on the distinction between "I write" and "I wrote" in the two sets of sayings.

Most writers explain the use of the verb in these two tenses as a matter of stylistic variation, perhaps to relieve the monotony of "I

---

[2]Haas, 54; similarly, Schnackenburg, 122f.

[3]The difference is obscured in the NIV and the TEV, which use the present tense throughout.

[4]Bruce, 57f. While Bruce regards the first set of clauses as the earlier draft, which is then elaborated in the second set, O'Neill, 20–22, thinks that the writer composed the first set on the model of the second, which he found in his source. O'Neill's argument rests on the fact that verses 12–13 are Christian while verse 14 could be Jewish in thought (although he has to emend the text to make this seem more convincing).

[5]One might see a remote parallel in the way in which the traditional Anglican order of service for Holy Communion manages to include the Lord's Prayer *twice* in slightly different versions. Bultmann's view (30f.) that the section was created by the author does nothing to explain its repetitive structure.

write" occurring six times over. In Greek it was possible to use the past (aorist) tense in a letter with the effect of a present tense: the writer projected himself forward in time to the situation of his recipient for whom the writing of the letter would be a past event. Hence, looking at things from the recipient's point in time, the correct tense would be "wrote" rather than "am writing."[6] In this way, John made use of a stylistic device to enable him to repeat certain things for emphasis. Other scholars have taken the difference in tenses more seriously. "I write" is most naturally understood of what the author is in process of writing: the letter as a whole, or the portion which he is just about to pen (cf. 1:4; 2:1, 7, 8). "I wrote" can refer to the part of the Epistle which he has just concluded (cf. 2:21, 26; 5:13). Brooke suggests that John is thinking first of the letter as a whole and then of the part which he has already composed, while de la Potterie holds that in verse 14 John is looking back merely to verses 12f. and repeating the point for emphasis.[7] The view that John was thinking of some previous composition when he says "I wrote," e.g. the Gospel or 2 John,[8] is generally discounted today.

It does not make a lot of difference to our understanding of the passage whether we use "because" or "that" to introduce John's statements. On the first view, John is writing the Epistle because certain things are true of his readers; consequently, they need the further instruction and are capable of obeying the injunctions which he is giving them.[9] This would fit in well with his statement in verse 21 that he is writing to his readers because they know the truth. The second view is favored by recent commentators who hold that what John is doing here is to make certain declarations about the Christian state of his readers.[10] On the whole, the former view is preferable; perhaps, however, Greek readers did not make the sharp distinction

---

[6]BD 334 and MH III, 73, deny that ἔγραψα can be used in this way; but see Schnackenburg, 125f., for evidence to the contrary.

[7]Brooke, 40–43 (cf. Westcott, 57f., for an over-subtle explanation of the same kind); I. de la Potterie, "La connaissance de Dieu dans le dualisme eschatologique d'après 1 Jn. 2, 12–14," in *Au service de la parole de Dieu. Mélanges offerts à M. A.-M. Charue,* Gembloux, 1968, 77–99, especially 80f.

[8]H. H. Wendt, "Die Beziehung unseres 1 Joh. auf den 2 Joh.," ZNW 21, 1922, 140–146, thought that the present passage referred back to 2 John. For the view that the Gospel is intended see Plummer, 98f.; Ross, 162f. The possibility of an earlier writing which is no longer extant is kept alive by Nauck, 125 n. 3, as part of his general view that John incorporated an earlier set of antitheses in the present Epistle.

[9]Westcott, 58; Brooke, 43f.

[10]Schnackenburg, 123; Haas, 55; B. Noack, "On 1 John 2, 12–14," NTS 6, 1959–60, 236–241; I. de la Potterie, *op. cit.,* 78–80.

between the two uses of the conjunction which springs to the mind of the grammarian!

The most important general problem concerns the different words used to describe the readers. Elsewhere the writer addresses *all* his readers as children (2:1, 18; *et al.*). Here he addresses them as children,[11] fathers, and young men.

One solution is that John is thinking of three different groups in the church. (a) He may have in mind literal children, young men, and old men.[12] If so, the order in which the groups are named is slightly odd. (b) The three groups may be metaphorical of three stages in Christian experience—young converts, those mature in the faith, and those somewhere in between.[13] Again, the order is odd, and there is nothing to indicate that the writer is developing a metaphor. A further difficulty, common to most explanations of the wording, is that, while a certain appropriateness can be seen in the qualities attributed to each of the three groups, some of the qualities overlap[14] and all of them should be true of all believers. Nevertheless, it is possible to associate new converts with a fresh knowledge of the forgiveness of sins, mature Christians with a deep knowledge of God, and young men with vigorous strength to overcome evil.

' A second type of solution is that the writer addresses *all* his readers as children, and then proceeds to address two particular groups within the church as a whole. (c) Thus "fathers" and "young men" may represent two groups of church officials, roughly equivalent to the elders and deacons found in other New Testament churches.[15] (d) Alternatively, the two groups may cover the older and younger members of the church.[16] This manner of speaking is found elsewhere in the New Testament (1 Tim. 5:1f.; Tit. 2:1-8; 1 Pet. 5:1-5). It is not so very different from the previous suggestion since the older men tended to be regarded as leaders. One possible

---

[11]John uses τεκνίον in verse 12 (cf. 2:1, 28; 3:7, 18; 4:4; 5:21), and παιδίον in verse 14 (cf. 2:18). Westcott, 60f., holds that the former word suggests kinship and the latter subordination, but the difference is probably insignificant.

[12]Windisch, 115, mentions this as a possibility.

[13]Stott, 96; Bruce, 58f.

[14]With the best will in the world, it is difficult to see any real distinction between verse 14a and b.

[15]Houlden, 70f. Cf. C. Spicq, "La place ou le rôle des jeunes dans certaines communautés néotestamentaires," RB 76, 1969, 508–527 (especially 524).

[16]So most commentators. I. de la Potterie, *op. cit.*, 86–91, thinks that the writer means "everybody, from the fathers to the young men," and lists qualities that should be found in all Christians. But his analogies for this inclusive usage (Jer. 31:34) are not compelling.

objection is that there is no mention of the middle-aged, but in fact this category did not exist in the language of New Testament times and one was either young or old.[17] The difficulty with either of these explanations is again that what is said of each group could be true of all, and indeed what is said of the children in verse 14a is virtually a repetition of what is said of the fathers.

(e) A third type of solution is favored by Dodd, who thinks that the writer is simply using a rhetorical device to indicate qualities, appropriate to the three stages of life, which ought to be true of all believers. All Christians should have the innocence of childhood, the strength of youth, and the mature knowledge of age.[18]

A choice between these possibilities is not easy. On the whole, the third type of solution (e) has most to commend it. Our difficulties probably arise because the writer is using a traditional scheme of expression which is not particularly relevant to his present purpose. It is possible that the distinction between the three groups mentioned had greater significance in the earlier use of the scheme, but that here the writer has made use of it more to express general spiritual truths that ought to apply to all his readers. In other words, the material may originally have been used in the manner (c) or (d), but here in the Epistle it is being used in the manner (e).[19]

12 John, then, addresses his readers as children, just as he does elsewhere in the Epistle, to express their need of instruction and their state of dependence upon God and upon teachers such as himself. They are people whose sins have been forgiven; they have fulfilled the condition laid down in 1:9, and as a result of their confession of their sin, they know the joy of forgiveness. Forgiveness, however, does not depend on human confession in the sense that this secures favor and pardon from God; it is granted "on account of his name," a phrase which directs our minds back to what John has said about the blood of Jesus and his role as advocate and offering for sin (1:7; 2:1f.),[20] and which also leads forward to the need for

---

[17]Cf. C. Spicq, *op. cit.* (In any case the word "middle-aged" has no specific meaning in English and is virtually a synonym for "old.")

[18]Augustine, cited by Chaine, 161; Dodd, 37–39; Morris, 1263. One does not need to adduce parallels from Hellenistic mysticism (CH 11:20; 13:11), as Dodd does, to accept this view.

[19]There is probably not a lot of difference between views (b) and (e) in practice, as is seen by the way in which Bruce, 58, has to express the hope that all the children of God have come to know him as Father.

[20]Cf. Matthew 10:22; 24:9; John 15:21; Revelation 2:3. There may be a reference to the forgiveness and knowledge of God associated with the new covenant (Jer. 31:34) (I. de la Potterie, *op. cit.*, 91–96).

belief in his name (3:23; 5:13). The act of forgiveness is expressed by a perfect tense; John is thinking of the conversion of his readers, whereas in 1:9 his thought was more of the continual forgiveness for which the Christian daily prays.[21] If John is thinking here of new converts, the appropriateness of this statement is manifest. The experience of forgiveness is the center of the Christian experience of conversion. "No man can properly rank as a Christian, in the sense of the New Testament, who has not received the forgiveness of sins, or who is not conscious that through its impartation something has happened of decisive moment for his relation to God," wrote H. R. Mackintosh.[22] In a day when many find the essence of Christianity elsewhere John's "recall to fundamentals"[23] deserves attention.

13 The description of a group of older Christians as "fathers" is unparalleled in the New Testament; when the word is not being used literally (e.g. Eph. 6:4), it refers to ancestors or older men who are now dead (e.g. 2 Pet. 3:4). We can, however, see its use as a title of respect to an older generation in Acts 7:2; 22:1.[24] Elsewhere such people are simply called "elders" or "older men." It is possible that a group of church leaders is meant (see above), but probably the writer is thinking simply of the mature Christian experience of older people. They know (literally, have come to know) the One who is from the beginning. This description repeats what was said of all true Christians in 2:3f. Only the characterization "who is from the beginning" is new, and it is not absolutely certain whether the reference is to God the Father or to Jesus, both of whom have existed from eternity past.[25] Since the Father is specifically mentioned in verse 14a, it is probable that we should see a reference to Jesus here, otherwise we are faced with an awkward repetition. Nobody doubted that the Father was from the beginning; it was more significant for John to stress the pre-existence of Jesus.[26] Perhaps, here as elsewhere, John was not drawing a very

---

[21]For this use cf. Luke 5:20, 23; 7:47f.; John 20:23. Windisch, 115f., notes that if the reference is to the baptism of children, this cannot have been infant baptism because they are also said to have come to know the Father.

[22]H. R. Mackintosh, *The Christian Experience of Forgiveness*, 1927, 2. I take the opportunity of commending this largely forgotten book.

[23]The phrase is taken from the heading to 1 John in the NEB.

[24]The warning in Matthew 23:9 must have been taken in the spirit rather than in the letter by John. There is a distinction between the proper respect for older people and the uncritical adulation of a particular teacher which Jesus condemns.

[25]There is no doubt that ἀπ᾿ ἀρχῆς here must refer to the beginning of time and not to the beginning of the Christian era or the readers' Christian experience (*pace* I. de la Potterie, *op. cit.*, 94–96).

[26]A reference to God is found by Stott, 97; Bruce, 58; (possibly Dodd, 38).

clear distinction between experience of God and experience of Jesus, since in practice these are so closely associated as to be virtually indistinguishable. What does matter is that the readers should be assured of their knowledge of the Godhead. It is difficult to believe that this knowledge is peculiar to older Christians, unless we take the saying to refer to maturity and depth of knowledge, but there is nothing in the actual phraseology to suggest this.[27]

It is more plausible to see a connection between the characteristics of youth and the quality ascribed to the young believers. Youth is associated not only with strong desires that need to be overcome (2 Tim. 2:22) but also with the strength to overcome them (Isa. 40:30—admittedly with the proviso that even young men need divine supplies of strength). Here the young men are said to have overcome the evil one. The masculine form indicates that the reference is to Satan (cf. 2:14; 3:12; 5:18f.), who is the source of evil and exercises his sway over the world, the realm of darkness. The use of the perfect tense is arresting. The victory has already been won, although there is still fighting to be done. John is thinking of the victory over the evil one which takes place at conversion, a victory due to the power of Jesus who conquered Satan by his death and resurrection. Here again, then, is something which should be true of all Christians. The thought is a new one in the Epistle; it will be taken up again in 4:4; 5:4f., but in its immediate context it prepares the way for the thought of overcoming worldly temptations which is implicit in 2:15–17; the thought of overcoming false teaching is not actually expressed in the section which immediately follows (2:18–27), but it is found in 4:4, which takes up the same subject, and therefore we may be justified in seeing here too a preparation for that theme. Christians must be victorious not only over moral and spiritual seduction but also over the attractions of false teaching.

14 These thoughts are now repeated,[28] and the effect is to emphasize the points already made. But there are variations in the wording. Only the second statement reappears unchanged. The children,[29] however, are now described as those who have come to

---

[27]O'Neill, 20, wishes to adopt the reading τὸ ἀπ' ἀρχῆς (B), which would refer to "the ancient teaching." If speculation is permitted, one might wonder whether John's *Vorlage* had ἐγνώκατε αὐτὸν ἀπ' ἀρχῆς—the thought that the fathers had known him (Jesus) from the beginning (i.e. for a long time; cf. v. 7) would be a fitting one, but unfortunately there is no evidence for this conjecture.

[28]The NIV follows the verse division in editions of the Greek New Testament. The AV, RV, RSV, and NEB put the first statement of verse 14 into verse 13. The AV follows the inferior Greek text γράφω in this statement.

[29]A different word from that in verse 13. See n. 11.

know the Father. What was stated with a certain conditional element in verse 3 is now expressed much more as a concrete fact. To know the Father is of course the privilege of a child (Mt. 11:25 par. Lk. 10:21), and in this sense all Christians are children. They also, as fathers, have come to know the One who is from the beginning. As young men, they are now explicitly said to be strong, and the reason for their strength is given: the word of God lives in them. This is a positive expression of what was denied in the case of merely nominal believers in 1:8; 2:4. Reception of God's word is a source of spiritual strength which goes beyond the force of mere teaching. If we are right in seeing a reference to the Father and the Son in the two earlier statements in the verse, we may well be tempted to associate the power of the Word of God with the Spirit (Eph. 6:17) in an implicit reference to the three Persons of the Trinity. It is by this personal, subjective power that the objective victory of Jesus over the evil one becomes a reality for believers. Here is the basis for the important command which is to follow.

It is good for Christians to be reminded in this way of their spiritual standing. Too often we have to hedge such declarations with conditions: "We can be sure we know him—*if* we obey his commands" (2:3). Of course this is necessary to avoid complacency and moral laxity. But it is possible to make Christian salvation into a very precarious possession that needs to be re-possessed every moment; such a faith lacks self-confidence. It is good to remember that in the last analysis our salvation depends on the promise and power of God, so that we can boldly declare that we have peace with God and that we know whom we have believed. John's statements here are meant to awaken such confidence among his readers (cf. 5:13), but the importance of Christian assurance is one of the notes in this Epistle which has aroused surprisingly little echo among expositors. Nor should we be reticent in expressing the joy that comes from this knowledge:

> Let those refuse to sing
> Who never knew our God;
> But servants of the heavenly King
> May speak their joys abroad.[30]

15 The set of statements about the Christian standing of the readers is followed somewhat abruptly by an important warning. It is worth stressing that the warning is directed to the loyal members

---

[30]I. Watts, "Come ye that love the Lord."

of the church, whose spiritual status is unquestioned, rather than to those known by John to be in real spiritual danger. Paul's warning is always timely: "If you think you are standing firm, be careful that you don't fall!" (1 Cor. 10:12). It is only too easy for those who are consciously and vigorously opposed to false teaching and its associated temptations to find that they are unconsciously affected by it; a person who publicly condemns, say, pornography can still take a secret delight in it. As a good pastor John warned against such dangers. He was writing to people who enjoyed fellowship with God and who loved their fellow Christians. Now he found it necessary to warn them against an attitude which could ruin their fellowship and land them in spiritual destruction, namely love of the world.

What John means will become fully clear in the explanation which he offers in the next verse. The word "world" has already appeared in verse 2 where it must signify the world of mankind which through its sin stands in need of reconciliation to God. It is a word which can be used in various senses. It can refer in quite a neutral way to the created universe which God made to be "very good" (Gen. 1:31). But in the writings of John "world" signifies more usually mankind organized in rebellion against God, so that the word carries a negative sense. It is under the control of the evil one (1 Jn. 5:19; cf. Jn. 12:31; 14:30). It lies in darkness (Jn. 1:5; 12:46) and sin. It is, therefore, under divine judgment (Jn. 9:39), but at the same time it is the object of divine love; God so loved the sinful world that he gave his Son to save it (Jn. 3:16). The believer's situation is one of tension. On the one hand, he can be regarded as separate from the world, since he no longer stands under its judgment and has passed from death to life. He now lives in the sphere of light and no longer in the darkness. On the other hand, he himself is part of the world, and he is exposed to its temptations that would pull him away from God and into sin.[31] John's fear is lest Christians may be attracted by such temptations.

Two important points emerge in the light of this background. The first is that when John speaks of the world here, he is thinking of the source of opposition to God and temptation to sin. He is not thinking of the material universe or its contents as such. Nor is he thinking of the people in the world as people. There is no suggestion

---

[31]See N. H. Cassem, "A Grammatical and Contextual Inventory of the Use of κόσμος in the Johannine Corpus with Some Implications for a Johannine Cosmic Theology," NTS 19, 1972–73, 81–91; Schnackenburg, 133–137; Bruce, 60–64. For the evil character of the world see *Testament of Issachar* 4:6.

that the Christian is to hate the material world or its inhabitants, or that he should refrain from contact with them. This would, of course, be an absurdity. Even if man cannot live on bread alone, he cannot live without bread—and without the structures of society that make it possible to grow crops, bake bread, and distribute it. It would be equally absurd to deny the pleasure given by the world. One may cite the extreme attitude of the Essenes, who were said to refrain from intercourse with their wives while they were pregnant, in order to demonstrate that they married not for pleasure but to produce children.[32] We cannot, however, avoid the pleasures of life in the world, and certainly God did not intend life to be miserable but "very good." It follows that here John is thinking of the attractions of a life lived in opposition to the commandments of God, one in which God's laws for the use of the world and the things in it are disobeyed. "Worldliness" means "disobedience to God's rule of life," and its presence is to be discerned by asking, "What is God's will?" and not by making a human list of taboos.

The second point is that the word "love" here must mean something different from what it did in 2:10. There, and in other references to loving other people, it signifies outgoing care and compassion; it is the kind of love which is concerned for the benefit of the person loved. Here, however, the thought is of the pleasure which the person hopes to get from the object of his love. To love, in this sense, is to be attracted by something and to want to enjoy it; the thought is of appetite and desire (cf. Jn. 3:19; 12:43; 2 Tim. 4:10). It should be emphasized that desire for pleasure is not necessarily selfish and wrong. We are so created by God that we have appetites and desires which need to be satisfied, and the satisfying of them produces pleasure. When I am hungry, I need food; I want a meal, and the eating of food produces a pleasure that is perfectly proper. There are, however, occasions when the satisfaction of my desires may be sinful. A desire to murder somebody is clearly sinful, and so too could be my desire to enjoy a good meal when I could share my resources with poor, starving people. What I have to ask myself is whether my "love" for things and people is sinful.

John's command is grounded in the fact that love for the world and love for the Father are incompatible. This follows clearly from what we have said. To love the world, in John's sense, is to love what is opposed to God by definition. "Friendship with the

---

[32]Josephus, *Bellum Judaicum* 2:161.

world is hatred toward God," says James (Jas. 4:4). This is surely the sense here, although some commentators think that John is saying that the person who loves the world has never really experienced the love which God has for him, or has shut up his heart against it.[33]

16 John now proceeds to explain more fully why love for the world is incompatible with love for God. It is because everything in the world is not from God but from the world itself. Its origin lies in the world, viewed as a system organized in opposition to God. The things in the world share in the character of the world. But this is a staggering statement. Surely the world was created by God (Jn. 1:3): how, then, can everything in it be opposed to God and said not to stem from him? Is everything in the world so tainted that the believer is not to desire it? The answer to these questions becomes clear when we consider the kind of specific things which John has in mind. These show that he is thinking of the world insofar as it has become fallen and rebellious, the source of desires which stand in opposition to the love of God. The language may seem exaggerated, but it is timely: *anything* in the world can become a source of sinful desire, even though it is good in itself. John is here expressing what used to be called "total depravity," by which is meant not that the world is as bad as it can possibly be but that its badness is universal.

John lists three typical features of the sinful world. The first is "the cravings of sinful man," literally "the desire of the flesh," i.e. the desire that comes from the flesh. In itself "desire" is a morally neutral word. It takes on a good or bad connotation from the context, and here it plainly has the latter force.[34] The same is to some extent true of "flesh," which can mean no more than the substance of which man is made and hence refer to various aspects of human, bodily life. But the fleshly body can be the source of sensual desires and lusts, whether for food and drink or for sexual gratification. It is, therefore, possible to take the phrase here to be a reference to the desire for sensual pleasure, especially sexual desire.[35] This would give a contrast with the more "refined" desires which follow in John's brief list. Certainly the first-century world was noted for its sensuality, and the New Testament writers generally were aware of

---

[33]Bultmann, 33; cf. NEB. See, however, Schnackenburg, 127; Wengst, 73 n. 172. Haas, 58, thinks that both senses may be present. Cf. 2:5; 3:17; 4:9, 12; 5:3.

[34]For the good sense see Matthew 13:17; Philippians 1:23; 1 Thessalonians 2:17; for the more common bad sense see Mark 4:19; Romans 1:24; Galatians 5:16; Ephesians 2:3; 1 Peter 2:11.

[35]Schnackenburg, 129f.; E. Schweizer, TDNT VII, 141 n. 317.

this fact and warned their readers against it. But it is perhaps more likely that John is here using "flesh" in its Jewish and biblical sense of the nature of man as a whole as a worldly being separated from and opposed to God; for Paul in particular "flesh" designates "the outlook orientated towards the self, that which pursues its own ends in self-sufficient independence of God."[36] It is the whole nature of sinful man which is comprehended in this phrase, and not merely his bodily, sensual desires. Any and every desire of man in his rebellion against God is what is meant.[37] The NIV translation as "the cravings of sinful man" is accordingly justified.

The second feature of the world is the lust of the eyes. The eyes are often the source of desire, and the thought here is of the greed which is aroused by what one sees. One may think particularly of the desire to watch things which give sinful pleasure, as in the case of pornography, or of the tendency to be captivated by outward, visible splendor and show, but more probably the basic thought is of greed and desire for things aroused by seeing them.[38]

The third feature is pride in possessions. The word for "possessions" is literally "life," a word that can be used of the things that support life (cf. Mk. 12:44).[39] The word "pride" refers to boasting and arrogance, but it conveys a strong hint of the ultimate emptiness of boasting; it means the braggadocio which exaggerates what it possesses in order to impress other people. E. K. Simpson claims that bogus assumption lies at the base of the word, and comments: "When the apostle John abandons, as here, his spare vocabulary for a polysyllabic noun, there must be cogent reasons for his procedure. He is contemplating the unregenerate world as a Vanity Fair, and the full strength of his expression can be brought out only by some such translation as the *charlatanry* or *make-believe* of life."[40]

We may regard the first of these three features as the inclusive

---

[36]A. C. Thiselton, NIDNTT I, 680.

[37]Bultmann, 33f.; Haas, 58. See especially N. Lazure, "La convoitise de la chair en 1 Jean 2, 16," RB 76, 1969, 161-205, for a convincing case that John's thought is molded here by the Old Testament and Judaism, and not by Hellenistic ideas. Schnackenburg, 129, draws attention to the association of the "evil impulse" with the flesh in the Qumran literature (1QS 11:9, 12; 1QH 10:22f.; 13:13-16). Similarly, Wengst, 69f., who draws attention to the parallel with 3:17.

[38]Cf. *Testament of Reuben* 2:4; Matthew 5:27-29.

[39]βίος is used similarly in 3:19. Commentators dispute whether we have a subjective genitive (pride which belongs to and springs from possessions; Schnackenburg, 130 n. 6) or an objective genitive (pride in possessions; AG). The former view gives the same construction in all three phrases, but this is not a decisive consideration. Once again it is probably a case of grammarians attempting to be too precise.

[40]E. K. Simpson, *Words Worth Weighing in the Greek New Testament*, London, 1946, 18.

concept, filled out in the other two. Selfish human desire is stimulated by what the eye sees and expresses itself in outward show. And this is not from God but from the world, for it expresses a sense of human self-sufficiency and independence from God and of human greed over against the needs of other people (3:17). Clearly all people need possessions, and therefore it cannot be wrong to want and take pleasure in and what God has provided for our needs. But when I begin to desire more than other people, to covet whatever I see, to boast of what I have, and to claim that I am self-sufficient, then my desires have become perverse and sinful, and I stand condemned. John's teaching stands as a timeless warning against materialism.[41]

Some commentators have seen a parallel to John's three sinful attitudes in the motives which animated Eve when she yielded to temptation: she saw that the forbidden tree was good for food, that it was a delight to the eyes, and that it was to be desired to make her wise.[42] The correspondence, however, is not especially close.

17 Now comes the climax to John's appeal. It is foolish to desire the world because the world and its desires are passing away. John has already reminded his readers that the era of darkness is coming to an end (2:8), and Paul also stated that "this world in its present form is passing away" (1 Cor. 7:31). The coming of the light is the sign of the beginning of the new era and the end of the old. With the world there will also depart desire for it.[43] Since the other part of the contrast is presented in personal terms ("the man who does the will of God") it is possible that "desire" is a case of the abstract noun representing the concrete reality, the person who desires the world. The desire, as it were, carries away the man who harbors it to share in its destruction. Permanence belongs to the person who does the will of God. He will remain standing amid the storms of judgment (Mt. 7:21, 24–27).

Many people are tempted to live for the moment, to conform to the way of life of a material world, and either to question the

---

[41]For other, more subtle types of worldliness, such as sharing the political, social, and economic presuppositions of the world and adapting the gospel to some contemporary tendency or philosophy, see Bruce, 60–64.

[42]Westcott, 62f.; Smith, 178; and Ross, 166, drew a parallel with the three temptations of Jesus and with the three chief vices in mediaeval ethics—*voluptas, avaritia*, and *superbia* (but see Brooke, 47f., for criticism). Houlden, 74, finds "an almost complete parallel" in the three nets of Satan in CD 4:17f.—riches, fornication, and profanation of the temple; the parallel in surely very forced.

[43]The αὐτοῦ is omitted by A 33 1739 *pc* h sa arm, but this may be a deliberate omission to generalize the thought (Metzger, 710).

temporary character of material life or to hope that there will be no judgment. It is a natural tendency to make oneself comfortable here in the present real world rather than to deny oneself here in hope of a better life hereafter. But John's reply would be that the judgment is taking place already; even now the world is in process of dissolution; men are blind if they do not realize what is going on before their very eyes (cf. Lk. 12:54–56). For John it is indeed already "the last hour" (2:18).[44]

A WARNING AGAINST ANTICHRISTS (2:18–27)

18. *Dear children, this is the last hour; and as you have heard that the antichrist is coming, even now many antichrists have come. This is how we know it is the last hour.   19. They went out from us, but they did not really belong to us. For if they had belonged to us, they would have remained with us; but their going showed that none of them belonged to us.*

20. *But you have an anointing from the Holy One, and all of you know the truth.[a]   21. I do not write to you because you do not know the truth, but because you do know it and because no lie comes from the truth.   22. Who is the liar? It is the man who denies that Jesus is the Christ. Such a man is the antichrist—he denies the Father and the Son.   23. No one who denies the Son has the Father; whoever acknowledges the Son has the Father also.*

24. *See that what you have heard from the beginning remains in you. If it does, you also will remain in the Son and in the Father.   25. And this is what he promised us—even eternal life.*

26. *I am writing these things to you about those who are trying to lead you astray.   27. As for you, the anointing you received from him remains in you, and you do not need anyone to teach you. But as his anointing teaches you about all things and as that anointing is real, not counterfeit—just as it has taught you, remain in him.*

[a]Some MSS read *and you know all the truth.*

A completely new section starts here. It has a slight link with what has just preceded. The writer has told his readers that the world is passing away; he now bids them note that it is in fact approaching its end. It is the last hour, as various signs make clear. But this thought

---

[44]Schnackenburg, 132, disputes that the end of the world is in mind here, and thinks that the accent lies on the permanence of eternal life rather than the catastrophe facing the world. See, however, de Jonge, 98 and n. 148.

of the nearness of the end is at most a bridge, and the writer's main concern is with the rise of a group of opponents of the Christian faith. They need to be exposed for what they really are, and the readers need to be warned against their teaching, although if in fact they are being taught by God they should have the spiritual discernment not to be led astray.

18 The beginning of the new section is signalled by a fresh address to the readers as "dear children" (cf. 2:14). There is no particular force in the appellation; it merely illustrates the fatherly concern felt by a genuine teacher for those who are still like children in their understanding and need his instruction. He announces that it is the last hour.[1] Although this word can mean a short period or point of time, it can refer to a period of some length (Jn. 4:23; 16:2). While the phrase "the last day" refers more specifically to the final point in world history, the day of the coming of Christ and the judgment, the last hour has a sense more like that of "the last days."

But what precisely did John have in mind with this phrase? Early Christians certainly regarded the whole period between the first and second advents of Jesus as constituting the last days: in Peter's Pentecost sermon the prophecy of Joel concerning the outpouring of the Spirit is deliberately linked with the last days (Acts 2:17; contrast Joel 2:28; cf. Heb. 1:2; 1 Pet. 1:20). Now that the last period in world history had been inaugurated by the coming of Jesus, it could not be long before the end. It is also possible, however, that John was thinking of the final stage in the last days (cf. 1 Tim. 4:1; 2 Tim. 3:1; Jas. 5:3; 1 Pet. 1:5; Jude 18); time had hurried past since the beginning of the church and now it was the last hour before the end. Most commentators adopt this view.[2] It fits in with the fact that John saw various events happening around him which had been prophesied by Jesus as being still future.

Commentators who adopt the former view do so in view of the fact that the end still has not come. If John felt that the minutes were rapidly ticking by, the slow rolling on of the centuries would suggest that he was mistaken. Hence the attractiveness of the first

---

[1]Although there is no article with ἐσχάτη ὥρα, we should translate "the last hour," and not "a last hour" (Westcott, 69; Morris, 1266): John uses ἐσχάτη with ὥρα without the article on the analogy of phrases with an ordinal numeral (e.g. Jn. 4:52; Mt. 20:3, 5; 27:45; BD 256).

[2]Brooke, 51; Schnackenburg, 141f.; Bruce, 64; Haas, 62. For the view that the period since the first coming of Christ is meant see Calvin, 255f.; Ross, 168. See also the discussion in Stott, 107–109, who holds that John was expressing a theological truth rather than making a chronological statement.

view, although even in this case it is passing strange that the last days inaugurated by the first coming of Jesus have dragged on for so long. It is not surprising that some scholars assure us that we cannot share the eschatological hopes of the New Testament writers.[3] If we feel that we are living in the last days now, it is for different reasons. For us the history of the world stretches further back than John could ever have imagined, so that the age of man is but a tiny appendix to the long and remote ages of prehistory. The prophets of doom assure us of the imminent end of human civilization if we do not learn to curb the growth of population, to slow down our use of world resources, and to arrest the pollution of the environment. It is not difficult for us to share John's point of view; the problem is whether we have a theological basis for doing so which will take into account the shift in time.

It must be noted, first, that John does not commit himself to any time-scale. Like the New Testament authors generally he does not delimit precisely the expected date of the parousia.[4] He was content to stress the urgency of the time in which he lived. Second, we have good authority for not measuring God's time by our clocks: "with the Lord a day is like a thousand years" (2 Pet. 3:8).[5] Third, the New Testament teaching is that we should be ready for the coming of the Lord at any time; every hour is the hour of crisis, and the Lord will come when he is least expected. F. F. Bruce has drawn attention to a remarkable passage from J. H. Newman, who speaks of the course of things as having changed direction since the coming of Jesus. It "has (if I may so speak) altered its direction, as regards His second coming, and runs, not towards the end, but along it, and on the brink of it; and is at all times near that great event, which, did it run towards it, it would at once run into. Christ, then, is ever at our doors."[6] Till the coming of Christ the course of history ran direct toward the goal:

history

――――――――――――――――→   coming of Christ

[3]See the appendix on "The Return of Christ" in E. Best, *The First and Second Epistles to the Thessalonians,* Naperville/London, 1972, 359–371.

[4]A. L. Moore, *The Parousia in the New Testament,* Leiden, 1966, 156f.

[5]But it should be noted that our difficulty is that the New Testament suggests that the time is short *by human standards* and not simply by God's standards.

[6]J. H. Newman, "Waiting for Christ," in *Parochial and Plain Sermons,* London, 1896, 241, as cited by Bruce, 65.

Now since the coming of Jesus it has taken a sharp bend:

```
                                        E
                    coming        ↑   N
    history         of Christt          D
    _____|
```

This is a helpful analogy. It preserves the sense of urgency and imminence found in the New Testament on the basis of the principle that God is capable of extending the last hour (for the excellent reason in 2 Pet. 3:9) while retaining his own secret counsel on its duration.

But John's main concern was with the evidence that would prove to his readers that they were living in the last hour. He rests his case on the fact that they had heard a prophecy of the coming of "antichrist." We have already come across this term in 2 John 7 to describe people who deny that Jesus Christ has come in the flesh, and verse 22 indicates that the same people are in mind. They are opposed to the true teaching about Christ. The word could also signify people who stand in the place of Christ and claim that they are Christ. Within the New Testament the term is used only in the Johannine letters.[7] John's use may be traced back to two possible roots. First, in the teaching of Jesus about the future there is a warning about the coming of "false Christs and false prophets" who "will appear and perform signs and miracles to deceive the elect—if that were possible" (Mk. 13:22 par. Mt. 24:24). Such persons are clearly opposed to Jesus as the Christ, but here they appear to be either prophets who declare untruths or persons who falsely claim that they themselves are Messiahs. We may compare the imagery of the beast and the false prophet in Revelation 13; 19:20, where the false prophet promotes the worship of the beast. But this passage in Revelation leads us to the second possible root of John's language in the expectation of one particular arch-opponent of Christ, the Anti-Christ *par excellence*. This expectation is reflected in the coming of the "man of lawlessness" in 2 Thessalonians 2:1–12 and possibly also in "the abomination that causes desolation" in Mark 13:14. These figures stand in a succession of such pictures in Jewish and Christian writings which portray the final opponent of God. It is a

---

[7] 1 John 2:18, 22; 4:3; 2 John 7. See further on 2 John 7; Brooke, 69–79; Schnackenburg, 145–149; W. Bousset, *Der Antichrist*, Göttingen, 1895; E. Lohmeyer, RAC I, 450–457; B. Rigaux, *L'Antéchrist et l'opposition au royaume messianique dans l'Ancien et le Nouveau Testament*, Paris, 1932.

striking fact that there is no pre-Christian evidence for the application of the title "Antichrist" to this figure. Nevertheless, many scholars hold that John has taken up the apocalyptic hope (or rather, fear) of the coming of this figure and has made it the basis of his language here. But (they claim), whereas the original prophecy spoke of the coming of *the* Antichrist, John has "demythologized" the idea by seeing the fulfilment of the prophecy in the coming of many antichrists who were already present in the church.[8] It is probable that this is the wrong way of putting it. John talks about persons who deny that Jesus is the Christ and says that persons who talk in this way are possessed by the spirit of the antichrist (4:3). He also says here that his readers have heard that the antichrist is coming, and that even now[9] many antichrists have come. It seems, therefore, that he regarded the false teachers of his day as being possessed by the spirit of the antichrist, whose own coming still lay in the future. The basis of his teaching is the prophecy of the coming of several opponents of Christ, and he relates this to the coming of the antichrist. He has not demythologized the figure of the antichrist, nor does he deny the future coming of the antichrist, but he is much more concerned with the present fact of false teachers in the church who have the spirit of the antichrist. The difference from Mark 13:22 is that here the antichrists do not appear to be claiming that they themselves are the true Christ: the thought is purely the negative one of their denial that Jesus is the Christ, as is apparent from verse 22.

19 So far John has not indicated the identity of the antichrists. Now he tells his readers that they are people who have gone out from their midst. This can only mean that they had once been members or adherents of the church, but had now departed from it, presumably to set up their own group.[10] This situation is a different one from that envisaged in 3 John 7 where John's own friends were being pushed out of the church by Diotrephes, and the two situations should not be confused. Here it is a case of the voluntary departure of those who held views opposed to those of John. But although these people had gone out from the church, it did not follow that

---

[8]John has "rationalized the myth"; Dodd, 49. Cf. Bultmann, 36.
[9]The force of καὶ νῦν is that already what was prophesied for the future is taking place in fact; cf. Schnackenburg, 144.
[10]Bultmann's claim, 36, that they still understood themselves as legitimate members of the congregation is hard to substantiate. Wengst, 12–14, asserts that they were still in the church, and translates, "Aus unserer Mitte heraus sind sie aufgetreten." But 2:19b surely indicates that they had not remained "with us," i.e. in the church.

they had at one time truly belonged to it.[11] They had been only apparent members. Here is one of the clearest expressions in the New Testament of the way in which we must distinguish between the church visible, composed of those who outwardly belong to it, and the church invisible, composed of those whom the Lord knows to be his (2 Tim. 2:19). "The statement permits recognition of the distinction between the empirical and the true congregation: false members are therefore to be found in the empirical congregation. The sentence is thus also an admonition to critical examination and certainly to self-examination as well."[12]

It is not clear how these people got into the church in the first place. Possibly they had at one time made a Christian profession, but now it had become apparent that they did not attach an orthodox interpretation to it, or more probably they had abandoned the confession and were now openly campaigning against it. They had "run ahead" and were not continuing in the teaching of Christ (2 Jn. 9).

John, however, believes that if they had truly been members of the church they would have remained within it.[13] If they ever had made a confession of faith, it had been an empty one. But a person who makes a genuine confession can be expected to persevere in his faith, although elsewhere John warns his readers against the danger of failure to persevere.[14] It is when a person departs from the church that the falsity of his faith becomes apparent. The last clause is ambiguous in expression, and it is not clear whether John is thinking of the antichrists in particular (NIV) or making the more general point that not all who appear to belong to the church truly belong to it; perhaps he is combining both thoughts.[15]

---

[11]ἐξ ἡμῶν is ambiguous; it can denote both origin ("they went out *from* us") and membership of a group ("they belong *to* us") (Haas, 63).

[12]Bultmann, 37.

[13]John uses the pluperfect (without augment) with ἄν in the main clause of a hypothetical condition. According to MH I, 148, "the pluperfect expresses the continuance of the contingent result to the time of speaking." Where the aorist would have given the sense, "they would have remained" (i.e. in the past), the pluperfect gives the sense, "they would have remained—until now." Cf. Acts 26:32.

[14]Note the warnings in 2:24 and 2 John 8; I. H. Marshall, *Kept by the Power of God*, Minneapolis, 1975, 187.

[15]It is unlikely that ἵνα is used imperatively (MH III, 95). Rather the sentence is elliptical: after ἀλλ᾽ supply ἐξῆλθαν or τοῦτο ἐγένετο. The ὅτι clause is expressed ambiguously. (1) The subject may be the false teachers, giving "all of them are not of us" or "not all [i.e. none] of them are of us" (Westcott, 72; Brooke, 54; Chaine, 169). (2) The subject may be the congregation: "not all [*sc.* the members of the congregation] are [truly] of us" (cf. NEB; Windisch, 117; Dodd, 52). But the change of subject is awkward, and the translation "not all" = "only some" is forced. (3) Heise,

20 English translations express a contrast at the beginning of this verse between the antichrists who have left the church and the true members to whom John is writing ("But you . . . ").[16] Perhaps, however, we should translate the conjunction by "and." Verse 19 has in effect indicated that the members of the church should recognize the falsity of the heretics and their teaching by the fact that they have left the church; now verse 20 states that in addition they should know by virtue of their spiritual insight that what they taught was not the truth.

It is possible that the heretics laid claims to special sources of knowledge. By contrast the writer assures his readers that they possess an anointing in virtue of which they know the truth. The word "anointing" (Gk. *chrisma*) may be a deliberate pun on the word "antichrist" (*antichristos*), for both words are connected with the name "Christ" (*Christos*). These are all derived from the Greek verb *chriō*, "to anoint," and "anointing" means the substance (oil) used to anoint somebody.[17] In Old Testament usage anointing was symbolical of the reception of the Spirit (1 Sam. 16:13; Isa. 61:1), and when Jesus is said to have been anointed, it is his reception of the Spirit at his baptism which is meant (Acts 10:38; cf. Lk. 4:18). It is, therefore, not surprising that the majority of commentators think that the anointing here is the Spirit who comes to teach believers and to guide them into all truth. R. Schnackenburg has observed how what is said here in 1 John about the anointing is paralleled by what is said in John 14:17; 15:26; 16:13 about the activity of the Paraclete, the Holy Spirit.[18] In the same way Paul describes the work of God in the believer: "He anointed us, set his seal of ownership on us, and put his Spirit in our hearts as a deposit, guaranteeing what is to come" (2 Cor. 1:21f.).

It is unlikely that the picture of anointing was derived from some actual act of anointing with oil, whether at the baptism of new converts or at some later point, although there is evidence that this

---

136, attempts a combination of thoughts: "es musse offenbar werden dass sie, wie überhaupt leider nicht alle, nicht zu uns gehören." The first of these views is best, taken with Schnackenburg's suggestion, 151, that πάντες is added to make it clear that the false teachers, one and all, are not true Christians. See Haas, 64, for a clear discussion.

[16]καί can have an adversative force, "and yet" (BD 442[1]); cf. Schnackenburg, 151.

[17]The noun does not mean "act of anointing" (*pace* Brooke, 55). It is found only in this passage (2:20, 27) in the New Testament; the verb χρίω occurs in Luke 4:18; Acts 4:27; 10:38; 2 Corinthians 1:21; Hebrews 1:9.

[18]Schnackenburg, 151–154; Heise, 138–140.

practice developed at a later stage.[19] It is possible that a heretical practice is reflected. Later Gnostics laid claim to a special anointing not shared by other Christians.[20] However, we have no definite evidence of this practice in the first century, and the fact that Paul uses the metaphor independently speaks against John's having derived the idea from the practices of his opponents.

A different understanding of the metaphor was introduced to English readers by C. H. Dodd.[21] He argued that the anointing oil refers to the Word of God which teaches the truth to believers and which is objective in its testimony to the truth. Because they have received the Word of God, the true believers have come to know the truth, and therefore they have the antidote to false teaching. There is much to be said for this interpretation. Thus it has been observed that in the two passages 2 Corinthians 1:21f. and Ephesians 1:13 there is a parallelism in thought between the ideas of being sealed with the Spirit and given the earnest of the Spirit; it is, therefore, tempting to conclude that the thought of being anointed in the former passage is equivalent to that of hearing and believing the Word of God in the latter. Further, the thought of teaching by the "anointing" (v. 27) fits in nicely with the identification of the anointing as the Word of God. Finally, John says that the anointing remains in his readers in the same way as he speaks about the Word of God or the truth remaining in them (1 Jn. 2:14; 2 Jn. 2).[22] All this adds up to a strong case that the anointing is to be identified with the Word of God. Above all, when understood in this way, John's statement is free from the danger of subjectivism. The false teachers could lay claim to spiritual illumination: how, then, could John's readers know for sure that their spiritual experience was of superior quality? If it is simply a matter of comparing claims to spiritual illumination, one

---

[19]For Gnostic use see Hippolytus, *Refutatio omnium haeresium* 5:7:19; 9:22; Origen, *Contra Celsum* 6:27; *Pistis Sophia* 86, 112, 128, 130; *Acts of Thomas* 27, 157; *Odes of Solomon* 36:6; *Apocryphon of John* 30:14-20; *Gospel of Truth* 36:17-26; *Gospel of Philip* 68, 95; cited by I. de la Potterie, "Anointing of the Christian by Faith," in I. de la Potterie and S. Lyonnet, *The Christian Lives by the Spirit*, Staten Island, 1971, 79-143 (80 n. 4) (= "L'onction du chrétien par la foi," Bib 40, 1959, 12-69).

[20]De la Potterie points out that the references are all in *Christian* Gnostic texts, and that probably the idea was borrowed from orthodox Christianity and not vice versa. Wengst, 48-50, holds that the heretics claimed an exclusive anointing for themselves in terms of the teaching function of the Spirit.

[21]Dodd, 58-64. The interpretation goes back to R. Reitzenstein, *Die hellenistischen Mysterienreligionen*, Leipzig, 1927³, 396f.; *Die Vorgeschichte der christlichen Taufe*, Leipzig, 1929, 184.

[22]De la Potterie, *art. cit.*, 101-108.

person's claim may be as good as another's. But if John rests his case on his readers' possession of the objective testimony of the Word of God, as handed down in the church, then clearly his case rests on a solid foundation.[23]

Nevertheless, it remains difficult to think of the Word of God, handed down and preached in the church, as being described under the metaphor of anointing. Moreover, the parallels which we saw between what is said here about the anointing and what is said in John 14–16 about the Spirit cannot be simply laid aside. Consequently, we should probably take the step of combining the two interpretations of our passage. The anointing is the Word taught to converts before their baptism and apprehended by them through the work of the Spirit in their hearts (cf. 1 Thess. 1:5f.). This view has been cogently presented by I. de la Potterie, who sums up: "The anointing is indeed *God's word*, not as it is preached externally in the community, but as it is received by faith into men's hearts and remains active, *thanks to the work* of the *Spirit*."[24] This gives a satisfying view of the passage. The antidote to false teaching is the inward reception of the Word of God, administered and confirmed by the work of the Spirit.

The gift itself comes from "the Holy One." It is possible that this is a reference to God the Father, the Holy One of Israel (Ps. 71:22; and frequently), but here it is virtually certain to be a reference to Jesus, the Holy One of God (Mk. 1:24; Jn. 6:69; cf. Acts 3:14).[25] Elsewhere Jesus is the giver of the Spirit, who is here associated with the Word (Acts 2:33).

As a result of this gift John can say to his readers, "all of you

---

[23]"The appeal to the indwelling Spirit easily declines into an appeal to the individual experience of 'inspiration'. If such experience is made the criterion, persons with little grasp of the central truths of the Gospel may mistake their own 'inspirations' (or bright ideas) for the truth of God, and so the corporate, historical tradition of Christianity is imperilled. Our writer found that this was actually happening within his sphere of influence (see iv. 1–6). If, on the other hand, we are referred to the Gospel itself, which is a recital of what God did for us in the life, teaching, death and resurrection of Jesus Christ—to the Gospel not as merely heard, believed and remembered, but as livingly apprehended and retained as a power in our lives—then there is an objective standard by which the faith of the Church is kept true to what is distinctive in the Christian revelation. The interior testimony of the Holy Spirit is confirmation of the *datum* in the Gospel (see iv. 13)" (Dodd, 63f.).

[24]I. de la Potterie, *art. cit.*, 114f. The same view is adopted by de Jonge, 109–114; cf. Barclay, 79–82. The objections to Dodd's view made by Stott, 109f., do not disturb the reformulation of the hypothesis by de la Potterie.

[25]The sequence of pronouns in 2:27f. is strong evidence that Jesus is meant here. Morris, 1266, claims that the Holy Spirit is meant.

know the truth." Literally the Greek states "all of you know," and the object "the truth" is supplied in the NIV from verse 21. It is slightly strange that the verb has no object, and in fact a number of MSS have a different text: "you know all things." The commentators are not certain which of these readings is original, but it is more probable that John is stressing that all of his readers know the truth than that he is emphasizing their knowledge of all things.[26] The antichrists have no monopoly of truth, no matter how superior they may regard themselves as being in comparison with ordinary Christians. It is the privilege of every true Christian to have knowledge from the Spirit.

21 John reinforces what he has just been saying.[27] The warning tone which he is using might suggest that he is doubtful whether his readers do in fact have Christian knowledge; perhaps he is afraid that on hearing about the presence of heretics in the church they may timidly begin to ask, "Is it I?" And so he reassures them. He is not addressing them as people who do not know the truth, but as those who do know it.[28] Consequently, they should realize that no false statement[29] comes from the truth.[30] If people utter heretical

---

[26]πάντες is attested by S B P sa, and supported by Schnackenburg, 154; Bultmann, 37 n. 10; Haas, 66. πάντα is defended by Windisch, 117; Nauck, 95 n. 6; W. Grundmann, TDNT IX, 572. In favor of πάντα it is argued: (a) οἴδατε requires an object; (b) in verse 27 the anointing is said to teach about *all* things; (c) to know the truth (v. 21) is tantamount to knowing all things; (d) the accusative could have been altered under the influence of John 16:30 to avoid the impression that disciples stand on the same level of knowledge as Jesus; (e) the accusative could also have been altered by assimilation to verse 19. In favor of πάντες, however, it can be argued: (a) it is parallel to πάντες in verse 19; (b) the stress is on the fact of knowing rather than on the object of knowledge; (c) the temptation to scribes to supply an object to οἴδατε would have been strong; (d) the text could have been altered by assimilation to John 14:26. On the whole, it is most plausible that πάντες is original, and that πάντα is a grammatical correction by scribes which was suggested by the context and parallel passages. The arguments for scribal alteration in the opposite direction are much weaker.

[27]ἔγραψα is an epistolary aorist; cf. 2:14.

[28]The Greek conjunction ὅτι, found three times in this verse, is translated "because" the first two times in most English versions, and "that" by Schnackenburg, 141, 154 n. 6; Bultmann, 38 n. 13; Haas, 66f. See 2:12–14 for a similar problem of interpretation. Schnackenburg argues that ἔγραψα should have an object, and therefore the meaning "that" should be adopted. De Jonge, 115, finds no reason why the author should want to underline what he has just said, and apparently prefers "because." The writer is not giving instruction to his readers because of their ignorance (after all they have the anointing!) but because he can build on the fact of their knowledge of the truth.

[29]πᾶν . . . οὐκ is tantamount to οὐδέν; cf. 2:23; 4:3; it may be a Semitic construction (Moule, 182), but could be an ordinary Greek construction with the negative attached to the verb rather than (as in English) to the nominative (MH II, 433f.). See also on 2:19.

[30]The third ὅτι in the verse may be (a) causal (if the preceding instances are causal;

statements, this is an indication that they are not possessed of the divine anointing. The readers ought to be able to recognize such people for what they are. They have no share in divine reality and consequently their statements are false.

22 One falsehood in particular characterizes those who do not come from the truth. It is so obviously a falsehood that John expects his readers to recognize it as such, and hence to draw the conclusion that the people who hold to it cannot possibly have any share in God the Father (v. 23). He makes his point with a rhetorical question. Who is the liar *par excellence*? It is the person who denies that Jesus is the Christ.[31] In the following verse the writer speaks of those who deny "the Son," and it is likely that he regarded "Christ" and "Son" as virtually equivalent terms. He uses similar expressions elsewhere with regard to heretical teaching. "Every spirit that acknowledges that Jesus Christ has come in the flesh is from God, but every spirit that does not acknowledge Jesus is not from God" (4:2f.). "Many deceivers, who do not acknowledge that Jesus Christ has come in the flesh, have gone out into the world" (2 Jn. 7). In our comments on the last of these quotations we saw that it was unlikely that the writer was combatting a Jewish denial that the Messiah was to be equated with Jesus, a problem which is prominent in the Gospel (Jn. 4:29; 7:26–31, 41–43). His controversy is not with Jews from outside the church, but with people who had at one time been members of the church.[32] Most commentators see some connection with the views of heretics who denied the reality of the incarnation. Ignatius of Antioch attacked heretics who denied that the Son of God truly became incarnate in Jesus.[33] Similarly, Irenaeus attacked

---

NIV; Westcott, 68; Brooke, 57); (b) "recitative," dependent on ἔγραψα (Schnackenburg, 154 n. 6); or (c) "recitative," dependent loosely on οἴδατε: "[and know] that no lie is of the truth" (RSV; cf. Chaine, 171; Bultmann, 38 n. 13). The first interpretation can be excluded: John is not writing *because* no lie comes from the truth. The second interpretation is a possible one: John is writing that no lie comes from the truth. The third interpretation gives the best sense. The readers know that no lie comes from the truth. Consequently, since the antichrists tell lies, they cannot come from the truth (vv. 22f.). The construction is elliptical and harsh, but not impossible.

[31]The clause following ἀρνούμενος contains the actual words of the denial in accordance with Classical Greek idiom (BD 429): "he denies [by saying] that Jesus is *not* the Christ." English idiom drops the negative.

[32]De Jonge, 119.

[33]Ignatius, *Letter to the Smyrnaeans*, stresses that Jesus was "truly of the race of David according to the flesh, but Son of God by the Divine will and power, truly born of a virgin and baptized by John. . . , truly nailed up in the flesh. . . . He suffered truly, as also He raised Himself truly; not as certain unbelievers say, that He suffered in semblance" (1f.). He goes on to confess his belief that Jesus was in the flesh even

a heretic called Cerinthus who held that the Christ descended upon Jesus at his baptism and departed again before he suffered and died.[34] In the view of these heretics the heavenly Christ did not suffer and die, nor did he shed his blood to be our Savior. Now it is true that there are other features of the teaching of Cerinthus which are not reflected in 1 John, so that we cannot simply identify the heretics with Cerinthus and his colleagues. Nevertheless, this aspect of the Cerinthian heresy still appears to give the closest parallel to that of John's opponents.[35] The difficulty is that we do not know what they taught positively; John is content to tell us what they denied. Did they give their allegiance to Jesus as a mere man? Or did they, on the other hand, believe in the Messiah/Son of God but deny that he had become incarnate and died for human sin? On the whole, it seems most probable that they accepted Jesus in some sense, but denied that he was the Messiah and Son of God, i.e. that he was permanently united with the divine Son. It is unlikely that they believed in the heavenly Messiah but denied his incarnation in Jesus.[36]

As a result of their denial that Jesus was the Christ, John could fittingly say that their attitude was that of antichrist. Any person who takes up this position can be said to be antichrist, just as Jesus could address Simon Peter individually with the words, "Out of my sight, Satan!" when he tempted him to turn aside from the path of the cross (Mk. 8:33). But to deny that Jesus is the Christ is to deny that he is the Son of God.[37] Consequently the antichrist can be

---

after the resurrection, and ate and drank with the disciples as one in the flesh, although he was united spiritually with the Father (3). See especially Schnackenburg, 20–22, who thinks that this gives the closest parallel to the heresy combatted by John.

[34]See the citation above, 70–71 n. 7.

[35]The link with Cerinthianism is denied by Schnackenburg, 19f., who notes that various features of Cerinthus's teaching appear to be absent: his differentiation between a higher and a lower god, Christ and Jesus being descended respectively from these; his rejection of the incarnation on the grounds that the virgin birth was impossible; his rejection of the sacrifice of Christ on the grounds that the spiritual cannot suffer. Cf. de Jonge, 122f., who argues that only in 2:22 does a distinction between Jesus and Christ appear; it is, however, implicit in 4:2f.; 5:1; 2 John 9. Schnackenburg's point is that the heretics rejected the Christian doctrine of redemption and hence saw no need of redemption, whereas Cerinthus worked from the Gnostic spirit/matter distinction. It is, however, difficult to interpret 5:6 in any other sense than as an attack on views similar to those of Cerinthus.

[36]The writer attacks those who do not continue in the teaching of Christ (2 Jn. 9), which may mean teaching about the Messiah, i.e. about his identity with Jesus. If so, the point would be that the heretics were unconcerned about the Messiah.

[37]For the equivalence of these terms in the Johannine Epistles see M. de Jonge, "The

more closely defined as one who denies the Son. John, however, speaks of denial of "the Father and the Son." We do not know whether the heretics denied the Fatherhood of God in so many words; it is improbable that they did so. But John is quite clear in his mind that denial of the Son is implicitly denial of the Father. He explains the point in the next verse.

We should, however, pause to note that for John the height of heresy is to deny that Jesus is the Messiah, the Son of God and Savior. To reduce Jesus to the status of a mere man, or to allow no more than a temporary indwelling of some divine power in him is to strike at the root of Christianity. Modern thinkers may have more refined ways of stating similar denials of the reality of the incarnation. It may be doubted whether they are any more immune to John's perception that they take the heart out of Christianity.

23 For the person who denies that Jesus is the Son has no share in God the Father. If the heretics thought that they could "have" God[38] without believing in Jesus, they were completely mistaken. It is only through the Son that we know that God is Father, and it is only through the Son and his propitiatory death that we can have access to God as Father. Thus to deny that Jesus is the Son is to deny the Christian doctrine of God, or at least to deprive it of its essential basis. The Christian doctrine of a personal, fatherly God is dependent on the revelation of God given in Jesus. Those who reject Jesus as the source of knowledge of God deprive themselves of access to the Christian God and are left with a bare abstraction. Conversely, however, acceptance of Jesus as Son automatically leads to personal communion with God as Father. There are only two courses, confession and denial. Moreover, what a man is prepared to confess with his lips is what he believes in his heart: Christian confession—whatever cost it may involve—is of decisive importance. John's thought is moving toward exhortation to his readers to hold fast to their Christian confession, and not to be swayed by the persuasions of the heretics.

24 He continues with an emphatic "as for you" (TNT), which has disappeared in most English translations. The readers are contrasted with the false teachers who have lost their grip on the

---

Use of the Word ΧΡΙΣΤΟΣ in the Johannine Epistles," in *Studies in John presented to Professor Dr. J. N. Sevenster,* Leiden, 1970, 66–74. See further W. Grundmann, TDNT IX, 570f.

[38]On the use of ἔχω here see above, 73 n. 16. The second clause in the verse was accidentally omitted by homoioteleuton in K L *al*; TR; cf. AV.

truth, and they are urged to let the teaching which they have received in the past continue to control their thinking and action. "From the beginning" refers most naturally to the commencement of their own Christian lives. The antidote to heresy is a return to the teaching given at the beginning.

This thought is common in other Christian documents of the same period (1 Tim. 6:3; 2 Tim. 1:13; 4:3f.; Tit. 1:9; 2 Pet. 3:2; Jude 17, 20). Written toward the end of the apostolic period, they all counsel holding fast to the teaching given in the past which constitutes "sound doctrine," the "faith that God has once for all entrusted to the saints" (Jude 3). Two points, however, must be noted. On the one hand, the writer is not saying that anything handed down from the past is true and reliable simply because of its antiquity. He regards the teaching given at the beginning as issuing from the Lord through the apostles and hence bearing the stamp of divine revelation; it is "the word of Christ" which is to "dwell in you richly" (Col. 3:16).[39] On the other hand, while the writer is clearly opposed to new fashions and innovations in doctrine which are false, he would no doubt allow that what has been handed down as "truth unchanged, unchanging" may need to be re-expressed in fresh ways if it is to make the same impact on modern readers as it made on its first readers. The art of translation is to reproduce by means of the receptor language the same impression on the readers as was made by the statement on its original readers in its original language. What is true of different languages is also true of presenting the gospel to people in different ages and cultures.

So important is this stress on the need to hold fast to the original Christian message that John repeats it for emphasis: "if what you have heard from the beginning remains in you"; the NIV, however, avoids what might seem to be an ungainly repetition in English by substituting "if it does."[40] Such adherence to Christian doctrine has as its result that the readers themselves will remain in the Son and the Father. The form of expression, using "remain," is deliberate; and the thought repeats that of verse 23 where confession of the Son was the condition for "having" the Father also. Now it becomes clear that acceptance of the original Christian message involves confession of Jesus as the Messiah and Son of God, and that such confession leads to fellowship with him and with the

---

[39]Cf. Schnackenburg, 158f.

[40]Haas, 69f., argues that the solemn repetition should be preserved in translation.

Father. It is significant that "remain" expresses a continuing relationship. It is not enough merely to have heard and assented to the
message in time past. The message must continue to be present and
active in the lives of those who have heard it. They must continually
call it to mind and let it affect their lives. This is why continual study
of the Word and participation in Christian instruction is so important
for perseverance in the faith.

25 For those who let God's Word remain in them there is an
appropriate reward. Here[41] is what Jesus has promised to us,[42] says
John: it is eternal life.[43] This is the only use of the word "promise"
in the Johannine writings. It is a term used especially to refer to the
prophetic elements in the Old Testament which make promises that
have already been fulfilled or are sure to find fulfilment.[44] Elsewhere
in the New Testament, especially in the Pastoral Epistles, we hear of
the promise of life (1 Tim. 4:8; 2 Tim. 1:1), and this is said to have
been promised by God (Tit. 1:2; Jas. 1:12). The thought is of the
eternal life of heaven which is promised by God to those who serve
him faithfully in this life. Here, however, the promise is probably
traced back to Jesus himself (Jn. 10:10, 28). It is not clear whether
John is thinking of eternal life primarily as a future blessing, so that
this verse promises a reward additional to that given in verse 24.
There is something to be said for the view that John is explaining
that the experience of remaining in the Son and the Father is, precisely, eternal life—available here and now. This would fit in with
the teaching of the Gospel where eternal life is a blessing which
commences to be enjoyed in this present life (Jn. 3:36; 6:40, 47); it
also fits in with the definition of eternal life in John 17:3 as knowing
the Father and the Son.[45] Naturally the future dimension (cf. 2:17) is
not lacking on this interpretation.

---

[41]The αὕτη refers forward to ἐπαγγελία and is put in the same gender (BD 132¹).
Nevertheless, the phrase καὶ αὕτη links the clause closely with what precedes (cf.
1:4/5) and suggests that the writer is still talking about the same theme.
[42]ἡμῖν is read by most authorities; ὑμῖν, found in B *al* h, is a scribal slip, or deliberate
assimilation to verse 24 (Schnackenburg, 159 n. 4).
[43]ζωήν is accusative by "inverse attraction" to the case of the relative pronoun ἥν
(BD 295).
[44]See, for example, Acts 2:39; 13:23, 32; 26:6; 2 Corinthians 1:20; Galatians 3:22;
Ephesians 3:6; Hebrews 6:12; J. Schniewind and G. Friedrich, TDNT II, 576–586. In
the present verse ἐπαγγελία must be concrete: the content of the promise.
[45]Schnackenburg, 159f., argues for the future meaning on the grounds that the author
is giving his readers a motive for perseverance and remaining in fellowship with God;
cf. de Jonge, 125f. Bultmann, 40, recognizes the elements of "already" and "not yet"
in eternal life both here and in the Gospel.

26 John has made his point, but so that his readers may be left in no doubt whatever he now repeats and summarizes what he has said, first with reference to the heretics, and then (v. 27) with regard to the spiritual resources of his readers. "I am writing" is literally "I wrote," and refers back to verses 18–25. There is, however, a new element in the summary. John describes the heretics as "those who are trying to lead you astray" (cf. 2 Jn. 7).[46] Previously he described them simply as opponents of Christ and purveyors of falsehood. Now he brings out what was implicit in his earlier description: the heretics were trying to lead the faithful members of the church astray also. It was not enough for the readers to recognize that there were heretics around; it was vital for them to realize that the heretics constituted a danger to themselves. The prophecy of Jesus about false Christs and false prophets who would appear and try to deceive the elect (Mk. 13:22) was in course of fulfilment. The church needed to heed the Master's warning: "So be on your guard; I have told you everything ahead of time" (Mk. 13:23).

27 The readers should not be deceived by the false teachers because John himself has warned them (v. 26). But there is an additional,[47] stronger reason: the readers themselves[48] have received the anointing given by Jesus,[49] and it is still at work in their hearts. The Word of God has been conveyed to their hearts by the Spirit, and this is the ultimate safeguard against falling away into heresy. The thought is the same as in verse 24, but whereas in that verse the readers were told to *ensure* that their initial teaching remained in them, here they are told that it *does* remain in them. Bultmann comments that the indicative form includes the imperative:[50] the promise of divine grace does not exclude the need for human response and effort. Those who have such inward instruction do not need anybody to teach them. Manifestly they do not need to listen to false teachers, inside or outside the church. John appears to be saying rather that they do not need instruction from teachers such as himself—and yet this is precisely what he gives them! This is an

---

[46]The participle has a conative force. For the verb see 1:8; 3:7; Mark 13:5f.; H. Braun, TDNT VI, 228–253, especially 245f.

[47]This is the force of the connective καί.

[48]The pronoun ὑμεῖς is strongly emphasized. It has been explained as being brought forward for stress from the relative clause (cf. BD 475[1]), but it is perhaps better explained as a hanging nominative (BD 466[1]).

[49]αὐτοῦ probably refers to Jesus, as in 2:20. Note the emphatic use of the pronoun in verse 27b.

[50]Bultmann, 41.

interesting paradox, which may shed some light on the fact that John also tells his readers that those born of God cannot sin and at the same time exhorts them not to sin. In the present case, two points may clarify what he means. On the one hand, Schnackenburg stresses that the instruction given by church teachers must be accompanied by inner teaching by the Spirit which enables the hearers to sift out and accept what is true.[51] On the other hand, Bruce comments that the Spirit's instruction comes through teachers who themselves possess the anointing; Christians possessed by the Spirit give one another mutual instruction, without which no single individual can appreciate the whole of God's truth (Eph. 3:18).[52]

The last part of the verse is an exhortation to hold fast to the teaching given by the Spirit rather than to be tempted by the false teachers.[53] Three reasons are given for doing so, expressed in a slightly cumbrous fashion. First, the anointing which the readers have received is a sufficient source of knowledge; it gives instruction about all things. We may legitimately take "all things" to mean "all that you need to know": there is no suggestion of omniscience here! Second, John emphasizes that the teaching so given is reliable, and is not a lie.[54] Third, John reminds his readers that they were instructed to abide in Christ.[55] So, finally, he urges them to remain in Christ,[56] which means that they will remain in the true teaching.[57]

[51]Schnackenburg, 161.
[52]Bruce, 76f.
[53]This seems to be the force of the connective ἀλλ'. Haas, 72, notes that it may be transitional or adversative. It seems to contrast the lack of need for human teachers with the full teaching given by the anointing.
[54]"Real" represents an adjective in Greek (ἀληθές), while "counterfeit" represents a noun (ψεῦδος), i.e. "a lie." See Westcott, 80. There is a contrast with the lies of the false teachers (cf. v. 21).
[55]The exegesis assumes that the content of ἐδίδαξεν is a command to remain in Christ, and that Christ is the implied antecedent of αὐτῷ. The latter point is demanded by the parallelism with verse 28, although Bultmann, 41 n. 31, takes the reference to be to the anointing. For the former point see Schnackenburg, 162; Haas, 72.
[56]μένετε must be imperative (*contra* Westcott, 81).
[57]We have taken verse 27b as one sentence (Westcott, 79f.). A number of scholars prefer to divide it into two sentences: "As his anointing teaches you about everything, so it (now referring to the teaching) is true and no lie. And just as it has taught you: abide in him" (Haas, 72; Schnackenburg, 161; so apparently Bultmann, 41 n. 34). The objections to this view are: (a) In the first sentence the logic is not clear, and the main clause receives an undue stress; (b) the possibility of dividing up the clauses in this way depends on understanding the καί before ἀληθές as an example of καί in apodosis (cf. BD 442[7]). The parallels cited are 2:18; John 15:9; 17:18; 20:21; cf. Romans 1:13; Matthew 18:33, but in each of these cases the καί accentuates a pronoun which is compared with a pronoun in the subordinate clause; this is hardly the case here.

So again the antidote to falling into false ideas of the Christian faith is to be found in holding fast to the initial statement of Christian truth given in the apostolic witness, as this is confirmed in our hearts by the anointing given by the Spirit. It cannot be otherwise with a religion based on a historical, once-for-all revelation. Granted that the Lord has yet more light to break forth from his Word, it is nevertheless from the Word that new understanding issues, and any new doctrine which is not in harmony with the Word is self-condemned.

THE HOPE OF GOD'S CHILDREN (2:28–3:3)

28. *And now, dear children, continue in him, so that when he appears we may be confident and unashamed before him at his coming.*

29. *If you know that he is righteous, you know that everyone who does what is right has been born of him.*

3:1. *How great is the love the Father has lavished on us, that we should be called the children of God! And that is what we are! The reason the world does not know us is that it did not know him.* 2. *Dear friends, now we are children of God, and what we will be has not yet been made known. But we know that when he appears,[a] we shall be like him, for we shall see him as he is.* 3. *Everyone who has this hope in him purifies himself, just as he is pure.*

[a]Or *when it is made known.*

John's connection of thought is not very clear at this point, and a number of commentators put the major break at the end of verse 28 or verse 29 rather than at the end of verse 27. We saw that there was a clear break at the end of verse 17, after which John wrote about the danger of the antichrists and their false teaching and assured his readers that they possessed the antidote. This line of thought extends to verse 27, after which the antichrists disappear from consideration (they will soon reappear!), and John's attention is directed to the positive encouragement of his readers by placing the hope of the coming of Jesus before them and drawing certain conclusions from it. No doubt the antichrists and the temptation they constitute are still in John's mind; he wants to encourage his readers to remain steadfast in their faith, and so he places before them the fact of the coming of Jesus as both a tremendous source of hope for the children of God and also the basis of an exhortation to holy living. The accent is thus moving away from the temptation to false belief to the temptation to sinful living.[1]

28 "And now" is simply a way of marking a new section,[2] and "dear children" is one of John's frequent ways of addressing his readers (2:1, 12). In the previous verse John had counselled them to remain in Christ, and he now achieves an easy transition to his next line of thought by a repetition of this phrase which serves to underline and emphasize its importance. Remaining in Christ is the antidote to false belief and unchristian behavior. But now John strengthens this appeal by reminding his readers of the coming revelation of Jesus. Although the time of his coming is uncertain, the fact of his coming is certain.[3] Two words are used to describe it. First, there is the verb "to appear," which John has already used to refer to the first coming of Jesus (1:2; cf. 3:5, 8). The word is actually the passive form of the verb "to reveal" and conveys the thought of the invisible becoming visible. The first coming of Jesus was the revelation of the previously hidden Word of God in human form, so that those with eyes to see could confess, "We have seen his glory, the glory of the one and only Son, who came from the Father, full of grace and truth" (Jn. 1:14). Now he is again hidden from view, although he is spiritually present with his disciples, but one day he will again be revealed from heaven.[4] The other word used to describe this event is "coming"; it is the Greek word *parousia,* which has been taken over into theological English. This word was used for the visit of a ruler to some part of his dominions, an occasion for celebration and rejoicing. Even today, although we have become accustomed to seeing the face of the monarch or president on TV, people will still turn out in great numbers on state occasions to see and cheer the ruler; how much more must this have been the case in the ancient world where to see the emperor was possibly the event of a lifetime. It is this kind of atmosphere which is conveyed by this word. It conceives of the return of Jesus to this world in visible splendor, like a monarch. For the Christian the parousia is associated with the resurrection of the dead, the gathering of Christ's

---

[1]For the various suggested divisions of the Epistle at this point, see the Introduction, section 3. Our division is accepted by Brooke, 79; Schnackenburg, 162f.; Stott, 115; Bultmann, 43f.; de Jonge, 128; Houlden, 84; Bruce, 77f.

[2]νῦν is logical and not temporal, as in John 17:5; 2 John 5; BD 442[15].

[3]The use of ἐάν, "if," does not place the *fact* of the coming in doubt, but merely its time and circumstances; it is equivalent to ὅταν, which has replaced it in some inferior MSS; see John 12:32; 14:3; AG, *s.v.* 1d.

[4]For the eschatological use of φανερόω cf. Colossians 3:4; 1 Peter 5:4.

people to be with him, and the apportionment of final destiny.[5] These are the thoughts which are present here. Jesus is coming, and his advent spells hope and encouragement for his people, but it is possible that some of them may find his coming unwelcome. Those who are looking forward to his appearing, the people who are now remaining in him, will be confident in his presence.

> Bold I approach the eternal throne,
> And claim the crown through Christ my own

sang Charles Wesley[6] with a confidence which we may find astounding and even immodest, but this is a correct deduction from John's words. The thought here is of the confidence with which a person may enter into the royal presence and speak with the king without any fear.[7] It is a natural confidence, since it arises out of an existing relationship expressed in prayer.[8] Such people will not share the fate of those who will be ashamed before Christ at his coming. This may be taken to mean that they will shrink back in shame as they realize their unworthiness to come into his holy presence. But it is more likely that it means that they will be put to shame by Christ; they will be disgraced openly.[9] For them the coming of Jesus will mean judgment and rejection.

It is sometimes suggested that if the Christian has a sense of the invisible presence of Jesus with him, exhortations to good be-

---

[5]παρουσία occurs here only in the Johannine literature, but is common in Paul (1 Cor. 15:23; 1 Thess. 2:19; 3:13; 4:15; 5:23; 2 Thess. 2:1, 8, 9); see also Matthew 24:3, 27, 37, 39; James 5:7f.; 2 Peter 1:16; 3:4, 12; A. Oepke, TDNT V, 858–871; G. Braumann, NIDNTT II, 898–901. The thought is thoroughly Johannine, and the theory of R. Bultmann, which assigns all future eschatological statements in both John and 1 John to a redactor, is unnecessary and unconvincing. See especially John 5:25–29 for a Johannine exposition of the elements associated with the parousia of the Son of man.
[6]"And can it be that I should gain," *The Methodist Hymnbook,* London, 1933, No. 371.
[7]παρρησία originally indicated the democratic right of a citizen to express his opinion. It is used of confidence to speak in God's presence in Job 27:10 LXX. Thus it can be applied to prayer (see n. 8). See the excellent article by H. Schlier, TDNT V, 871–886, and the briefer summary by H.-C. Hahn, NIDNTT II, 734–737.
[8]1 John 3:21; 5:14; Hebrews 4:16; 10:18.
[9]The two possibilities arise because ἀπό can be taken to mean "from" (its usual meaning) or may be equivalent to ὑπό (Lk. 6:18; 8:43, *et al.*; BD 210²). MH IV, 136, notes that the phrase αἰσχύνομαι ἀπό is septuagintal (Isa. 1:29 B; Jer. 12:13). Cf. Isaiah 45:24; 1 Enoch 63:11 ("Their faces shall be filled with darkness and shame before that Son of Man, and they shall be driven from his presence"); Philippians 1:20. The thought is of judgment by Christ rather than of psychological feelings in his presence (Schnackenburg, 165; cf. Haas, 74; Bultmann, 44 n. 4). The middle form, "to shrink back in shame," is defended by Westcott, 82; Brooke, 66. For the contrast of παρρησία and αἰσχύνομαι, cf. Proverbs 13:5.

havior in the light of the coming of Jesus as judge are not going to make much difference for him. What fresh moral impetus can the thought of the second coming of Jesus add to the fact that he is already with us and sees what we do? Is not the sanction of final judgment superfluous? The objection is a valid one, but it may be suggested that John has preserved the proper balance. His point is that the future coming of the Lord means hope for those who are in union with him now; it is the natural climax to their present relationship. Those who will be ashamed when he comes are the people who did not live in union with him on earth, those who were merely nominal in their allegiance to him, and their rejection at his coming will be the final confirmation of a life of spiritual separation from him. It is right that the Christian who lives in union with Christ now should long for his nearer presence (Phil. 1:21–23), and that the person who has cut himself off from living in union with Christ should fear the day when that separation becomes final and irremediable.

29 The train of thought here is not entirely clear. John has been speaking of the possibility of judgment at the parousia. The judgment is by One who, as the readers know,[10] is righteous,[11] and therefore the expected statement is: "If you do not want to be ashamed at his coming, be righteous," or "If the judge is righteous, those who will be confident when he comes will be the righteous (therefore, be righteous)." There is no difference in meaning between the adjective "righteous," used to describe Jesus, and the verbal form "does what is right," used to describe Christians. Both expressions refer to correct moral behavior, acceptable to God.[12]

However, the thought is not as simple as this. What John says is that "everyone who does what is right has been born of him." A new idea is introduced here, that of spiritual birth; it figures prominently in the rest of the Epistle (3:9; 4:7; 5:1, 4, 18; cf. Jn. 1:13; 3:6,

---

[10]The fact that the clause begins with "if" does not make it hypothetical or doubtful; the construction is simply a rhetorical way of comparing two pieces of knowledge. It is not clear whether οἶδα and γινώσκω are used as synonyms or not. Older commentators take οἶδα to refer to knowledge which is intuitive or absolute, on the basis of which the readers can have further experimental knowledge (γινώσκω) by means of observation (Westcott, 82; Brooke, 68f.; Law, 364–367). The point is that if the readers know that Christ is righteous, they ought also to recognize that persons born of God will be righteous.

[11]Clearly it is Jesus who is in mind, as in verse 28. See also n. 13.

[12]ποιεῖν τὴν δικαιοσύνην is a Jewish type of expression (Ps. 99:4; 106:3; 119:121), similar to ποιεῖν τὴν ἀλήθειαν (1:6). See Matthew 6:1; Romans 10:5; and Acts 10:35; Hebrews 11:33; James 1:20.

8). The thought is that believers stand in a new relationship to God,[13] analogous to that of children to a father. This is a common picture elsewhere in the New Testament, and has its basis in the Old Testament where God's people are said to be related to him, like children to a father, and the thought is of his fatherly care for them and their filial duty of obedience toward him.[14] The metaphor is taken further when it is expressed in terms of begetting and birth: Christians have received new life from God by a creative act comparable with physical begetting. This is as far as the metaphor can be taken: we never hear in the Bible of a female partner in the act of spiritual birth. The point of the metaphor is rather to indicate that spiritual life comes from God through the agency of the Word and the Spirit. The Christian is thus placed in the same relationship to God as is occupied by Jesus, although John preserves the distinction by reserving the name of "Son" for Jesus and referring to Christians simply as "children" of God.[15]

There are two difficulties about what John says at this point. First, there is the substitution of the idea of being born from God for the idea of remaining in Christ. The new expression has probably been introduced in anticipation of the use of the metaphor in 3:9. At the same time, perhaps it was an easy equivalent for John to use with reference to Christians as those who have received a divine anointing, and to this extent the way had already been prepared for its

---

[13]Although the first part of the verse referred to Christ (n. 11), it is probable that ἐξ αὐτοῦ in the second part of the verse refers to God. It was probably so self-evident to him and his readers that spiritual birth was from the Father that he was not conscious of gliding from one antecedent for αὐτοῦ (Christ, 2:28, 29a) to another (God, 2:29b). Nevertheless, some commentators feel that the transition is so awkward that the author must have been using pre-formulated phrases which he has not edited with sufficient care (Schnackenburg, 166f.).

[14]Deuteronomy 1:31; 8:5; 14:1; 32:6; Psalm 103:13; Proverbs 3:12; Isaiah 63:16; 64:8; Jeremiah 31:9, 20; Hosea 11; Malachi 1:6; 2:10. See O. Hofius, NIDNTT I, 615–621.

[15]Both Jesus and Paul, however, speak of men as sons of God (Mt. 5:9; Rom. 8:14; Gal. 3:26; 4:4–7). For spiritual birth elsewhere in the New Testament see 1 Peter 1:3, 23; Titus 3:5.

The question of the origins of John's terminology is an important one, but cannot be pursued here in detail. Although the thought of men having a filial relationship to God is found in the Old Testament, the idea of spiritual birth is absent, and there is little that is relevant in Judaism. But the language of rebirth is to be found in the mystery religions and Gnosticism. Many scholars claim that here a Hellenistic idea has been imported into Christianity (Dodd, 68; Bultmann, 45–47). This is combatted by Schnackenburg, 175–183, who admits the similarity in terminology, but holds that the idea developed in connection with the Christian understanding of baptism and the gift of the Spirit. See further Windisch, 122f.; K. H. Rengstorf and F. Büchsel, TDNT I, 665–675.

use.[16] The New Testament has a variety of expressions to describe Christians, and the various writers use them in what sometimes seems to be a fairly indiscriminate manner, and no embarrassment is felt in switching from one to another.

Second, the major difficulty is that the statement made by John seems to be back to front. We expect John to say "everyone who has been born of him does what is right (and therefore is acceptable at the parousia of the righteous One)." Instead he says that doing what is right is the sign of spiritual birth. Hence doing what is right gives assurance that we shall have confidence before him at his coming. What John is trying to stress is that doing what is right is the consequence of spiritual birth; hence if a person does what is right, this is a sign of spiritual birth. Naturally, this does not mean that any morally upright person is a child of God, even though he makes no religious profession;[17] when John says that "Everyone who loves has been born of God" (4:8), he does not mean that atheists who love are really Christians. John is quite clear that being a Christian is dependent on believing in Jesus Christ and loving one another (3:23), and his other remarks must be understood in this context. Here he has in mind the problem of testing the truth of claims to be true Christians within the church, and he asserts that true righteousness (the kind shown by Jesus) is possible only on the basis of spiritual birth. So the readers themselves can take comfort that, if they do what is righteous, this is a sign that they are born of God, and hence that they can have confidence for the day of judgment.[18]

3:1 John now proceeds to bring the ideas of the new birth and the parousia into conjunction with each other. He describes the wonder of the present status of believers as God's beloved sons, and then comments on their even higher position which is to be revealed at the parousia. This status is no less real for being unrecognized by the sinful world. And the thought of "such amazing bliss" in store for us should not only "constant joys create" but also act as an incentive to holy living.

From the thought of the new birth, then, John's thought moves to the great love shown by God, as a result of which we have become his children. The train of thought has an interesting parallel in John 3 where the conversation with Nicodemus about the new

---

[16]The transition from one phrase to the other is eased by the fact that in both anointing and the new birth the Word and the Spirit are the operative factors.
[17]So rightly Alexander, 76.
[18]See Houlden, 88.

birth from above through which alone men can enter the kingdom of God is followed by the magnificent declaration of the divine love which sent God's only Son so that we might have eternal life. John's appeal to his readers to consider the greatness of God's love has been lost in the NIV; contrast the TEV, "See how much the Father has loved us!"[19] A slightly unusual word is used to express the sense "how great,"[20] and John speaks of the Father "giving" his love, as if it were a gift to be received. The NIV catches the sense well by using the verb "lavished" to express the meaning, but it is perhaps given most felicitously in a Scottish paraphrase, based on a rendering by Isaac Watts:

> Behold the amazing gift of love
> The Father hath bestowed
> On us, the sinful sons of men,
> To call us sons of God![21]

The "love package" contains our title to be called children of God.[22] Jesus promised a blessing for those who make peace: "they will be called sons of God" (Mt. 5:9). This blessing is now generalized, and covers all disciples. (We may legitimately argue in the opposite direction that if all disciples are sons of God, then all disciples ought to be makers of peace.) The picture is that of legitimation: by naming the child as his son, the father acknowledges that it is indeed his child.[23] There is no legal fiction in this. But, lest any readers might draw this false conclusion, John emphasizes that

---

[19]The Greek has ἴδετε with an indirect statement as a means of arousing the readers' attention. The NIV (cf. the NEB) has chosen to achieve a similar effect by using an exclamatory clause (Haas, 76).

[20]ποταπός usually means "of what a kind" (Lk. 1:29; 7:39), but here has the force "of what a size" (Mk. 13:1).

[21]The original verse by Watts is:
> Behold what wondrous grace
> The Father hath bestowed
> On sinners of a mortal race,
> To call them Sons of God.

The Scottish paraphrase is by William Cameron, "who with little original poetical gift himself had an almost infallible knack in improving the verses of other writers" (J. Moffatt, Handbook to the Church Hymnary, London, 1927, 164f.). For the full version see The Church Hymnary (third edition), London, 1973, 396.

[22]Cf. 3:2, 10; 5:2; John 1:12; 11:52; Romans 8:16; 9:8; Philippians 2:15. The term has the same force as υἱός (cf. n. 15). It is appropriate that earlier in the verse God is described as ὁ Πατήρ, a form used almost exclusively by John (but see Mt. 11:27 and par.; Mk. 13:32 and par.; Bultmann, 47 n. 14).

[23]On the rite of legitimation see G. Fohrer, TDNT VIII, 344f.

those whom God names as his children really are such.[24] The new birth is a reality. Once again, John is expressing the assurance which believers can possess here and now of their standing in God's sight.

Because we are God's children the world does not recognize us, since it did not recognize him either.[25] In fact the world hates the children of God (3:13), just as it hated Jesus (Jn. 15:18f.), since they do not belong to the world. This very fact is a further proof that the readers are children of God: the way in which the world does not recognize them as being on its side is proof that they belong to God. Thus this comment, which at first sight may seem irrelevant, has a part to play in strengthening the readers' assurance. Christians who are persecuted sometimes feel cut off from God because they are in a difficult and unpleasant situation, and they may be tempted to give up their faith; on the contrary, the very fact that they are being persecuted should strengthen their faith since it is an indication that the evil world recognizes that they have passed from death to life.[26]

2 The fact that we are now children of God has been thoroughly established, but the author repeats it once again in order to place it in contrast with what he is going to say about the Christian's future hope. More precisely, the contrast is between the known and the unknown, but our knowledge of our present state enables us to say that our future state will be something even more wonderful. Now we are sons of God: but an even higher status awaits us in the future. Already we have some inkling of what the Christian life is like, and so we can dimly guess at the future state. One is reminded of a similar type of argument propounded by Charles Wesley:

[24]The words καὶ ἐσμέν were omitted in the later MSS (K L *al;* TR) on which the AV was based, but are amply attested in earlier MSS. They may have appeared redundant to scribes, and in any case the passive "to be called" is often tantamount to "to be" (e.g. Mt. 2:23; 5:9; AG, *s.v.*).

[25]διὰ τοῦτο may be regarded as referring backward, so that verse 1a gives the basis for the statement in verse 1b; the ὅτι clause then gives a further explanation of the main clause (Westcott, 96; Bultmann, 48 n. 17; Haas, 77). Most translations, however, including the NIV, regard διὰ τοῦτο as referring forward to the ὅτι clause, so that the reason why the world does not know Christians is that it did not recognize him. There is not a lot of difference in meaning between the two ways of understanding the sentence, but the former way gives a better connection with the context. It is not clear whether the final αὐτόν refers to the Father (cf. v. 1a) or to Jesus (Dodd, 69; Bultmann, 48). Westcott, 97, suggests that "God in Christ" is meant. We have met similar ambiguities earlier in the Epistle.

[26]The thought is similar to Romans 8:35f. where Paul points out that persecution does not separate us from God: it is the sign that we belong to God.

And if our fellowship below
In Jesus be so sweet,
What heights of rapture shall we know
When round His throne we meet.[27]

And Paul also cites the words: "No eye has seen, no ear has heard, no mind has conceived what God has prepared for those who love him" (1 Cor. 2:9). For the moment, however, we live in the period of "not yet," and we must await a fuller revelation of our intended status.[28]

But although we await this revelation, we can nevertheless have a good idea of what our future state will be. We know that when he appears, we shall be like him.[29] At the parousia (2:28), we shall become like Jesus. This, of course, is what we already are: we are children of God, we live in the light, and we are free from sin. John does not state explicitly in what new ways we shall be like Jesus at the parousia. But we may assume that the privileges which we now enjoy in a partial manner will then be ours fully and completely. Not only so, but we may also recollect that our hope is to see Jesus in his glory (Jn. 17:1, 5, 24) and therefore our hope is to share his glory, a hope that is clearly expressed by Paul (Rom. 8:17–19; Phil. 3:21; Col. 3:4). The process of glorification, already begun here and now in the lives of believers (2 Cor. 3:18), will reach completion. John states finally that this transformation will take place because we shall see

---

[27]*The Methodist Hymnbook,* No. 745.

[28]The NIV adopts the generally accepted punctuation of the verse. F. C. Synge, "1 John 3, 2," JTS ns 3, 1952, 79, proposed placing a stop after ἐφανερώθη, giving the rendering: "Now we are the children of God, and he has not yet been revealed. We know what we shall be, for, if he is revealed, we shall be like him, for we shall see him as he is." This rendering has found its way into the NEB margin, but has otherwise not attracted any support. Schnackenburg, 170 n. 5, rightly observes that it disturbs the parallelism of the verse.

[29]The NIV text and margin give the two possibilities of understanding the subject of φανερωθῇ as either Jesus or "it" (*sc.* what we shall be). In favor of the second interpretation it is argued: (1) the change in reference of φανερόω from verse 2a ("it") to verse 2b ("Jesus") is improbable; (2) the introduction of Jesus into a context describing the Father (v. 1) is unlikely; (3) the person whom we are to be like is God, not Jesus (Schnackenburg, 170; Haas, 78f.). These reasons are unconvincing. John has already used φανερόω of the parousia in verse 28, and a change in meaning would be strange; there is, however, nothing unusual in the same verb being used in a different sense in an intervening sentence; in both cases the contexts make clear which sense is present. Further, it is difficult, if not impossible, to give a clear sense to "if/when it is revealed." A reference to Jesus is not at all strange, since, as we have seen, John can switch rapidly from Father to Son and vice versa. It is also more probable that our future likeness is to the Son (Chaine, 179) rather than the Father (de Jonge, 135f.).

him as he is.[30] The thought is that the effect of seeing Jesus is to make us like him, just as a mirror reflects the image of the person in front of it: "we, who with unveiled faces all reflect the Lord's glory, are being transformed into his likeness with ever-increasing glory" (2 Cor. 3:18).

3 All this is a solid basis for Christian confidence and joy, and it is one of John's aims to strengthen this aspect of his readers' faith. Living in a hostile world, and perhaps with their confidence shaken by the secession of a sizable number of their fellow-church members who proclaimed that they possessed the truth, they needed to be encouraged. John does this by telling them of their privileges as Christians and developing the thought of their hope which rests on Christ.[31] But, as so often in Christian teaching, doctrine has moral implications. Although John has just told us that seeing Jesus will make us like him, it is also true that the condition for seeing Jesus is that we should be morally fit to come into his presence. "Blessed are the pure in heart, for they will see God" (Mt. 5:8).[32] John was aware that his readers needed to achieve this purity of heart, and therefore he encouraged them to seek to be pure, and so to be like Jesus.[33] The word "pure" is found only here in the Epistle. It was used to denote

---

[30]The construction is ambiguous. (1) ὅτι ὀψόμεθα . . . may depend on ἐσόμεθα: "we know that because we shall see him we shall be like him." The thought then is that seeing Jesus produces likeness to him (2 Cor. 3:18; Col. 3:4). (2) ὅτι ὀψόμεθα . . . may depend on οἴδαμεν: "our knowledge that we shall be like him rests on the fact that we shall see him." This may mean: (a) Likeness to Jesus results from the fact that, as we know, we shall see him. This is the same as view (1). (b) The fact that we are to see him means that we shall be like him, since being like him is the condition for seeing him. This is the thought in Matthew 5:8, and it comes out clearly in the exhortation in verse 3; cf. 4:17. This interpretation is much less likely; it depends on the unexpressed premise that we must be like him in order to see him. In favor of (2a) Schnackenburg, 172, cites the parallel in 3:14 which must undoubtedly be understood in this way. Since views (1) and (2a) give the same result, it may be that John himself could not have distinguished clearly which construction he was using. The origins of the ideas of seeing God and becoming like him have been sought in pagan religion (Windisch, 120; W. Bousset, *Kyrios Christos*, Nashville, 1970, 220–227). However, the concept of seeing God is fully at home in Judaism (cf. Ps. 11:7; 17:15; 42:1–5; SB I, 206–215), as is that of becoming like him (SB III, 777); see Chaine, 180; Schnackenburg, 171–173.

[31]ἐλπὶς ἐπ' αὐτῷ means "hope resting on, i.e. in, him (Christ)"; BD 235[2] and 187[6]. The concept of "hope" is not found elsewhere in the Johannine literature (except Jn. 5:45).

[32]The tension between these two statements is perhaps to be explained in terms of the distinction between moral fitness for the presence of Christ and the divine reward which is granted at the parousia.

[33]For the use of ἐκεῖνος to refer to Jesus see 2:6. The change of pronoun does not mean that αὐτῷ must refer to God rather than Jesus.

the outward spotlessness of objects or persons involved in worship (Jn. 11:5), but in a Christian context it is obviously moral purity that is meant.[34] The following verses show that for John purity meant freedom from sin. Those who hope to come into the presence of the pure Son of God must themselves be pure. Here, then, we have the moral outworking of the continuing spiritual union with Jesus with which this section of the Epistle began.

The importance of this section as a whole is that it draws attention to the reality and the incompleteness of Christian experience. Christians who are in doubt about their standing need to be reassured that those who do what is right have been born of God and belong to him. They have all the privileges of God's children. At the same time, however, they need to be warned against any self-satisfaction or feeling that they have achieved all that is possible in Christian experience. To think in this way is to ignore the dimension of hope. It is to suggest that God has already done all that he can do, and that he has no further moves open to him. Worse still, it is to acquiesce in the present sorry state of the world and of ourselves, the situation in which the true light is shining but only in the midst of darkness. We have to be reminded of the hope of a future consummation and encouraged to live in the light of that great event.

A. M. Hunter cites the saying of a farm laborer, engaged in a lowly task, to Robert Louis Stevenson: "Him that has aye something ayont (or, as the English would say, 'always something ahead of him') need never be weary." Hunter applies this to the spirit of 1 Peter,[35] but it is equally true of this passage in 1 John. Without the dimension of hope life is empty.

Perhaps no other version brings out the significance of the section so well as the paraphrase whose opening verse was quoted earlier:

> *Concealed as yet this honour lies,*
> *By this dark world unknown, —*
> *A world that knew not when he came,*
> *Even God's eternal Son.*
>
> *High is the rank we now possess;*
> *But higher we shall rise;*
> *Though what we shall hereafter be*
> *Is hid from mortal eyes.*

[34]For ritual purity see Exodus 19:10; Numbers 8:21; John 11:55; Acts 21:24, 26; 24:18; for moral purity see James 4:8; 1 Peter 1:22, *et al.*; F. Hauck, TDNT I, 122–124.
[35]A. M. Hunter, *Introducing the New Testament*, London, 1945, 99.

Our souls, we know, when he appears,
Shall bear his image bright;
For all his glory, full disclosed,
Shall·open to our sight.

A hope so great, and so divine,
May trials well endure;
And purge the soul from sense and sin,
As Christ himself is pure.

THE SINLESSNESS OF GOD'S CHILDREN (3:4–10)

4. *Everyone who sins breaks the law; in fact, sin is lawlessness.*
5. *But you know that he appeared so that he might take away our*
sins. And in him is no sin. 6. *No one who lives in him keeps on*
sinning. No one who continues to sin has either seen him or known
him.
    7. *Dear children, do not let anyone lead you astray. He who does*
what is right is righteous, just as he is righteous. 8. *He who does*
what is sinful is of the devil, because the devil has been sinning
from the beginning. The reason the Son of God appeared was to
destroy the devil's work. 9. *No one who is born of God will con-*
tinue to sin, because God's seed remains in him; he cannot sin,
because he has been born of God. 10. *This is how we know who*
the children of God are and who the children of the devil are: Any-
one who does not do what is right is not a child of God; neither is
anyone who does not love his brother.

In the preceding section John has been stressing the importance of
continuing in Christ, doing what is right, and purifying oneself in
anticipation of his coming. Now he deals more closely with the
negative side of all this, the need for believers to abstain from sin
and the possibility of their doing so. The world is divided into the
children of God and the children of the devil, characterized by righteousness and sin respectively: it follows that the children of God
cannot and must not sin. In the following section John will turn from
the negative, moral imperative to the positive aspect of righteousness, expressed in love for one another.

    4   The discussion begins somewhat abruptly with defini-
tions of sinners and sin. The word "sin" was last used in 2:12, but
now we have a succession of five verses in which it is repeatedly
used. John's concern is to make it clear to his readers that sin is what
he calls "lawlessness," and he hammers the point home by repeti-

175

tion. But why did John have to emphasize this point, and what is the significance of it? It seems most likely that the readers were being tempted to regard sin as a matter of indifference: to fall into sin was not a serious matter. At the beginning of the letter we saw that there were people in the church who claimed to be sinless, and that John had the task of showing them that they were not in fact free from sin, and that they needed to seek cleansing and forgiveness. Perhaps these same people argued that even if they did commit sin, it was not a matter of any great moment. After all, as John himself taught, there was ready pardon for the person who confessed his sin. Paul had to face a similar problem with people who argued that Christians could sin with impunity and God would be gracious to them (Rom. 6:1). But both Paul and John were emphatic that this was not the case. To argue in this way reflected a false understanding of sin.

What, then, is sin? What John says here has been understood in two slightly different ways. According to the traditional understanding of the passage John is saying that sin is a moral (or, rather, an immoral) action, consisting in the breaking of God's law—and this is why it is so serious.[1] Elsewhere we find the same equation of sin and lawbreaking.[2] But there is some reason to doubt whether this is precisely what John meant. The word "lawlessness" occurs only here in the Epistle, and the word "law" is completely absent. This makes it hard to see why John introduces the idea of lawbreaking as such at this point, and why its use would have counted as an argument with his readers. It has been suggested that the Greek word used here has a different connotation. It is used in 2 Thessalonians 2:3, 7 to describe "the man of lawlessness" who will be opposed to Christ at his second coming. This and other references suggest that the word was associated with the final outbreak of evil against Christ and that it signifies rebellion against the will of God.[3] To commit sin is thus to place oneself on the side of the devil and the antichrist and to stand in opposition to Christ. If this view is correct, the idea of

[1]So, for example, Westcott, 102; Stott, 122; Houlden, 92.
[2]ἀνομία and ἁμαρτία are equivalent expressions in Psalm 32:1f. (Rom. 4:7f.) and Jeremiah 31 (38):34 (Heb. 10:17).
[3]In the LXX ἀνομία translates a number of words for "sin," and the link with the law is weak. A number of passages in Jewish texts regard ἀνομία (Heb. 'āwel, 'awlāh) as hostility to God in an eschatological context (T.Dan 5:4–6; T.Naph. 4:1; 1QS 1:23f.; 3:18–21; 4:19f., et al.). See further Matthew 7:23; 13:41; 23:28; 24:12; Mark 16:14f. For this interpretation see especially I. de la Potterie, "Le péché, c'est l'iniquité (I Joh., III, 4)," Nouvelle Revue Théologique 78, 1956, 785–797; revised and translated in I. de la Potterie and S. Lyonnet, The Christian Lives by the Spirit, 37–55; cf. Schnackenburg, 186f.; Bultmann, 50; de Jonge, 141–143; Haas, 81.

"law" contained in the Greek word, according to its etymology, has been obscured and the stress falls more on the idea of opposition to God which is inherent in disregarding his law.[4] The advantages of taking the word in this way are that it fits in with John's earlier teaching on the presence of antichrists in the world, and that it associates this section of the letter closely with the immediately preceding section: one cannot hope for the appearing of Christ and at the same time persist in the sin which signifies rebellion against him. Sin is not a matter of isolated peccadillos: it is an expression of siding with God's ultimate enemy—the devil (vv. 8–10).

5   A further reason why the Christian should not sin[5] is that God's opposition to it is to be seen in the coming of Jesus. It is universally known, says John,[6] that Jesus[7] appeared in this world in order to take away sins.[8] The verb here means "to take away" sins, rather than "to atone for" sins, but if we ask how Jesus takes away our sins, the answer must be that he does so as the Lamb of God whose blood atones for sin. John's language here echoes John 1:29 where Jesus, the Lamb of God, takes away the sin of the world.[9] But the writer's purpose here is not so much to assure his readers that their sins have been taken away as to indicate that the One who came to take away sins must obviously stand in opposition to sin. Not only so, but his opposition to sin is further indicated by his own lack of sin.[10] He is the Righteous One (2:1), and the Pure One (3:3), a thought which is amply confirmed elsewhere in the New Testa-

[4]For this shift in meaning we may perhaps compare the New Testament usage of ἡ βασιλεία τοῦ Θεοῦ, where the idea of God's *rule* or *kingdom* appears to have dropped into the background compared with that of God's powerful intervention to save and bless his people.

[5]The NIV translates the connective καί by "but," which expresses the contrast with verse 4 but obscures the fact that the two verses are parallel in intention.

[6]οἴδατε refers to elementary Christian knowledge, perhaps acquired in the instruction of new converts (Schnackenburg, 187).

[7]Greek ἐκεῖνος; cf. 2:6.

[8]Some MSS add ἡμῶν (S *pm* vg sy^p co; TR), possibly influenced by 2:2; 4:10 (Metzger, 712). *Diglot* accepts the reading, presumably as being in accordance with Johannine style, despite the poor external attestation.

[9]To "bear sin" is to remove or forgive it (αἴρω, 1 Sam. 15:25; 25:28) or to atone for it by bearing its consequences (λαμβάνω, Num. 14:34; Ezek. 18:19f.; ἀναφέρω, Num. 14:33; Isa. 53:11f.). If the former rendering gives the correct meaning of the verb in the present context, we have still to ask in what way the sin is removed. No answer is given in the present context, but since in John 1:29 it is the Lamb of God who takes away sin, we are bound to think of his representative bearing of sin and the consequent atoning power of his death (cf. 1 Jn. 2:2; 4:10; 1 Pet. 2:24); see SB II, 363–370; J. Jeremias, TDNT I, 185f.; K. Weiss, TDNT IX, 60f.

[10]It is significant that John uses the present tense to refer to the sinlessness of Jesus; it is not simply his earthly life that is in mind but his eternal character as the Son of God.

ment.[11] It follows that, at the very least, his people should be opposed to sin. But John is even more emphatic.

6 Nobody who lives in Christ does sin, claims John. And, lest we should be in any doubt on the point, he reinforces it by denying its antithesis: anybody who does sin has neither seen him nor come to know him. The same thing is said in a different form in verse 8 and verse 10, and, most clearly of all, John affirms in verse 9 that a person who has been born of God *cannot* sin, because he has been born of God. John thus appears to be stating that the Christian is sinless. But this at once raises difficulties of two kinds. The first is that elsewhere in this Epistle John allows for the possibility of sin by believers (1:8, 10; 2:1; 5:16), and also that much of what he says is in the form of exhortation to his readers not to sin but to practice righteousness (2:1, 15, 29; 3:12, 18; 5:21). Clearly John did not regard what he says here as being incompatible with the possibility, and indeed the fact, of sin in the lives of his readers. The second fact is that what John allows for in his readers is confirmed by our own personal experience. Few Christians would claim to be sinless in practice or free from the fear of yielding to temptation. The vast majority of Christians would have to confess their own continuing sinfulness, and many Christian theologians would deny any theoretical possibility of sinlessness.[12] How, then, is the present passage to be explained?

(1) We can begin by ruling out the possibility that John is making a statement which in his belief was true of only one group of Christians. Nothing suggests that he had in mind a group of "super-Christians," living a Christian life of a higher quality than is possible for other believers. His language is absolute, and refers to what is true of everyone.

(2) A second type of explanation is concerned with the possibility that John is referring to some particular type of sin. J. R. W. Stott cites the view of J. H. A. Ebrard that wilful and deliberate sin is in mind, as opposed to the involuntary sins and errors into which a Christian may fall without intending consciously to sin against God.[13] But this explanation is older than the nineteenth-

---

The thought is not of his fitness to take away sin, but rather of his total opposition to sin, a character which should be shared by believers.

[11]2 Corinthians 5:21; Hebrews 4:15; 1 Peter 3:18; cf. John 8:46; 1 Peter 2:22.

[12]So especially B. B. Warfield, *Perfectionism,* Philadelphia, 1931–32; L. Berkhof, *Systematic Theology,* Grand Rapids/London, 1958, 537–540.

[13]Stott, 134.

century commentator. It goes back at least as far as John Wesley in whose sermon on this text sin is defined as "an actual, voluntary transgression of the law; of the revealed, written law of God; of any commandment of God, acknowledged to be such at the time that it is transgressed."[14] It may, then, be allowed that a Christian can commit errors and involuntary sins, but this need not take away the possibility of a life of conscious, complete conformity to the will of God. But this solution faces three difficulties. One is that by itself it is an inadequate solution to the problems of the text. Wesley himself has to admit that even saintly people (he cites David and Peter) could commit gross, deliberate sins, and therefore he has to admit that, even with this limited definition of sin, the text represents an ideal rather than something that is universally true of all believers. The second difficulty is that it is notoriously difficult to distinguish between voluntary and involuntary transgressions; we can never be sure that even our best deeds are entirely free from selfish motives, or that our errors were in no way due to our own fault. And, third, the crucial objection is that there is no indication that John is working with such a limited definition of the term sin. He is talking about all sin.

This last-mentioned objection also holds good against the suggestion that what John means here is "sin that does not lead to death," as opposed to the "sin that leads to death" (5:16f.); on this view, the sin that leads to death is something that can be committed only by unbelievers, whereas the sins committed by believers do not count as sins. Since immediately after these verses John states that believers do not sin (5:18), it is argued that two different concepts of sin must be in view, and that it is only the "sin that leads to death" which is in John's mind when he says that believers do not sin.[15] Whatever be the right interpretation of this difficult passage, it is unlikely that John's readers could be expected to anticipate the definitions given in it at this earlier point in the Epistle. It remains true that John is talking here about sin in general.

---

[14]J. Wesley, *Sermons on Several Occasions*, London, 1944, 178; see further, *A Plain Account of Christian Perfection*, Naperville/London, 1952; for the Wesleyan view see R. N. Flew, *The Idea of Perfection in Christian Theology*, Atlantic Highlands, NJ/Oxford, 1934; W. E. Sangster, *The Path to Perfection*, London, 1943; H. Lindström, *Wesley and Sanctification*, London, 1950; I. H. Marshall, "Sanctification in the Teaching of John Wesley and John Calvin," EQ 34, 1962, 75–82.

[15]D. M. Scholer, "Sins Within and Sins Without: An Interpretation of 1 John 5:16–17," in G. F. Hawthorne (ed.), *Current Issues in Biblical and Patristic Interpretation*, Grand Rapids, 1975, 230–246, especially 244f.

(3) A third type of solution is represented by the translation offered by the NIV, which stresses that the verbs are in the present tense and takes them in a continuous sense: "no one who lives in him *keeps on* sinning." The explanation is thus that the believer does not sin habitually. He may sin on occasion; indeed advocates of this view note that in 2:1 the aorist tense, which can express a single act, is used. But he will not make sin his deliberate habit. This is perhaps the most popular understanding of the passage among British commentators.[16] It has the merit of providing a view of the life of the believer which is consistent with New Testament teaching generally: the Christian is a person whose heart is set on pleasing God and who therefore cannot make sin his way of life, even if he may lapse from his high intent.

But this view is not free from difficulty. It involves translators in stressing the present continuous form of the verb in a way which they do not do elsewhere in the New Testament. It has also been observed that in 5:16 John uses the present tense of the sins of believers, and that therefore his practice is not consistent. Further, John says that the believer does not sin because God's seed remains in him (3:9) and the Son of God keeps him safe (5:18). But it is hard to see why God preserves him from some sins, but not from all sins. We must, therefore, wonder whether an important point of interpretation can be made to rest on what has been called a grammatical subtlety.[17]

(4) So we turn to a fourth type of solution, which in one way or another suggests that what John is depicting here is the ideal character of the Christian. The simplest form of this view is that the verse depicts what ought to be the character of the Christian. The saying is to be "explained by the analogy of (the Apostle's) way of speaking throughout the Epistle of the ideal reality of the life of God and the life of sin as absolutely excluding one another," says Alford.[18]

This basic thought can then be developed in various ways. Thus Dodd in particular has argued that the writer's absolute way of writing was dictated by the polemical situation in which he found himself. He was writing from a different point of view from that of chapter 1. Some of his opponents thought that they were already

---

[16]Westcott, 104; Ross, 183; Stott, 135f.; Morris, 1265.
[17]See the criticisms by S. Kubo, "1 John 3, 9: Absolute or Habitual?", *Andrews University Seminary Studies* 7, 1969, 47–56 (summarized in NTA 14, 1969, § 290).
[18]Alford, 465.

perfect, and it is their moral complacency which is attacked in the strongest terms in chapter 1: "if we claim to be without sin, we deceive ourselves." Others, however, thought that it did not matter whether they were virtuous or not. To combat this point of view, "the author uses all the resources of antithesis to set forth the essential polarity of ethical religion. God and the devil, children of God and children of the devil, doing right and doing wrong—these represent absolute contraries. . . . To claim to be a child of God, and yet to be indifferent to moral obligations, is to confuse the whole issue. Of the personal problem raised for one who acknowledges all this, and yet is conscious of sin, he is not at the moment thinking."[19] Thus the strong language of John is due to the exigencies of polemic, and may perhaps be described as pardonable exaggeration.

Another, complementary way of regarding John's statements is to see them as implicit imperatives. They are statements of what Christians ought to be, and are thus injunctions to them to approach the ideal. This feature will obviously be present in any attempt to interpret John's teaching as the presentation of an ideal.

Other scholars have suggested that there is an implicit condition in John's statement. "No one who lives in him keeps on sinning": the implication is that so long as a person abides in Christ, he will be free from sin.[20] There is good pastoral advice here. The best counsel for a person who is faced by temptation to sin may well not be, "Don't do it," which directs the person's mind toward the temptation itself, but rather, "Live in Christ," which turns the person's attention positively toward his Savior and diverts it from the temptation. It is as our hearts are filled with love by the Spirit that they become incapable of harboring sinful desires. Nevertheless, it is to be noted that while verse 6 may well be taken in this way, there is difficulty in interpreting verse 9 in the same way, since it says that anyone born of God cannot sin.[21]

It would seem that this view too is not without difficulty. We may perhaps make further progress by asking what ideas may lie behind John's teaching here. Dodd and others have observed that in Jewish literature of the time we can find the expectation that when

---

[19]Dodd, 78–81.
[20]Classically put by Bede: *"in quantum in eo manet in tantum non peccat"* ("in so far as he abides in him, he does not sin"; cited by Alford, 465). Similarly, Brooke, 86; cf. Plummer, 124; Bruce, 90; Houlden, 94. For these commentators the statements express a hope or state a moral ideal: it is unthinkable that a Christian should sin, and so Christians ought not to sin.
[21]See the criticisms made by Stott, 132–134.

God inaugurates the Age to Come it will be characterized by perfection, and those found worthy of admission to it will be free from sin.[22] This hope is of course squarely founded on expectations already found in the Old Testament: "I will put my spirit within you, and cause you to walk in my statutes and be careful to observe my ordinances" (Ezek. 36:27).[23] In view of the teaching in the New Testament generally, it would not be surprising if the early church concluded that the age of fulfilment had come, and that therefore God's people could now expect to be sinless. The texts under review thus express the eschatological reality brought about by the coming of Jesus.

We may now conclude that our texts express the possibility which is placed before every believer, the possibility of a life free from sin. At the same time, however, it is necessary to observe that what is said from the point of view of the realization of God's promises must be carefully qualified. Paul found it necessary to deal with people in the church at Corinth and Philippi who thought that they were experiencing the life of the Age to Come in all its fulness and could regard themselves as "perfect." He had in effect to remind them that the Christian lives "between the times," in the period of overlap between the end of the old age and the beginning of the new, the period when the Christian is still subject to temptation, mortality, and imperfection. Yet in the midst of this situation the Christian can grasp the new life of the Spirit and is being changed into the likeness of Christ; only at the consummation will the process be completed. John shares (not unnaturally) the same basic outlook, as we have already seen (2:8). He is only too well aware of the presence of temptation and of the danger of Christians succumbing to its attraction. Indeed, he protests against any claim by Christians to be free from sin. What he is describing here therefore is the eschatological reality, the possibility that is open to believers, which is both a fact ("he cannot sin") and conditional ("[if he] lives in him"). It is a reality which is continually threatened by the tensions of living in the sinful world, and yet one which is capable of being realized by faith.[24]

---

[22]"And then there shall be bestowed upon the elect wisdom, And they shall all live and never again sin, Either through ungodliness or through pride: But they who are wise shall be humble" (1 Enoch 5:8); cf. *Testament of Levi* 18:9; 1QS 4:20–23; *Psalms of Solomon* 17:32.

[23]Cf. Jeremiah 31:33f.

[24]See especially I. de la Potterie, "The Impeccability of the Christian according to I John 3, 6–9," in I. de la Potterie and S. Lyonnet, *The Christian Lives by the Spirit,*

Despite its apparent subtlety this view is probably the most satisfactory of the various alternatives which we have discussed. Its strength is that it builds on the general understanding of God's eschatological action found in early Christianity; at the same time it avoids limited definitions of the nature of sin. Further, it fits in with the rest of John's teaching. John summons believers to become what they are, in the same way as Paul urges the "saints" to live as saints. Sinlessness is not a negative virtue: it includes full observance of God's positive commands. John speaks of Christians as those who do observe God's commands, and yet he has to counsel them to keep those very commands. A person who does not love his brother is not a child of God (3:10); nevertheless, believers need to be exhorted to love their brothers (3:11; 4:7). "Become what you are," is John's message.

We can regard this verse as a practical conclusion to what John has been saying in the previous verses. Sin is incompatible with being a child of God. God's intention is that the believer should be free from sin. Consequently, it can also be said that if a person does continue in sin, it is a sign that he is lacking in true Christian experience. Here John appears to be thinking of the Christian confession which might be made by a person whose way of life belies what he says. "I have come to know him" is an apt description of Christian conversion (cf. 2:4). "I have seen him" is a less obvious form of confession, since it can safely be said that few, if any, of John's readers could have seen the earthly Jesus. The same kind of language is used in 3 John 11, where the point is put negatively, with respect to God: "Anyone who does what is evil has not seen God." Clearly, "seeing" with the eyes is not meant.[25] John is thinking

---

175–196. See also Dodd, 79f. De Jonge, 151–154, notes particularly how in the intertestamental literature God's people will be known as his children in the last days, and claims that "being born of God" (v. 9) is a similar expression. Windisch, 121f., recognizes correctly the nature of the eschatological hope of perfection expressed here, but goes astray in claiming that it cannot be harmonized with John's earlier statements about the sinfulness of Christians. Bultmann, 51–53, emphasizes the twofold nature of the situation: the new birth of the Christian (v. 9) gives him the possibility of sinlessness, but this possibility becomes a reality only on the condition of abiding in Christ (v. 6). H.-M. Schenke, "Determination und Ethik im ersten Johannesbrief," ZTK 60, 1963, 203–215, draws attention to the way in which statements about the Christian's sinlessness and exhortations to right conduct lie side by side in the Epistle; the problem is accordingly that of the relationship between determinism and obligation.

[25]There is thus a contrast with the literal seeing of Jesus in 1:1–3, and also with the impossibility of seeing God (4:20); cf. John 6:40, 62; 12:44f.; 14:19; 16:10, 16f.; W. Michaelis, TDNT V, 361–366.

rather of "seeing" the significance of Jesus as the one who reveals the unseen God. The perfect tense of the verb will then denote the initial act of conversion which leads on to a continuing experience. John's point is that nobody can go through such an experience and remain capable of sinning. In fact, however, as our own experience demonstrates, it is all too easy to "see" Jesus Christ and yet fall back into sin. John is again stating the "ideal," and his statement, though indicative and factual in terms of syntax, is logically an imperative or statement of obligation.

7 All this is in a sense clear enough: the incompatibility of being a Christian and continuing in sin could not be more sharply expressed. Nevertheless, there must have been people who contested John's statement and who were trying to mislead the congregation. So John repeats and amplifies the point in terms of fatherly counsel. He begins by looking at the positive side of the matter. It looks as though the church contained people who claimed to be believers and perhaps even called themselves "righteous," which would be an understandable self-description, drawn from the Old Testament.[26] If so, the word may have been used in a rather formal way to express "belonging to the divine sphere"[27] rather than to describe people who were, or tried to be, righteous in conduct. But John insists on the fact that the proper use of the adjective is as a description of people who actually do what is righteous. In this way they are like Jesus.

8 John has been talking of sin in terms of rebellion against God. Now he goes over the same ground once again, this time bringing out the fact that sin is instigated by the devil. There is a close parallelism between verses 4–6 and 8f.; in each case John states the nature or origin of sin, shows how the Son of God is opposed to sin, and then draws the conclusion that believers cannot and should not sin.[28] The person who sins belongs to the devil's side or draws his inspiration from him.[29] This follows from the fact that right from the very beginning the devil has been active in sin:[30] consequently he

[26]Daniel 12:3; Matthew 25:37, 46; 1 Peter 3:12; 4:18; Hebrews 12:23; Revelation 22:11.
[27]Houlden, 88.
[28]Stott, 121.
[29]The meaning of ἐκ τοῦ διαβόλου is not certain. It may express belonging to the devil or originating from him.
[30]The present tense is used of an activity begun in the past and still continuing. ἀπ' ἀρχῆς may mean: (1) from the beginning of the devil's existence (Bultmann, 52 n. 35); (2) from the beginning of human sin (Schnackenburg, 189); (3) "all along" (Brooke, 88). Probably view (3) should be adopted, although John has the story of the fall in mind.

must be regarded as the originator and instigator of sin. Presumably John, who is well acquainted with the early chapters of Genesis (v. 12), is making the identification between the devil and the serpent which we find in Revelation 12:9; 20:2.[31] Two ideas are then used to bring out the relationship between sinners and the devil. One is the idea of paternity: sinners can be said to have their origin in the devil as their father (Jn. 8:44), since they show the family likeness. The other idea is that of the two spirits, found in the Qumran texts, according to which men are dominated either by the spirit of truth or by the spirit of perversity.[32] Men cannot be neutral: they must belong to one side or the other. John is doing his best to make it absolutely clear that persons who fail to do righteousness do not belong to God but to God's enemy.

That the actions of the devil and his children are opposed to God is now stressed once again (cf. v. 5) by a further reference to the work of Jesus. The Son of God appeared in the world for the express purpose of undoing the work of the devil. Here John assumes the reality of the incarnation, which was accepted by his adherents but doubted by his opponents (2:22f.). It was *God's* Son who acted against the devil—and from this the attitude of God the Father can be deduced. Readers familiar with John's Gospel would need no proof that Jesus came to defeat the devil (Jn. 12:31), but the thought is common enough in the New Testament (Mt. 4:1–11; 12:25–29; Lk. 10:18; Rev. 12:7–12; 20:1–3).[33] The actual word used here, however, "to destroy" is somewhat unusual: the task of Jesus was to undo whatever the devil had achieved, to thwart whatever he tries to do. No doubt it is his "work" of temptation and enslaving men that is in view.[34]

9 Still following the same pattern of thought as in verses 5f., John draws the conclusion that those who are on the same side as the Son of God, the great opponent of the devil, cannot follow the devil's way and live in sin. He takes up the idea of being born of God, which was introduced in 2:29, where it was said positively that those who do what is right demonstrate that they are God's children. Later on we shall be told that God's children are characterized by love for one another (4:7), belief in Jesus (5:1), and victory over the world (5:4). Now the same point can be made negatively: a person

---

[31]On the devil see further 3:12; 5:18f., where he is "the evil one"; Stott, 136–138.
[32]1QS 3:13–4:26.
[33]R. Leivestad, *Christ the Conqueror,* Naperville/London, 1954.
[34]F. Büchsel, TDNT IV, 336. Cf. Ignatius, *Eph.* 19:3; 13:1.

who is born of God does not sin.[35] John makes his statements in absolute terms: the way in which he can interchange subjects and predicates indicates that there is a one-to-one correspondence between those who are born of God and those who do what is right, love one another, believe in Jesus, overcome the world, and refrain from sin. There are no shades of grey here: it is a case of belonging to the light or the darkness, to God or the devil, to righteousness and love or to sin.

It is this divine birth which is the explanation of the moral character of a child of God. He does not continue in sin because God's seed remains in him. It is possible to take "God's seed" to mean "God's offspring"; such a person cannot sin because he abides in God.[36] But this interpretation has found little favor, and most commentators take "seed" to refer metaphorically to a divine principle of life which abides in the believer. John is using the metaphor of a seed planted in the heart which produces new life, just as in Jesus' parable of the sower the seed planted in receptive soil is the Word of God which "grows" into eternal life.[37] There is some doubt whether the seed is intended to signify the Holy Spirit (Jn. 3:6, 9) or the Word of God (Lk. 8:11; Jas. 1:18, 23; 1 Pet. 1:23, 25). Probably these two ideas are to be linked together, just as was the case in John's description of the "anointing" of believers (2:20, 27).[38] The Spirit is operative in the preaching of the Word which

[35]John uses πᾶς . . . οὐ . . . as an equivalent to οὐδείς . . . (Moule, 168, 182). The NIV rendering "will continue to sin" translates a present indicative, and is open to the same objections as the corresponding rendering in verse 6.
[36]So Moffatt; RSV margin; Alexander, 86f. The use of σπέρμα collectively in this sense is well attested (Lk. 1:55; Gal. 3:29; Jn. 8:33, 37). The objections are that on this view σπέρμα ought to have the article, and that the rendering produces a tautology. Neither of these objections is convincing. Bruce, 92, retains this as a possible interpretation of the passage.
[37]The metaphor must not be pressed too far, or else the believer becomes merely the soil in which the plant of eternal life grows.
[38]For taking "seed" as the Spirit see Brooke, 89; Schnackenburg, 190f.; for taking it as the Word see Dodd, 77f.; and for a combination of Word and Spirit see Ross, 185; de Jonge, 148–151 (primarily, Word); S. Schulz, TDNT VII, 545. Others think more generally of the divine principle of life or the new nature of the believer (Westcott, 107; Bultmann, 52; cf. Bruce, 92). Parallels have been sought with Hellenistic ideas of the implanting of a divine principle in man (Dodd, 76f., cites CH 1:12–15, 24–26; Philo, *Quod deterius potiori insidiari solet* 22; *De vita Mosis* 1:279; Hippolytus, *Refutatio* 5:26–28; 5:8:28f.; Irenaeus, AH 1:1:10, 12–13; Clement, *Excerpta ex Theodoti* 38, 40, 49, 53). See further Windisch, 122f.; Bultmann, 52 n. 36. De Jonge, 150, and Schnackenburg, 191, remain sceptical over against attempts to derive John's thought from Hellenism and Gnosticism, the former stressing the close relationship of John's language to that used elsewhere in the New Testament in connection with baptism.

produces the new birth in the hearts of those who hear it and respond with faith (1 Thess. 1:5f.). As a result of the continuing presence of the Word in the believer's heart through the Spirit he cannot
sin. Whatever is born of God must share God's character, and his
opposition to sin. It should be unthinkable for such a person to sin.

10 The conclusion of the whole matter is now drawn.[39] In
the light of all that has been said it is possible to distinguish who are
the children of God and who are the children of the devil by what
they do. The test offered is the negative one. A person who does not
do what is right is not a child of God. And lest there be any doubt
about what this means, John amplifies his statement in terms of love
for one's brothers—the theme which he will develop more broadly
in the next section.

Here, then, the readers have a criterion by which to test
people who claim to be children of God or "righteous" people—and
also, at the same time, to test themselves. For those who wish to be
God's children the lesson is obvious. They must examine themselves to see whether they do what is right. This could be hard
advice for a believer who is all too conscious of his own sins and is
lacking in confidence; he could well be tempted to doubt his own
status as a child of God. Hence it is not surprising that commentators have attempted to water down John's teaching to refer merely
to the believer's freedom from habitual sin. But we must not misin-
terpret the text for pastoral reasons. Properly interpreted, the text
remains a source of comfort.[40] John is describing the ideal character
of the Christian, ideal in the sense that this is the reality intended by
God for him, even if he falls short of it while he still lives in this
sinful world. The person who is conscious of the new beginning that
God has made in his life will seek to let that divine ideal become
more and more of a reality. He knows that he cannot claim
sinlessness—for he has already read the first chapter of this
Epistle—but at the same time he can claim God's power to enable
him not to sin. This is the tension in which the Christian lives, and
John has portrayed it realistically. The believer, conscious of sin,
need not, therefore, lose heart: this section is a promise of what God
intends him to be, and he looks forward to the time when he shall be

[39]ἐν τούτῳ refers both forward and backward: in view of what has just been said it
is clear who are the children of God . . . , namely in view of the principle that anyone
who does not do what is right . . . (Windisch, 123; Schnackenburg, 192 n. 2). See
2:5 n.
[40]Houlden, 96f., finds John's statements impossible to reconcile with the fact of
sinfulness among his readers.

like Christ at his appearing. To maintain the balance between warning believers of the seriousness of their falling into sin and consoling those who are overwhelmed by their sins is not easy; John's attention moves from the one to the other, and we must allow both types of statement to have their full effect.

BROTHERLY LOVE AS THE MARK
OF THE CHRISTIAN (3:11–18)

11. *This is the message you heard from the beginning: We should love one another.* 12. *Do not be like Cain, who belonged to the evil one and murdered his brother. And why did he murder him? Because his own actions were evil and his brother's were righteous.* 13. *Do not be surprised, my brothers, if the world hates you.* 14. *We know that we have passed from death to life, because we love our brothers. Anyone who does not love remains in death.* 15. *Anyone who hates his brother is a murderer, and you know that no murderer has eternal life in him.*

16. *This is how we know what love is: Jesus Christ laid down his life for us. And we ought to lay down our lives for our brothers.* 17. *If anyone has material possessions and sees his brother in need but has no pity on him, how can the love of God be in him?* 18. *Dear children, let us not love with words or tongue but with actions and in truth.*

Having established that the children of God are characterized by righteousness and freedom from sin, John now describes them as people who love one another. But, although this is their character (v. 14), it is nevertheless necessary to urge them to love one another (vv. 11, 18). The nature of brotherly love is illustrated negatively by the contrast with Cain who murdered his brother and positively by the example of Jesus Christ who laid down his own life for us. Each of these illustrations is followed by a corollary. Thus believers must not be surprised if they are hated by people like Cain, and they must avoid the feelings of hatred which are tantamount to murder. In the same way, the positive example of Christ's self-sacrifice leads to an appeal for a practical love which goes beyond feelings to costly sharing of one's possessions with the needy. In this way the paragraph is both an appeal for love and an explanation of the nature of love by contrast with its opposite, hatred.

11 The passage is closely linked with the preceding discussion by the linking phrase at the end of verse 10 which is now clarified with a "because" clause.[1] "This is the message" is a repetition of the opening phrase at the beginning of the main body of the Epistle.[2] The statement that "God is light" is now balanced by the imperative "Love one another."[3] This is no new message. The readers have heard it "from the beginning," i.e. of their Christian experience.[4] John is appealing to the traditional nature of the message to emphasize its importance and its truth to his readers who may have been tempted to ignore it in view of the bad example presented by John's opponents. This is the first use in the Epistle of the words "to love one another" (3:23; 4:7, 11, 12; 2 Jn. 5), but the phrase means exactly the same as "to love one's brother" (2:10; 3:10, 14; 4:20f.).[5] John has already made it clear that only those who love their brothers live in the light of God's presence and revelation (2:10), and he now develops this basic thought. Although he speaks of "one another," it is primarily love of one's Christian brothers which he has in mind; this is where Christian love must start. The command to do this goes back to the teaching of Jesus himself (Jn. 13:34f.; 15:12), and hence belongs to the foundation of Christian teaching.

12 As often, John underlines his point by contrasting it with its opposite. Christians are not to be[6] like Cain, the first attested murderer, who drew his inspiration from the evil one, the devil, who is himself the archetypal murderer (Jn. 8:46).[7] The story of Cain

---

[1]ὅτι can function as a coordinating conjunction, equivalent to "for" (BD 456[1]).

[2]Cf. 1:5. The word ἀγγελία is found only in these two places in the New Testament. The variant ἐπαγγελία has considerable support (S 1799 al [h r] bo Lcf), but is due to substitution of the more common word; the text is attested by A B vg sa.

[3]ἀγγελία almost means "command"; the ἵνα clause is an indirect command. αὕτη points forward to the ἵνα clause.

[4]Nevertheless, the command is older than the beginning of the Christian era or the readers' Christian experience, as is shown by the writer's use of Cain as an implicit example of disobedience to the command. Since ἀπ' ἀρχῆς goes with ἠκούσατε, however, it must refer primarily to the beginning of the readers' knowledge of the Christian message, although there may just be an echo of the broader meaning (1:1; Haas, 87). The aorist ἠκούσατε refers to the action of hearing "regarded as a completed whole irrespective of its duration" (Haas, 87).

[5]John speaks in the plural of loving one another and in the singular of loving one's brother; only in 3:14 does he speak in the plural of our loving our brothers.

[6]Literally, "Not as Cain was from the evil one. . . ." Cf. John 6:58; 2 Corinthians 8:5.

[7]The reference to Cain is the only specific Old Testament allusion in 1 John. There is no need to seek some special reason for the use of the Old Testament here; the example was a sufficiently familiar one; cf. Matthew 23:35 par. Luke 11:51; Hebrews 11:4; 12:24; Jude 11; O. H. Steck, *Israel und der gewaltsame Geschick der Propheten*, Neukirchen, 1967. In particular, it is unlikely that there is implicit polemic against a glorification of Cain, such as was practiced by the late second-century sect of Cainites.

The verb σφάζω is often used of violent killing (Rev. 6:4, 9 *et al.*).

shows what failure to love one's brother can lead to—sheer murder—and thus stresses that all hatred is embryonic murder. Jesus did not say that the person who hates his brother has already committed murder in his heart, but he did speak about hatred in the same context as his statement that whoever looks at a woman lustfully has already committed adultery in his heart, and he indicated that the penalty for hatred was the same as that for murder (Mt. 5:21–28). John is simply bringing out the implications of his teaching. But he goes beyond Jesus in asking the question: why do people commit murder?[8] Although he phrases his question in terms of Cain's motive, the following verses make it plain that he is already beginning to think of the reasons why believers are the objects of hatred from the world. The answer given, that his own actions were evil while his brother's were righteous, does not simply mean that Cain killed him because he was inherently wicked. Rather, as a wicked person he hated a good person. According to the story in Genesis, Cain's sacrifice was regarded as unacceptable by God, while Abel's sacrifice was acceptable: Cain's action was evil, while his brother's was righteous. We may, therefore, conclude that John saw Cain's motive as being envy of his brother. He saw that righteous acts won God's approval, and he was angry that this was so.

13 In what is almost a parenthetical comment John reminds his readers that they must show love despite the fact that they will be the objects of hatred by the world. He addresses them as "brothers," a description which is appropriate in the context of discussion of brotherly love and which also indicates that his readers belong to the community of God's people who can expect to be persecuted. They are not to be surprised[9] if the world hates them. For the same situation is present as in the case of Cain and Abel. The world's actions are evil, while those of believers are righteous, and hence the world acts from envy and anger against believers. John clearly has in mind not simply people outside the church who may persecute Christians but also people within the church whose lack of love demonstrates that they are not truly believers.

14 At first sight, the connection of thought is not clear. What John has just been saying is that persons who murder their

---

[8]χάριν can be used as a preposition (normally following the noun it governs) with the sense, "for the sake of, on behalf of, on account of"; cf. Luke 7:47; *1 Clement* 31:2.
[9]It is not clear whether we should read καὶ μή at the beginning of the verse (S C ᵛⁱᵈ P Ψ 1739 r 65 syᵖ arm eth) or simply μή; see Metzger, 712. θαυμάζετε is constructed with εἰ, meaning "that" or "if": hatred by the world is thus a possibility rather than an inevitable fact (BD 454¹).

brothers, like Cain, belong to the evil one; it is implied that persons who hate their brothers belong to the realm of death. Consequently, John is now able to make the converse statement, one which is full of assurance for his readers. We know,[10] he says, that we have passed from death to life because we love our brothers. The proof that a person possesses eternal life is that he shows love for his brothers. But note that John says something more significant than that. He is implicitly asserting that once his readers were in a state of death, from which they have now been transferred to life. John never suggests that some people are by nature endowed with spiritual life; on the contrary, a process of spiritual birth is necessary. It should be emphasized that spiritual life does not result from loving our brothers. Love for our brothers is the evidence, not the basis, for spiritual life.[11] We find the basis in a saying in the Gospel: "I tell you the truth, whoever hears my word and believes him who sent me has eternal life and will not be condemned; he has crossed over from death to life" (Jn. 5:24). It follows that the converse is true: the person who does not show the evidence of loving his brothers is still in the realm of darkness and death.[12] It is from such people that the readers can expect hatred.

15   The final statement in verse 14 is reinforced by a further consideration. This was implicit in the connection between the statements in verses 12 and 13 which spoke of murder and hatred respectively. Now John takes up the thought implied in Matthew 5:21f. and states quite bluntly that hatred is tantamount to murder. Hatred is the wish that the other person was not there; it is the refusal to recognize his rights as a person, the longing that he might be dead. We may not like to put the point quite so frankly, but it is good that the real character of hatred should be so unambiguously displayed, so as to warn us against it. If I hate somebody, I am no different from a murderer in my attitude toward him. Such a person shares the nature of the devil, the archetypal murderer, and therefore it should come as no surprise that such a person cannot possibly

---

[10]οἴδαμεν (cf. 3:2, 5; 5:13, 15, 18, 19, 20) is an appeal to the common Christian knowledge or experience of the readers.

[11]The first ὅτι clause after οἴδαμεν is a noun clause, expressing the content of what we know. The second ὅτι clause is a causal clause which qualifies οἴδαμεν and expresses the ground of knowledge; it is not to be construed with μεταβεβήκαμεν to express the reason for the transfer. Wengst, 67 n. 152, however, argues that verse 14c shows that love is the basis for eternal life, not in the sense that love *merits* life, but that love *is* life; both are God's gift.

[12]After ὁ μὴ ἀγαπῶν (S A B 33 *pc* lat arm) many witnesses supply an object: τὸν ἀδελφὸν (αὐτοῦ); this is clearly secondary (Metzger, 712).

possess eternal life. Hatred is incompatible with spiritual life. Put otherwise, the person who hates another wants to deprive him of life; such a person clearly does not belong to the realm of life.[13]

16 From this wretched picture of hatred and murder John turns to consider positively the nature of love. It was a necessary inquiry then, and it remains so today. The word "love" can have a variety of meanings, and it is necessary to know exactly what any given writer means by it. Most people associate Christianity with the command to love, and so they think that they know all about Christianity when they have understood its teaching in terms of their own concept of love. John found it necessary to explain clearly to his readers what he meant by love, and we can profit from his exposition.

John defines love by giving an example of what he means: This is how we know what love is,[14] by observing that Jesus Christ laid down his life for us. The language used here would at once recall to readers of the Gospel the picture of the Good Shepherd in John 10; although the word "love" is not used in this connection in John 10, the contrast with the hired man who does not care for the welfare of the sheep brings out the point that the shepherd's willingness to lay down his life for the sheep is due to his concern for their welfare.[15] But the idea of love is expressed with all desirable clarity in the saying that the greatest example of love is seen when a man lays down his life on behalf of his friends (Jn. 15:13). Love means readiness to do anything for other people. In both cases the thought is of Jesus' approaching death. This is particularly evident in the saying about the Good Shepherd, since it is unusual for a shepherd to die for his sheep: here the reality is bursting through the boundary of the metaphor. In the present context the actual wording used, to lay

---

[13]For the whole section cf. *Testament of Gad* 4:6f.: "For as love would quicken even the dead, and would call back them that are condemned to die, so hatred would slay the living, and those that had sinned venially it would not suffer to live. For the spirit of hatred worketh together with Satan, through hastiness of spirit, in all things to men's death; but the spirit of love worketh together with the law of God in long-suffering unto the salvation of men." For further parallels see Windisch, 124f.

[14]ἐν τούτῳ clearly refers forward to the ὅτι clause (2:5 n.). ἐγνώκαμεν is used in the perfect of the abiding knowledge of the nature of love which began when the readers heard and responded to the gospel. τὴν ἀγάπην is used absolutely: some late MSS added the clarification τοῦ Θεοῦ (AV has "of God" in italics, showing that it has no real MS authority).

[15]John 10:11, 15, 17f.; cf. 11:50f.; 13:37f. for the thought of laying down one's life. See further Romans 5:8; Galatians 2:20; Revelation 1:5 for the revelation of divine love in the death of Jesus.

down one's life, is significant. It indicates that one is prepared to give up one's own life in order that others may live.[16] Love means saying "No" to one's own life so that somebody else may live. Finally, it should be noted that the laying down of life is done for the benefit of the other person.[17] The death of Jesus is not simply a demonstration of love in the sense that we might gaze on the spectacle of the crucified Son of God and say, "He must have loved very much in order to suffer all that." This is not how we know love. Rather, the point is that we experience the benefit of life given to us as a result of the death of Jesus, and so we realize that the love was for us. The point has been put simply and effectively by J. Denney:

> If I were sitting on the end of the pier on a summer day enjoying the sunshine and the air, and some one came along and jumped into the water and got drowned "to prove his love for me", I should find it quite unintelligible. I might be much in need of love, but an act in no rational relation to any of my necessities could not prove it. But if I had fallen over the pier and were drowning, and some one sprang into the water, and at the cost of making my peril, or what but for him would be my fate, his own, saved me from death, then I should say, "Greater love hath no man than this." I should say it intelligibly, because there would be an intelligent relation between the sacrifice which love made and the necessity from which it redeemed.[18]

John is not concerned here to spell out how the death of Jesus saves us, or what benefits accrue to us from it; his immediate point is that the self-giving involved in Jesus' death for our sakes shows us in concentrated form the meaning of love. There is no need to define love: it is enough to point to the supreme example of it.

But now John goes on to make the devastating claim that we too ought to lay down our lives for our brothers. This claim would

[16]The Greek phrase appears to be based on a Semitic phrase, which can also be translated by δοῦναι τὴν ψυχὴν αὐτοῦ (Mk. 10:45). It may represent *nāṭan napšô* (SB II, 537) or *śîm napšô* (Isa. 53:10; J. Jeremias, TDNT V, 708, 710; VI, 496). Jeremias notes that the phrase can mean "to hazard one's life" (so in Jn. 10:11, generically of any good shepherd) or "to give one's life" (so in Jn. 10:15, 17f., of Jesus) (TDNT VI, 496 n. 104). See further C. Maurer, TDNT VIII, 155f., who agrees with Jeremias that this phrase is the Johannine equivalent to Mark 10:45b, and that it is based on the Hebrew text of Isaiah 53:10; in other words, the sacrifice made by the Good Shepherd is described in terms of the Suffering Servant.
[17]ὑπέρ is used to express the beneficiaries of the action; cf. Mark 14:24 and par.; Romans 5:8; 2 Corinthians 5:15; Galatians 2:20; Hebrews 2:9; 1 Peter 2:21, *et al.* With the thought of the shepherd in the background, it is probable that the preposition indicates not merely that Jesus laid down his life for our benefit, but also that he acted in place of us: he died in order that we might not die.
[18]J. Denney, *The Death of Christ,* London, 1951, 103.

also have been familiar to readers of the Gospel who knew that Jesus
had commanded his disciples to love one another just as he had
loved them (Jn. 15:12). The example of Jesus' love is indeed an
example, a pattern to be followed.[19] Admittedly, we do not know
precisely what John had in mind when he spoke of this supreme
sacrifice. Clearly he was not thinking of believers atoning for the sins
of other people. Perhaps he was thinking of the possibility of laying
down one's own life to save other people in time of persecution or of
being prepared to lay down one's life in the service of the gospel.
But most probably he was thinking of the limit to which one may
have to go in self-abnegation, and his statement is a way of saying
that love must be prepared to meet the needs of others whatever the
cost in self-sacrifice.

17 Certainly John brings us down to earth with a bump in his
very next statement. Readiness to lay down one's life is a high ideal,
to which we may enthusiastically consent: it is a fairly remote possibility, and, if it did arise, we could probably make the supreme
effort that would be required. Meanwhile, however, we are content
to live our present comfortable life until that supreme sacrifice is
demanded. No, says John, the moment is here now. If you have the
means of livelihood in the world[20]—and everybody who can afford
to buy this book comes into this category[21]—*and* you see a brother
in want, *and* you show no pity to him,[22] then the love of God cannot
possibly be in you.[23] It is not certain whether John means "God's
love channeled through us," or "our love for God," or (as is most
probable) "the type of love shown by God,"[24] but the point of the

---

[19]For Christ as an example see John 13:12-15; 1 Corinthians 11:1; Romans 15:2f.;
2 Corinthians 8:9; 10:1; Philippians 2:2-8; 1 Timothy 6:13; Hebrews 12:13f.; 1 Peter 2:21,
et al.; W. Michaelis, TDNT IV, 659-674; W. Bauder, NIDNTT I, 490-492 (with
bibliography).

[20]For βίος see 2:16. Here it signifies the resources needed for "the life of the world,"
i.e. "possessions" (AG); τοῦ κόσμου here has a neutral sense; it does not seem
necessary to say, with Schnackenburg, 199, that the word is added to indicate the
transience of possessions.

[21]Even those who borrowed the book from a library or a friend could probably
purchase it if they wanted to.

[22]Literally, "close the bowels against." In Hebrew thought the bowels were regarded
as the locus of compassion; cf. Genesis 43:30; Jeremiah 31:20; Proverbs 12:10; Sirach
30:7; Luke 1:78; Philippians 2:1; Colossians 3:12. In Greek thought, however, the
bowels were associated with anger; the LXX rarely uses σπλάγχνα to translate
Hebrew *rah°mîm,* but see 2 Maccabees 9:5f.; Sirach 30:7; *Testament of Zebulon*
5:3f.; H. Köster, TDNT VII, 548-559.

[23]Literally, "how does the love of God remain in him?"

[24]τοῦ Θεοῦ is regarded as (a) a genitive of origin by Bultmann, 56; Stott, 144;
Houlden, 101; Haas, 92; Wengst, 73 n. 172; (b) an objective genitive by Brooke, 97;

saying is unaffected. Christian love is love which gives to those in
need, and so long as we have, while our brothers have little or
nothing, and we do nothing to help them, we are lacking in the love
which is the essential evidence that we are truly children of God.
Nor is it simply a case of making a payment out of our bank balance
and thinking no more about it: John is talking about a *feeling* of pity
which expresses itself in action.

The down-to-earth, forceful character of John's comment
appears to have been obscured in one commentator's remarks on
this verse:

> Giving one's life immediately translates itself into the more manage-
> able and less stringent duty of generosity to the needy brother. It
> seems that the one is even equivalent to the other. We have moved
> from crisis to daily living. . . . Not only is there no sign of crisis in
> which martyrdom is likely to be required (despite the fact that the
> End is believed to be near), but the essentially critical nature of the
> demand, as marked by the Cross, is softened, without comment or
> explanation, into an ethical programme. . . . Here we are in the
> presence of Christian life which is settled and established, at least to
> the extent that virtue is esteemed most characteristically in the
> shape of kindness with material goods. Love of the brothers and
> giving one's life now find this quite concrete—and unheroic?—
> expression.[25]

On the contrary, it must be affirmed that, at least in the present
situation, it would be inappropriate for Christians to think that they
had accomplished their Christian duty by being ready for an—
unlikely—act of martyrdom.[26] The need of the world is for food,
clothing, and jobs, for those who have these things to share with
those who have not. John betrays no suggestion that the world is
divided into "haves" and "have nots," and that this is how God
intended it to be. Rather, the person who has is lacking in Christian
love if he does not share with the brother in need. The tragedy is that
we have not learned to take this seriously. The need of the world is
not for heroic acts of martyrdom, but for heroic acts of material

---

Bruce, 101f.; and (c) a genitive of quality by Schnackenburg, 200. (d) Westcott, 115,
combines all three possibilities. John does not, however, teach that our love for
others is simply God's love flowing through us, and in the present context there is
no mention of our love for God. Hence the thought is probably of our showing a love
like the love which God showed to us, and inspired by his love. See 2:5, 15; 4:9, 12; 5:3.
[25]Houlden, 100.
[26]It is far from clear that John was in fact thinking of martyrdom.

sacrifice. If I am a well-off Christian, while others are poor, I am not acting as a true Christian.

18 So John rounds off this section of his letter (and prepares the way for the next) by a call to his readers to love not merely by saying kind things but above all by action. Their love is to be demonstrated "in truth," which is a call not just for actions to prove the reality of their inward feelings but also for a love which is in accord with the divine revelation of reality in the love shown by Jesus.[27]

ASSURANCE AND OBEDIENCE (3:19–24)

19. This then is how we know that we belong to the truth, and how we set our hearts at rest in his presence 20. whenever our hearts condemn us. For God is greater than our hearts, and he knows everything.

21. Dear friends, if our hearts do not condemn us, we have confidence before God 22. and receive from him anything we ask, because we obey his commands and do what pleases him. 23. And this is his command: to believe in the name of his Son, Jesus Christ, and to love one another as he commanded us. 24. Those who obey his commands live in him, and he in them. And this is how we know that he lives in us: We know it by the Spirit he gave us.

This passage can be regarded as the conclusion to the preceding part of the letter and also as a bridge to the remaining part. Its main purpose is to give assurance to the readers, on the basis of which they may have confidence to approach God in prayer. Yet, although John emphasizes that our assurance ultimately depends on God himself, nevertheless he insists that we must continue to keep his commands to believe in Jesus and to love one another. When we do this, the Spirit inwardly assures us of our spiritual position. The passage is a difficult one to follow, since it relates the divine and human aspects of assurance in a paradoxical fashion.

19, 20 John begins by looking back to what he has just written, and declaring that obedience to the injunction to love one another is the basis for knowing that we belong to the truth.[1] Doing

---

[27]For the view that ἀλήθεια means more than "reality" see Haas, 13f., who thinks that the context (v. 19) strongly suggests this deeper meaning; otherwise the word is somewhat tautologous after ἔργῳ.

[1]As in verse 13 it is uncertain whether the verse should begin with καί (omitted by A B *al* it vg bo Clem); UBS brackets the conjunction. If accepted, it links this verse

what is characteristic of the realm of truth is the sign that we belong to that realm.[2] The NIV obscures the fact that the verb "we know" is in the future tense. John is not thinking of our continual assurance that we belong to God, but rather of the coming of a crisis of belief when we want to know whether we belong to God. In such a situation we are to examine ourselves to see whether we are keeping the command given to us by God.

This thought will reappear in verses 22b–24, but first of all John has two further points to mention. It may happen that when a person engages in this self-examination he is alarmed by the result. He considers his life and can only conclude that he falls short of the divine standard. He does not love his brothers as fully as he should. He cannot claim that freedom from sin of which John spoke earlier. How can he possibly belong to the truth when he feels that his actions belie it? John says that we can set our hearts at rest[3] whenever[4] they condemn us. The connection of clauses in the NIV

---

more closely to what precedes.

More important is the question whether ἐν τούτῳ gathers up what has just been said in verse 18 (cf. v. 14) (so most scholars) or refers forward to the second ὅτι clause (i.e. v. 20) (Nauck, 78–83). In favor of the second view is that ἐν τούτῳ usually refers forward (see 2:3 and 2:5 n.), but there are cases where it may refer backward (see 3:10; 4:17; 5:2; Jn. 16:30), and so this argument loses its force. It can also be urged that the ground of knowledge is unlikely to be an imperative or exhortation, "let us love"; but again it can be urged that the indicative is present in verse 14, and that John means, "by our obedience to this exhortation we shall know. . . ."

[2]For "belonging to the truth" cf. 2:21. The phrase refers to belonging to the divine sphere of reality, and is synonymous with "being born of God" and similar phrases.

[3]The verb πείθω usually means "to persuade" somebody to do something, or "to convince" somebody that something is true. The former meaning is clearly irrelevant here. The latter is possible linguistically, but is unlikely in the context, since it is not clear what is the object. If the thought is that we shall persuade our hearts that God is greater than our hearts and knows everything, the question arises as to *how* we know this; it is not at all obvious how verse 18 can form the basis for this statement, and it is equally unclear how verse 19a can form a basis for verses 19b–20, which are concerned with the situation where we do *not* know that we belong to the truth. Hence this translation is unacceptable. O'Neill, 43, suggests that the verb means "to stir up," i.e. to make our consciences sensitive, but this is possible only if verse 20a (ὅτι ἐὰν . . . καρδία) is excised as a gloss, for which there is not the slightest evidence. However, πείθω has a well-attested meaning, "to reassure, appease, set at rest" (2 Macc. 4:15; Mt. 28:14), and this gives a good sense here.

[4]The word ὅτι occurs three times in verses 19f. (1) At its first occurrence it must mean "that," introducing a direct statement. (2) Its force at its second occurrence is debatable: (a) If it means "that" (providing an object for πείσομεν), it renders ὅτι [3] redundant. (b) Similarly, if it means "because" (giving the grounds for πείσομεν . . .), it makes ὅτι [3] redundant. (c) The difficulty is avoided if ὅτι [2] is taken as the neuter of the relative pronoun ὅστις (i.e. ὅ τι) and linked with the immediately following ἐάν (equivalent to ἄν) so as to mean "whatever" (cf. NIV "whenever"). (3) If we adopt view (2c), then at its third occurrence ὅτι signifies "because."

suggests that we can pacify our troubled heart, i.e. our conscience,[5] by our obedience to the command. For God understands us better than our own hearts know us, and in his omniscience he knows that our often weak attempts to obey his command spring from a true allegiance to him. But it is also possible to make a break at the end of verse 19a and begin a new thought: "And we shall set our hearts at rest in his presence whenever our hearts condemn us, for God is greater than our hearts, and he knows everything."[6] If we adopt this view, the thought is that even if we have no grounds for assurance in ourselves, nevertheless we can commit ourselves confidently to the mercy of God who knows all things.[7] Neither of these ways of understanding a difficult sentence is quite free from problems, but fortunately the difference in meaning is not great, and the main thought is clear. The thought is similar to that expressed by Paul: "I care very little if I am judged by you or by any human court; indeed, I do not even judge myself. My conscience is clear, but that does not make me innocent. It is the Lord who judges me. Therefore, judge nothing before the appointed time; wait till the Lord comes. He will bring to light what is hidden in darkness and will expose the motives of men's hearts. At that time each will receive his praise from God" (1 Cor. 4:3-5). Here Paul is making it clear that judgment is not finally exercised by other men or even by our own conscience; it is God who will exercise judgment and apportion condemnation or praise. So here too John is telling his readers that they can safely entrust themselves to the judgment of God who knows all about them, and consequently they can set their hearts at rest, even though they feel self-condemned.

On what sort of occasion did John's readers need this kind of

[5]In Hebrew thought the heart is tantamount to the conscience, there being no separate word in Hebrew for "conscience" (cf. 1 Sam. 24:5). The use of the singular for the plural is idiomatic.

[6]Cf. de Jonge, 175. A number of commentators (Windisch, 125; Bultmann, 56f.) hold that the difficulties of interpretation are due to textual corruption, but this is an unnecessary conclusion. On the passage as a whole see especially Westcott, 115-118; Haas, 93-95; C. Spicq, "La justification du charitable (1 Jo. 3, 19-21)," Bib 40, 1959, 915-927.

[7]God's knowledge of all things includes his knowledge of us, which is better than our knowledge of ourselves. The point is not that God is merciful and forgiving (which, of course, John assumes), but that he has the full knowledge on which to base a just verdict concerning us. Consequently, we have grounds for confidence. The view of some of the early fathers and of Calvin, 278f., that John's point is the greater severity of God's judgment, compared with our own standards (1 Cor. 4:3-5), is quite inappropriate in the present context. See further W. Pratscher, "Gott ist grösser als unser Herz. Zur Interpretation von 1 Joh. 3, 19f.," TZ 32, 1976, 272-281.

reassurance? They want to set their hearts at rest "in his presence." This phrase could refer to standing in the presence of God on the day of judgment (4:17), an occasion which might well fill the heart of a man with foreboding. But the context here is one of prayer: dare we approach God with our requests if we feel guilty before him? On the whole, it seems more likely that this is what is in John's mind (cf. 1 Thess. 1:3; 3:9).[8] We then have a smooth transition to verse 21.

To be sure, the occasion can be generalized. What John says here can be extended to any and every occasion when the believer is in doubt about his situation before God. No matter how much his heart may condemn him, God still welcomes and forgives the man who seeks his forgiveness and casts himself upon his mercy. And even when we are no longer capable of conscious faith in God and tread the dark valley of severe physical or mental illness, this God will still hold us in his hand: "The Lord knows those who are his" (2 Tim. 2:19).

21 It is obvious that so long as our hearts condemn us[9] we have no confidence to come before God. Confidence is the characteristic that we need to have at the parousia (2:28), but it is something that we also want now so that we can pray to God.[10] If we can set our hearts at rest by remembering that God is greater than our hearts and knows everything, then our hearts will no longer[11] condemn us, and we shall be able to approach God with boldness. Such boldness is expressed in making requests to God.

22 Not only so, but we receive from God anything we ask. This astonishing statement ranks with the statements about the believer's sinlessness (3:6, 9) and his perfection in love (2:5; 4:17) in presenting an eschatological reality that seems far removed from our humdrum and often disappointing experience. Behind it stands the promise of Jesus, "You may ask me for anything in my name, and I

---

[8]Bultmann, 56 n. 59, holds that the sense of ἔμπροσθεν αὐτοῦ is forensic, "before God as judge," although he is not apparently thinking of the final judgment. Schnackenburg's argument, 202 n. 7, that the phrase means simply "in the presence of," since the context is one of divine grace, is less persuasive. The point is surely that the sinner who fears divine judgment discovers that the judge is merciful and forgiving.

[9]The text is uncertain, but the meaning is basically unaffected: the basic problem is whether ἡμῶν should be read after καρδία and/or after καταγινώσκῃ; for details see Metzger, 713f.

[10]On παρρησία see 2:28 n.

[11]The sense of the clause must be "when our heart therefore *no longer* condemns us" (Bultmann, 58; my italics). There does not seem to be any need for the complicated explanation in Schnackenburg, 203 and n. 3.

will do it. . . . I tell you the truth, my Father will give you whatever
you ask in my name" (Jn. 14:14; 16:23; cf. 15:16). Manifestly such
statements are capable of misunderstanding: though we are encouraged to have faith that will move mountains, a prayer that an awkward mound in my garden will smooth itself out is unlikely to be
answered by some kind of miraculous bulldozing operation. Later in
the Epistle John makes it clear that "if we ask anything according to
his will, he hears us," thus emphasizing that our prayers must be in
accordance with God's will. This may seem to be a circular statement: surely if we ask God to do his will, he is going to do it anyway
since it is his will to do so. But the point is surely rather that we
ought to ask for those things which are in accordance with God's will
rather than for those things which arise from selfish motives. And
this is brought out in the present context by the qualification that we
are people who "obey his commands and do what pleases him." We
may observe the same collocation of answered prayer and obedience
to God's commandments in the other Johannine sayings on the same
theme (Jn. 14:15; 15:14, 17). The Christian is to be a person who
obeys the commandments (2:3) and pleases God,[12] just as Jesus
always did what pleased God (Jn. 8:29). This could make answered
prayer seem to be a *quid pro quo*—God repays us in accordance
with what we give him—but such a thought is excluded by the fact
that John is thinking of the relationship between the Father and his
children (3:1), a relationship characterized by love in which all
thoughts of our doing good simply in order to win advantages or of
God granting favors merely to those who please him are excluded. If
verses 21–22a state the eschatological reality, verse 22b draws our
attention to its imperfect realization in the lives of those who fail to
live as true children of God. John's purpose is to encourage us to
enter fully into the filial relationship in which God delights to hear
and answer the requests of his children. The more fully we enter into
that relationship, the more will our asking be in accordance with
his will.

23 Having spoken of the need to obey God's commands,
John now expresses clearly what this means. He sums up the commands as one command, which is then expressed as having two

---

[12]For ἀρεστός cf. John 8:29; Acts 6:2; 12:3. See further the use of the verb in Romans
8:8; 1 Corinthians 7:32–34; 1 Thessalonians 2:4, 15; 4:1; 2 Timothy 2:4, and of
εὐαρεστέω (Heb. 11:5f.; 13:16) and εὐάρεστος (Rom. 12:1f.; 14:18; 2 Cor. 5:9;
Eph. 5:10; Phil. 4:18; Col. 3:20; Tit. 2:9; Heb. 13:21); W. Foerster, TDNT I, 455–457;
H. Bietenhard, NIDNTT II, 814–817.

parts; in this way the fundamental unity of the two parts is made quite clear.[13] It is possible for readers of 1 John to gain the impression that the sum-total of Christianity is love for one another, and hence to claim that anybody who shows love is a Christian. This misunderstanding would be avoided if sufficient attention was paid to this key verse which shows that belief and love go together, and that neither is sufficient without the other. John has already made plain the nature of Christian love as the fulfilment of Christ's command (Jn. 13:34; 15:12, 17). So far he has not actually used the *word* "believe," although the *idea* is to be found in his earlier teaching on the need to acknowledge the Son and the danger of denying him (2:22f.). Later on, however, the theme of belief will become a central one in the Epistle, and the present verse is transitional in function. Thus with its stress on faith and love this verse announces two of the main themes of the remainder of the Epistle. There is a certain stress here on the thought of right belief: the readers are to believe in the name of Jesus Christ, the Son of God,[14] a stress that is demanded by the situation in which false beliefs about Jesus were prevalent. Belief in the name of Jesus means believing that his name contains the power which it signifies, so that the question is not simply one of right belief, but of trust in the One who is the object of the Christian confession. A Jesus who is not the Son of God and the Christ would not be able to save the readers from their sins and bring them into the light of God's presence. A Jesus who is less than the Jesus of the apostolic witness is incapable of doing what that witness ascribes to him: he may be a moral and spiritual guide, but he cannot atone for

[13]Cf. 2 John 4–6 and nn.; 1 John 2:3–8.

[14]John here uses πιστεύω with the dative, which usually signifies believing that something is trustworthy and true rather than making an act of personal committal (usually expressed by πιστεύω εἰς) (Brooke, 104f.). Many recent scholars (Chaine, 194; Schnackenburg, 206f.; Bultmann, 59 n. 79; Bruce, 100) hold that the two constructions are virtually indistinguishable in meaning; cf. 5:13. Schnackenburg suggests that the two constructions are due to the synonymous use of he'ᵉmîn bᵉ and lᵉ in Hebrew. R. Bultmann, TDNT V, 203 and n. 221, admits that there is a linguistic distinction, but, *ibid.*, 210–212, claims that there is no material distinction. However, I have tried to show that in the Gospel πιστεύω with the dative can be used to express mere intellectual credence unaccompanied by personal commitment (*Kept by the Power of God*, Minneapolis, 1975², 182f. and n. 16). The present verse is an exception to the rule, in that commitment to Jesus is clearly meant, but the choice of construction may indicate that John has the heretics in mind and is thinking particularly of intellectual acceptance of the true confession about Jesus. The aorist πιστεύσωμεν is perhaps used of the initial act of confession, by contrast with ἀγαπῶμεν, which indicates a continuing attitude.

human sins, give spiritual help in time of temptation, or offer any assurance of eternal life after death.

24 Finally, John again makes the point that obedience to God's commands is the condition for communion with God (cf. vv. 18f.). He uses the plural "commands" perhaps to bring out the point that the one command to believe and love expresses itself in a multiplicity of subordinate commands which express its meaning in concrete terms. The person who is obedient lives in God,[15] and God lives in him. This formula, similar to Paul's language about the mutual indwelling of Christ and the believer,[16] indicates the closest possible union between man and God. It is noteworthy that in 2:6 we were told that the person who lives in him ought to walk as Jesus did. Now we are told that the person who obeys his commands lives in him. Later we shall read that if we love one another, God lives in us (4:12). It would seem to follow that obeying God's commands is not so much the condition of living in him, as rather the expression of our spiritual life; yet this expression may fail to appear, with the result that our spiritual life is in jeopardy, and therefore we can be commanded to obey God's commands. Spiritual life and obedience are thus two sides of the one coin.

But just as we may be tempted by the voice of an accusing conscience to wonder whether we are in a right relationship with God and so may need a divine assurance (vv. 19f.), so if we base our assurance on our imperfect obedience to God's commands, we may well feel that we do not live in him. John, therefore, names a further and more sure source of confidence. We can know that God lives in us by the Spirit whom he has given us (cf. 4:13). The presence of the witness of the Spirit brings us the assurance that we need (cf. Rom. 5:5; 8:14–16). John does not explain how this assurance manifests itself. Is he thinking of the way in which the believer realizes that he can confidently address God as Abba, Father? Or is it some inner consciousness of being loved by God? Or is it some "charismatic" experience of the power of the Spirit? John has not told us, and in this there may be an element of divine wisdom. Had John named some particular manifestation of the Spirit, it would have been tempting for us to regard the *experience* as the important

---

[15]The context strongly suggests that ἐν αὐτῷ refers to God rather than to Christ (Bruce, 100f.), although here, as elsewhere, John may not be distinguishing too sharply between the Father and the Son (cf. Jn. 14:23).

[16]See Romans 8:10; 2 Corinthians 13:5; Galatians 2:20; Colossians 1:27; and 2 Corinthians 5:17; 12:2; Philippians 1:13; 3:9, *et al.*; A. Oepke, TDNT II, 541–543; M. Harris, NIDNTT III, appendix (forthcoming).

thing and even to make one particular type of experience the *sine qua non* for testing the faith of ourselves and others. We shall be wise not to insist on some particular evidence of the Spirit's presence as being indispensable.

THE SPIRITS OF TRUTH AND FALSEHOOD (4:1–6)

1. *Dear friends, do not believe every spirit, but test the spirits to see whether they are from God, because many false prophets have gone out into the world.* 2. *This is how you can recognize the Spirit of God: Every spirit that acknowledges that Jesus Christ has come in the flesh is from God,* 3. *but every spirit that does not acknowledge Jesus is not from God. This is the spirit of the antichrist, which you have heard is coming and even now is already in the world.*

4. *You, dear children, are from God and have overcome them, because the one who is in you is greater than the one who is in the world.* 5. *They are from the world and therefore speak from the viewpoint of the world, and the world listens to them.* 6. *We are from God, and whoever knows God listens to us; but whoever is not from God does not listen to us. This is how we recognize the Spirit*[a] *of truth and the spirit of falsehood.*

[a]Or *spirit*

Appeals to the witness of the Spirit are useless if we cannot be sure that it really is the Spirit of God who is bearing testimony. John's opponents also laid claim to spiritual inspiration. But the mark of true inspiration is confession that Jesus Christ has come in the flesh. Any teaching which denies this is inspired by antichrist. There are thus two spirits in the world, representing truth and error, and it is not surprising that the world, inspired by antichrist, does not accept the witness of believers. Yet believers can remain confident because God is greater than their adversary; they have in fact already overcome the false prophets.

1   The present section, verses 1–6, is a self-contained unity, clearly separate from what follows. It is linked with what precedes by the catchword "spirit," which joins verses 3:24 and 4:1. It is not absolutely clear whether the mention of the Spirit in 3:24 led John to develop the thought in this new section or whether in anticipation of this section he included the linking phrase in 3:24. On the whole, the latter is more likely.[1] With this section John returns to a theme

[1]Dodd, 94, adopts the former view; Windisch, 126, Schnackenburg, 208, and de Jonge, 178f., the latter. De Jonge argues that verse 24b is so different in theme from the preceding section that it appears to be a link added to join on the next section.

which he has already discussed, that of the coming of the antichrists with their false christological confession. But the theme is taken up in a slightly different form. Here it is a question of the claims which were made by John's opponents that their teaching rested on inspiration by the spirit. It is tempting to ascribe any unusual phenomenon to the power of God, and in the early church there was a tendency to regard any kind of unusual "spiritual" gift such as tongues or prophecy as being inspired by the Spirit of God, and therefore a sign of the validity and truth of what was said by the person possessed of the gift. Consequently Paul had to warn the members of his churches to "try" the spirits.[2] The reality of demonic spirits was not questioned, as the various stories of exorcisms in the Gospels and Acts indicate. Christians, however, needed to be reminded that demonic activity could penetrate their churches. The fact that a statement was attributable to inspiration by the spirit did not prove that it was the Spirit of *God* which was at work. So John too found it necessary to remind his readers that not every "spirit" was to be believed. The word "spirit" here must mean either "utterance inspired by a spirit" or "person inspired by a spirit." In the latter case the thought is perhaps of the individual spirit of a prophet, which might be inspired by God or Satan.[3] Since this is the case, the members of the church must not believe what is said by inspired individuals without first testing whether the spirits are from God. There is a real danger of deception since many false prophets have gone out into the world. Such prophets had been the subject of warnings by Jesus (Mt. 7:15; Mk. 13:22); we have already seen how John regarded them as manifestations of antichrist (2:18). They went out, like Christian missionaries (2 Jn. 7), in order to win converts for their cause. The important problem is: how do you test such people?[4]

2 Here is the answer[5] to the problem. John presents the positive evidence for recognizing[6] when a prophet is inspired by the Spirit of God. The test is the confession of faith made by the person

[2]1 Corinthians 12:1–3; 14:29; 1 Thessalonians 5:20f. See further *Didache* 11–12; Hermas, *Mandate* 11.

[3]Schnackenburg, 220; cf. E. Schweizer, TDNT VII, 435 and n. 689, 448f. The plural "spirit" thus does not refer to a multiplicity of divine spirits or even of evil spirits but to a multiplicity of human beings who may be inspired in their spirits by the Spirit of God or the spirit of falsehood (so rightly Bultmann, 61). That "spirit" does not mean "spirit-inspired utterance" is evident from the personification in verses 2f.

[4]For δοκιμάζω in this sense cf. 1 Thessalonians 5:21; *Didache* 11:11; 12:1; Hermas, *Mandate* 11:7; *1 Clement* 42:4.

[5]ἐν τούτῳ refers forward (2:5 n.).

[6]γινώσκετε is to be taken as indicative.

who claims to be inspired by the Spirit.[7] It is not absolutely certain how the wording of the confession should be understood. The NIV takes the confession to be "[I acknowledge] that Jesus Christ has come in the flesh." Alternatively we may translate "[I acknowledge] Jesus Christ as come in the flesh."[8] The wording of the confession is similar to that in 2 John 7 (see also 1 Jn. 5:6). In both cases the emphasis lies on the reality of the incarnation, the fact that the Word became flesh (Jn. 1:14; cf. 6:51–55). There was a true union of the divine Word, the Son of God, with a human personality in Jesus Christ. With the NIV rendering the stress is more on belief in the fact of the incarnation as a historical event; with the alternative rendering the stress is rather on the human "state" of Jesus, and indeed on his continuing human state. The incarnation was not a temporary event but the permanent union of God and man in Jesus Christ. Moreover, to say that Jesus Christ came "in the flesh" is to say that he was truly united with human flesh rather than that he merely came into a human body and indwelt it (possibly only for a limited period). We should no doubt take "has come" as a verb implying the coming of Jesus Christ from God; the pre-existence of Jesus Christ before the incarnation is presupposed.[9]

In 1 Corinthians 12:3 Paul tells us that nobody can utter the Christian confession "Jesus is Lord" except by the inspiration of the Spirit. Paul too was dealing with the question of allegedly inspired

---

[7]For ὁμολογέω cf. 2:23; 4:17; 2 John 7; of confessing sin, 1:9.

[8]ὁμολογέω can be used absolutely (Jn. 12:42); with a ὅτι clause (4:15; Jn. 1:20); with a single accusative (1:9; 2:23; 4:3); or with a double accusative (4:2; 2 Jn. 7; Jn. 9:22). Here, since there is no indication that any part of the phrase is to be taken predicatively, it is best to adopt the second rendering in the text (Schnackenburg, 220f.; Haas, 102). In view of the parallelism with verse 3 this understanding seems preferable to that adopted in the NIV, although the difference in meaning is slight. The translation "[I acknowledge] Jesus as the Christ come in the flesh" produces a difficult separation of the two proper names. Stott, 155f., argues in its favor that it fits in with the view that the opponents of John regarded the Christ as a divine aeon which came upon Jesus at his baptism; John claimed, however, that it was not that the Christ entered the flesh of Jesus but rather that Jesus was the Christ come in the flesh. Although this view is improbable from a grammatical point of view, it may just be possible to take the phrase to mean "(acknowledge) Jesus (as) Christ (and as) come in the flesh," thus giving each part of the formula its full meaning. But the rendering adopted in the text is adequate to make the point which Stott is concerned to defend; to speak of "Jesus Christ as come in the flesh" is to state that there was a union of the earthly and the heavenly from the moment of incarnation.

[9]The verb "to come" naturally does not always carry this implication, but the thought of Jesus being sent from the Father or coming from the Father is sufficiently common to give us a probable background for the present statement (Jn. 1:9; 3:19, 31; 8:14, et al.).

utterance; having pointed out that denial of Christ is incompatible with divine inspiration, he makes the positive point that acknowledgment of Jesus as Lord is possible only under the inspiration of the Spirit. Paul, therefore, was not specifically putting forward a test of doctrinal orthodoxy, although his formula could be used in that way. John's confession is certainly meant for use in this manner, and the fact that it is different from the Pauline confession indicates that it has been formulated to meet the need of a particular situation. To some extent confessions are formulated in the light of the need to exclude particular errors, and existing forms of words, true in themselves, may need to be reformulated more precisely in order to bring out the full intended meaning and to guard against their being used in a sense which is felt to be inadequate or even incompatible with their intended meaning. The full implications of "Jesus is Lord" are incompatible with many heresies, both ancient and modern. The framers of this formula would not have accepted "I regard Jesus as my ultimate concern (but not as having the metaphysical status of 'Son of God')" as a correct exegesis of the formula; but in order to exclude such wilful twisting of the meaning it may be necessary to express the confession in more precise terms. In the same way, it is possible that John's opponents thought that they could confess Jesus as Lord but without accepting the fact that he was the Word incarnate, and therefore John had to stress that the confession must be made in this particular form.

John's test is not an infallible one. Jesus himself had to protest against people who called him "Lord" and yet did not do what he said (Mt. 7:21–23; Lk. 6:46). Mere confession with the mouth is not necessarily a guide to the belief of the heart. John's test is accordingly relevant to a particular situation in which it was possible to regard certain people as inspired by the spirit of evil because of their faulty confession. In other circumstances a different form of words may be the test point. Ultimately, however, the whole of the Epistle furnishes the characteristics of genuine Christianity: faith, love, and righteousness are all relevant to the question, and concentration on any one of them to the exclusion of the others is bound to be misleading.

3 Having given the positive evidence that a man's spirit is inspired by the Spirit of God, John now deals with the converse. A person who does not acknowledge Jesus is not from God. The abbreviated form of the confession, "[I acknowledge] Jesus" indicates that personal allegiance to Jesus is what is at stake. But such al-

legiance involves readiness to make the fuller confession found in verse 2, which indicates clearly who the Jesus is in whom a person puts his trust. If a person claims to believe in Jesus, it is proper to ask, "Is your Jesus the real Jesus?" For it is all too easy for us to make a picture of Jesus which is congenial to our taste but leaves out vital aspects of the New Testament presentation of him. Ancient scribes thus thought it necessary to fill out the confession in this verse on the lines of verse 2.[10] A more important textual point is that a number of authorities have a text which may be translated, "Every spirit that annuls Jesus is not from God." While this rendering has not found its way into the English versions of the New Testament (except that of R. A. Knox, which is based on the Latin Vulgate), it has found considerable favor among commentators. Nevertheless, it is probably due to a gloss or marginal comment by a scribe who was trying to bring out the precise way in which Jesus was denied.[11]

[10]The short text is supported by A B 1739 r vg bo Iren[lat] Clem. The wide variation in wording of the alternative readings listed in UBS is sufficient proof that they are all secondary expansions (Metzger, 714).

[11]In place of μὴ ὁμολογεῖ, read by most authorities, including the early evidence of Polycarp, *Phil.* 7:1, the variant λύει is attested by 1739[mg] ar c dem div p vg Iren[lat] Clem Orig[lat] Lucifer Prisc[⅓] Aug mss[acc. to Socrates] Fulgentius. The majority text is supported by Westcott, 163–166; Brooke, 110–114; Windisch, 126f.; Dodd, 96; Nauck, 57; Alexander, 103; Stott, 156; Houlden, 107; Bruce, 105 (apparently); de Jonge, 185–187; Balz, 189f. The variant is regarded as original by A. Harnack, "Zur Textkritik und Christologie der Schriften des Johannes," *Sitzungsberichte der Preussischen Akademie der Wissenschaften, Philosophisch-historische Klasse*, 1915, 534–573 (556–561), reprinted in *Studien zur Geschichte des Neuen Testaments und der alten Kirche*, Berlin, 1931, I, 105–152 (132–137); A. Rahlfs, "Mitteilungen. 9," TLZ 40, 1915, 525; F. Büchsel, TDNT IV, 336; AG 485b; BD 428[4]; O. A. Piper, "I John and the Didache of the Primitive Church," JBL 66, 1947, 437–451 (440–444); Chaine, 197f. (with hesitation); Schnackenburg, 222; Bultmann, 62; Vawter, 410. The term λύω, "to loosen, set free, destroy, abolish, annul," cannot mean "to separate the divinity from the humanity of Jesus" in a New Testament document, although it was so taken in early christological controversy. It must mean here "to annul (the true teaching about) Jesus (by spurning it)" (AG) or "to abolish Jesus" (i.e. regard him as of no account) (Bultmann). Piper suggested "to curse Jesus" on the analogy of 1 Corinthians 12:3. Knox, 410 n., interpreted it of the disuniting of Jesus and Christ.

   In favor of this reading it is argued: (1) The attestation is very old, going back to the mid-second century. (2) The grammatical irregularity of using μή with the indicative ὁμολογεῖ suggests that this reading is not original. (3) λύει is a pregnant expression, while μὴ ὁμολογεῖ is a colorless substitution. (4) The sharp continuation in verse 3b demands the stronger word. (5) It is easier to explain the scribal alteration of the more difficult word to bring the saying into conformity with verse 2.

   On the other hand, it can be argued: (1) The attestation of the traditional text is equally ancient (Polycarp), and the variant appears only in the mg. of one Greek MS. (2) The use of μή with ὁμολογεῖ is possibly a generalizing use (cf. 2 Pet. 1:9); cf. BD 428[4] with Appendix; de Jonge, 186 n. 342. (3) λύει is not so much pregnant as

The spirit which John condemns is that of the antichrist.[12] It is thus a sign of the last days and the final rebellion of evil against Jesus Christ. The readers already knew from the teaching of Jesus to expect this to happen;[13] now it was already in the world, exercising its evil influence. John is in no doubt that denial of the apostolic confession about Jesus Christ is not merely intellectual error, still less "advanced theology"; it represents the very spirit of rebellion against God and can only be condemned.

4 Other people may be taken in by the false teachers who deny Christ, but John does not believe that his "children" will do so. They have their source in God (cf. 3:10),[14] and consequently they have the inner power of the truth to enable them to withstand error. In this sense they can be said to have "overcome" the upholders of false teaching. This probably does not mean that they have physically driven them out of the church; rather they have proved victorious over the temptation to accept false doctrine.[15] False belief is as much a sin as unrighteous behavior or lack of love. Victory over it, however, is not due to any innate strength of believers but rather to the fact that the One who lives in them is greater, i.e. more powerful, than the one at work in the world. God[16] is mightier than the evil one.[17]

---

downright difficult. (4) For John failure to confess Jesus was the mark of antichrist (2:22). (5) The variant reading probably arose in anti-gnostic controversy. The traditional text could have arisen as a variant only when the meaning of λύει had become unclear, but in fact it is equally early. But the variant could easily have arisen as a means of sharpening the text of 1 John for controversy (Brooke, 114). De Jonge, 186 n. 342, suggests that it was due to a misreading of the traditional text.

[12]The omission of πνεῦμα in the phrase τὸ τοῦ ἀντιχρίστου is possibly a device to avoid suggesting that there is a "spirit" of antichrist comparable with the Spirit of God. It allows a generalizing interpretation (Westcott, 143).

[13]See 2:18 and n.

[14]In the light of 3:10 ἐκ τοῦ Θεοῦ ἐστε probably means more than merely belonging to God, and signifies having one's origin in God, i.e. being born of God; cf. 5:19.

[15]Cf. 2:13f.; 5:4f.; Romans 12:21. Elsewhere νικάω is used of overcoming Satan and the hostile world (Jn. 16:33; Rev. 2:7; 5:5; 12:11; 17:14; 21:7, et al.).

[16]The change from the neuter form "spirit" to the masculine pronoun indicates that God is meant, especially since the latter is said to be in believers (3:24; 4:12, 15f.).

[17]Since the false teachers are identified as antichrists, John can hardly say that antichrist is in them; he means that the devil inspires them (cf. 3:10 for a similar contrast between the children of God and of the devil). Schnackenburg, 224, thinks that John spoke of the devil being "in the world" rather than "in them" (as we might have expected), to avoid suggesting that the devil is "in" men in the same realistic way as God is in believers. But it is perhaps more likely that the change of phrase is meant simply to indicate that people who deny Christ are to be identified with the sinful world.

5   John has just spoken of the power at work in the world. He has already said that the false prophets have gone out into the world. But, lest there should be any confusion, he emphasizes that the false prophets belong to the world, and are therefore inspired by the evil power at work in the world. The world is their mission field in the sense that people who already are in the world and under its influence listen gladly to them and are confirmed in their errors (cf. Jn. 15:19a). "World" thus means both mankind united in opposition to God and the evil attitude characteristic of such people.[18] Those who deny Christ thus show that they belong to this evil world and are not from God.

6   What John has just said in verse 5 enables him to draw the lines of demarcation all the more clearly. Over against the false prophets there stands the Christian community of true believers, including John and his readers; possibly the thought is particularly of the teachers in the church.[19] They belong to God (cf. v. 4), and it follows that anybody else who knows God will listen to their message with approval, while anybody who does not belong to God will not listen to them. Hence it is by their response to the preaching of the true church[20] that it is possible to discern those who are directed by the Spirit of truth, i.e. the Holy Spirit,[21] and the spirit of falsehood or error.[22]

Thus John has given us two tests of truth and falsity: the confessions that men make and their responses to the message of the church. His way of putting the matter might lead to the conclusion that he views mankind as being divided into two groups: either men

[18]The word "world" has several nuances of meaning; in verse 3 it means more the area inhabited by men, but in verse 4 it refers rather to sinful mankind, while in verse 5 the stress is more on the sinful principle found in such people.

[19]The change to the first person ἡμεῖς strongly suggests that teachers are in the front of John's mind, although the rest of the church is not excluded (Dodd, 100: "the Church as a whole, speaking through its responsible teachers").

[20]ἐκ τούτου, used only here by John, refers backward to the immediately preceding statements, rather than primarily to the more remote verses 2f.

[21]For this description see John 14:17; 15:26; 16:13. The meaning of πνεῦμα has shifted from verses 1–3 where by metonymy it meant "person inspired by the spirit."

[22]πλάνη means both "error" and "cause of error" (Eph. 4:14; *Diognetus* 12:3; see H. Braun, TDNT VI, 228–253, especially 245f.; W. Günther, NIDNTT II, 457–461). A close parallel to the present verse is given by the *Testament of Judah* 20:1, which speaks of the two spirits which wait upon man, the spirit of truth and the spirit of deceit; in the *Testament of Reuben* 2 there are seven spirits of deceit; cf. *Testament of Asher* 6:2. Similar, but not identical teaching is found at Qumran, where men are controlled by the spirits of truth and perversity (1QS 3:15–26; 4; see the critical comments in Braun, 297–300; also Schnackenburg, 209–215).

belong to God and so respond to the preaching, or they belong to the world and are incapable of responding to the preaching. This conclusion would then suggest that John accepted the sort of dualism found in some Gnostic systems of thought, according to which some men possess the divine spirit, while others do not. One might draw an analogy with certain types of predestinarian theology which divide men into two groups, one of which responds to the gospel because God has chosen them to do so, while others cannot respond because God has not chosen them.[23] It is, however, doubtful whether John was here facing the problem of the unconverted and trying to find an answer to the problem of why some respond to the gospel and others reject it. It is more likely that he is thinking of the situation in the church where there were true and false teachers with their adherents, and he is arguing that the response gained by the false teachers is due to the fact that those who accept their teaching are themselves animated by the spirit of error.[24] Since John issues warnings to his readers against being taken in by the false teachers (2:24; 2 Jn. 7-11), he appears to have reckoned with the possibility of true believers going astray.[25]

GOD'S LOVE AND OUR LOVE (4:7-12)

> 7. *Dear friends, let us love one another, for love comes from God. Everyone who loves has been born of God and knows God.* 8. *Whoever does not love does not know God, because God is love.* 9. *This is how God showed his love among us: He sent his one and only Son[a] into the world that we might live through him.* 10. *This is love: not that we loved God, but that he loved us and sent his Son as an atoning sacrifice for our sins.* 11. *Dear friends, since God has so loved us, we also ought to love one another.* 12. *No one has ever seen God; but if we love each other, God lives in us and his love is made complete in us.*

> [a]Or *his only begotten Son*

Somewhat abruptly John turns from his discussion of true and false spirits to present his readers with a further appeal to love one another. He has already made it plain that love is one of the evi-

---

[23]Cf. Dodd, 100-102.
[24]Schnackenburg, 225f.
[25]I. H. Marshall, *Kept by the Power of God*, 187.

dences of the new birth. Now he goes on to claim that Christians ought to love one another because God has loved them, giving the supreme demonstration of the meaning of love in the sending of his Son as an atoning sacrifice for sin.

7 In the context of an appeal for love, it is appropriate that John addresses his readers as "dear friends," literally "beloved."[1] He has already described Christians as people who love their brothers (2:10; cf. 2 Jn. 5) and appealed to them to love one another (3:11, cf. 18, 23). Now he returns to the theme, urging his readers to act in accordance with their Christian status. The thoughts expressed largely repeat what John has already said. This is probably for the sake of emphasis, but nevertheless John has new things to say. Thus he begins by grounding his appeal in the fact that love comes from God. It has its origin in God and belongs to the divine sphere.[2] The beginning of love is to be found in the love shown by God, and the true nature of love is to be discovered by considering what love means in the case of God (4:9f., 19). But if love belongs to the divine sphere, it follows that anybody who shows love must belong to that sphere; he has been born of God and now lives in the knowledge of God.[3] John does not say, "everyone who has been born of God loves," which would have the effect of laying an obligation on the readers. Rather he is making two parallel statements: (all) love comes from God; therefore all lovers have been born of God. John is here concerned with definition, not with exhortation.

To be sure, the statement is open to misunderstanding. One might conclude that anybody who shows love is a child of God, regardless of whether he actually believes in Jesus Christ as the Son of God. This misunderstanding can only arise, however, if we take this statement and wrench it out of its context in the letter. John makes it plain enough elsewhere that the true child of God *both* believes *and* loves (3:23). Nevertheless, we might still want to ask how it is possible for people who do not believe in Jesus Christ to

---

[1]Cf. 4:11. However, John uses this form of address in a variety of contexts, and his motivation for using it appears to lie basically in his affection as a pastor for his readers.

[2]Both of these nuances are present in the phrase ἐκ τοῦ Θεοῦ ἐστιν.

[3]For birth from God see 2:29; 3:9; for knowing God see 2:3f., 13f.; 3:1, 6; 4:6. Here John uses the present tense (cf. 4:6; 5:20) to bring out the thought of a continuing relationship; in verse 8, however, he uses the aorist when speaking of a person who has never come into the experience of knowing God (cf. 2:3f. and n. for the use of the perfect to express the continuing relationship arising from a conversion experience).

love one another—as they manifestly do. There *is* love outside the Christian church, and sometimes non-Christians seem to love one another better than Christians do. How is the existence of such love to be explained, and what does its presence indicate regarding the status before God of those who show it? Has John been shutting his eyes to the facts of life? A theological answer to the question would be phrased in terms of the doctrines of creation and common grace. It is because men are created in the image of God, an image which has been defaced but not destroyed by the Fall, that they still have the capacity to love. Moreover, through the preaching of the gospel men are well aware of the obligation to love one another, and they may be influenced by this preaching even though they fail to respond to the call to believe in Jesus Christ. Yet ultimately it is belief in Jesus Christ and love for God which matters. Human love, however noble and however highly motivated, falls short if it refuses to include the Father and Son as the supreme objects of its affection. It falls short of the divine pattern, and by itself it cannot save a man; it cannot be put into the balance to compensate for the sin of rejecting God. Love alone, therefore, is not a sign of being born of God.

8 As we have so frequently seen, John emphasizes his point by stating the converse. A person who does not love does not know God. His lack of love demonstrates that he does not belong to the divine sphere, since God is love. The implication is that knowledge of God as love leads men to love one another. A person cannot come into a real relationship with a loving God without being transformed into a loving person. John does not explain how this transformation comes about. He speaks of it as an obligation in verse 11, but he also implies that the love of God takes control of our natures and transforms us.

But it is the subordinate clause in this verse which carries the real emphasis and provides the theme for the next few sentences. "God is love" is rightly recognized as one of the high peaks of divine revelation in this Epistle. Logically the statement stands parallel with "God is light" (1:5) and "God is spirit" (Jn. 4:24) as one of the three great Johannine expressions of the nature of God. Some theologians give the impression that the present statement is superior to the other two, but there is no justification for doing this. We do wrong to exalt the love of God as his supreme feature just because it is more congenial to our thinking. Nevertheless, it is true that "God is spirit" describes his metaphysical nature, while "God is light" and "God is love" deal with his character, especially as he has revealed himself to men. It has been noted that to speak of God as love is not to reduce God to the status of an abstract quality. The statement refers to his action. Yet it signifies more than "God loves," for its effect is to claim that *all* God's action is loving. Since love is a personal activity, the statement stresses the personality of God to the fullest extent. At the same time, the immense gulf between God and men is expressed; of no man could it possibly be said that he *is* love. Only God is completely loving.

There is no need to enter into a historical survey of the teaching of Scripture on this point. It would merely demonstrate that this statement is simply the clearest expression of a doctrine of the nature of God that is attested throughout its pages. Equally it would show that outside the pages of Scripture there is no comparable picture of God.[4]

God is all-loving and, equally, all-holy (1:5). These two characteristics do not stand in opposition to one another but belong together and determine his actions. Consequently, it is not surprising that John does not stay on the level of abstract theological assertion but proceeds directly to speak of how God has showed his love.

9 John has already in fact told us "how we know what love is," and has thereby safeguarded his readers from the danger of confusing God's love with human substitutes of inferior quality (3:16). Now he goes over the ground again, but in such a way as to underline certain points and introduce fresh ones. His language is strongly reminiscent of John 3:16, and there can be no doubt that he is deliberately reminding his readers of that tremendous declaration. He stresses at the outset that the coming of Jesus, which is the supreme example of love, demonstrates *God's* own love. This thought was implicit in 3:16f., but needed to be stated explicitly. The way in which John puts the point shows that the coming of Jesus is the visible indication in our experience[5] of the hidden love of God.[6] Has there ever been a better attempt to illustrate the point than that

---

[4]On love see 3:16 n.; 2 John 1 n.; E. Stauffer, TDNT I, 21–55; G. Stählin, TDNT IX, 113–171; W. Günther, H.-G. Link, and C. Brown, NIDNTT II, 538–551; A. Nygren, *Agape and Eros*, New York/London, 1953[2]; C. Spicq, *Agape in the New Testament*, St. Louis, 1963–66; G. Outka, *Agape: An Ethical Analysis*, New Haven, 1972; Dodd, 107–110; Schnackenburg, 231–239; M. de Jonge, *Jesus: Inspiring and Disturbing Presence*, Nashville, 1974, 110–127.

[5]For the thought of the revelation of God taking place "in the midst" of believers see Luke 1:1; John 1:14; 1 Corinthians 11:19; 2 Corinthians 4:3 (so Schnackenburg, 229 n. 4, stressing the local sense). But ἐν ἡμῖν can also mean "to us" (BD 206[3]; 220[1]; Haas, 108). Westcott, 149, held that the phrase meant that God's love is revealed "in us" believers as the medium through which it becomes known to the world (so Brooke, 119). See further on verse 16.

[6]φανερόω conveys the thought of the manifestation of what was previously hidden.

in Helen Waddell's *Peter Abelard,* where we have the picture of a freshly felled tree?—the rings which appear on the cut face of the log are the visible cross-section of lines that run right up the trunk, hidden from view by the bark. So the cross of Jesus is the visible appearance in this world of love that stretches back beyond our vision into the depths of eternity.[7] God sent his one and only Son[8] into this world in order that we might obtain life[9] through him. Here we see the two factors which determine the nature of love: on the one hand, self-sacrifice, and, on the other hand, action done for the benefit of others. Although the actual word "give" is not used here (contrast 3:1; Jn. 3:16), the thought is obvious enough. John's use of his favorite verb "send" may have been dictated by a desire to emphasize the way in which the Son came from the heavenly sphere right into this sinful, rebellious world.

10 In the preceding verse John has described the character of God's love. Now he goes even further. Here, he says, is love—not just the love of God but love as such. There can be no explanation or definition of true love which does not start from God's love. We cannot begin to understand love by considering the nature of our love for God.[10] Rather love is to be seen in the prior act of God who loved us and expressed his love by sending[11] his Son as an atoning

[7]H. Waddell, *Peter Abelard,* London, 1933, 290.
[8]The word μονογενής is used of only children (Lk. 7:12; 8:42; 9:38; Heb. 11:17), and is applied to God's Son in John 1:14, 18; 3:16, 18. In the Old Testament the Hebrew word *yāḥîd,* "single, only," is sometimes rendered into Greek by ἀγαπητός, "beloved" (Gen. 22:2, 12, 16; Jer. 6:26; Amos 8:10; Zech. 12:10 LXX), and sometimes by μονογενής (Judg. 11:34 LXX; cf. the later Gk. versions of Gen. 22:2, 12; Jer. 6:26; Prov. 4:3; Josephus, Ant. 1:222; 5:264). This has suggested that μονογενής may contain the nuance "beloved," especially since an only child is particularly loved by his parents. It is not clear whether the -γενής part of the word retained any force: the NIV text assumes that the word simply meant "one and only," but the NIV margin (adopted in place of the text in the edition of the NIV produced for the Gideons) allows that the thought of God's begetting of the Son is present in the word. But the -γενής part of the compound is concerned with derivation or kind (γένος) rather than with birth (γεννάω). The English "only begotten" arose from Jerome's use of *unigenitus* to replace the Old Latin translation *unicus* in an effort to deny Arian claims that Jesus was not begotten by God. See D. Moody, "God's Only Son: The Translation of John 3:16 in the Revised Standard Version," JBL 72, 1953, 213–219; K.-H. Bartels, NIDNTT II, 725. Nevertheless, some scholars hold that John's use of the word may reflect the divine begetting of the Son which is clearly taught in 5:18, although they produce little tangible evidence to support this view (F. Büchsel, TDNT IV, 737–741; R. Schnackenburg, *Das Johannesevangelium,* Freiburg, 1965, I, 246f.).
[9]ζήσωμεν is an ingressive aorist. For the verb cf. John 5:25; 6:51, 57f.; 11:25; 14:19.
[10]The use of the perfect ἠγαπήκαμεν (B; most authorities have ἠγαπήσαμεν) perhaps stresses that it is not our continuing love for God which should be central but the love which he revealed historically to us (ἠγάπησεν, aorist) in Jesus (de Jonge, 198 n. 367).
[11]The change from the perfect (v. 9) to the aorist stresses the historic manifestation of the love rather than the continuing effects of God's act.

sacrifice for our sins.[12] In this phrase we find the deepest meaning of the term "love": love means forgiving the sins of the beloved and remembering them no more. This is what God has done for rebellious mankind: he pardons their sins against himself at his own cost. To remove this element from the biblical teaching on the nature of God's love is to water down the concept of love beyond measure. It is true that some writers have denied that a loving God needs to be propitiated for human sin and have suggested that this makes him less than loving. They have not realized that the depth of God's love is to be seen precisely in the way in which it bears the wounds inflicted on it by mankind and offers full and free pardon. The point was expressed once and for all by James Denney:

> So far from finding any kind of contrast between love and propitiation, the apostle can convey no idea of love to anyone except by pointing to the propitiation—love is what is manifested there; and he can give no account of the propitiation but by saying, "Behold what manner of love." For him, to say "God is love" is exactly the same as to say, "God has in His Son made atonement for the sin of the world." If the propitiatory death of Jesus is eliminated from the love of God, it might be unfair to say that the love of God is robbed of all meaning, but it is certainly robbed of its apostolic meaning. It has no longer that meaning which goes deeper than sin, sorrow, and death, and which recreates life in the adoring joy, wonder, and purity of the first Epistle of John.[13]

11 The recipients of such love have no choice as to their response. Their sins have been taken away by this gracious act of God. He has loved them in such a way[14] as to arouse adoring wonder at the magnitude of his sacrificial giving. They cannot do anything else but show love to one another.

Moralists have long puzzled over the problem of how a command can be generated out of a statement. How can "we ought to love one another" be logically based on "God loved us"?[15] John was no doubt unconscious of this problem. It was sufficient for him to claim that the recipients of divine love must demonstrate the same

---

[12]On the meaning of ἱλασμός see 2:2 n. The meaning of the word is clearly defined by its context in 2:2. Here the word is used almost incidentally in a discussion of divine love, and consequently the context is less precisely defined. It would, however, be false to argue from the absence of thoughts of judgment and wrath in the present context that the word has no connection with these concepts.

[13]J. Denney, *The Death of Christ,* London, 1951, 152.

[14]The use of οὕτως is a strong echo of John 3:16.

[15]For discussion of the logical relationship between "is" statements and "ought" statements see W. D. Hudson (ed.), *The Is-Ought Question,* New York/London, 1969.

love. He could not understand how a person could experience divine love and remain unmoved by the obligation to love other people in the same way as God had loved him; the connection is not so much through the logic of moral philosophy as through the constraint of experienced love which generates fresh love. It is significant that John does not say that experience of God's love should constrain us, to love him in return; rather he speaks of our obligation to love others. Although he is thinking primarily of love within the Christian fellowship, the fact that he starts from a statement of God's love for sinners strongly suggests that his vision is not limited to the church but extends to the world.

12 The logical structure of John's thought at this point is not crystal clear. Having stated in verse 11 that we ought to love one another, he wants to go on to say that if we fulfil this command, God lives in us and his love is made complete in us. But before he reaches this point he slips in a contrasting statement, against which his conclusion must be understood. Nobody, he says, has ever seen God. This is a familiar thought in the Old Testament, and it is taken up in John 1:18, a verse which is clearly in the author's mind here.[16] In John 1:18 a contrast is drawn between the invisibility of God and the fact of his revelation in his incarnate Son, Jesus Christ. Here the contrast is with the way in which God is made known to us in the context of mutual love. The statement has been thought to be out of context; it anticipates the point made in verse 20.[17] Nevertheless, its position here is deliberate. It may well have been the case that there were people around who claimed some kind of direct vision of God, perhaps through mystical experiences; possibly John's opponents claimed something of the kind.[18] But John insists that God is not to be known in this kind of way at all. It remains true, despite all claims to the contrary, that God cannot be seen. Nor does John go on to say

[16]Cf. John 5:37; 6:46; Exodus 33:20 is the classical reference; see W. Michaelis, TDNT V, 329–334; Jewish teaching generally adopted the same line, *ibid.*, 334–340. John's use of the verb θεάομαι here (contrast ἑώρακεν, Jn. 1:18) may reflect an ancient wordplay based on the etymological connection that was believed to exist between θεός and θεάομαι (P. W. van der Horst, "A Wordplay in 1 Joh 4, 12?", ZNW 63, 1972, 280–282).

[17]Houlden, 114; nevertheless, he admits that there is no textual evidence that the clause has been misplaced.

[18]Schnackenburg, 240f., draws attention to the apocalyptic idea of the heavenly ascent of the soul (1 Enoch 71; 2 Enoch 1ff.; T.Levi 2–5; 2 Bar.; 4 Ezra 1; Ḥag. 14b) and to the heavenly journey of the soul in Gnosticism (Mithras Liturgy 6, 9ff.; CH 1:24–26; Apuleius, *Metamorphoses* 11:23; A. Oepke, TDNT II, 449–460); he thinks that ideas of the latter kind may be in John's mind here.

that those who love one another will be granted a vision of God. Such a vision is reserved for the parousia (3:2). What does happen is that if we fulfil the command to love one another,[19] then we experience the presence of God in ourselves.[20] At the same time God's love is made complete in us. Here we have the same problem of interpretation as we faced in 2:5 and 3:17: does "his love" mean "God's love for us," or "our love for God," or "God's kind of love"? The first alternative is attractive in the present context (v. 9),[21] but it does not fit in with John's usage in 2:15 and 5:3. If we adopt the second alternative, then the thought is that loving one another is an essential part of truly loving God.[22] The third alternative avoids some of the difficulties in the first.[23] The point would then be that it is when we love others that God's love for us has its full effect in our lives, or that our love for God reaches full expression (since loving him involves fulfilling his command to love one another), or that the kind of love that God showed to us is being fully expressed in our lives. Decision between these possibilities is not easy, and it may well be that John himself would not have sharply distinguished between them.[24] On the whole it seems best to effect a combination of the first and third possibilities: when we love others, God's love for us has reached its full effect in creating the same kind of love as his in us.

John thus turns his back on mystical experience as the high point in religion. Not for him retreat from the world of men into the privacy of a vision of God. On the contrary, it is only when a person loves his fellow-Christians—on a very practical level (3:17f.)—that he fully experiences the love of God in his own heart and knows the presence of God with him. This does not mean that Christian duty is summed up in merely loving one another, as some would have us believe. John's point is that loving one another is indispensable in a religion which longs to have a true knowledge of God. We cannot

---

[19]The NIV has "each other," which might refer to men and God, but more probably is simply a slip for "one another."

[20]See 3:24 for the thought of God living in believers. Stott, 164, emphasizes that God's presence in us is not the result of our loving one another, but rather that our love for one another is the evidence that God lives in us. But the matter is not quite so simple; there would appear in fact to be a reciprocal relationship between God's part and ours.

[21]Brooke, 120; Bultmann, 68; Stott, 164; Haas, 110; Wengst, 73 n. 172.

[22]Chaine, 204; Dodd, 113: "love to God, which has no meaning apart from obedience, is completed in loving our fellows." Cf. Houlden, 114.

[23]Westcott, 152; Schnackenburg, 241.

[24]See 2:5 n. and especially de Jonge, 77f.

find God by withdrawing from the world and its obligation to love one another; but equally we cannot find God merely by trying to love one another. For true religion comes only through believing in Jesus Christ *and* accepting his command to love another.

ASSURANCE AND CHRISTIAN LOVE (4:13–5:4)

13. *We know that we live in him and he in us, because he has given us of his Spirit.* 14. *And we have seen and testify that the Father has sent his Son to be the Savior of the world.* 15. *If anyone acknowledges that Jesus is the Son of God, God lives in him and he in God.* 16. *And so we know and rely on the love God has for us.*

God is love. Whoever lives in love lives in God, and God in him. 17. *Love is made complete among us so that we will have confidence on the day of judgment, because in this world we are like him.* 18. *There is no fear in love. But perfect love drives out fear, because fear has to do with punishment. The man who fears is not made perfect in love.*

19. *We love because he first loved us.* 20. *If anyone says, "I love God," yet hates his brother, he is a liar. For anyone who does not love his brother, whom he has seen, cannot love God, whom he has not seen.* 21. *And he has given us this command: Whoever loves God must also love his brother.*

5:1. *Everyone who believes that Jesus is the Christ is born of God, and everyone who loves the father loves his child as well.* 2. *This is how we know that we love the children of God: by loving God and carrying out his commands.* 3. *This is love for God: to obey his commands. And his commands are not burdensome,* 4. *for everyone born of God has overcome the world. This is the victory that has overcome the world, even our faith.*

It is not easy to find a single strand of thought running through the Epistle at this point. On the whole it seems likely that John begins by summarizing the grounds on which a person may be sure that he is a Christian: he has received the Spirit, he knows that Jesus has come as the Savior of the world, and thus he has come to experience personally the love of God. John then develops again this thought of love by stating that when we show love, this is a sign that we know God and have communion with him. Consequently we can have confidence for the day of judgment, since there can be no place for fear of punishment in a relationship of love. But this relationship must be a real one, and real love of God exists only when we also love our fellow Christians. The need for brotherly love is obvious: anybody who loves a father is also bound to love his children—and to keep his commands. It might be suggested that this is not easy, but those who are born of God will in fact find that their faith gives them the power over temptations to go the way of the world and disobey God.

13 John has just told his readers that if they love one another this is a sign that God lives in them (v. 12). Now, in a manner somewhat similar to that in 3:24b, he states that we can know that God lives in us by the fact that he has given us the Spirit. He broadens out the statement in verse 12 by speaking not only of God living in us but also of our living in God.[1] Our knowledge that we have this relationship with God arises from the fact that he has given[2] us a share in the Spirit.[3] Thus to the practical test—do we love one another?—there is added the "psychological" test—have we received the Spirit? But how do we know that we have received the Spirit? In our earlier discussion of this point (3:24 n.) we concluded that various experiences might be in mind, such as confidence in prayer, inward conviction that we are God's children, and charismatic gifts. It is possible that the last of these is particularly in mind here: possession of the Spirit may lead to prophecy or other forms of utterance, but these may need to be tested by their fidelity to the apostolic witness.[4] This would explain the transition in thought to the next verse. In any case it is important to recognize that the grounds of Christian assurance and the tests of the reality of Christian experience are multiple: one cannot say that simply because a person professes true belief, or loves his fellow men, or claims to have charismatic experiences, he is a true Christian: it is the combination of these features in a harmonious unity that makes up true Christianity.

14 If our attempt to work out the connection of thought is correct, then it would seem that John is listing a further characteristic of the true Christian, by which he may be differentiated from those who rest their claims simply on charismatic experiences. The test for the reality of spiritual gifts is whether those who possess them also

---

[1] See 2:6, 24, 27, 28; 3:6, 24a.

[2] The use of the perfect δέδωκεν by contrast with the aorist ἔδωκεν in 3:24b does not seem to be a significant difference. The thought is of the continuing presence of the Spirit in the believer.

[3] ἐκ τοῦ πνεύματος is partitive; contrast 3:24b (BD 169).

[4] Haas, 110. The connection of thought would then be similar to that in 3:24/4:1–6.

hold to the apostolic faith. So John goes on to state that he and his readers have seen and now bear witness that the Father has sent his Son to be the Savior of the world. Although the wording is close to that of 1:1f., it seems likely that here we have the testimony of the church as a whole rather than merely of the original eyewitnesses of the earthly ministry of Jesus.[5] The confession which is made is similar to the statements made in verses 9f.[6] But where the previous statements described Jesus as an atoning sacrifice for sins, here he is called the Savior of the world. It is through being the former that Jesus can be the latter, and once again the universality of Jesus' sacrifice is implicitly brought out (cf. 2:2). The confession should remind us of the words of the Samaritans who discovered for themselves that Jesus "really is the Savior of the world" (Jn. 4:42).[7]

15 The fact that John has his opponents in mind is confirmed by the way in which he now applies the point made in verse 14. It is only if a person confesses that Jesus is the Son of God that he is joined to God in fellowship. In other words, the possibility of spiritual fellowship with God depends on the historical fact of the incarnation; we must confess that the Father sent the Son, and that the Son is Jesus. Clearly this is a confession which goes beyond mere recognition of the historical fact. To acknowledge that Jesus is the Son of God is not simply to make a statement about his metaphysical status but to express obedient trust in the One who possesses such a status. Nowadays the tendency is often to express obedient trust in Jesus while denying his metaphysical status as the

---

[5]Westcott, 153, suggests that "the emphatic pronoun . . . brings into prominence the experience of the Christian Society gathered up in that of its leaders"; similarly, Bruce, 111; de Jonge, 201. For the view that the original eyewitnesses are meant see Brooke, 121; Chaine, 205; Ross, 204; Stott, 166; Schnackenburg, 242. For the view that "the Church and its ministry continuing the apostolic witness to the Gospel" is meant see Dodd, 115. The first of these three views, which recognizes the primary reference to the apostles but stresses that the whole church is represented by them, does justice both to the language of personal experience and also to the link with verse 16 where the author places himself and his readers over against unbelievers.
[6]In both verse 10 and verse 14 the task of the Son is described by an appositional phrase.
[7]The term "Savior" is less common than might be expected in the New Testament. It appears in Luke 2:11; Acts 5:31; 13:23; Ephesians 5:23; Philippians 3:20; 2 Timothy 1:10; Titus 1:4; 2:13; 3:6; 2 Peter 1:1, 11; 2:20; 3:2, 18 with reference to Jesus, and in Luke 1:47; 1 Timothy 1:1; 2:3; 4:10; Titus 1:3; 2:10; 3:4; Jude 25 of God. Schnackenburg, 243f., notes that the title was used with reference to the Roman emperor and suspects that the Christian usage may have developed partly in contrast and opposition to this. It may also have been used to claim that Jesus was superior to other gods worshiped in the Hellenistic world; see further W. Foerster, TDNT VII, 1003–1021.

Son of God, or at least being agnostic about it. Both elements, however, remain necessary: belief that Jesus is the Son of God and obedient trust in him.

16 It is probably best to see this verse as a parallel statement to verse 14, expressing another basic Christian conviction.[8] The believer is sure of his faith because he has personally experienced the love of God. He has come to know it[9] and also to put his trust in it.[10] He is absolutely sure of its reality. The object is expressed somewhat strangely. Literally it is "the love which God has in us." This way of putting the matter suggests that John is thinking not merely of the love for us shown by God in the cross but also of the personal experience of his love in our hearts created by the Spirit (Rom. 5:5).[11]

There is some uncertainty whether the rest of the verse should be regarded as concluding the present train of thought, with a new paragraph beginning at verse 17, or as marking the beginning of a new topic.[12] On the whole it is more probable that verse 16b has the same function as verse 15: in both cases the comment draws a conclusion regarding the people who make the confession that has just been described. Since God is love, as has already been stated (v. 8), it follows that the person who lives in love lives in God and God in him. Stott rightly notes that living in love is the proof or result of living in God: it is not by loving that we come into fellowship with God, but as a result of our fellowship with him we live in love.[13] Commentators are uncertain whether John is referring to our living in God's love for us or our love for him and our brothers.[14] But it is probable that no differentiation is intended. John means that the true Christian lives in the sphere of love, both as the object of God's love and as a channel of that love to his brothers. More than one subse-

---

[8]On this view, verse 16 is not dependent on verse 15, nor is it a summary of verses 14f. (Haas, 111), nor is it a return to the point after the digression in verses 14f. (Schnackenburg, 242).

[9]Perfect tense: "we have come to know and still know."

[10]The use of πιστεύω with a direct object is unusual (Jn. 11:26; 1 Cor. 13:7); here the use of the accusative is determined by the preceding verb (Schnackenburg, 244).

[11]Bruce, 112. Westcott, 155, appears to think of the manifestation of love in the life of the church.

[12]The NIV begins a new section at verse 16b (similarly, Westcott, 156; Brooke, 122). Haas, 111, rightly argues, however, that the repetition of the formula of mutual indwelling (cf. vv. 13, 15) marks the end of the paragraph.

[13]Stott, 168.

[14]Most commentators think that human love is meant, but a human love that is modeled on and inspired by divine love.

quent writer has taken up the words of Dodd at this point: they deserve quoting at length, for they sum the matter up in magisterial fashion:

> The expression "to remain in love" is suggestive rather than exact. It is not clear whether the meaning is "to continue to live as the objects of God's love," or "to continue to love God," or "to continue to love our brothers." It is in fact impossible, according to the teaching both of this epistle and of the Fourth Gospel, to make a clear separation between these three modes or manifestations of love. The energy of love discharges itself along lines which form a triangle, whose points are God, self and neighbour: but the source of all love is God, of whom alone it can be said that He *is* love. Whether we love God or our neighbour, it is God's love that is at work in us—assuming, that is, that our love is that authentic *agapé* which is exemplified in God's gift of His Son, and in Christ's sacrifice for us all.[15]

Here, then, the three characteristics of the Christian emerge: possession of the Spirit, confession of Jesus as the Son of God, and living in the love of God. On this basis there can be erected a firm foundation for Christian hope.

17 This is what John now proceeds to do. Earlier he had spoken of a basis for confidence in approaching God in prayer (3:19–22), but now there is a more serious matter that claims attention. Perhaps confidence in prayer comes and goes; the vital question is whether we have confidence

> *. . . in that all-important day,*
> *When I the summons must obey,*
> *And pass from this dark world away. . . .*[16]

---

[15]Dodd, 117f.; echoed by Schnackenburg, 245; de Jonge, 203f. The rest of Dodd's comment is worth pondering: "The famous aphorism of 16b, in its English dress, readily lends itself to falsely sentimental interpretations, if it is detached from its total context. It does not mean that anyone who feels for another person any sort of liking, affection or passion, which we loosely include under the term 'love', is *ipso facto* in union with God. The true nature of divine charity is sufficiently defined by reference to the Gospels, and it is this love, or charity, that is meant."

This closely knit statement therefore places the reality of the Christian experience of God beyond question, guarding against the dangers of subjectivism on the one hand, and of mere traditionalism on the other; placing equal and co-ordinate stress on love to God, which is the heart of religion, and love to man, which is the foundation of morality, without allowing religion to sink to the level of mere moralism, or morality to be dissolved in mysticism. The passage is the high-water mark of the thought of the epistle" (*ibid.,* 118).

[16]R. Jukes, "My heart is fixed, eternal God," *The Methodist Hymnbook,* No. 403.

How may we be sure that "we may be confident and unashamed before him at his coming" (2:28)?

The NIV translation conceals the initial "By this" which indicates the way in which love is made complete among us.[17] As in verse 16 it is likely that the love of which John is speaking is the relationship of love which involves both God's love to us and our love to him.[18] This experience of mutual love is fully realized[19] in the fact that we can have confidence on the day of judgment.[20] John will explain more fully how this is the case in the next verse, when he comments that in a relationship of love between ourselves and our Judge there can be no fear of him as Judge but only the confidence which is born of love. But before reaching this principle he makes the comment that this confidence is possible because "in this world we are like him," i.e. Jesus. Although we are in the sinful world with its temptations, nevertheless we do not belong to the world but we stand in the same relationship to God as that of Jesus to his Father and we live as Jesus lived (2:6). Some scholars have seen a difficulty here in that we are not in fact like Jesus, and shall only become like him when we see him at the second coming (3:2); this difficulty is already reflected in the variations in wording introduced by some scribes, and has led some modern scholars to rewrite the text or to conclude that John is inconsistent.[21] It seems doubtful whether such expedients are necessary. We probably have here another example of that portrayal of the "eschatological reality" of the Christian life which we found particularly in 3:6, 9; John is stating the characteristic which ought to be found in every true Christian, namely that he is

---

[17]Most commentators take ἐν τούτῳ as pointing forward to the ἵνα clause (understood as a noun clause); cf. John 15:8 (Brooke, 123f.; Schnackenburg, 246; Bultmann, 72; Haas, 111). Westcott, 157, claimed that the phrase refers backward: "in this double communion (v. 16) love has been perfected, so that we may have boldness . . ." (cf. RSV). This seems more natural. See 2:5 n.

[18]The phrase has been taken to refer to God's love for us (Bultmann, 72; Haas, 111f.) or to our love for God (AV; Stott, 168). For the view that love as the divine mode of existence is meant, see Schnackenburg, 246.

[19]τελειόομαι here signifies "to come to full expression"; cf. 2:5; 4:12. The phrase μεθ' ἡμῶν is unusual. Westcott, 157, held that it was used to show that in perfecting his love God works along with men. The phrase may be a Hebraism, reflecting use of 'im (Brooke, 124) or 'ēṯ (Schnackenburg, 246). One may perhaps compare the use of μετά in greetings and blessings (AG, s.v., A II 1 c γ); cf. 2 John 3.

[20]For παρρησία see 2:28; 3:21; 5:14. For the day of judgment see Matthew 10:15; 11:22, 24; 12:36; 2 Peter 2:9; 3:7; cf. Jude 6. There is no need whatever to follow Bultmann, 72, in regarding the phrase as an ecclesiastical interpolation.

[21]See Houlden, 117–119, who notes that some minuscules replace "as he is, so we are" by "as he was spotless and clean in this world, so we too shall be"; less drastically S has "as he is, so we shall be." These alterations indicate the difficulty felt

like Jesus, but this is not incompatible with his urging his readers to let the ideal become a reality. Were it not so, our grounds for confidence might seem very slender and fitful.

18 Fear and love cannot coexist. This is why a person who stands in a relationship of love to God can look forward to the future day of judgment without fear and apprehension. One can argue whether the thought is of God's love for us or of our love for him. In the former case, we do not need to be afraid of One who loves us; in the latter case, we cannot love and fear simultaneously.[22] The second part of the verse may appear to support the second of these two possibilities, but probably the best interpretation lies in a combination of the two: in a relationship of mutual love there is no possibility of fear. Where there is a perfect relationship of love, it drives out all fear of God. This must be so, says John, because fear is bound up with punishment. Here again John's meaning is ambiguous. He may mean that the fear in question is fear of final retribution, and since the person who stands in a relationship of love to God stands in no danger of condemnation and judgment, it follows that he has no need to be afraid of God.[23] Alternatively, he may mean that fear is in itself a painful experience, and this too is incompatible with a loving relationship with God.[24] Either way, the thought is that God will not cause his children pain. If a person is afraid of God, this is because the love of God has not yet filled his heart and driven out all fear.

There is, of course, a place for fear in the life of the Christian. The word "fear" can be used in a somewhat weak sense to indicate that reverence for God which characterized believers under the old dispensation and which is still demanded in the new (Lk. 1:50; Acts 10:2, 22, 35; 13:16, 26; cf. 9:31; 2 Cor. 7:1; Eph. 5:21; 6:5; Col. 3:22; 1 Pet. 1:17). There is also a sense in which the believer must serve

---

by scribes in view of (a) the present tense ἐστιν describing Jesus, and (b) the present tense ἐσμεν describing our state. But these alterations fail to appreciate that Jesus still is what he was while on earth, namely in perfect union with God (Haas, 112), and that we also stand in this relationship of love with God. It is probable that in 3:2 the thought is more of sharing the glory of Jesus at the parousia, while here it is more of the relationship of love to God. Houlden himself admits that the teaching given here is comprehensible, especially if John 17 is taken as a fuller statement of the relationship between Christ and his followers on earth which is succinctly presented here.

[22]See above, 223 n. 18, for the same problem in verse 17.

[23]See Schnackenburg, 248 and n. 4, who notes that κόλασις is an eschatological term (Mt. 25:46).

[24]So Bultmann, 73f., who is thus able to claim that John has de-eschatologized the idea of κόλασις; similarly, J. Schneider, TDNT III, 816f. Haas, 113, rightly notes that both interpretations are possible; the fear of future pain is a present pain.

God "with fear and trembling" (2 Cor. 7:15; Eph. 6:5; Phil. 2:12). Clearly there is a distinction between reverence for God and fear of judgment. It is sadly the case, however, that our relationship to God can sometimes fall away from perfect love, and then we need to be reminded of his judgment to prevent us from falling further into sin. As long as I love my fellow-men, I have no fear of the law which forbids murder. It is only when I slip away from love and begin to hate them that I need the fear of the law to warn me against letting my hate turn into murderous action and to exhort me to return to love.[25]

19 But the main instrument which God uses to bring us back to a true relationship of love is not fear of his judgment but the fact of his love. We love because he first loved us. Our love for God[26] is based on God's prior[27] love for us, and is thus the response of gratitude. The more we realize how much God loved us, the more we shall realize our obligation to love him in return. It is, therefore, good for us constantly to renew our knowledge of God's love as we read of it in the Bible, as we hear it proclaimed in the worship of the church, and as we consider the ways in which our whole life has been molded by experiences of God's love and care for us.

20 Such love for God, however, must be expressed in brotherly love. If a person claims to love God and yet fails to love his fellow Christians, that person is manifestly a liar. For the biblical injunction is that we should love God and our brothers. Jesus summed up the commands of God[28] in this double requirement, and, according to John's Gospel, he laid particular stress on the need for brotherly love (Jn. 13:34). A person may deceive other men by declaring that he loves God; but since God cannot be seen, there is no direct way of telling whether he truly loves God. Even if he goes through the outward motions of devotion to God, prayer, attendance at worship, and so on, it may still be all empty show. But a person

[25]See further H. Balz and G. Wanke, TDNT IX, 189–219, especially 216; W. Mundle, NIDNTT I, 621–624.

[26]So A B 424^mg *al* vg^w; other MSS add αὐτόν or τὸν Θεόν, regarded as giving the correct sense by Bultmann, 75. Schnackenburg, 249, however, argues that love for one another is meant, since this is the theme of the following verses. But perhaps both God and our brothers are in mind (Haas, 114). The form ἀγαπῶμεν may be indicative (so most commentators) or subjunctive, expressing an exhortation (Schnackenburg, 249); the former seems more natural and gives the primary sense.

[27]πρῶτος has a comparative sense (Jn. 1:15, 30; BD 62). For the thought cf. *Odes of Solomon* 3:3 (Chaine, 203).

[28]ἀπ᾽ αὐτοῦ in verse 21 probably refers to God, since Jesus has not been mentioned in the context (Schnackenburg, 250 n. 2).

cannot so easily deceive others regarding his love for his fellow Christians; since they can be seen, the person's relation with them is also visible. (Admittedly, there is still the possibility of deception, since apparently loving acts may arise from false motives, but the possibility is not so great as in the case of love for the unseen God.) It follows that if a person is seen not to love his brothers, it is unlikely that he loves God. Indeed, he *cannot* love God, since one part of love for God[29] is love for one's brothers.[30]

21 The point is underlined by a final reminder that God's command to those who love him is that they also love one another (2:9; 3:10, 23). John's readers needed to have the point emphasized, no doubt because some of them failed to realize that love for God and love for one's brothers are inseparable. The lesson is still needed for modern readers. It is easy to have a kind of love for God which does not recognize the obligation to love one another. Such love for God falls short of being real love for him, since it fails to obey his commandments.

5:1 At first sight John seems to have moved to a fresh theme, that of faith and divine sonship, a view that is strengthened by John's concentration on faith in the following verses. But the second part of the verse is still concerned with love, and it is probable that the first part of the verse should be understood as an introduction to a further thought about love; nevertheless, it introduces an idea which will be taken up more fully once the author has concluded his exposition of the place of love.

He begins by affirming that everybody who holds the true confession of faith about Jesus has been born of God.[31] Faith is thus a sign of the new birth, just as love (4:7) and doing what is right (2:29; 3:9f.) are also indications that a person has been born of God. At the same time, however, faith is a condition of the new birth: "to all who received him, to those who believed in his name, he gave the right to become children of God" (Jn. 1:12). Here, however, John is not trying to show how a person experiences the new birth; his aim

[29]Bultmann, 76, wrongly claims that our love for God is expressed only in love for our brothers. On the contrary, love for our brothers is only part of the expression of our love for God, but an indispensable part.

[30]For the interpretation given above see Dodd, 124. The alternative, more commonly accepted, view is that if a person cannot love his fellow-men (which is easier, because he can see them), he cannot perform the more difficult task of loving the unseen God. Dodd rightly comments that John's concern is not with stages by which we learn to love God but with the tests by which it may be known whether we love him truly. Schnackenburg, 250, apparently combines the two views.

[31]John uses the perfect tense, as often, to indicate the present state of the believer.

is rather to indicate the evidence which shows that a person stands in the continuing relationship of a child to God his Father: that evidence is that he holds to the true faith about Jesus.

But this statement is merely preparatory to John's main point. He follows it up with a second preparatory statement, from which he will draw a conclusion in verse 2. It is surely self-evident that everybody who loves a parent also loves his child. A number of commentators think that the point is slightly less general; they take John to be saying that anybody who loves his own father will also love his father's other children, his own brothers and sisters.[32] This at least is the general rule and expresses what we normally expect to happen; the cases where people do not love their brothers and sisters are generally recognized to be contraventions of the intended natural order of things.

2 Now comes the conclusion. We would expect John to say, "Everybody who is born of God (the Father) must love his fellow Christians." But this is not what he says. His expression is more complicated. The NIV adopts one common interpretation of the text by finding a forward reference in the verse: "This is how we know that we love the children of God: by loving God and carrying out his commands."[33] This, however, is not what we would expect John to say. Normally he argues from the fact that we love our brothers to the fact that we love God; love for our brothers is the evidence and proof that we love God and keep his commands (3:14f., 17–19; 4:20). One way of getting better sense is to regard "we love" as a virtual statement of obligation: "This is how we know that we *ought* to love the children of God when we love God and keep his commands." But once we have adopted this sense of "we love" it is apparent that "this is" no longer refers forward. It must refer backward: "by this principle, namely that we must love our father's [other] children, we know that we ought to love the children of God whenever we love God and keep his commands." The content of loving God and keeping his commands is love for God's children, since love for God must involve love for his children.[34] So John is saying what we would

---

[32]So apparently Westcott, 177, and clearly Brooke, 129; Haas, 115. It would seem that John is stating a general rule of human experience rather than referring primarily at this point to the relation between God and his children (despite Chaine, 210; Bultmann, 76).

[33]Similarly, TEV; Brooke, 129; Stott, 173; cf. Bultmann, 77; Houlden, 123.

[34]See especially Dodd, 124f.; Schnackenburg, 252; Haas, 115. The objection that ἐν τούτῳ usually points forward in this Epistle (Brooke, 129) is false; it can undoubtedly refer backward (3:19). Bultmann, 77 n. 12, argues that this view causes

expect him to say, but he has expressed himself in a different manner. It is worth asking why John expressed himself like this. The most probable answer is that he wished to move on to the thought of keeping God's commandments, and therefore tried to include this idea, placing it at the end of the verse to form a link to his next statement.[35]

3 We already know that love for God is expressed in keeping his commandments (2:4f.; 2 Jn. 6; cf. Jn. 14:15, 21). Now we are reminded of the fact. It is an appropriate addition, for elsewhere John has shown us that God's commandments are summed up in the command to love one another. Here, however, the thought is a bridge, leading over to the main point that these commandments—and hence the duty of loving one another—are not burdensome. They are not beyond our ability to keep. Jesus offers us an easy yoke and a light burden (Mt. 11:30).[36] If we are tempted to think that the love and obedience demanded of Christians are beyond our powers, this verse comes as a welcome source of strength and encouragement.

4 How, then, can the believer keep God's commandments? John's answer is that he has been given the power by God to overcome the forces of temptation which would prevent his obedience. Everyone[37] born of God has overcome the world. The power that enables believers to overcome false prophets (4:4) also enables them

---

difficulties with the ὅταν clause, and that it is necessary to suppose an inversion of order, so that the sentence really means: "we always then love (also) the children of God when we truly love God (their Father and ours)." But the fact that the ὅταν clause comes last may be because John wished to create a link with the next verse.
[35]The last clause is rather awkwardly tacked on. ποιῶμεν is read by B *al* r vg sa; the variant τηρῶμεν is an assimilation of an unusual phrase (found only here in the NT) to the more usual form found in the next verse (Metzger, 715). Although the latter reading is adopted by *Diglot,* presumably on the grounds that B represents an elegant correction, it is hard to see why the correction was not made also in verse 3.

R. Kittler, "Erweis der Bruderliebe an der Bruderliebe? Versuch der Auslegung eines 'fast unverständlichen' Satzes im I. Johannesbrief," *Kerygma und Dogma* 16, 1970, 223–228, offers the improbable exegesis that we can only tell who are our brothers by actually loving people; see the criticism in de Jonge, 309.
[36]βαρύς here means not important (Mt. 23:23) but burdensome (Mt. 11:30; 23:4; Lk. 11:46; cf. SB I, 901–905; G. Schrenk, TDNT I, 556–558; W. Mundle, NIDNTT I, 260–262).
[37]"Everyone" is a translation of a neuter phrase (contrast 5:1), possibly meant in a generalizing sense (Jn. 6:37; 17:2). T. W. Manson, "Entry into Membership of the Early Church," JTS 48, 1947, 25–33, especially 27, suggested that the neuter was meant collectively (cf. Jn. 6:37) to express the whole body of those begotten of God. The neuter is also found in John 3:6; is it possible that the use is influenced by the fact that the Greek words for "child" are neuter?

to overcome the world with all its temptations. And what is this power? The means of victory[38] is our faith. The fact that we hold the true faith[39] from our hearts is the means whereby the power of the new world operates in us and enables us to overcome the world. It is striking that John says that we *have* overcome the world. Perhaps he is thinking of the completed victory of Jesus (Jn. 16:33) which repeats itself in the life of the Christian. Or perhaps we should take John's meaning to be: "this is the means of victory, namely what we believe about Jesus who has already overcome the world."[40] To believe that Jesus has been victorious is to have the power that enables us also to win the battle, for we know that our foe is already defeated and therefore powerless. And it is precisely faith that we need. To the natural man the power of evil appears uncontrollable, and to the weak Christian the force of temptation appears irresistible. It requires a firm belief in Jesus to enable us to dismiss this appearance of irresistible, uncontrollable evil as being merely appearance. Nor is such faith a means of escape from conflict; on the contrary it is right in the middle of evil's display of power that the believer is able to call its bluff and proclaim the superior might of Jesus. Such faith is far from being wish-fulfilment or sheer illusion. On the contrary, it rests foursquare on the fact that Jesus Christ has defeated death, and anybody who can defeat death can defeat anything.

> *Though the sons of night blaspheme,*
> *More there are with us than them;*
> *God with us, we cannot fear;*
> *Fear, ye fiends, for Christ is here!*
>
> *Lo! to faith's enlightened sight,*
> *All the mountain flames with light;*
> *Hell is nigh, but God is nigher,*
> *Circling us with hosts of fire.*[41]

---

[38]So AG, *s.v.*, where it is also noted that it was customary to speak of the emperor's νίκη as the power that granted him victory.

[39]It is clear from verse 1 and also from verses 5–12 that the author is concerned not with "faith" as a general attribute but with faith that specifically accepts the truth about Jesus; Bultmann, 78, rightly notes that the word here is used in the sense of confession.

[40]T. W. Manson, *art. cit.*, 27. The aorist participle νικήσασα can refer to Jesus' once-for-all victory.

[41]C. Wesley, "Earth, rejoice, our Lord is King," *The Methodist Hymnbook*, No. 246.

THE TRUE FAITH CONFIRMED (5:5-12)

5. *Who is it that overcomes the world? Only he who believes that
Jesus is the Son of God.*
6. *This is the one who came by water and blood—Jesus Christ.
He did not come by water only, but by water and blood. And it is the
Spirit who testifies, because the Spirit is the truth.* 7. *For there
are three that testify:*[a] 8. *the Spirit, the water, and the blood;
and the three are in agreement.* 9. *We accept man's testimony,
but God's testimony is greater because it is the testimony of God,
which he has given about his Son.* 10. *Anyone who believes in
the Son of God has this testimony in his heart. Anyone who does not
believe God has made him out to be a liar, because he has not believed the testimony God has given about his Son.* 11. *And this
is the testimony: God has given us eternal life, and this life is in
his Son.* 12. *He who has the Son has life; he who does not have
the Son of God does not have life.*

[a]Vulgate adds *in heaven: the Father, the Word and the Holy Spirit, and
these three are one. And there are three that testify on earth:*

In the opening verses of the chapter John has managed to bring
together the three main characteristics of those born of God—belief
in Jesus as the Christ, love for God and one another, and obedience
to the commands of God. He now defines once again the nature of
the true faith which alone gives victory over the world and its temptations and opposition. Jesus is the One who came by water and
blood, a fact corroborated by the Spirit. So there are three witnesses
to a true understanding of Jesus and in their united testimony they
bring us the Father's sure word concerning his Son. If a person
believes in Jesus, this testimony finds a place in his heart and issues
in the experience of eternal life. But anybody who disbelieves God's
testimony is making God out to be a liar and cutting himself off from
eternal life.

5 Verse 5 forms the bridge from John's discussion of the
power of faith to his setting out of the content of true faith and his
statement of the evidence which confirms it. Rhetorically he asks if
anybody can overcome the world[1] if he does not believe that Jesus is

---

[1]John's use of νικάω here is reminiscent of that in Revelation 2:7, 11, 17, 26; 3:5, 12,
21 (Schnackenburg, 256); in Revelation, however, the verb is used absolutely, of
maintaining one's faith and overcoming temptation even to the point of martyrdom,
whereas here the thought is of overcoming the world and its temptations to disobey
God's commands (see 2:13f.) and also of overcoming false teachers (4:4). In both
cases, believers follow the pattern set by Jesus (Jn. 16:33; Rev. 5:5; 17:14); see
O. Bauernfeind, TDNT IV, 942-945; W. Günther, NIDNTT I, 650-652.

the Son of God.[2] There is a slight shift in terminology. In verse 1 the content of true faith was that Jesus is the Christ, whereas here he is to be confessed as the Son of God. This suggests that for John the two titles are virtually synonymous; we may compare the similar oscillation between them in 2:22f. But the title "Son of God" is more appropriate here because John is thinking of the power of God revealed in his Son, Jesus; only the person who recognizes that Jesus is the Son of God can believe that Jesus supplies divine power to overcome the world.[3] The Son of God is the Savior, but only because he shares the power of God which is greater than that of the devil. To believe anything less about Jesus is to believe in somebody who does not have the ability to save us from the power of the godless world.

6 We now have a closer definition of Jesus: the person I am writing about, says John, is the One who came by water and blood,[4] namely Jesus Christ. To the modern reader this is a statement which obscures rather than clarifies the thought. Nevertheless, it was obviously meant to draw the readers' attention to facts which would act as convincing testimony (vv. 7f.) about the person of Jesus. We have already met the word "come" in the wording of the confessions in 2 John 7 and 4:2, where it refers to the coming of Jesus into the world as the incarnate Son of God.[5] John is not, of course, thinking narrowly of the mere moment when the incarnation became a reality at the birth of Jesus; he is thinking of the total act of his coming into the world. This enables us to understand what he means by Jesus coming "by water and blood." In all probability he is referring to the water of Jesus' baptism and the blood of his death.

[2]Literally, "Who is it that overcomes the world but he who believes that Jesus is the Son of God?" (RSV).
[3]For confession (and denial) of Jesus as the Son of God see 2:22f.; 3:23; 4:15; 5:10, 13.
[4]αἵματος is read by B K L Ψ al q vg syᵖ; TR. A few MSS read πνεύματος (43 pc Ambr). The combination αἵματος καὶ πνεύματος is read by S A 614 al syʰ co (and, in reverse order, by P 81 pc). The latter reading, i.e. "by water and blood and Spirit," was accepted by von Soden, and by Moffatt in his translation which forms the basis of Dodd's commentary. Dodd, 128 n., perhaps partly constrained by the need to comment on Moffatt's translation, observed that the reading, "as well as being strongly attested, gives a good sequence of thought," but that "the true text remains uncertain." The reading was also favored by T. W. Manson, "Entry into Membership of the Early Church," JTS 48, 1947, 25–33. The variant certainly gives quite good sense, preparing the way for verse 6b and for verse 8; the reference to the Spirit would be an allusion to the place of the Spirit in the coming of Jesus (see comments below on v. 6c). However, it seems more likely that scribes substituted πνεύματος for αἵματος under the influence of the baptismal narrative or of John 3:5, and then various conflations of the two readings developed (cf. Metzger, 715f.).
[5]See on 4:2 (n. 9).

He is claiming that Jesus Christ truly was baptized and truly died on the cross. The reason why John emphasized these two events in the life of Jesus is to be seen in the second part of the verse where he stresses that Jesus did not come by water only but by water and blood.[6] If we read, as it were, between the lines, it is not hard to guess that John's opponents accepted that Jesus Christ came by water but not by blood. We have already seen who these opponents were (see 2 Jn. 7; 1 Jn. 2:22 and nn.). They were people who held that the heavenly Christ descended upon Jesus at his baptism but withdrew from him before his death, so that it was only the earthly Jesus who died and not the heavenly Christ. Over against this heresy John emphasized that it was Jesus Christ—not simply a human Jesus—who experienced both baptism and crucifixion. John thus understood the baptism of Jesus in a different way from his opponents. They thought of the baptism as the point when Jesus received the heavenly Christ; but John argued that Jesus was already the Christ when he experienced his baptism, and therefore the Christ did not descend upon him at that point. What did descend, as we know from the Gospel, was the Holy Spirit (Jn. 1:32–34). Perhaps, therefore, this is why John speaks here of the water of Jesus' baptism rather than the Spirit which came upon him. He wants to emphasize that the person who went down into the Jordan and over whom John poured the baptismal water was Jesus Christ and not simply a human Jesus; perhaps too he deliberately omits mention of the coming of the Spirit upon Jesus, in case this should be misinterpreted by his opponents. Very probably these opponents held views similar to

---

[6]Although John does not actually mention the baptism of Jesus with water in his Gospel, he clearly implies this fact (Jn. 1:33); in the Gospel he was more concerned to stress the fact that Jesus received the Spirit. In the first part of the verse John uses the preposition διά to express the manner in which Jesus came (for this use see BD 223³). According to AG, s.v., A I 1, this "first of all refers quite literally to Jesus' passing *through* water at his baptism and *through* blood at his death. But, as a secondary mng., sense A III 1c may also apply: Jesus comes with the water of baptism and *with* the blood of redemption for his own." The former of these explanations is unlikely, since no good sense can be attached to the phrase "through blood"; the secondary meaning is also improbable in the context. In the second part of the verse John uses the preposition ἐν, which can also express manner or circumstances (see BD 219⁴). De Jonge, 214f., notes that the two prepositions may be used synonymously for the sake of literary variation or the latter may have been introduced to indicate that Jesus came bringing the water (of baptism) and the blood (of the Lord's Supper); this latter possibility would arise if John was combatting opponents who held false views of the Lord's Supper (cf. Ignatius, *Smyrn.* 7:1), but it is not clear that this was the case; probably, therefore, we should see nothing more than literary variation; cf. Haas, 119.

those of Cerinthus and other Gnostic heretics whose views are combatted by Ignatius and Irenaeus. Certainly it is difficult to find any
closer background to the present verse than this particular aspect of
the teaching of Cerinthus, although it may be that other heretics
shared his teaching at this point. The early church certainly believed
that John personally opposed Cerinthus.[7, 8]

The importance of what may appear to be a rather obscure
theological debate is that only on John's view of it can the death of
Jesus be the mighty act of God for our salvation. For John's opponents it was merely the human Jesus who died. All the force of
John's statements that "God showed his love to us" by sending his
Son to die disappears if the One who died was not in fact Jesus
Christ, the Son of God. And all John's teaching that Jesus Christ
offered a sacrifice for our sins and now acts as our advocate in
heaven likewise loses its meaning and force. As soon as we reduce
the death of Jesus to that of a mere man, so soon do we lose the

---

[7]See on 2 John 7 and especially on 1 John 2:22. For John's personal opposition to
Cerinthus, see Irenaeus, AH 3:3:4.

[8]See further L. Goppelt, TDNT VIII, 329f. Other views have been held of the significance of the water and the blood in this verse. The possibility that John was
referring to the sacraments of baptism and the Lord's Supper has often been raised
(see n. 6 above). This certainly cannot be the primary reference in the passage, since
John's concern here is with the reality of the historical manifestation of Jesus rather
than with his continuing presence in the church; further, the use of αἷμα as a designa-
tion for the Lord's Supper is unparalleled. It is just possible that a secondary reference
is intended (Chaine, 214): John would then be thinking of the baptism and death of
Jesus as these are witnessed to by the sacraments. A decision on the presence of this
thought as a secondary allusion is partly dependent on how we interpret verse 8.
On the whole, however, it seems unlikely that a sacramental allusion is present at
this point (see Brooke, 132; Schnackenburg, 258).

A second possibility is to interpret the present passage in the light of John 19:34,
where blood and water flow from the pierced side of the crucified Jesus. John
continues: "The man who saw it has given testimony, and his testimony is true.
He knows that he tells the truth, and he testifies so that you also may have faith"
(Jn. 19:35). But, as Brooke, 132f., rightly comments, it is impossible to see how this
verse can explain the words "not by water only, but by water and blood." Further,
the order of "blood and water" is reversed here in 1 John, and, despite the similarity
in terminology, the witness in John 19:34f. is that of the observer, not of the blood
and water. Although, therefore, we are "naturally reminded" of this incident (Bruce,
118), it is unlikely that John has it in mind here, not even as a secondary allusion
(despite Westcott, 181f.).

Other more general references to Jesus as the source of life-giving water (Jn. 4:10,
14) and blood (Jn. 6:53–56) are even more remote.

G. Richter, "Blut und Wasser aus der durchbohrten Seite Jesu (Joh 19, 34b),"
Münchener Theologische Zeitschrift 21, 1970, 1–21 (as summarized in NTA 15,
1970–71, No. 568), argues that "blood and water" refers to physical birth: the
Docetists denied that Jesus had a genuine human birth. Against this view see
Wengst, 19f.

cardinal point of the New Testament doctrine of the atonement, that *God* was in Christ reconciling the world to himself; in the last analysis, the doctrine of the atonement means that God himself bears our sins and shows that the final reality in the universe is his sin-bearing, pardoning love,[9] but if Jesus is not the Son of God, his death can no longer bear this significance. So-called theologies, which reduce talk of the incarnation to the status of myth,[10] may be attractive to modern men, but they take away our assurance that God's character is sin-bearing love.

So far John has been making assertions about the coming of Jesus. But how do we know that they are true? His opponents did not deny that a man called Jesus was baptized and crucified, but they attached a different significance to his baptism and crucifixion from that given by John. What evidence is there that John's interpretation is the correct one? In the third part of this verse[11] John claims that the Spirit is the witness, because the Spirit is truth.[12] What the Spirit says can be trusted because he speaks God's truth. It is, however, not clear to what John is referring here. Since he refers to the Spirit's activity in the present tense, the most obvious interpretation is that the Spirit presently testifies to us, in our inward hearts or through the preaching of the Word, that the baptism and death of Jesus point to his being the Christ and Son of God. This view fits in with what is said in the Gospel about the task of the Spirit of truth, which is to testify to Jesus (Jn. 15:26). Some commentators emphasize the way in which the Spirit works through the church, i.e. through the preaching and sacraments of the Word by means of which he bears testimony to the saving significance of Jesus.[13] Others stress more the way in which he convinces the individual believer in his heart of the truth of the gospel.[14] These two aspects, however, can scarcely

[9]J. Denney, *The Christian Doctrine of Reconciliation,* London, 1917, 330; see I. H. Marshall, "James Denney," in P. E. Hughes (ed.), *Creative Minds in Contemporary Theology,* Grand Rapids, 1966, ch. 7.

[10]J. Hick (ed.), *The Myth of God Incarnate,* Philadelphia/London, 1977.

[11]In the RV and RSV the last clause of verse 6 is renumbered as verse 7, and verse 7 becomes the first part of verse 8; the NIV follows the current modern versification.

[12]John must mean that the Spirit is able to bear (true) witness because the Spirit is truth. The Vulgate reads: "Et spiritus est, qui testificatur, quoniam Christus est veritas," i.e. "And the Spirit testifies that Christ is the truth." This reading, followed by the late Greek MS 61, is probably an error, due to the influence of John 14:6 (Schnackenburg, 259 n. 2).

[13]Dodd, 129, thinks that the reference is to inspired or prophetic utterance; more generally, Schnackenburg, 260, thinks of the witness of the Spirit in and through the church.

[14]Bultmann, 82f., thinks particularly of the witness of the Spirit being present in faith and confession. It is not a fact that can establish the correctness of faith, but

be separated from one another: it is as the Spirit speaks through the Word that he makes it convincing to the heart of the individual.

We may wonder, however, whether this is all that John meant. It is tempting to think of the activity of the Spirit in the life of Jesus. At his baptism the Spirit came upon him, and it was this fact which convinced John the Baptist that Jesus was the Son of God (Jn. 1:32–34). In the other Gospels the baptism of Jesus was accompanied by a heavenly voice which declared that he was God's Son (Mk. 1:11). The Gospel writers certainly did not believe that this meant that Jesus was adopted as God's Son at this point, and there is no evidence that this view was held by their predecessors.[15] It was a sign that the One being baptized was already God's Son. Could it be that the Spirit was regarded as the vehicle of the Father's voice to his Son?[16] If so, it could then be argued that the Spirit did in fact confirm the significance of the baptism of Jesus. Not only so, but the Spirit was certainly regarded as inspiring the Old Testament writers who prophesied the coming of Jesus as the Messiah and Son of God. In some or all of these ways it may be claimed that the Spirit was already bearing witness to Jesus during, and even before, his earthly life. Hence it is possible that John is thinking here of the activity of the Spirit who witnessed in the past to Jesus as the Son of God and who still bears his testimony, confirming to the believer what he has already said.[17]

7   So far John has spoken of one witness, the Spirit.[18] Now he introduces a corrective. There are in fact three witnesses. These are identified in the next verse as the Spirit, the water, and the blood. But users of the *Authorized Version* will be aware of a form of

---

faith as faith in the preached Word is its own source of assurance. Bruce, 119, stresses the inward witness of the Spirit in the believer's heart, but notes that this cannot be separated from his outward witness in the church. See also Chaine, 214f.

[15]It is true that the baptism is often regarded by modern scholars as having been originally understood as God's act of "adoption" of Jesus: so, e.g., F. Hahn, *Christologische Hoheitstitel*, Göttingen, 1964², 301f.; R. H. Fuller, *The Foundations of New Testament Christology*, London, 1965, 193f.; E. Schweizer, TDNT VI, 400. Nevertheless, it is very doubtful whether the story was ever understood in this way, except in Docetist circles.

[16]There does not seem to be any evidence, however, in favor of this speculation.

[17]For this interpretation see Dodd, 129: "In history, the descent of the Spirit was evidence of the Messiahship of Jesus. In the present experience of the Church, the activity of the Spirit is evidence of His power to baptize with the Spirit, and therefore of His divine Sonship"; *ibid.,* 130: "The Spirit is, as we have seen, both a factor in the historical life of Jesus, and a continuing factor in the experience of the Church."

[18]Although verses 7–8 speak of three witnesses, it seems probable that at this point John is thinking merely of the Spirit as bearing witness, as the use of τὸ μαρτυροῦν with the article suggests.

text which speaks first of three witnesses in heaven, and then of three witnesses on earth. The former three are the members of the Holy Trinity, the Father, the Word, and the Holy Spirit, while the latter three are the Spirit, the water, and the blood. This form of wording appears in no reputable modern version of the Bible as the actual text; most editions adopt the same practice as in the NIV of relegating the extra words to a footnote, while some (such as the RSV and NEB) totally ignore them. The words in fact occur in none of the Greek manuscripts of 1 John, except for a few late and worthless ones, and are not quoted by any early church writers, not even by those who would have joyfully seized upon this clear biblical testimony to the Trinity in their attacks on heretics; they probably owe their origin to some scribe who wrote them in the margin of his copy of 1 John; later they were erroneously regarded as part of the text. Beyond any shadow of doubt the wording of the NIV text represents what John actually wrote.[19] We must, therefore, confine our attention to the three witnesses of whom John did write, the Spirit, the water, and the blood.

[19]The facts concerning the so-called "Comma Johanneum" (i.e. the Johannine [interpolated] clause; *comma,* from Greek κόμμα, clause) have been frequently and fully discussed. See the excellent brief accounts in Bruce, 129f.; Metzger, 716–718; B. M. Metzger, *The Text of the New Testament,* New York/Oxford, 1964, 101f.; and more fully, Westcott, 202–209; Brooke, 154–165; Schnackenburg, 44–46 (with bibliography). The words "in heaven: the Father, the word and the Holy Spirit, and these three are one. And there are three that testify on earth" are usually said to be found in only four Greek MSS (61 88^{mg} 629 635^{mg}—so Metzger, 717; but UBS gives 61 88^{mg} 429^{mg} 629 636^{mg} 918). None of these is earlier than the fourteenth century. The passage is quoted by none of the Greek church writers, and it first appears in Greek in a council report of 1215. None of the ancient versions of the New Testament contains the words, except the Latin version. The words appear, with considerable variation (including inversion of the order of the two sets of witnesses), in some Old Latin and Vulgate MSS, but not in the earliest form of the Old Latin or in Jerome's edition of the Vulgate. They are attested by a number of Latin writers, the earliest certain reference being in the *Liber Apologeticus* of the Spanish writer Priscillian (*ob. c.* 385) or his follower Instantius. It is wholly improbable that such a weakly attested reading is an original part of the text of 1 John, and the added words cause a break in the sense. The addition appears to rest on allegorical exegesis of the three witnesses in the text; it was probably written in the margin of a Latin MS and then found its way into the text; later still the order of the two sets of witnesses was inverted and the text was translated back into Greek and was included in a few Greek MSS. Erasmus rejected it from the first two editions of his Greek New Testament; he said that he would include it if a single Greek MS could be produced containing the words. Such a MS (61), probably written in 1520, was produced, and Erasmus had to keep his word in his third edition (1522), although he protested forcibly; subsequently, he again omitted the words. But the words remained in the Vulgate, and modern Roman Catholic translations, based on the Vulgate rather than the Greek text, included them (so Knox); the most recent Roman Catholic translations (such as the Jerusalem Bible) omit them. There remains some doubt as to how far back the variant reading can be traced in the Latin tradition (Schnackenburg, 46; W. Thiele, "Beobachtungen

8   John, then, writes now of three witnesses; he personifies the water and the blood, placing them too as witnesses alongside the Spirit,[20] and he insists that they are united in their testimony.[21] The implication of this last remark is that their witness stands or falls together; a person cannot claim that he is accepting the witness of the Spirit if he rejects the witness of the water and the blood to the true character of Jesus.[22] The Spirit takes the first place in the list of the three witnesses, since it is he who witnesses through the water and the blood.[23] But what do the water and the blood signify in this context? The most obvious answer is that they mean the same thing as in verse 6, namely the water of Jesus' baptism and the blood shed at this death. It should only be for very good reasons that we reject this interpretation. Many scholars do in fact hold that the meaning must be different in this verse, since here John is talking of a present activity of witnessing, whereas the water and the blood signify past events.[24] But it is hard to see why past events cannot continue to

---

zum Comma Johanneum (1 Joh. 5, 7f.)," ZNW 50, 1959, 61–73), but this does not affect the basic issue. Elsewhere the Latin text of 1 John shows other interpolations and alterations (2:17; 4:3; 5:6, 20).

[20]It is striking that although Spirit, water, and blood are all neuter nouns in Greek, they are introduced by a clause expressed in the masculine plural: τρεῖς εἰσιν οἱ μαρτυροῦντες. Elsewhere John constructs τὸ πνεῦμα with masculine forms (Jn. 14:26; 15:26), although this happens under the influence of the masculine form ὁ παράκλητος. Here in 1 John he clearly regards the Spirit as personal, and this leads to the personification of the water and the blood.

[21]Greek εἰς τὸ ἕν εἰσιν, literally, "are to the one." The construction seems to be unparalleled (though see Jn. 11:52; 17:22f.); N. Turner states that the use of εἰς is Semitic (MH III, 254), and W. F. Howard holds that it is equivalent to *l*ᵉ predicative, i.e. "the three are one" (MH II, 462). Brooke, 137, paraphrases "are for the one thing, tend in the same direction, exist for the same object." The unanimity of the three witnesses fulfils the biblical requirement for reliable evidence (Deut. 19:15; cf. Jn. 8:17); see further H. Strathmann, TDNT IV, 498.

[22]Bruce, 120.

[23]Bruce, 120, cites C. Wesley:

His Spirit answers to the blood,
And tells me I am born of God

(*The Methodist Hymnbook*, No. 368). But a closer parallel is to be found (*ibid.*, No. 363):

Spirit of faith, come down,
Reveal the things of God;
And make to us the Godhead known,
And witness with the blood.
'Tis thine the blood to apply,
And give us eyes to see
Who did for every sinner die
Hath surely died for me.

Wesley is more concerned with soteriology than christology, but the essential point remains unchanged.

[24]H. Strathmann, TDNT IV, 498; Schnackenburg, 261; Haas, 120.

bear witness, in the same way as the Old Testament Scriptures can still bear witness to Jesus; we may perhaps compare Abel who "still speaks, even though he is dead." We would, therefore, maintain that in this verse the water and the blood have the same meaning as in verse 6.[25]

The commentators who think that the present tense excludes this interpretation hold that in this verse John is referring to the Christian sacraments of baptism and the Lord's Supper. These sacraments may be regarded as abiding witnesses to the historical baptism and death of Jesus respectively; through them the saving power of the Son of God is mediated to believers and thus they find confirmation in their own experience of the truth about the person of Jesus.[26] Such a view is open to the objection that there is nothing to indicate that there is a change of meaning from verse 6.[27] It is also open to the objection that the use of "blood" to mean the Lord's Supper is unparalleled.[28] Furthermore, it is difficult to see how Christian baptism testifies to the reality of Jesus' baptism. There are thus difficulties with this view, although the fact that it has such widespread support among commentators prevents us from ruling it out altogether as a possible interpretation. The most that can be said is that it is possible that John was speaking of the historical water and blood of Jesus' baptism and death, as these are symbolized in

---

[25]Brooke, 137; Ross, 212–215; Bruce, 120f. Stott, 179, stresses that the historic meaning is primary, but allows that there may be a sacramental allusion. N. Brox, *Zeuge und Märtyrer*, München, 1961, 87f., as cited by Schnackenburg, 261 n. 3, holds that the reference is merely to the historical facts as abiding witnesses to which fresh appeal can continually be made.

[26]Westcott, 182; H. Strathmann, TDNT IV, 488; Dodd, 131; Schnackenburg, 260–263; Bultmann, 80; Houlden, 128–130; Haas, 120.

[27]To suggest that this is "an instance of the Johannine capacity for making symbols bear more than one sense" (Houlden, 128) does not altogether relieve the difficulty.

[28]The objection is squarely faced by Houlden, 130. He notes that "where attention is drawn to one element alone to signify the whole rite, it is usually the bread or body which is singled out. . . . But in GJ vi itself there is the idiosyncrasy of speaking in terms of 'flesh' rather than 'body,' which is otherwise the usual eucharistic term; and at this early date there is no call to be surprised at a departure from what later became the dominant terminology. There was no list of approved technical terms!" The merit of this comment is that it directs us to John 6 where Jesus speaks of drinking his *blood* (Jn. 6:53–56) as well as of eating his flesh. This suggests that it would be possible for John to be speaking here of "the water, with which Jesus was baptized, and which is symbolically present in Christian baptism, and the blood, which Jesus shed, and which is symbolically present in the Lord's Supper." The reference would then be not to the sacramental elements themselves but to what they symbolize. However, on this view we would expect a reference to the Spirit bestowed at baptism rather than to water.

the water of Christian baptism and the wine of the Lord's Supper.[29]
9 The witness of the Spirit is God's testimony to Jesus.
Normally we accept human testimony. But God's testimony is
greater than that of men (cf. Jn. 5:36); it is about something far more
important.[30] Therefore (John implies) we ought to accept God's testimony. For, he goes on to say, this is the nature of God's testimony,
namely that he has borne testimony to his Son.[31] In other words,
John is saying that we ought to accept God's testimony precisely
because it is God's testimony, and that this testimony concerns his
Son; the supreme importance of the fact that Jesus is the Son of God
is thus brought out. Because it is God who has borne testimony to
Jesus and declared him to be his Son, it follows that acceptance of
Jesus as the Son of God is of fundamental and decisive importance.

But what exactly is this testimony given by God? Three possibilities have been suggested, and it is not easy to decide between

---

[29]Other interpretations of the passage have been offered. Windisch, 133, stated that
three "mysteries" are meant: baptism (Jn. 3:5), the Eucharist (Jn. 6:54ff.), and the
reception of the Spirit (2:20; Jn. 20:22f.). This suggestion has the merit of attempting
to account for the mention of the Spirit in a manner analogous to the water and the
blood. However, Windisch has to invert the order, Spirit, water, and blood, to make
his point. A novel solution to this problem was proposed by T. W. Manson, "Entry
into Membership of the Early Church," JTS 48, 1947, 25–33, and developed by
Nauck, 147–182. They drew attention to the way in which reception of the Spirit may
precede baptism with water (Acts 10:44–48), to the way in which the Lord's Supper
may immediately follow baptism (e.g. in Pliny's letter), and to the practice of anointing candidates *before* baptism in the Syriac church. All this suggested a possible rite
of Christian initiation in which anointing, baptism, and the Lord's Supper followed
one another, corresponding to the mention of the Spirit, water, and blood in 1 John.
Parallels were found in contemporary Jewish practice, notably in the initiation of
candidates to join the Qumran sect (1QS 3:6–12), in the consecration to the priest-
hood described in the *Testament of Levi* 8:4f., and in the initiation of the Jewish
proselyte described in *Joseph and Aseneth*. The conclusion drawn was that 1 John
reflects an early pattern of Christian initiation which survived in the Syriac church,
and that 1 John probably came from Syria. This intriguing theory has failed to win
any followers (see the comments by Schnackenburg, 263; Bruce, 120f.; de Jonge, 217
n. 407, and Houlden, 130–132). Schnackenburg notes that there is no evidence for the
practice of anointing before baptism in the New Testament; one would have expected
John to use the word χρῖσμα instead of πνεῦμα if this is what he meant; and the function
of the Spirit is different from that of the water and the blood in this passage, since it
bears testimony through the water and the blood. Schnackenburg's second point is
weak (since John speaks of water and blood, not baptism and Lord's Supper, it would
be appropriate for him to speak of the Spirit rather than anointing in this context),
but his other points are valid.
[30]John's use of μείζων here (cf. 3:20; Jn. 5:36) conveys the two ideas of greater
significance and greater trustworthiness (Schnackenburg, 264 n. 1; Haas, 121). The
εἰ clause does not imply any doubt; the NIV rightly turns it into a statement of fact.
[31]αὕτη should be taken as pointing forward to the ὅτι clause (Westcott, 185f.;
Brooke, 138).

them. First, it is natural to assume that John is referring in another way to the threefold testimony which he has just been describing.[32] It is, however, a difficulty for this view that the tense in verses 6–8 is present, whereas here it is perfect. Nevertheless, this is not an insuperable obstacle, since we have seen that in verse 6 the thought is of the historic acts of witness to Jesus as the Son of God in his lifetime; through these, it could be said, God was bearing witness to his Son.[33] There is, however, a further problem. In John 5:31–40 Jesus refers to various testimonies concerning himself: there is his own testimony, that of John the Baptist, that of his own works, and that of the Scriptures. The testimony of God appears to be distinct from these others, although of course God stands behind the other witnesses. So, it can be argued, a divine witness other than the threefold witness of the Spirit, water, and blood is meant here. Since, however, it is the Spirit who is the essential witness, testifying through the water and the blood, and since the Spirit is God's instrument of revelation, it seems perfectly possible that John is simply speaking of the Spirit's testimony in a different way. Commentators who do not accept this point must postulate a second interpretation of God's testimony. They argue that John has not told us what this testimony is; he is content simply to record the fact of it. The best that can be suggested is that it is connected with the stories and sayings of Jesus recorded in John's Gospel.[34] This is not very helpful. Still less helpful is the suggestion that God's testimony is nothing but the event of faith itself.[35] A third possibility is that John is speaking of the "inner witness" of the Spirit in the heart of the believer to the truth of what he hears in the proclamation of the Word. But this understanding is exposed to the difficulty that John is here speaking of a past act of God; furthermore, John does not elsewhere use the term "testimony" to refer to an inward witness by the Spirit.[36] It seems best, therefore, to accept the first interpretation.[37]

---

[32]So the NEB. This understanding does not depend on taking αὕτη to refer backward to verse 8, which is an unlikely construction.

[33]The obstacle is naturally greater for commentators who think that in verse 8 the reference is primarily to the sacraments.

[34]Schnackenburg, 270; see his whole excursus on the problems of this section, "Das Gotteszeugnis und der Glaube," 267–271, which sets out well the difficulties in traditional interpretations of the passage. Chaine, 216, refers to the Father's testimony by the works of Jesus and the prophecies recorded in John.

[35]Bultmann, 82; cf. R. Bultmann, *Theology of the New Testament,* New York/London, 1955, II, 77f.

[36]Schnackenburg, 268–270.

[37]Bruce, 121. So apparently de Jonge, 220: "This testimony of God does not stand

10 If God's witness is about his Son, it follows that anybody who believes in the Son of God is thereby accepting God's witness. The NIV translation "has this testimony in his heart" may suggest that the thought is of receiving an inward confirmation of faith from God. The believer receives the inward witness of the Spirit.[38] It is, however, doubtful whether this is the meaning conveyed by the Greek text, especially when we compare this clause with its antithesis in the second part of the verse. The contrast is between accepting what God has said and rejecting it. It is, therefore, more likely that John is simply stating that to believe in the Son of God is to accept and keep God's testimony.[39] The converse is that a person who does not believe God and rejects his testimony to his Son[40] has made him out to be a liar and stands self-condemned. It is inconsistent to profess belief in God, as John's opponents did, and yet to disbelieve what God has said.[41] Belief in God and in his Son, Jesus Christ, are inseparably joined.

11 The question whether we accept God's testimony or not is not a merely academic one. On our answer to it depends the question whether or not we participate in eternal life. For what God's testimony means[42] is that he has given us eternal life; but this life is given only in his Son.[43]

12 Hence it follows inevitably that if a person accepts the

---

alongside that of the three witnesses, but lays the foundation for it and works through it."

[38]Brooke, 139; Stott, 181f.

[39]The phrase ἔχειν ἐν ἑαυτῷ means "to hold fast"; cf. Revelation 6:9; 12:17; 19:10. The reading ἑαυτῷ (S Ψ 049 88 1739 al) is preferred by UBS to αὐτῷ (K al; TR; cf. αυτω, A B P), although both are grammatically possible and convey the same meaning (BD 283). It is perhaps more likely that an original αυτω was differently understood as a reflexive (αὐτῷ, an obsolete form in Hellenistic times, MH II, 180f.) or as a personal pronoun; cf. Metzger, 718.

[40]In verse 10a John uses πιστεύειν εἰς of believing in the Son of God; in verse 10b he uses πιστεύειν with the dative of believing God, i.e. accepting his testimony, and πιστεύειν εἰς of accepting the testimony which God has given; this last usage is unique and implies personal belief in the object of the testimony (Westcott, 187).

[41]Admittedly, John's opponents might have questioned whether God did in fact give the testimony which John ascribes to him.

[42]Verse 11 does not give the content of the testimony (as the NIV translation suggests), unless we take the meaning to be: "The witness which God bore consisted in the fact that He gave life to men, by sending His Son that men might have life in Him" (Brooke, 140). In any case the receiving by men of eternal life is not the content of the witness, since this would involve John in a vicious circle of proof (Schnackenburg, 270). The verse must be taken to indicate what the meaning or effect of the testimony is: the sending of the Son leads to eternal life.

[43]The statement is clearly meant to be exclusive, as verse 12 demonstrates; hence the addition of "only" is justified.

Son he receives eternal life, but if he refuses to accept the Son[44] he does not have life.

The long theological discussion of the nature of faith thus has a significant practical conclusion. Eternal life is not possible apart from true belief in Jesus as the Son of God. Those who deny that Jesus is the Son of God have cut themselves off from the life of God, no matter how much they may protest that they possess it. For the life that God gives is available only through his Son. He alone is the way, the truth, and the life; no one can come to the Father except through him (Jn. 14:6).

CHRISTIAN CERTAINTIES (5:13–21)

13. I write these things to you who believe in the name of the Son of God so that you may know that you have eternal life. 14. We have this assurance in approaching God, that if we ask anything according to his will, he hears us. 15. And if we know that he hears us—whatever we ask—we know that we have what we asked of him.

16. If anyone sees his brother commit a sin that does not lead to death, he should pray and God will give him life. I refer to those whose sin does not lead to death. There is a sin that leads to death. I am not saying that he should pray about that. 17. All wrongdoing is sin, and there is sin that does not lead to death.

18. We know that anyone born of God does not continue to sin; the one who was born of God keeps him safe, and the evil one does not touch him. 19. We know that we are children of God, and that the whole world is under the control of the evil one. 20. We know also that the Son of God has come and has given us understanding, so that we may know him who is true. And we are in him who is true—even in his Son Jesus Christ. He is the true God and eternal life.

21. Dear children, keep yourselves from idols.

John has at last reached the end of what he wants to say; he has shown clearly the differences between the true believer and the false, and now he concludes by reiterating his purpose, which was to assure those of his readers who believed in Jesus as the Son of God of their possession of eternal life. Such people can be sure of an

[44]John says "does not have the Son *of God*," thereby indicating once again the enormity of the offense, and the impossibility of having God as Father without accepting his Son.

answer to their prayers, a point which leads the author into a brief discussion of the problem of interceding for those who fall into sin. Finally, he sums up the great truths which he has discussed earlier in the Epistle, the realities of God's keeping power, of divine sonship, and of communion with God. Yet the hortatory note is maintained to the end, and the Epistle closes with an appeal to his readers not to be led astray into false religion.

13 We are fortunate that John has given us in his Gospel a statement of his purpose in writing it (Jn. 20:31). In the same way he here summarizes his purpose in the composition of this Epistle. He was writing to a church in which there had arisen divergent teaching regarding the nature of Christian belief. Such a situation was calculated to make the members wonder whether they really possessed eternal life; some of those who professed belief in Jesus as the Son of God must still have wondered whether they were right in their belief, and whether their experience of eternal life was not a mere delusion. Having demonstrated to the readers that eternal life is to be found only in Jesus Christ, the Son of God (vv. 11f.), John now sums up by saying that the effect of what he has written[1] should be to give assurance to believers[2] that they do possess eternal life.[3] John was therefore writing not to persuade unbelievers of the truth of the Christian faith but rather to strengthen Christian believers who might be tempted to doubt the reality of their Christian experience and to give up their faith in Jesus. Those who believe in the name of Jesus[4] can be sure of their possession of eternal life.

---

[1]Commentators differ as to whether ταῦτα refers back to the Epistle as a whole (Westcott, 188; Dodd, 133; Bultmann, 83; Haas, 124) or to the immediately preceding section (vv. 5–12, Schnackenburg, 273; vv. 1–12, Brooke, 142). In favor of the latter view is the way in which verse 13 takes up the language of verses 11f. and emphatically applies it to the readers. In favor of the former view is the striking parallel with the language of John 20:31 which gives the purpose of the Gospel as a whole. One or two scholars have thought that verse 13 marks the original conclusion of the Epistle, what follows being in the nature of a postscript or redactional addition (Windisch, 134; Dodd; Bultmann), but it is more probable that it is an intended part of the Epistle as a whole (Nauck, 133–146). Assuming the latter view, verse 13 then functions as the introduction to this concluding section and acts as a bridge from the preceding section. In content, therefore, it sums up the Epistle as a whole, but in function it serves to link verses 5–11 with verses 14–21.

[2]The placing of τοῖς πιστεύουσιν...at the end of the sentence is deliberately emphatic; cf. John 1:12.

[3]The separation of αἰώνιον from ζωήν by the verb is for emphasis.

[4]For belief in the name of Jesus see John 1:12; 2:23; see also 1 John 3:23 where the writer uses πιστεύω with the dative, and the note on that verse. Here full commitment to Jesus, as the One who can do what is expressed by his name, is meant.

14 One important result of the believer's assurance of eternal life is that he can have confidence and boldness[5] in relation to God.[6] In particular this applies to the situation of making requests to God in prayer. John has already told his readers: "we have confidence before God and receive from him anything we ask, because we obey his commands and do what pleases him" (3:21f.). Now he repeats this assurance. God will hear us in respect of anything we ask of him. To "hear" means to hear favorably;[7] God will answer our prayers. To be sure, there is a condition attached. Such prayer must be offered by those who remain in Jesus and let his words remain in them (Jn. 15:7); it must be offered in the name of Jesus (Jn. 14:13f.; 15:16; 16:23–26). Yet it is common Christian experience that such prayer is not always answered. Even Jesus himself knew the experience of pouring out his soul to God in order that he might not have to drink the cup of suffering, but he had to accept that what he wished might not be God's will and so to pray: "Yet not what I will, but what you will" (Mk. 14:36). So too the Christian must offer his prayers "according to his will." We do not always know what is God's will for us or for the people we pray for; but we have the joyful assurance that whatever is God's will for us will be done. At the same time, we are warned against the offering of prayers which we know will not be according to God's will; prayer for sinful or selfish motives, however much we may attempt to disguise them, is excluded.

But, if prayer is to be made according to God's will, why pray at all? Surely his will is going to be accomplished, whether or not we pray for it to be done? To speak in such terms is to assume that God's will must be understood in a static kind of way, as if God has made a detailed plan beforehand of all that is going to happen—including the fact that we are going to pray in a particular way and at a particular time. But while the Bible does speak of God's plan and purpose for the world, to speak in such deterministic terms is inconsistent with the freedom which the Bible itself assigns to God's children, and it wreaks havoc upon the biblical idea of the personal relationship which exists between God and his children.[8] The point is rather that the believer must seek to submit

---

[5]Cf. 3:21.
[6]αὐτόν means God, as the NIV assumes.
[7]Cf. John 9:31; 11:41f.; W. Mundle, NIDNTT II, 175, 178.
[8]See my essay, "Predestination in the New Testament," in C. Pinnock (ed.), *Grace Unlimited*, Minneapolis, 1975, 127–143.

his will to God's by saying, "Your will be done" (Mt. 6:10). It is as we freely yield ourselves to God that he is able to accomplish his will through us and our prayers. In a very real sense, therefore, the accomplishment of God's will in the world does depend on our prayers. Through prayer we make ourselves instruments of God's will, and at the same time, in a manner that lies beyond human comprehension, he is able to act powerfully to answer our prayers. When we learn to want what God wants, we have the joy of receiving his answer to our petitions.[9]

15 This point is now underlined. If we know that God hears our prayers,[10] whatever we may ask for, we can be equally sure that we have obtained[11] whatever we have asked for. This statement can be taken to mean: "Our petitions are granted at once: the results of the granting are perceived in the future."[12] Doubtless this is true of some requests that we make. Many of our prayers are concerned with future events, and the answers to them can only be future. But perhaps John means what he says. The spiritual gifts for which we ask in prayer are directly available to us.[13] In any case, the point is that God's children can be certain of an answer when they pray according to God's will. "I tell you," said Jesus, "whatever you ask for in prayer, believe that you will receive it, and it will be yours" (Mk. 11:24). We need today to recover that confidence.

16, 17 John has just described one of the most important fruits of Christian assurance, namely confidence in prayer. It is possible to regard what follows in verses 16f. as simply an example of such prayer, due to the author's habit of gliding from one topic to another by association of ideas.[14] But it is unlikely that John was simply giving an illustration of what he meant. On the contrary, it would seem that he has been deliberately leading up to this as his main topic. Throughout the Epistle he has been warning his readers against falling into sin, and stressing that sin is the characteristic of those who are not born of God. He has drawn the lines between believers and unbelievers as clearly as possible.

[9]See further on 3:22.
[10]John has ἐάν followed by the indicative (cf. Lk. 19:40; 1 Thess. 3:8), a colloquial usage (BD 372¹ᵃ).
[11]ἔχομεν, literally "we have"; the present tense expresses possession rather than reception.
[12]A. Plummer, as cited by Stott, 186.
[13]So Schnackenburg, 275.
[14]Schnackenburg, 273.

Now, as he attempts to reassure his readers that they are children of God, the question of their sin once more arises, and he takes it up again, arguing that the prayers of believers can secure life for their fellow Christians when they fall into sin.

John describes a situation in which one of the members of the church sees another member[15] committing what is described as "a sin that does not lead to death." In this situation he is to intercede[16] for his brother, and thus God[17] will grant him life. John emphasizes that this possibility applies only in the case of those whose sin does not lead to death.[18] For there is also the possibility of sin that does lead to death, and it is not about such sin that he is recommending intercession.[19] Then he reminds his readers that all wrongdoing is sin, but nevertheless there is a kind of sin which does not lead to death.

[15]The word ἀδελφός must signify another member of the church. Stott, 190, defends a broader view, "neighbor," or a nominal Christian. But there is nothing in John's usage to suggest that "neighbor" is a possible meaning here.

[16]The future tense is equivalent to a gentle imperative or expresses what John assumes will happen as a matter of course (Brooke, 146). αἰτήσει is here used of intercession in prayer; for the concept of intercession in the Old Testament and Judaism see Genesis 18:27–33; 20:7; Exodus 32:11–14, 31f.; 34:8f.; Numbers 14:13–19; 2 Kings 19:4; Jeremiah 37:3; 42:2 (contrast 7:16; 11:14; 14:11f.; 15:1); Amos 7:1–6; 2 Maccabees 7:37f.; 15:14; 4 Maccabees 6:28f.; 17:21f.; 4 Ezra 7:102–115; *Testament of Reuben* 1:7; *Testament of Judah* 19:2; *Testament of Benjamin* 3:6; 10:1; *Testament of Gad* 5:9; 2 Enoch 64:4; *Assumption of Moses* 11:17; 12:6; N. Johannson, *Parakletoi*, Lund, 1940; Schnackenburg, 275f. For intercession in the New Testament see G. P. Wiles, *Paul's Intercessory Prayers*, New York/Cambridge, 1974. The view that ἐρωτάω here means "to ask questions" (*sc.* about degrees of sin) (P. Trudinger, "Concerning Sins, Mortal and Otherwise. A Note on 1 John 5, 16–17," Bib 52, 1971, 541f.) is highly improbable.

[17]It is not clear whether the subject to be supplied with δώσει is "God" (NIV; Westcott, 191f.; Schnackenburg, 276; Stott, 186) or "he" (the intercessor; Brooke, 146; Bultmann, 87 n. 16; Haas, 127). Those who favor the latter interpretation argue that a change in subject is awkward and that there is a parallel in James 5:20. God is then understood to act through the intercessor. But it is unusual to speak of one man giving another life, and the thought is surely of God's answer to prayer (see D. Scholer, "Sins Within and Sins Without: An Interpretation of 1 John 5:16–17," in G. F. Hawthorne [ed.], *Current Issues in Biblical and Patristic Interpretation*, Grand Rapids, 1975, 230–246, especially 239f. and n. 53).

[18]Although John commences by thinking of an individual case, he adopts a generalizing plural at the end of the sentence; for the loosely attached participle cf. 5:13; John 1:12.

[19]This rather cumbrous rendering is meant to emphasize that John is *not* saying: "I say that he should not pray about that." "The writer does not forbid such intercession. He merely abstains from commanding it" (Brooke, 147). λέγω can be used to express a command. Attempts to find a distinction between αἰτέω, used in the first part of the verse, and ἐρωτάω (Westcott, 192; G. Stählin, TDNT I, 192f.; H. Greeven, TDNT II, 806) are fanciful (D. Scholer, *op. cit.*, 243 n. 62).

The basic problem here is that of the two kinds of sin mentioned by John. He obviously could assume that his audience knew what he was writing about, and therefore he had no need to explain what he meant. Presumably, therefore, he did not mean anything particularly recondite. We may begin by noting that the terminology used here, sin that leads to death, is found in a number of Jewish writings, but there it refers to sins which lead to the physical death of the sinner.[20] Although the New Testament knows cases of persons who suffered physical death for their sins, it seems unlikely that this is what is meant here.[21] Presumably in that case the fact that a sin was of this kind would be recognized only by the severe illness or actual death of the person concerned. But there is no indication that John was thinking of death in this sense.[22] A more profitable approach is to observe that in the Old Testament and Judaism there was a well-recognized difference between two kinds of sin, the unconscious or unwitting sins, for which forgiveness was provided by the annual sacrifice on the Day of Atonement, and deliberate or witting sins, for which the sacrificial ritual provided no forgiveness.[23] The latter could be atoned for only by the death of the sinner. This distinction between sins which could be forgiven and those which led to the death of the sinner may well be part of the key to the problem.

But what kinds of sin fall into these two categories? Here we turn to the evidence of the Epistle itself. It is plain that the author is most concerned about the sins which are incompatible with being a child of God, and these are summed up in denial that Jesus is the Son of God, refusal to obey God's commands, love of the world, and hatred of one's brothers. Such sins are characteristic of the person who belongs to the sphere of darkness rather than the sphere of light. This would lead us to the conclusion that by sin that leads to death John means the sins that are incompatible with being a child of God. The person who consciously and de-

---

[20]Numbers 18:22; Deuteronomy 22:26; Isaiah 22:14; *Jubilees* 21:22; 26:34; 33:13, 18; *Testament of Issachar* 7:1; *Soṭa* 48a (SB III, 779; cf. IV 2, 659).

[21]Cf. Acts 5:1–11; 1 Corinthians 5:3–5; 11:30. Hence it has been suggested that John is forbidding praying for those who have physically died (Bruce, 124f., as one possibility; more strongly, S. M. Reynolds, "The Sin Unto Death and Prayers for the Dead," *Reformation Review* 20, 1973, 130–139).

[22]Law, 139; D. Scholer, *op. cit.*, 234f.

[23]Leviticus 4:2, 13, 22, 27; 5:15, 17f.; Numbers 15:27–31; Deuteronomy 17:12; Psalm 19:13. See further 1QS 5:11f.; 8:21–9:2; CD 3:14f. See Nauck, 133–146; I. H. Marshall, *Kept by the Power of God*, 34–38, 41f.

liberately chooses the way that leads to death will surely die. Sin that leads to death is deliberate refusal to believe in Jesus Christ, to follow God's commands, and to love one's brothers. It leads to death because it includes a deliberate refusal to believe in the One who alone can give life, Jesus Christ the Son of God. By contrast, sins that do not lead to death are those which are committed unwittingly and which do not involve rejection of God and his way of salvation. The sinner is overcome by temptation against his will; he still wants to love God and his neighbor, he still believes in Jesus Christ, he still longs to be freed from sin.[24]

This explanation of the two kinds of sin meant by John gives a satisfactory meaning to the passage. But it still leaves a number of points to be cleared up.

First, there is the question why one Christian should intercede for another Christian if his sin is not one that leads to death. If his sin does not lead to death, why does his brother need to pray that he may have life? John does not answer this question, and any answer must be speculative. The clue is supplied by verse 17 where John reminds his readers that all wrongdoing is sin, and yet there is sin that does not lead to death. Sin remains sin, and sin is dangerous, because it is the characteristic of life apart from God. Sin remains a blemish on the life of God's children. Further, we have not been able to isolate any particular types of sin which fall into either of the two classes. The sins of believers include disbelief in Jesus Christ, failure to keep God's commands, and lack of love for their brothers. Indeed, there are no other sins than these. The line between unconscious and conscious sins is thus hard to define. Let it be plainly said that if there were no forgiveness for deliberate sins, then we would all be under God's condemnation, for which of us has not sinned deliberately since our conversion and new birth? Hence, there is always the danger that a person who sins unconsciously or unwittingly may move to the point of sinning

---

[24]For this view see especially Nauck, *ibid.*; Brooke, 146f.; Chaine, 219f.; Alexander, 127f.; de Jonge, 225–228; I. H. Marshall, *op. cit.*, 188–190. Many commentators think that John's language is too vague to allow of definite interpretation (Schnackenburg, 277; Bultmann, 87). D. Scholer, *op. cit.*, 234, argues against this view (a) that there is no indication that John was thinking of inadvertent and deliberate sins; and (b) that this view assumes wrongly that the sin unto death is one committed by believers. In reply it may be urged that the sin of apostasy is by its very nature deliberate, and that it is those who have committed the sin who are *ipso facto* not or no longer believers. Scholer is unable to offer a satisfactory alternative explanation of what kind of sins do not lead to death.

deliberately and then of turning his back completely on God and the way of forgiveness. Because of this danger it is essential that Christians should pray for one another lest any of their number should cross the line that leads to open and deliberate rejection of the way of life. No sin is of such a kind as to prevent forgiveness, provided that we repent of it. We are to pray for our brothers that they will repent of all sin. When we do this, we have God's promise that he will hear our prayers. We also have the example of Jesus himself who interceded for Peter when he lapsed into denying his Master (Lk. 22:23).[25]

In the case of open refusal to repent and believe, however, the sinner is on the way to death. In such cases, John does not require his readers to pray for the offender. The early church took much more seriously than we do the possibility that a person may sin beyond hope of redemption. It would seem that where a person himself refuses to seek salvation and forgiveness there is not much point in praying for him. Nevertheless, it must be carefully observed that sin which leads to death need not necessarily be sin that inevitably results in death, that John does not absolutely forbid intercession in such cases, and that elsewhere in the New Testament the application of strict discipline and even excommunication always had in mind the possibility of the ultimate repentance of the sinner.[26]

A further question is whether the sin that leads to death can be committed by those who are truly God's children. There is no doubt that when John wrote about it, he was thinking primarily of those who had left the church and whose lives were characterized by deliberate refusal to believe in Jesus Christ and to love their brothers. But did John think that believers could fall away into such a state? A number of scholars have tried to show that this could not have been John's meaning. Thus it has been argued that the people in question had merely masqueraded as believers but had never at any point truly believed in Jesus. Consequently, the sin that leads to death is to be understood as a sin of unbelievers which believers cannot in principle commit.[27] However, this point

[25]See especially Bruce, 125.
[26]1 Corinthians 5:5; 1 Timothy 1:20; Schnackenburg, 278; I. H. Marshall, *op. cit.*, 212f.
[27]Stott, 186–191, argues that neither type of sinner is a true believer, since "brother" can refer to merely nominal members of the church and since a true believer cannot receive "life," for the true believer has already passed from death to life (3:14; so Morris, 1270). Commentators usually assume that John is thinking of the

must remain doubtful. The fact that John needed to warn his readers against the possibility of sinning and failing to continue in the truth and in the doctrine of Christ (2:24; 2 Jn. 7–11) suggests that he did not altogether exclude the possibility that a person might fall away from his faith into apostasy.[28] Nevertheless, it was his clear expectation that his readers would continue in their faith without falling away from it.[29]

John's teaching raises problems when we consider our contemporary practice in intercession. On the one hand, it is not characteristic of the modern church prayer meeting (if we hold one at all) that we pray for specific members who have fallen into sin by name. Even the sharing of experiences practiced in the early Methodist class meetings is no longer found today. We have become reticent about confessing our own faults publicly, and we are given still less to praying publicly for the faults of our friends. Our social situation is different from that of John's church, and it would be folly to try to follow his teaching literally in changed circumstances. On the other hand, we find it hard to accept that we should not pray for unbelievers and especially for those who have lapsed from a Christian faith which they once professed. It is no comfort—indeed it is downright cruelty—to tell the parents of children who have rebelled against the faith which they once accepted that there is no point in praying for them. Indeed, C. H. Dodd goes so far as to

---

restoration of fulness of eternal life and fellowship with God which is threatened by any act of sin (Schnackenburg, 276f.; D. Scholer, *op. cit.*, 240). Scholer claims that the person who sins unto death is not a "brother" and is not described as such; he is a non-believer who hates believers and does not confess Christ. This is a correct statement of the present state of the person whose sin leads to death; whatever he was before, he is certainly not a believer now. J. E. Rosscup, "Paul's Teaching on the Christian's Future Reward with Special Reference to I Corinthians 3:10–17" (Unpublished Thesis, Aberdeen, 1976), 447 n. 89, adopts Stott's position, and claims that the use of the present participle refers to the sin of the unsaved person.

[28]I. H. Marshall, *op. cit.*, 186–190.

[29]John's teaching has some connection with Jesus' saying about the sin against the Holy Spirit (Lk. 12:10 and par.; on which see I. H. Marshall, *The Gospel of Luke*, Exeter, 1978, *ad loc.*). It is also linked with the teaching of Hebrews 6:4–6; 10:26–31 which refers to the awful possibility of a person spurning the Son of God and profaning the blood of the covenant. We may also refer to Hermas, *Similitude* 6:1–4, which describes how the angel of self-indulgence and deceit destroys the souls of God's servants, some unto death and some unto corruption. For the former there is no hope of repentance, but for the latter there is hope. "Corruption then hath hope of a possible renewal, but death hath eternal destruction." Despite the unwillingness of some scholars to link all these passages together, there seems little doubt that all these texts refer to the possibility of sinners becoming hardened in their sin and rebelling against the grace of God; they cut themselves off from salvation.

suggest that we may quietly drop what John says here about not praying for certain types of sinner: "We cannot think that it can ever be contrary to the will of Him who came to call sinners to repentance that we should pray for even the worst of sinners (who may after all be—ourselves)."[30]

How, then, are we to interpret John's advice? Surely we are to take from it a reminder that we have in fact become so unconcerned about the sins of our fellow Christians that we have ceased even to think about praying for them. John's words are a challenge to the quality of our intercession for others. If it is out of place for us to pray publicly about other people's sins, at least we should be more concerned for their spiritual welfare and pray positively for it in public, while in our private prayers we may also intercede more specifically for those who fall into sin.[31] At the same time, we may note that while John says that God will certainly answer prayer for the brother who does not sin to death, he does not rule out the possibility of answered prayer for the person who commits sin that does lead to death. "If we have in mind any case where, to our limited view, such a prayer seems unlikely to be answered, we may recall what Jesus said when a man had refused what looked like his only chance of salvation—For men it is impossible, but not for God; anything is possible for God (Mark x. 27)."[32]

18 Having concluded his exhortation to the members of the church to pray for one another that they may be saved from sin, John comes to the vigorous statement of belief which forms the climax of his letter. He takes up his keyword from verse 13: "I write these things to you...so that you may *know*." In a series of three affirmations he declares the content of this Christian knowledge which should characterize his readers. It may be significant that the Greek word which he uses expresses a state of knowledge rather than the action of coming to know something.[33] John is declaring what he and his fellow Christians know for certain, and his readers ought to be able to include themselves in the number of those whose Christian faith is a matter of certainty and assurance.

First, he declares once again that anyone who is born of God does not commit sin.[34] This is a statement with which we are

[30]Dodd, 137.
[31]It should be noted that John does not in fact speak of public prayer. He is speaking about what one Christian should do when he sees another in need of prayer.
[32]Dodd, 137.
[33]See Westcott, 82, 112, 188, 193.
[34]NIV, "does not continue to sin," as in 3:6, 9.

251

already familiar from 3:6, 9. We saw that it describes the eschatological reality which should characterize the life of the child of God. It is, therefore, all the more significant that John's affirmation follows directly upon his warning about the need to pray for brothers who fall into sin. We are not to seek to evade the paradox by assigning the two statements to different sources or by denying that John is talking about believers in verses 16f., or by claiming that "sin" has two different meanings in the two verses. Rather, John is well aware of the sad facts of life in a sinful world; his statement that the child of God does not sin is at once a promise and a demand. But how is this sinlessness possible? The answer given is that the One who was born of God keeps him safe, and so the evil one[35] cannot lay hold of him and overpower him.[36] He will face satanic attacks and temptations, but he is defended by One who is stronger than Satan. The translation adopted by the NIV takes "the one who was born of God" to be Jesus, and this is very probably the correct rendering.[37] Nevertheless, some early manuscripts have "himself" instead of "him" as the object of the verb "keep safe"; if this reading is adopted, we should have to understand the clause to mean: "but he who is born of God (i.e. the believer) keeps himself free (i.e. from sin)."[38] This is less likely, as are other interpretations of the clause found in some modern commentators.[39]

[35]Cf. 2:13f.; 3:12; 5:19.
[36]ἅπτομαι means to lay hold of somebody in order to harm him (Job 2:5; Ps. 105:15; Zech. 2:8; T.Jud. 3:10; 1 Esdr. 4:28).
[37]Westcott, 194; Brooke, 148f.; Dodd, 138; Windisch, 135 (with hesitation); Chaine, 222; Stott, 192; Bultmann, 88f. (with hesitation); Bruce, 126; Haas, 128. In favor of this view is the change in aspect from ὁ γεγεννημένος, perfect (the child of God), to ὁ γεννηθείς, aorist. Further, on this view, the pronouns αὐτόν and αὐτοῦ refer consistently to the believer. Finally, the thought of Jesus keeping his disciples is found in John 17:12; cf. Revelation 3:10. The objections to this view are that ὁ γεννηθείς is a unique phrase to apply to Jesus, and it is difficult to know why it is adopted here (Schnackenburg, 281). Yet it can be urged that John is here bringing out the way in which the Son identifies himself with his followers (Haas, 128).
[38]αυτον is read by A* B and αὐτόν by 330 614 r vg sy^h bo; the reflexive ἑαυτόν is read by S A^c K P Ψ 33 81 1739 al; Brooke, 148f., argues that an original ἑαυτόν is unlikely to have been changed to the apparently more difficult αὐτόν, while Schnackenburg, 280, claims that with the reflexive pronoun we should expect some explanation of what the believer keeps himself from (cf. 2 Cor. 11:9; 1 Tim. 5:22; Jas. 1:27; Jude 21). No value can be attached to the variant ἡ γένεσις for ὁ γεννηθείς ([1852] 2138 latt sy^h).
[39]Schnackenburg (1st edition), 251f., adopted the translation, "the one who is born of God holds fast to him (sc. God)" (similarly, AG, s.v. τηρέω, 3; Houlden, 133). However, this is a most odd rendering of τηρέω (Rev. 3:3; Eph. 4:3; 2 Tim. 4:7 and Rev. 16:15 are hardly par.), and Schnackenburg, 280, has abandoned it in favor of

19 John's second declaration is a reminder of the fact that mankind is divided into two camps, those who belong to God and those who belong to the evil one. But, whereas verse 18 merely stated something that is true of anybody who is born of God, John's second declaration now states that this principle is true of himself and his readers: we know that *we* are children of God[40] and can therefore claim the promises made to those born of God. By contrast, the world is in the power of the evil one.[41]

20 If mankind is divided into these two camps, how is it possible for a person to find his way from one to the other? How could the church ever come into existence in a world that lies under the control of Satan? John's third great declaration gives the answer. God's Son—none other than Jesus—has come into the world.[42] He has brought us understanding of the truth[43] so that we may know[44] the One who is true, namely God.[45] It is interesting that here the task of Jesus is clearly presented as that of bringing knowledge through which we can be saved. Such a conception of the work of Jesus could be misunderstood in terms of Gnosticism, the ancient religion which claimed that salvation comes through knowledge of the truths brought by the Revealer. But the knowledge of which John speaks is different from that offered by Gnosticism. Throughout this Epistle he has insisted on the real incarnation of

---

a different view, proposed by K. Beyer, *Semitische Syntax im Neuen Testament*, Göttingen, 1962, I:1, 216f. On this view ὁ γεννηθείς ἐκ τοῦ Θεοῦ is a hanging nominative phrase expressing a condition, which is taken up by αὐτόν; the subject of τηρεῖ is then to be taken as God: "Whoever has been begotten of God—he (*sc.* God) keeps him, so that the evil one does not touch him" (Bultmann, 88f., hesitates between this interpretation and that given in the text). De Jonge, 229, rightly objects that John is not likely to have got his syntax into such a mess, and also questions the force of the alleged parallels (Jn. 17:2; cf. 7:38; 1:3).

[40]Literally, "we are of God"; cf. 3:9f.; 4:7.

[41]κεῖμαι is "to lie (in the power of)" (AG, *s.v.*). τῷ πονηρῷ is undoubtedly to be taken as masculine (cf. v. 18). For the thought see Luke 4:6.

[42]For ἥκω see John 8:42, from which verse it is clear that John is thinking of the coming of the Son of God into the world from the heavenly sphere.

[43]διάνοια occurs only here in the Johannine literature; it refers to the mind or knowledge.

[44]Instead of γινώσκωμεν (K *pm*; TR) a number of important MSS have γινώσκομεν (S A B L P *al*). Although BD 369[6] regard the indicative as nothing more than an error (cf. Westcott, 196: a corrupt pronunciation), there is sufficient evidence elsewhere of the indicative (especially the future indicative) after ἵνα in New Testament MSS to suggest a different verdict. Brooke, 151, speaks of "a vulgarism" subsequently corrected by scribes. De Jonge, 231, n. 445, follows a suggestion of J. de Zwaan that the use here is pregnant: "so that we may know him who is true (just as we do in fact know him)."

[45]That God is meant is clear from the continuation of the verse: "even in *his* Son."

the Son of God, whereas the Gnostics would only allow that the Son of God *seemed* to be united with Jesus. Moreover, John has insisted on the death of Jesus to make an atoning sacrifice for our sins, whereas the Gnostics understood man's need in terms of ignorance rather than of sin, and hence saw no need for atonement. Finally, John insists on the need for belief in Jesus, whereas faith was in effect replaced by knowledge in Gnostic types of religion. Despite these differences from Gnosticism, however, it remains true that Christianity is a religion based on revelation. It is this important element which is expressed here. Of himself man cannot find the way to God and eternal life; he needs a revelation from God himself. So God has sent his Son to reveal the truth, and those who accept the revelation come to know the true God.[46] Not only so, but we can be said to be "in" the true One (2:5, 24). This happens insofar as we are in his Son, Jesus Christ. For to be in the Father is to be in the Son. As John has emphasized earlier, one cannot have the Father unless one also has the Son (2:23). For the Father and the Son are so closely joined to each other that the Father cannot be known apart from the Son, nor the Son apart from the Father. Since it is the Son who came to be the Revealer, it follows that the only way to the true God is through belief in the Son. It is equally true that a person who believes in the Son is necessarily brought into fellowship with the Father. It is true that some people today attempt to have a religion which acknowledges Jesus but questions the reality of God the Father. This can happen only when it is denied that Jesus is the Son of God—the very mistake that John had to combat so energetically in this Epistle. For the last time John hammers home the point. He—Jesus[47]—is the true God and

---

[46]For John's relation to Gnosticism see (briefly) E. D. Schmitz, NIDNTT II, 403–405.

[47]The NIV rightly adopts the view that οὗτος refers back to Jesus (Chaine, 224; Schnackenburg, 291; Bultmann, 90; de Jonge, 232f.; Bruce, 128; Haas, 129f.). Older commentators held that οὗτος referred back to "the true One"; "The pronoun gathers up the revelation indicated in the words which precede: This Being—this One who is true, who is revealed through and in His Son, with whom we are united by His Son—is the true God and life eternal" (Westcott, 196; similarly, Brooke, 152f.; Windisch, 135f.; Stott, 195f.). Dodd, 140, claims that the pronoun sums up all that the Epistle has said about God. In favor of the view that God is meant, it can be observed that οὗτος need not refer back to the immediately preceding phrase (cf. 2:22; 2 Jn. 7); it is also true that it is the knowledge of God which constitutes eternal life (Jn. 17:3). On the other hand, this view makes the text rather tautologous: "we are in him who is true....He is the true God." Further, it is Jesus who is the source of eternal life (1:2; Jn. 11:25; 14:6), and it is fitting that at the climax of the Epistle, as at the beginning and climax of the Gospel (Jn. 1:1; 20:28), full deity should be ascribed to Jesus. It is precisely because Jesus is the true God that the person who is in him is also in the Father.

eternal life. Here, as in the Gospel (Jn. 1:1; 20:28; cf. 1:18 NIV mg.), John declares that Jesus is the true God. He does so, not in the sense that the Father and the Son are identical with each another,[48] but in the sense that "in Christ we have to do with God."[49] John's Jesus is the One who said, "Anyone who has seen me has seen the Father" (Jn. 14:9), and "I am the way—and the truth and the life" (Jn. 14:6). It is no doubt this passage which John has in mind as he writes these words.

21 If what John has just said is true, it is of the utmost urgency that his readers should avoid anything that would lead them astray from this God who has revealed himself in Jesus. So, for the last time, John addresses himself to his readers and warns them: "keep yourselves from[50] idols." This last word, introduced abruptly and forming the abrupt ending of the letter, has caused difficulty to readers. Nowhere in the letter has John spoken of the danger of worship of the material images and false gods whose cults flourished in the world of his readers. It is true that elsewhere in the New Testament the danger of idol worship and its accompanying temptations is a matter for urgent warning,[51] but it would be surprising if John were to introduce this theme so suddenly at the end of his Epistle. Two possibilities of interpretation arise. One is that John is referring to false conceptions of God.[52] Having emphasized that Jesus is the true God, John warns against being misled into the worship of any other alleged manifestation or representation of God. Alternatively, we may note how in the Dead Sea Scrolls sin and idolatry are closely linked together, so that the latter may possibly be regarded as a synonym for the former; in this case, John is saying to his readers, "keep yourselves from sin."[53] But the association of sin with idolatry does not mean that idolatry can be used without further ado as a synonym for sin. Probably, therefore, we should adopt the former interpretation. In content, however, the two interpretations are not so very different. The adoption of false gods or conceptions of God is usually associated with sin. John

---

[48]It is quite clear that for John the Father and Son are distinct beings, although they belong so closely together that on occasion, as we have seen, it is not clear to which of them he is referring.

[49]Haas, 130.

[50]For φυλάσσω ἀπό cf. Luke 12:15; 2 Thessalonians 3:3; *Testament of Reuben* 4:8.

[51]Acts 17:29; Romans 1:23; 1 Corinthians 8:5f.; 10:14; 1 Thessalonians 1:9; Revelation 13:15.

[52]Bruce, 128. See also Bultmann, 90f., who takes εἴδωλα in the sense of false gods (1 Cor. 8:4, 7; 1 Thess. 1:9).

[53]See 1QS 2:11, 17; 4:5; 1QH 4:15; CD 20:9f.; Nauck, 137f.; Schnackenburg, 292f.; de Jonge, 233f. See the discussion in Braun, 304f.

urges his readers to have nothing to do with false ideas of God and the sins that go with them. Today, it is fashionable to imagine that religion and morality are separable and independent; one can be good and righteous without belief in Jesus as the Son of God. John would remind us that apart from Jesus Christ there is no real understanding of the truth and no power to live according to the truth. But Jesus Christ is the true God and the way to eternal life.

INDEX OF SUBJECTS

Abel 190, 238
Advocate 116f., 233
Age to Come 182
Anoint, anointing 52, 153–55, 162–64, 239
Antichrist 71, 150–53, 158, 208
Apostasy 132, 250
Apostle 10, 44, 89
Appear 103, 165, 177, 185
Aristion 43
Asia Minor 47
Assurance 53–55, 122–24, 141, 166, 174, 196–203, 218–29, 242–56
Atone, atonement 7, 15, 34f., 41, 117–19, 177, 201f., 211, 214f., 234

Baptism 17f., 153, 155, 158, 168, 231–35, 237–39
Basilides 17–22, 70f.
Beginning 35f., 38, 67f., 100f., 129, 139, 141, 160, 184, 189
Believe, belief 54, 201, 204, 226, 228–31, 241, 243
Binitarian formula 64
Birth 52, 167–71, 185–87, 211, 226–29, 252
Bishops 11, 60, 90
Blood 112, 118f., 231–39
Brothers, itinerant 83, 85
Brothers, brotherly love 131f., 183, 187–96, 225–27, 246

Cain 50, 188–90
Cerinthus 17–22, 47, 70f., 158, 233
Children 60f., 65, 84, 115, 135, 137–41, 148, 165, 169–72, 183, 185–88, 208, 227
Christ 15, 53, 70, 72f., 157–59, 201, 205f., 232–35, 255
Church 36, 85, 88–90, 151f.
Cleanse, purify 112–14

Command, commandment 36, 38, 66–68, 120–31, 143, 196, 200–02, 219, 225–30
Confess 70, 113, 159, 204–07, 220f.
Conscience 198
Covenant 50

Darkness 36, 53, 109–12, 129–33, 142
Dead Sea Scrolls 51, 255; see also Qumran and Index of Extrabiblical Literature
Deceive 113, 162, 184
Demetrius 4, 81, 92f.
Deny, denial 157–59
Devil 175, 184–87, 189; see also Evil one
Diotrephes 4, 11–14, 43, 88–93, 151
Docetism 12, 17–22, 39f., 52, 101, 233
Dualism 41, 50, 53f., 109

Elder 11–14, 42–46, 59f., 82
Elder, John the 42–48, 59–77, 81–95
Episcopacy 10–14
Eschatology, eschatological 36f., 147–51, 164–75, 182f., 199, 223
Essenes 143
Eve 146
Evil one 140f., 189, 252f.; see also Devil
Example 92, 128, 194
Expiation 117
Eyes 145
Eyewitness 44f., 106f.

Faith, see Believe, belief
Faithful 85, 114
False, falsehood 69f., 74, 135, 150f., 204, 208f.
Father 115, 137–41
Father, God as 63f., 66f., 73, 103f., 106, 108, 116, 127, 141, 143, 157, 159–61, 170, 220
Fear 223–25

Fellowship 15, 104–08, 110–12, 220
Flesh 70f., 101, 144f., 205
Forgive, forgiveness 113f., 138f., 215
Friends 94, 128, 211

Gaius 3f., 9f., 13, 81, 83–86, 88f., 91–95
Glory 172
Gnostic, Gnosticism 12f., 15, 17–22, 34, 52, 70f., 109, 121, 127, 154, 158, 168, 186, 210, 233, 253f.
God 34f., 53, 108f., 121–23, 212f., *et passim*
Good Shepherd 192
Gospel of John 31–42, 44–47, 51f.
Grace 63
Greeting 59–64, 75–77, 81–84, 94f.

Hate 131f., 189–91
Heart 197–99
Hellenistic 52, 138, 145, 168, 186, 220
Heresy, heretic 11, 16, 39f., 74, 90, 157f.
Holy One 155
Hope 37, 164–75
Hour 37, 148–50

Idols 255f.
Incarnation 7, 17, 53, 70f., 157–59, 205, 231–35, 253–55
Independency 89
Intercession 116–19, 248f.

Jesus *passim*
Jews 16f.
Johannine "school" 45f.
John, Epistles of
    Aramaisms 51
    Authorship 42–48
    Canonicity 48f.
    Date of composition 47f.
    Destination 47
    Early history 48f.
    Greek 2
    Hebraisms 51, 63, 111, 167, 201
    Rearrangement 27f.
    Redaction 27–30
    Relationships between the Johannine writings 31–42
    Situation of 1 John 4f., 14–22
    Situation of 2 John 3, 9–14
    Situation of 3 John 3f., 9–14
    Sources 28–30
    Structure of 1 John 22–27
    Style 32f., 51, 135
    Syllable analysis 27
    Thought 49–55

Joy 65, 76, 84, 105
Judge, judgment 34f., 142, 166, 198, 222–25

Know, knowledge 15f., 62, 121–26, 139–41, 183, 196f., 209, 211f., 221, 253

Lady, the chosen 10, 60f., 66
Lawlessness 175–77
Letter writing 9f., 59–61
Life 34f., 102–06, 161, 191f., 214, 241–44, 246–48
Light 36–38, 53, 108–12, 129–33
Live 65f., 68, 83f., 110–12, 127f., 132f.
Lord's Supper 238f.
Love 53f., 61–64, 66–68, 82, 85, 123–26, 131–33, 134, 142–44, 169f., 187–96, 201, 210–29

Menander 19
Mercy 63f.
Message 189
Messiah, see Christ
Missionaries 83–87, 89, 91, 93
Monepiscopate 90
Muratorian Canon 48
Murder 188–92

Name 86f., 138, 210, 243
New 37f., 67, 128–31

Old 37f., 129f.
Old Testament 49f.
Only 214
Orthodox, orthodoxy 10–12, 16, 39, 54, 70, 72f., 74

Parousia 34, 130, 148, 151, 165–79
Pastoral Epistles 13, 81
Peace 63, 94
Perfect, perfection 7, 124–26, 199, 216f., 223–25
Perseverance 72, 152
Peshitta 49
Philoxenian version 49
Possessions 145, 194–96
Prayer 82f., 199f., 244–51
Preachers 70, 74f., 87, 88
Predestination 53f., 210, 244
Pride 145
Promise 161
Prophecy, prophet 16, 46, 204, 209
Propitiation 34, 117, 215
Pure, purity 173f.

Qumran 30, 50f., 145, 185, 239

Remain, abide 127, 160–62, 222
Resurrection 15
Revelation, reveal 103, 165, 172, 213f.
Revelation of John 41–44; 46
Reward 72
Righteous, righteousness 53f., 114, 116f.,
    167–69, 184, 187f., 190

Sacraments 238
Sacrifice 117, 211, 214f., 233
Savior 220
Secede, secession 4f., 15, 151f.
See 35, 92, 101, 104, 106f., 172f., 183f.,
    216, 225f.
Seed 52, 186f.
Shame 166f.
Signs 34f.
Simon of Cyrene 18
Sin 34, 112–20, 138f., 142–46, 175–88,
    215, 245–52, et passim
Sin unto death 7, 179, 245–51
Sinlessness 15, 53f., 113, 175–88, 199,
    251f.
Son of God 4f., 15–22, 53, 64, 73, 104–06,
    112, 157–60, 185, 201, 205, 211, 214,
    220–22, 230–35, 239–43, 253–55
Spirit, spirits 203–10

Spirit, Holy 34f., 53, 75, 153–56, 202–06,
    209, 218f., 232–41
Strength, strong 140
Stumble 132

Teach 72f., 162f.
Teachers, false 15f.
Test 203f.
Testimony 83, 93, 103, 220, 231–41
Tests of life 5
Thanksgiving 82
Truth 31, 61–66, 82, 84, 87, 93, 110f., 124f.,
    129f., 153–57, 163, 196f., 209f., 234,
    253–55

Unity 107
Unrighteousness 114

Victory 208, 228–31

Water 18, 231–33, 236–39
Will of God 146, 244f.
Witness, see Testimony
Word 53, 99–108, 124, 141, 154f., 161, 205
World 119, 142–47, 171, 190, 194, 208f., 214,
    220, 223, 228–30, 253
Wrath 117f.

Young men 137f., 140f.

INDEX OF AUTHORS

Alexander, J. N. S. 169, 186, 207, 248
Alford, H. 180f.
Ambrose 31
Apuleius 216
Argyle, A. W. 33
Aurelius a Chullabi 49

Baltensweiler, H. 26
Balz, H. 19, 207, 225
Banks, R. J. 119
Barclay, W. 85, 155
Bardy, G. 18
Barrett, C. K. 9, 46
Bartels, K.-H. 214
Bartlet, V. 88
Bauder, W. 92, 194
Bauer, W. 11f., 90
Bauernfeind, O. 230
Beck, B. E. 33
Beck, H. 63
Becker, J. 39
Behm, J. 41, 112, 116
Bergmeier, R. 31
Berkhof, L. 178
Bertram, G. 66
Best, E. 149
Betz, O. 116
Beyer, K. 253
Bietenhard, H. 200
Boismard, M.-É. 50, 122
Bornkamm, G. 10, 13, 40, 42, 45, 46, 60
Bousset, W. 150, 173
Braumann, G. 166
Braun, H. 29, 50, 162, 209, 255
Brooke, A. E. 16, 22f., 31f., 47–49, 60, 62, 65,
    68f., 72, 76, 87f., 93, 101, 103, 113, 124f.,
    128–30, 132f., 136, 146, 148, 186, 194, 201,
    207f., 213, 217, 220f., 223, 227, 233,
    236–39, 241, 243, 246, 248, 252–54

Brown, C. 61, 63, 213
Brown, R. E. 39f., 50, 116
Brox, N. 238
Bruce, F. F. 19, 23, 30, 48f., 72, 102–04, 125f.,
    135, 137–39, 142, 146, 148f., 163, 165, 181,
    186, 195, 201f., 207, 220f., 233, 235–40,
    247, 249, 252, 254f.
Büchsel, F. 16, 29, 168, 185, 207, 214
Bultmann, R. 10, 12, 18, 28–31, 36f., 39, 60,
    62f., 65f., 69, 73, 82–84, 87, 90, 93, 102f.,
    107, 109, 112, 122f., 125–27, 130, 132, 135,
    144f., 151f., 156f., 161–63, 165f., 168,
    170f., 176, 182, 184, 186, 194, 198f., 201,
    204, 207, 217, 223–27, 229, 234, 238, 240,
    243, 246, 248, 252, 253-55

Calvin, J. 61, 114, 124, 148
Cameron, W. 170
Campenhausen, H. F. von 11, 14
Cassem, N. 142
Chaine, J. 48, 84, 122, 138, 152, 157, 172f.,
    201, 207, 217, 220, 225, 227, 233, 235, 240,
    248, 252, 254
Charles, R. H. 31
Charlesworth, J. H. 50
Charue, A.-M. 136
Chrysostom 49
Clark, A. C. 33
Clavier, H. 118
Clement of Alexandria 48f., 186
Coenen, L. 42, 60f.
Conzelmann, H. 35f., 63, 100, 109, 133
Craig, T. 11
Cullmann, O. 64
Cyprian 61

Deissmann, A. 87
Delling, G. 101, 125
Denney, J. 193, 215, 234

Dibelius, M. 35
Dobschütz, E. von 28, 30
Dobson, J. H. 105
Dodd, C. H. 11, 23, 31f., 49, 60, 62, 64, 74, 82, 87, 89, 93, 102, 107, 117f., 125–27, 130, 138f., 151f., 154f., 168, 171, 181f., 186, 203, 207f., 210, 213, 217, 220, 222, 226f., 231, 235, 238, 243, 251f., 254
Doty, W. G. 9
Dunn, J. D. G. 119

Ebrard, J. H. A. 178
Ellis, E. E. 83
Eltester, W. 101
Erasmus 236
Esser, H.-H. 63, 67
Eusebius 31, 42f., 45, 47–49, 93

Farmer, W. R. 76
Feine, P. 41
Feuillet, A. 25f.
Flew, R. N. 179
Foerster, W. 18, 44, 61, 63, 71, 200, 220
Fohrer, G. 170
Forestell, J. T. 41
Fortna, R. T. 39
Francis, F. O. 99f.
Friedrich, G. 161
Fürst, D. 70
Fuller, R. H. 235
Funk, R. W. 9, 76

Goppelt, L. 233
Grant, R. M. 19
Grayston, K. 102
Greeven, H. 246
Grundmann, W. 71, 156, 159
Günther, W. 61, 209, 213, 230
Guthrie, D. 41–43

Haas, C. 25, 27, 62, 82–84, 102f., 111, 122, 125f., 130, 132, 135f., 144f., 148, 152f., 156, 160, 163, 166, 170–72, 176, 189, 194, 196, 198, 205, 213, 217, 219, 221, 223–25, 227, 232, 237–39, 243, 246, 252, 254f.
Haenchen, E. 12f., 29f., 42, 50–52, 72, 90
Häring, T. 23
Hahn, F. 235
Hahn, H.-C. 166
Hall, D. R. 87
Hanse, H. 73
Hanson, A. T. 50
Harnack, A. von 13f., 207
Harris, M. 202

Hauck, F. 104, 127, 174
Hawthorne, G. F. 179, 246
Heise, J. 10, 31f., 122, 126f., 132, 152f.
Héring, J. 51
Hermas 85, 204, 250
Hick, J. 234
Hill, D. 118
Hippolytus 18, 48, 151, 186
Hofius, O. 64, 168
Hooker, M. D. 16
Horst, P. W. van der 216
Hort, F. J. A. 22
Houlden, J. L. 22, 29, 32, 39, 65, 87, 102f., 125f., 137, 146, 165, 169, 176, 181, 184, 187, 194f., 207, 216f., 223f., 227, 238f., 252, 254
Howard, W. F. 32–34, 237
Hudson, W. D. 215
Hunter, W. M. 45, 174

Ignatius 18f., 47f., 74, 101, 158, 185, 232
Irenaeus 14, 18, 20, 47–49, 70f., 157f., 186, 233

Jeremias, G. 39
Jeremias, J. 64, 117, 177, 193
Jerome 31, 49
Johannson, N. 246
Jones, P. R. 23, 27
Jonge, M. de 19, 26f., 29f., 39f., 42, 45, 48, 103, 125, 147, 155–58, 161, 165, 172, 176, 182, 186, 198, 203, 207f., 213f., 217, 220, 228, 232, 239f., 248, 253, 255
Josephus 143, 214
Jülicher, A. 28
Jukes, R. 222
Justin Martyr 44, 48, 85

Käsemann, E. 12f., 29, 40, 42, 44, 90
Katz, P. 49
Kauder, E. 71
Keyes, C. W. 9, 93
Kilpatrick, G. D. 130
Kittler, R. 228
Klein, G. 33, 36–38
Knox, R. 236
Knox, W. L. 33
Köster, H. 194
Kubo, S. 180
Kümmel, W. G. 23, 32, 42

Law, R. 18, 22, 27, 32, 129, 167
Lazure, N. 145
Leivestad, R. 185
Lewis, C. S. 61

Lindars, B. 16, 39f.
Lindström, H. 179
Link, H.-G. 61, 213
Lohmeyer, E. 41, 150
Lohse, E. 59
Luck, U. 83
Lyonnet, S. 154, 176, 182

Mackintosh, H. R. 139
Malatesta, E. 23f., 27, 62
Manson, T. W. 49, 228f., 231, 239
Marshall, I. H. 12, 72, 128, 152, 179, 201, 210,
   234, 244, 247–49, 250
Maurer, C. 193
Metzger, B. M. 72, 76, 128f., 146, 177, 190f.,
   199, 207, 228, 231, 241
Michaelis, W. 41, 83, 92, 183, 194, 216
Michel, O. 70
Moffatt, J. 31f., 34, 42, 49, 139, 170, 186, 231
Moody, D. 214
Moore, A. L. 149
Morgenthaler, R. 33
Morris, L. 60, 112, 118, 124, 138, 148, 155,
   180, 249
Moule, C. F. D. 104, 129, 156, 186
Müller, D. 83
Müller, U. B. 19
Mullins, T. Y. 66
Munck, J. 43, 45
Mundle, W. 225, 228, 244

Nauck, W. 29f., 47, 50, 132, 136, 156, 197,
   207, 239, 243, 247f., 255
Neufeld, V. H. 64
Newman, J. H. 149
Nicol, W. 39
Nicole, R. R. 118
Noack, B. 136
Nygren, A. 213

Oepke, A. 166, 202, 216
O'Neill, J. C. 30, 51, 112, 135, 140, 197
Origen 48f.
Outka, G. 213

Papias 14, 42–46, 48, 93
Philo 186
Pinnock, C. 244
Piper, O. A. 29, 207
Pliny 239
Plummer, A. 43, 60, 93, 136, 181, 245
Polycarp 48, 65, 207
Polycrates 47
Potterie, I. de la 136–39, 154f., 176, 182

Pratscher, W. 198
Preisker, H. 29

Quell, G. 61f., 64

Rad, G. von 63
Rahlfs, A. 207
Reicke, B. 26
Reitzenstein, R. 154
Rengstorf, K. H. 73, 168
Reynolds, S. M. 247
Richter, G. 233
Riesenfeld, H. 118
Rigaux, B. 150
Robinson, J. A. T. 47
Ross, A. 18, 43, 60, 75, 136, 146, 148, 180,
   186, 220, 238
Rosscup, J. E. 250

Salom, A. P. 33
Sangster, W. E. 179
Schenke, H.-M. 183
Schlier, H. 166
Schmauch, W. 28
Schmitz, E. D. 254
Schnackenburg, R. 11, 13, 16–19,
   24–27, 29–32, 40, 45–47, 51f., 64–66,
   68–70, 72, 76, 82–85, 91, 93f., 101–03, 107,
   113, 115, 122, 125–27, 130, 132, 135f., 142,
   147f., 150f., 153, 156–58, 160f., 163, 165f.,
   168, 172f., 176f., 184, 186f., 194f., 199, 201,
   203–05, 207–10, 213f., 216f., 220–27, 230,
   233f., 236–41, 243, 245f., 248–50, 252, 254f.
Schneider, J. 224
Schniewind, J. 161
Scholer, D. M. 179, 246–48, 250
Schottroff, L. 52
Schottroff, W. 122
Schrage, W. 133
Schrenk, G. 61, 64, 67, 228
Schulz, S. 186
Schweizer, E. 10, 34, 83, 144, 204, 235
Seesemann, H. 66, 104, 127
Sevenster, J. N. 27, 159
Sibinga, J. S. 27
Simpson. E. K. 145
Smith, D. 43, 60, 146
Soden, H. F. von 231
Spicq, C. 137f., 198, 211
Stählin, G. 94, 132, 213, 246
Stauffer, E. 61, 213
Steck, O. H. 189
Stevenson, R. L. 174
Stibbs, A. M. 112

INDEX OF AUTHORS

Stott, J. R. W. 18, 43, 48, 62, 64, 93, 103, 109, 124–26, 137, 139, 148, 155, 165, 176, 178, 180f., 184f., 194, 205, 207, 217, 220f., 223, 227, 238, 241, 245f., 249f., 252, 254
Strathmann, H. 103, 237f.
Streeter, B. H. 10, 45
Synge, F. C. 172

Tacitus 107
Teeple, H. M. 39
Tertullian 48
Theodore of Mopsuestia 49
Thiele, W. 236
Thiselton, A. C. 145
Thyen, H. 39
Tomoi, K. 27f.
Tröger, K.-W. 20
Trudinger, P. 246
Turner, N. 237

Vawter, B. 49, 83, 207
Vielhauer, P. 9, 12, 28f., 31, 33, 36

Waddell, H. 214
Wanke, G. 225
Warfield, B. B. 178

Watts, I. 141, 170
Weir, J. E. 102
Weiss, K. 20f., 177
Wendt, H. H. 100, 136
Wengst, K. 18, 20f., 38, 40, 107, 125, 131, 144f., 151, 191, 194, 217, 233
Wesley, C. 119, 166, 171, 229, 237
Wesley, J. 125, 179
Westcott, B. F. 18, 22, 68, 84f., 90f., 93, 101, 103, 112, 114, 117–19, 122, 125f., 129, 132f., 136f., 146, 148, 152, 157, 163, 166f., 171, 176, 180, 195, 198, 207f., 213, 217, 220f., 223, 227, 233, 236, 238f., 241, 243, 246, 251–54
Wilson, R. M. 15
Wilson, W. G. 32f.
Windisch, H. 18, 29, 89, 93, 137, 139, 152, 156, 168, 173, 182, 186f., 192, 198, 203, 207, 239, 243, 252, 254
Wurm, A. 16

Yamauchi, E. 15
Young, N. H. 118

Zahn, T. 43
Zimmerli, W. 63
Zwaan, J. de 253

263

INDEX OF BIBLICAL REFERENCES

GENESIS
1:1 — 100
1:31 — 142
17:1 — 66
18:27–33 — 246
20:7 — 246
22:2, 12, 16 — 214
43:30 — 194

EXODUS
19:10 — 174
32:11–14 — 246
32:31f. — 246
33:20 — 216
34:8f. — 246

LEVITICUS
4:2, 13, 22, 27 — 247
5:15, 17f. — 247
16:21 — 113
19:18 — 129

NUMBERS
8:21 — 174
14:13–19 — 246
14:33, 34 — 177
15:27–31 — 247
18:22 — 247

DEUTERONOMY
1:31 — 168
8:5 — 168
14:1 — 168
17:12 — 247
19:15 — 93, 237
22:26 — 247
32:4 — 114
32:6 — 168

JOSHUA
24:7 — 107
27:10 — 166

JUDGES
11:34 — 214

1 SAMUEL
2:12 — 122
15:25 — 177
16:13 — 153
24:5 — 198
25:28 — 177

2 SAMUEL
13:15 — 61

1 KINGS
2:4 — 66
8:46 — 115

2 KINGS
5:18 — 118
19:4 — 246
20:3 — 66

1 CHRONICLES
28:9 — 122

JOB
2:5 — 252
4:17 — 115
15:14–16 — 115
36:12 — 122

PSALMS
11:7 — 173
14:3 — 115
17:15 — 173
19:13 — 247
25:11 — 118
27:1 — 109
32:1f. — 176
32:5 — 113
36:9 — 109
42:1–5 — 173
71:22 — 155
99:4 — 167
103:13 — 168
104:2 — 109
105:15 — 252
106:3 — 167
119:121 — 167
130 — 50

PROVERBS
3:12 — 168
4:3 — 214
12:10 — 194
13:5 — 166
20:9 — 115
28:13 — 113

ECCLESIASTES
7:20 — 115

ISAIAH
1:3 — 122
1:29 — 166
5:13 — 122
22:14 — 247
40:30 — 140
45:24 — 166
49:6 — 109
53:6 — 115
53:10 — 193

53:11	117	MATTHEW		1:24	155
53:11f.	177	2:23	171	4:19	144
54:1–8	60	3:6	113	7:3	60
61:1	153	4:1–11	185	7:5	60,66
63:16	168	4:16	109	8:31	60
64:6	115	5:8	173	8:33	158
64:8	168	5:9	168,170f.	10:27	251
		5:14–16	109	10:45	193
JEREMIAH	50	5:21f.	191	11:24	245
6:26	214	5:21–28	190	12:32	61
7:16	246	5:27–29	145	12:44	145
9:6, 24	122	6:1	167	13:1	170
11:14	246	6:10	245	13:5f.	69, 162
12:13	166	7:12	68	13:22	69, 150, 162, 204
14:11f.	246	7:15	204	13:23	162
15:1	246	7:21	146	13:32	170
31:9	168	7:21–23	206	14:24	193
31:20	168,194	7:23	176	14:36	244
31:33f.	182	7:24–27	146	16:14f.	176
31:34	122, 137f., 176	9:11	75		
37:3	246	10:8	87	LUKE	
42:2	246	10:15	223	1:1	213
		10:22	138	1:29	170
EZEKIEL		11:19	75	1:47	220
18:19f.	177	11:22, 24	223	1:50	224
36:27	182	11:25	141	1:55	186
		11:27	170	1:78	194
DANIEL		11:30	228	2:11	220
4:1	51	12:36	223	2:32	109
9:20	113	13:17	144	4:6	253
12:3	184	13:41	176	4:8	153
		16:22	117	5:10	104
HOSEA		16:23	132	5:20, 23	139
4:1f.	122	18:33	163	5:31	83
11	168	20:3, 5	148	6:18	166
		23:4	228	6:46	206
JOEL		23:5–12	90	7:10	83
2:28	148	23:9	115, 139	7:12	214
		23:13ff.	61	7:18	102
AMOS		23:28	176	7:39	170
2:10f.	107	23:35	189	7:47	190
7:1–6	246	24:3	166	7:47f.	139
8:10	214	24:9	138	8:11	186
		24:12	176	8:42	214
MICAH		24:20–28	90	8:43	166
7:18–20	114	24:24	150	9:38	214
		24:27, 37, 39	166	10:5f.	74
ZECHARIAH		25:37	184	10:18	185
2:8	252	25:46	184, 224	10:21	141
12:10	214	27:45	148	11:51	189
		28:14	197	12:1–3	61
MALACHI				12:4	94
1:6	168	MARK		12:10	250
2:10	168	1:11	235	12:15	255

THE EPISTLES OF JOHN

12:54–56	147	4:10	233
15:27	83	4:22	101
18:13	117	4:23	148
19:40	245	4:24	212
20:36	103	4:29	157
21:16	65	4:42	220
22:23	249	4:52	148
24:39	101	5:21–29	35
		5:23	40
JOHN		5:24	35, 103, 191
1:1	35, 100f., 254f.	5:25	214
1:1–18	34, 40, 101	5:25–29	166
1:2	104	5:31–40	240
1:3	101, 144, 254	5:36	239
1:4	103	5:37	216
1:4–9	109	5:44	63
1:5	142	5:45	173
1:9	205	6	238
1:12	170, 226, 243, 246	6:37	101, 228
1:13	40, 167	6:39	101
1:14	63f., 71, 165, 205, 213f.	6:40	161, 183
1:15	225	6:46	216
1:16f.	63	6:47	161
1:17	64	6:51	215
1:18	214, 216, 254	6:51–55	205
1:18–35	108	6:51–58	40
1:19	130	6:53–56	233
1:20	205	6:54ff.	239
1:29	41, 119, 177	6:57f.	215
1:29–34	40	6:58	189
1:30	225	6:61	132
1:32	21	6:62	183
1:32–34	232, 235	6:64	35
1:33	232	6:69	154
1:34	21	7:16f.	66
1:36	41	7:26	72
1:47	61	7:26–31	157
1:49	40	7:28	41
2:23	243	7:38	253
3	169	7:41–43	157
3:3–8	103	8:12	66, 109, 130
3:5	231, 239	8:14	205
3:6	40, 101, 167, 186, 228	8:17	237
3:8	168	8:19	41
3:9	186	8:29	200
3:16	103, 142, 213–15	8:33, 37	186
3:16–18	40	8:42	253
3:18	214	8:44	185
3:19	130, 143, 205	8:46	178, 189
3:19–21	109	8:47	92
3:20	112	8:53	51
3:21	111	8:55	41
3:31	205	9:5	109, 130
3:32	108	9:17	51

9:22	205	14:7	40f.
9:31	244	14:9	255
9:39	142	14:10, 11	127
9:41	113	14:13f.	244
10:7, 9	34	14:14	200
10:10	161	14:15	67, 200, 228
10:11	41, 192f.	14:15–17	62
10:14–18	130	14:16	63
10:15, 17f.	41, 192f.	14:17	153, 209
10:28	161	14:19	183, 214
10:32	91	14:20	127
11:5	174		
11:9f.	132		
11:25	103, 214, 254		
11:26	221		
11:27	40		
11:41f.	244		
11:50f.	192		
11:50–52	41		
11:52	170		
11:55	174		
12:31	142, 185		
12:32	165		
12:35	66, 133		
12:35f.	109, 130		
12:40	133		
12:42	205		
12:43	143		
12:44f.	183		
12:46	109, 130, 142		
12:47f.	35		
13	128		
13:6	91		
13:12–15	194		
13:13	46		
13:15	128		
13:34	37, 67, 129, 201, 225		
13:34f.	189		
13:37f.	192		
14–16	116, 155		
14:3	165		
14:6	34, 73, 93, 103, 242, 254		

14:21	67, 228	19:11	113	23:26	59, 74
14:23	127, 202	19:30	21, 40	24:18	174
14:26	156, 237	19:31–37	40	26:6	161
14:27	63	19:34	233	26:32	152
14:30	142	19:34f.	233	27:3	94
15–16	40	19:35	93, 233		
15–17	39	20:19	63, 94	ROMANS	
15:4–10	127	20:21	63, 94, 163	1–15	34
15:5	34	20:22f.	239	1:5	86
15:7	244	20:23	139	1:10	83
15:8	87, 223	20:24–29	40, 101	1:13	163
15:9	163	20:26	63, 94	1:23	255
15:10	67	20:28	254f.	1:24	144
15:11	105	20:31	40, 243	3:23	115
15:12	201	21	40	3:25	114, 117
15:12f.	130	21:24	43, 93	4:7f.	176
15:13	192			5:3–9:30	34
15:14	200	ACTS		5:5	202, 221
15:14f.	94	2:17	148	5:8	192f.
15:16	200, 244	2:33	155	6:1	116, 176
15:17	200f.	2:39	161	6:4	66
15:18f.	171	3:14	117, 155	6:8	34
15:19	209	4:13	44	8:4, 7	255
15:21	41, 138	4:27	153	8:8	200
15:22, 24	113	5:1–11	247	8:10, 14–16	202
15:26	153, 209, 234, 237	5:20	103	8:14	168
15:27	35	5:31	240	8:16	170
16:1	132	5:41	86	8:17–19	172
16:2	148	6:2	200	8:26	114
16:3	41	7:2	139	8:34	116
16:4	35	7:52	117	8:35f.	171
16:10	183	9:13	108	9:8	170
16:13	153, 209	9:31	224	10:5	167
16:16f.	183	10:2, 22	224	12:1f.	200
16:17	65	10:33	85	12:13	85
16:23	200	10:35	167, 224	12:21	208
16:23–26	244	10:38	128, 153	13:8–10	67
16:24	105	10:44–48	239	13:12	130
16:25	102	11:30	60	14:13	132
16:30	156, 199	12:3	200	14:18	200
16:33	63, 208, 229f.	13:16	224	15:2f.	194
17	40	13:23	161, 220	15:24	86
17:1	172	13:26	224	15:27	104
17:2	51, 101, 228, 253	13:32	161	15:33	94
17:3	41, 161, 254	14:23	60	16:1f.	93
17:5	165, 172	15:3	86	16:20	94
17:10	101	15:29	94		
17:12	252	17:29	254	1 CORINTHIANS	
17:17	115	18:1–4	87	1:9	104
17:18	163	19:18	113	1:23	102
17:21, 23	127	20:38	86	2:9	172
17:24	51, 172	21:5	86	3:10–17	250
17:26	127	21:24, 26	174	4:3f.	93
18:19	72	22:1	139	4:3–5	198

4:14	84, 115	3:22	161	3:20	200
4:16	92	3:26	168	3:22	224
4:17	115	3:29	186	3:23	85
5:3–5	247	4:4–7	168		
5:5	249	4:19	84, 115	**1 THESSALONIANS**	
6:6	85	4:25	60	1:1	63
7:31	130, 146	5:6	133	1:2f.	65
7:32–34	200	5:16	144	1:3	199
8:5f.	255	6:6	87	1:5f.	155, 187
9:11f., 14	87	6:10	85	1:6	92
10:12	142	6:16	63, 94	1:9	255
10:14	255			2:4	200
11:1	92, 194	**EPHESIANS**		2:9	87
11:19	213	1:13	154	2:12	86
11:30	247	2:3	144	2:14	92
12:1–3	204	2:8	85	2:15	200
12:3	205	3:6	161	2:17	144
13:7	221	3:18	163	2:19	166
14:19	85	4:3	252	3:8	245
14:29	204	4:14	209	3:9	199
14:35	85	5:1	92	3:13	166
15:23	166	5:10	200	4:1	200
15:50	71	5:21	224	4:15	166
16:2	83	5:23	220	5:20f.	204
16:6, 11	86	5:26	114	5:23	94, 166
16:17	65	6:4	139		
		6:5	224f.	**2 THESSALONIANS**	
2 CORINTHIANS		6:17	141	2:1	166
1:16	86	6:23	94	2:1–12	71
1:20	161			2:3, 7	176
1:21	153	**PHILIPPIANS**		2:8, 9	166
1:21f.	153f.	1:7	104	3:3	255
3:3	76	1:13	202	3:7	92
3:18	172f.	1:20	166	3:16	94
4:3	213	1:21–23	167		
4:4–6	71	1:23	144	**1 TIMOTHY**	
4:5	102	1:28	85	1:1	220
5:9	200	2:1, 2–8	194	1:2	63, 115
5:15	193	2:12	225	1:20	249
5:17	202	2:15	170	2:3	220
5:21	178	2:16	103	3:2	85
6:1	86	2:22	84	4:1	148
7:1	114, 224	3:9	202	4:7	252
7:15	225	3:20	220	4:8	161
8:5	189	3:21	71, 172	4:10	220
8:9	194	4:9	94	5:1f.	137
10:1	194	4:10	65	5:10	85
11:9	252	4:18	200	5:13	91
12:2	202			5:17	60
13:5	202	**COLOSSIANS**		5:22	252
13:11	94	1:10	86	6:3	160
		1:27	202	6:13	194
GALATIANS		3:4	165, 172f.	6:16	109
1:3	63	3:12	194		
2:20	192f., 202	3:16	160		

268

2 TIMOTHY

1:1	161
1:2	63
1:10	220
1:13	160
2:14	91
2:19	152, 199
2:22	140
3:1	148
4:3f.	160
4:10	61, 143

TITUS

1:2	161
1:3	220
1:4	104, 220
1:8	85
1:9	160
2:1–8	137
2:9	200
2:10, 13	220
3:4	220
3:5	168
3:6	220
3:13	86

PHILEMON

	81
10	115

HEBREWS

1:1f.	102
1:2	148
1:3	114
1:9	153
2:9	193
2:17	117
4:15	178
4:16	166
5:3	118
6:4–6	250
6:12	92, 161
8:11	122
8:12	117
9:5	117
10:2	114
10:6, 8	118
10:17	176
10:18	118, 166
10:23	114
10:26	118
10:26–31	250
11:4	189
11:5f.	200

11:17	214
11:33	167
12:13f.	194
12:23	184
12:24	189
13:2	85
13:7	92
13:11	118
13:16	200
13:20	94
13:21	200

JAMES

1:1	59, 74
1:12	161
1:18	186
1:20	167
1:23	186
1:27	252
4:4	144
4:8	114
5:3	148
5:7f.	166
5:14	60
5:16	113
5:20	246

1 PETER

1:3	168
1:5	148
1:17	224
1:20	148
1:22	174
1:23	168, 186
1:25	186
2:11	144
2:21	128, 193f.
2:22	178
2:24	177
3:12	184
3:18	117f., 178
4:9	85
4:18	184
5:1	43, 60
5:1–5	137
5:4	165
5:13	60f.
5:14	94

2 PETER

1:1	220
1:9	207
1:11	220
1:16	166

1:19	130
2:9	223
2:20	220
3:2	160, 220
3:4	139, 166
3:7	223
3:8	220
3:9	150
3:12	166
3:18	220

1 JOHN

1:1	35, 51, 104, 189
1:1f.	220
1:1–3	106, 183
1:1–4	5, 34, 43, 45
1:2	100, 102, 104, 165, 254
1:3	51, 100, 102, 105, 121
1:4	35, 136
1:5	27f., 36, 66, 121, 189, 212f.
1:5f.	128
1:5–10	28
1:5–2:27	28
1:6	15, 51, 112, 121, 124, 127, 131, 167
1:6f.	66
1:6–10	30
1:7	28, 30, 50, 66, 113f., 118, 121, 138
1:7–2:9	50
1:8	15, 114f., 124, 132, 134, 141, 162, 178
1:9	28, 114, 119, 134, 138f., 205
1:10	15, 124, 132, 134, 178
2:1	50, 84, 136f., 165, 177f., 180
2:1f.	138
2:2	28, 122, 142, 177, 215, 220
2:3	48, 126f., 134, 141, 197, 200
2:3f.	67, 125, 128f., 139, 211
2:3–5	124
2:3–8	201
2:4	15, 121f., 141, 183
2:4f.	28, 132, 228
2:5	34, 51, 61, 123, 126, 144, 187, 192, 195, 197, 199, 217, 223, 254
2:5f.	126
2:6	66, 126, 173, 202, 219, 223

2:7	10, 35f., 100, 129, 136, 140	3:1	48, 115, 200, 211, 214	4:1–6	27, 71, 155, 219
2:7f.	37, 67, 122	3:2	28, 37, 51, 82, 170, 191, 217, 223f.	4:2	15, 30, 32, 48, 70, 113, 126, 207, 231
2:7–17	128	3:3	37, 127, 177	4:2f.	48, 157f., 204
2:8	30, 36, 51, 67, 132, 136, 146, 182	3:4	29	4:2–7	92
2:9	15, 82, 121, 132, 226	3:4–6	184	4:3	70f., 113, 151, 156, 205, 209, 237
2:9f.	69	3:5	127, 165, 185, 191	4:4	34, 115, 127, 134, 137, 140, 209, 228, 230
2:9–11	28, 128	3:6	92, 113, 122, 127, 181, 186, 199, 209, 211, 223, 251f.	4:5	28, 135
2:10	51, 143, 189, 211			4:6	28, 211
2:11	66	3:6–10	29	4:7	28, 82, 167, 183, 185, 189, 226, 253
2:11f.	128	3:7	115f., 127, 137, 162		
2:12	115, 134, 137, 165, 175	3:8	35, 50, 165, 178	4:7–21	27
2:12f.	135f.	3:8f.	184	4:8	27f., 169, 211, 221
2:12–14	27, 50f.	3:8–10	177	4:9	124–26, 144, 195, 217
2:13	122, 134, 140	3:9	35, 113, 167f., 178, 180f., 183, 199, 211, 223, 251f.	4:9f.	119, 211, 220
2:13f.	35, 101, 208, 211, 230, 252			4:10	28, 117f., 126, 177, 220
2:14	122, 134–37, 139, 148, 154, 156	3:9f.	226, 253	4:11	82, 189, 211
		3:10	92, 178, 208, 226	4:12	28, 125, 144, 189, 195, 202, 208, 219, 223
2:15	69, 124f., 131, 195, 217	3:11	10, 69, 100, 183, 211		
		3:11f.	67, 126, 129, 170, 183, 188f., 197	4:13	30, 35, 106, 126, 155, 202, 221
2:15–17	16, 27, 110, 134f., 140			4:13f.	107
2:16	194	3:11–24	27	4:14	106, 115, 221
2:17	30, 161, 164, 237	3:12	35f., 50, 140, 185, 191, 252	4:15	64, 70, 113, 205, 221, 231
2:17f.	27	3:13	128, 171, 191, 196	4:15f.	208
2:18	10, 25, 71, 134, 137, 147, 163, 204, 208	3:14	35, 103, 173, 188f., 191, 197	4:16	27f., 122, 213, 223
2:18–25	162	3:14f.	28, 227	4:17	28, 126f., 173, 197, 199, 205, 221
2:18–27	71, 140	3:16	61, 122, 126f., 213	4:17f.	125
2:19	10, 14, 17, 69, 72, 92, 99, 113, 153, 156	3:16f.	213	4:18	115
		3:16–18	67	4:19	48, 211, 227
2:20	16, 35, 162, 186, 239	3:17	125, 131, 144–46, 217	4:20	35, 69, 125, 183, 216, 227
2:21	92, 136, 197	3:17f.	217		
2:22	15, 71, 150, 208, 232f., 254	3:17–19	227	4:20f.	189
		3:18	62, 115, 137, 188, 197, 211	4:21	27f., 67, 225
2:22f.	19, 73, 185, 201, 231			5:1	15, 27f., 158, 167, 185, 228f.
2:23	10, 28, 32, 64, 70, 73, 106, 113, 156f., 160, 205, 240	3:18f.	202		
		3:19	126, 145	5:1–12	28, 243
		3:19f.	202	5:2	126, 170, 197
2:24	28, 35, 51, 100, 152, 162, 210, 219, 250, 254	3:19–22	222	5:2f.	125
		3:20	30, 92, 239	5:3	10, 124f., 144, 195, 217
		3:21	34, 82, 166, 223, 244	5:4	28, 30, 51, 167, 185
2:26	10, 136	3:21f.	244	5:4f.	101, 134, 140, 208
2:27	16, 30, 35, 127, 153f., 164, 186, 219	3:22	67, 245	5:5	15
		3:22–24	197	5:5–8	71
2:27f.	27, 155	3:23	66f., 129, 139, 169, 189, 211, 226, 231, 243	5:5–11	243
2:28	90, 115, 127, 137, 163, 168, 172, 199, 219, 223			5:5–12	229, 243
		3:24	30, 35, 67, 126, 203, 208, 217, 219	5:6	15, 30, 70f., 93, 158, 205, 237f., 240
2:28f.	27f.				
2:29	27f., 116, 164, 185, 211, 226	3:24–4:1	28	5:6f.	47
2:29–3:10	30	4:1	16, 25, 82	5:6–8	240
		4:1–3	10, 209		

5:7	69, 234
5:7f.	30, 231, 235
5:8	51, 93, 231, 233f., 240
5:10	28, 64, 231
5:11f.	243
5:12	28
5:13	5, 105, 116, 136, 139, 191, 201, 231, 246, 251
5:14	34, 166, 223
5:14–21	28, 243
5:15	191
5:16	178, 180
5:16f.	50, 179, 252
5:17	114
5:18	113, 167, 179f., 191, 253
5:18f.	140, 185
5:19	142, 191, 211, 237
5:20	127, 130, 191, 211, 237
5:21	115, 137

2 JOHN

1	10, 69, 76, 82, 85, 121f.
1–3	82
2	51, 62, 154
3	62, 82, 223
4	10, 62, 67, 82, 84, 110
4–6	69, 90, 123, 201
4–11	64
5	66f., 128f., 165, 189, 211
5f.	10, 35f.
6	228
7	10, 15, 30, 32, 48, 113, 150, 157, 162, 204f., 231–33, 254
7f.	49
7–11	88, 210, 250
8	10
9	10, 16, 28, 32, 152, 158
10f.	10
11	49
12	3, 94, 105

3 JOHN

1	62, 128
3	62, 65f., 85
3f.	66
4	62, 115
5	82
5f.	84
7	69, 151
8	152
9	83
9f.	85
10	88
11	82, 183
12	81, 104
13f.	76
14	3
15	63

JUDE

2	63
3	104, 160
11	189
17	160
18	148
20	160
21	252
25	220

REVELATION

1:1, 4	44
1:5	192
1:9	44
2:3	138
2:7	208, 230
2:11	230
2:14	132
2:17, 26	230
3:3	252
3:5	230
3:10	252
3:12, 21	230
5:5	208, 230
6:4	109
6:9	109, 241
12:7–12	185
12:9	185
12:11	208
12:17	60, 241
13	71, 150
13:15	255
16:15	252
17:14	208, 230
19:10	241
20:1–3	185
20:2	185
21:7	208
21:14	46
22:11	184

INDEX OF EXTRA- AND NONBIBLICAL LITERATURE

ACTS OF THOMAS
27   154
157   154

AMBROSE, EPISTLE
11:4   31

APOCRYPHON OF JOHN
22   44
30:14–20   154

APULEIUS,
  METAMORPHOSES
11:23   216

ASSUMPTION OF MOSES
11:17   246
12:6   246

1 BARUCH
4:30–37   60
5:5   60

2 BARUCH
78:2   63

1 CLEMENT
31:2   190
42:4   204

CLEMENT, EXCERPTA
  EX THEODOTI
38, 40, 49, 53   186

CLEMENT, STROMATEIS
2:15:66   48

CORPUS HERMETICUM
1:12–15   186
1:24–26   186, 216
11:20   138
13:11   138

COVENANT OF
  DAMASCUS (CD)
3:14f.   247
20:9f.   255
20:28f.   113

CYPRIAN, DE UNITATE
6   61

DECRETUM
  GELASIANUM
  31

DIDACHE
11   86
11f.   10, 204
11:11   204
12:1   204

1 ENOCH
5:8   182
71   216

2 ENOCH
1ff.   216
64:4   246

EPISTLE TO DIOGNETUS
10:3   48
12:3   209

1 ESDRAS
4:28   252

EUSEBIUS, HISTORIA
  ECCLESIASTICA
3:23:3f.   47
3:24:17   48, 49
3:25:2   48, 49
3:25:2f.   49
3:25:3   31
3:31:2f.   47
3:39:3   93
3:39:4   43
3:39:5–7   43
3:39:15   45
3:39:17   48
5:24:3f.   47
6:14:1   48
6:25   48, 49
7:25   42

4 EZRA
1   216
7:102–115   246

GOSPEL OF PHILIP
68   154
95   154

GOSPEL OF TRUTH
27:14   48
31:4f.   48
36:17–26   154

HAGIGA
14b   216

HERMAS, MANDATE
11   204
11:7   204

HERMAS, SIMILITUDE
6:1–4   250
9:27   85

HIPPOLYTUS,
  REFUTATIO OMNIUM
  HAERESIUM
5:7:19   154
5:8:28f.   186
5:26–28   186
7:27:10   18
9:22   154

IGNATIUS, LETTER TO
  THE EPHESIANS
7:2   48
9:1   74
13:1   185
19:3   185

IGNATIUS, LETTER TO
  THE MAGNESIANS
9f.   19
11   19

IGNATIUS, LETTER TO
  THE SMYRNAEANS
1f.   157
1–3   19
2f.   101
3   158
4:1   74
6:2   19
7:1   232
7:2   74

IGNATIUS, LETTER TO
  THE TRALLIANS
9f.   19

IRENAEUS, ADVERSUS
  HAERESES
1:1–10   186
1:12–13   186
1:16:3   49
1:23:5   20
1:24:4   18, 71
1:26:1   18, 71
2:22:5   47
3:3:4   18, 47, 233

3:16:5   48
3:16:8   48, 49

JEROME, DE VIRIS
  ILLUSTRIBUS
9   31, 49
18   31

JOSEPH AND ASENETH
                            239

JOSEPHUS, ANTIQUITIES
1:222   214
5:264   214

JOSEPHUS, BELLUM
  JUDAICUM
2:161   143

JUBILEES
1:21   132
21:22   247
26:34   247
33:13, 18   247

JUDITH
5:20   132

JUSTIN, APOLOGY
1:67   85

JUSTIN, DIALOGUE
81   44
123:9   48

2 MACCABEES
4:15   197
7:37f.   246
9:5f.   194
15:14   246

3 MACCABEES
7:16   73

4 MACCABEES
6:28f.   246
17:21f.   246

MITHRAS LITURGY
6, 9ff.   216

ODES OF SOLOMON
3:3   225
36:6   154

ORIGEN, CONTRA
  CELSUM
6:27   154

ORIGEN, IN JOANNEM
5:3   48, 49

PESAḤIM
10:56   107

PHILO, QUOD DETERIUM
  POTIORI INSIDIARI
  SOLET
22   186

PHILO, DE VITA MOSIS
1:279   186

PISTIS SOPHIA
86, 112, 128, 130   154

POLYCARP, PHILIPPIANS
1:1   65
1:23f.   176
7   48
7:1   207

PSALMS OF SOLOMON
17:32   182

1QH
4:15   255
10:22f.   145
13:13–16   145

1QS
1:5   111
1:9f.   109
1:24–2:1   113
2:11, 17   255
2:12, 17   132
3:6–12   239
3:13–4:26   209
3:15–26   209
3:18–21   176
4   209
4:5   255
4:19f.   176
4:20–23   182
5:11f.   247
5:25   66
7:18   66
8:5   66
8:21–9:2   247

11:9, 12   145

SIRACH
5:5f.   119
30:7   194

SOṬA
48a   247

TACITUS, AGRICOLA
45   107

TERTULLIAN,
 ADVERSUS
 MARCIONEM
5:16:4   48

TESTAMENT OF ASHER
6:2   209

TESTAMENT OF
 BENJAMIN
3:6   246

10:1   246

TESTAMENT OF DAN
5   73
5:1   51
5:4–6   176

TESTAMENT OF GAD
4   51
4:6f.   192
5:9   246

TESTAMENT OF
 ISSACHAR
4:6   142
7   73
7:1   247

TESTAMENT OF JUDAH
3:10   252
19:2   246
20:1   209

TESTAMENT OF LEVI
2–5   216
8:4f.   239
18:9   182

TESTAMENT OF
 NAPHTALI
4:1   176

TESTAMENT OF REUBEN
1:7   246
2   209
2:4   145
4:8   255
6:9   51

TESTAMENT OF
 ZEBULON
5:3f.   194

WISDOM OF SOLOMON
12:2   91